GOLF IN AMERICA

Project Director: Margaret L. Kaplan
Designer: Bob McKee
Photo Editor: John K. Crowley

This 1994 edition is published by Harry N. Abrams, Incorporated,
New York
A Times Mirror Company

Printed and bound in Hong Kong

Library of Congress Cataloging-in-Publication Data

Golf in America : the first one hundred years / by George Peper,
 general editor, with Robin McMillan and Jim Frank.
    p.   cm.
  Includes bibliographical references and index.
  ISBN 0–8109–8123–8
  1. Golf—United States—History.   I. Peper, George.
II. McMillan, Robin. III. Frank, James A.
GV981.G65 1994   94–4490
796.352′0973—dc20

Copyright © 1988 Harry N. Abrams, Inc.

GOLF
IN AMERICA
The First One Hundred Years

BY GEORGE PEPER, GENERAL EDITOR,
WITH ROBIN MCMILLAN AND JAMES A. FRANK

ABRADALE PRESS

HARRY N. ABRAMS, INC., PUBLISHERS

TO ANDY DEMPSEY, WHO LOVED THE
GAME OF GOLF, LOVED THE BUSINESS
OF PUBLISHING, AND PURSUED BOTH
WITH UNCOMMON ZEAL AND
UNWAVERING INTEGRITY

CONTENTS

ACKNOWLEDGMENTS

One hundred heroes are honored in this book, and at least one hundred helped create it.

First among them are the people at *GOLF Magazine.* Early in 1986, Peter Bonanni had barely begun his duties as publisher when I walked into his office and hit him with the notion of *GOLF Magazine* leading a hundredth anniversary celebration "of the game, by the game, and for the game." From that day forward, I was no longer the most enthusiastic crusader for the Centennial of Golf in America, Pete was. Without his inspired leadership and hard work, neither the celebration (of which this book is a part) nor *GOLF Magazine* (from whose editorial offices this book has sprung) would have achieved the remarkable successes they have during the past several months.

Since Bonanni and I are both hopeless golf addicts, we were blessed to be reporting to two kindred spirits at Times Mirror Magazines, the late Andy Dempsey, then president and chief executive officer, and Jim Kopper, the executive vice president and group publisher. The Centennial enterprise might easily have stopped at these decision-makers' doors. Instead, that is where it got its launch. Perhaps it had something to do with the fact that Kopper is a member of Inwood Country Club and Dempsey of Winged Foot, the sites of two of Bobby Jones's U.S. Open victories. Whatever the reason, both executives instantly embraced the Centennial, and in early 1987 Dempsey added several hundred thousand dollars' worth of editorial pages to *GOLF Magazine* for the purpose of celebrating golf's history and traditions in a series of ten Centennial inserts. He also agreed to allow a number of *GOLF Magazine* staff people to do after-hours work on the preparation of this book.

And oh, did they work! Over the past several years, *GOLF* has won more awards for its editorial excellence than all other golf publications combined, and it is thanks to the same people who poured their hearts and minds into this book. Senior Editor Robin McMillan edited fifty thousand of these hundred thousand words—the profiles of the fifteen "Players of the Decade" and the biographical sketches of all the "100

Heroes of American Golf," many of which he wrote himself. Executive Editor James A. Frank wrote thirty of those sketches, five of those profiles, and also produced the comprehensive chapter on golf equipment, "From Hickory Cleeks to Metal Woods," while helping me in a variety of behind-the-scenes editorial tasks, from tracking down photographs and writing captions to tracing the whereabouts of the sixty-two living Heroes.

Two associate editors, David Barrett and J.B. Mattes, wrote the bulk of the rest of the profiles and sketches, and our Senior Editor for Instruction, John Andrisani, contributed the chapter on "The Learning Process." Before taking on this assignment, John was extremely knowledgeable in his area. Now, after months of research and writing the history of instruction in America, he is a bona fide authority. The same can be said about each of the aforementioned editors on the respective subjects they tackled.

Surely no one spent more time with this manuscript than our own Managing Editor, Pauline Crammer. Long after most of us thought the book was "handed in," Polly pored over our word-processed pages, checking and rechecking them for accuracy and consistency. Even, in some cases, for inconsistency. For instance, the first golf club in America calls itself St. Andrew's (with an apostrophe), whereas the original Royal and Ancient Golf Club in Scotland is St. Andrews (no apostrophe). Keeping punctuation on the correct side of the Atlantic was just one of Polly's myriad tasks.

Several quasi-members of our staff also added mightily to the book. Contributing Editors Mike Bryan and Tom Doak each wrote a chapter, as did frequent contributor Jim Finegan, each exhibiting the thoroughness and style for which we value' them. For two more chapters we are grateful to an expert on the history of women's golf, Sarah Ballard (on loan from *Sports Illustrated*), and an expert on the history of men's golf (particularly U.S. Open Championships), the pseudonymous Carson Codd.

We were fortunate, indeed, to be able to enlist the services of knowledgeable people, but in no case more fortunate than in the chapter on the media, where our author was Joseph Murdoch. The co-founder of the Golf Collectors' Society, Murdoch is without question the number one authority on golf books and literature. His private collection of golf books is one of the finest in the world.

A handful of people quarreled with our assertion that American golf began with John Reid in 1888. Yet no one was able to advance a more credible date. And with published history books by Herbert Warren Wind, H.B. Martin, and Charles Blair Macdonald backing us, and authorities such as Joe Murdoch in our corner, we were never shaken in our conviction that the hundredth birthday party is smack on schedule.

Another leading collector-historian, Gary Wiren, allowed us to photograph some of his vast collection of antique golf clubs; George and Susan Lewis were gracious in allowing us to photograph much of their "Golfiana"; Bill Carey, the resident golf historian of southern Florida, happily shared both his knowledge and his photographs; and Ray Davis, curator of the World Golf Hall of Fame in Pinehurst, was both generous and tireless in unearthing old and previously unpublished photographs.

We are also indebted to the golf associations that supported the Centennial—the PGA of America, PGA Tour, LPGA Tour, and National Golf Foundation—for use of their research facilities and photograph archives. Although the USGA did not officially take part in the Centennial, it was helpful to the cause of this book. We are particularly grateful to Janet Seagle, curator of the USGA Museum, for her assistance in procuring dozens of photographs and for allowing us to take photographs of many of the museum exhibits.

The first chapter of this book—and for that matter, the first chapter of golf in this country—could never have been written without the cooperation of the St. Andrew's Golf Club. A hundred years after its founding, the members were kind in allowing us to visit their valuable archives both for research on the text of the book and for access to several photographs and rare documents.

The photographs are the true joy of this book, and the list of sources is lengthy. Most of the older shots came either through the USGA or the World Golf Hall of Fame. The majority of the color photographs are by GOLF Magazine's staff photographer Leonard Kamsler. But at least a few of the other contributors deserve our thanks. They are Frank Christian, Tom Doak, John Kelly, Jeff McBride, Brian Morgan, and Fred Vance.

Two illustrators also merit special mention—Ron Ramsey and Walt Spitzmiller. Ramsey, the art director of GOLF Magazine, happens to be one of the most talented portrait illustrators in New York. Another golf fanatic, he spent his free evenings for the better part of a year meticulously rendering likenesses of each of the 100 Heroes, a heroic achievement in itself. Spitzmiller, perhaps the most sought-after sports artist in America, painted the fifteen stunning portraits of the "Players of the Decade."

With an earlier GOLF Magazine book, Golf Courses of the PGA Tour, the people at Harry N. Abrams, Inc., proved that they know how to present this game in book form more beautifully and professionally than any other publisher, and with Golf in America they've topped themselves, thanks to the tireless efforts of executive editor Margaret Kaplan, designer Bob McKee, photo editor John Crowley, photo researcher Alexandra Truitt, and production director Shun Yamamoto.

The penultimate thank you goes to the many sponsors who saw the merit in helping us celebrate the history and traditions of the game. Without their support, the Centennial might have taken place, but the party would never have been the success it was. We therefore owe our appreciation to the people at American Airlines; Ben Hogan Company; Best Products; Buick; Casio, Inc.; Chrysler; Clubman (Neslemur); John Deere; Foot-Joy, Inc.; Golf Pride Grips/ Eaton Corp.; Independent Insurance Agents of America; Izod Lacoste Golf & Tennis; Jaguar Cars Inc.; Jeep; Lynx Golf Inc. and Daché; MacGregor Golf Company; Michelob; Pella Windows and Doors/Rolscreen Company; RJR Nabisco, Inc.; Times Mirror Company; Titleist; True Temper Sports; U.S. Historical Society; Wilson Sporting Goods Company. Bill Neff at Ohlmeyer Communications and Dave Strand at GOLF Magazine were instrumental in attracting this corporate support, and for their work in this and several other areas of the Centennial, we are deeply grateful.

But our final and most sincere gratitude goes not to any of the people who contributed to the making of this book. It goes instead to the people who are in it. To the heroes both named and unnamed, who, in every decade along the way, played the game and loved it, nurtured it yet left it substantially as they had found it.

The world in which we live today bears little resemblance to America in the 1880s. But the simple and wonderful virtues of golf are intact. It is to the guardians of those virtues and to the enduring appeal of golf that we all owe our ultimate debt, as well as our promise to continue preserving this, the greatest game of all.

George Peper
New York City
November 15, 1987

In the city of Yonkers, New York, on the twenty-second day of February—Washington's Birthday—1888, six men assembled in a hillside cow pasture with a selection of strange-looking implements and quietly conducted an experiment. Today, precisely one hundred years later, twenty million gratefully addicted Americans can look back on that moment as the start of the most beguiling recreational pastime this nation has ever embraced—the game of golf.

It was an unlikely game, introduced at an unlikely time. America during the 1870s and 1880s was in the midst of what one historian called the "dark ages," a drab and uncertain period of no particular consequence. There were no horseless carriages, no flying machines, no moving pictures, and no incandescent lamps. We were a sober, somber nation, working hard for wages that were low. Grover Cleveland, who had been solidly elected president three years earlier, was about to be voted out of office in favor of the Republican Benjamin Harrison. The country was torn by labor strikes in an atmosphere of dissatisfaction and uncertainty, particularly in the Northeast.

On that fateful day in February, the *New York Daily Tribune* carried more than a dozen accounts of assaults and murders—with revolvers, knives, blackjacks, and poison. In New England, floods from a midwinter thaw increased the restlessness of factory workers who believed their future happiness lay in the fertile pastures of western Pennsylvania and Ohio. Farmers there, in turn, had begun to doubt the value of their soil and looked toward the wheat and cornfields of Kansas and Iowa for their salvation. The mentality and movement of America were westward, and a steady stream of covered wagons continued down the dusty road to the land of promise and golden opportunity.

Few men had the time or resources for outdoor amusement. Cricket had come from England but had failed to gain accep-

tance except among the elite. In 1875 both lawn tennis and polo had been introduced in Boston and Newport, but they, too, had been slow to gain adherents. We had a tendency to look with suspicion upon any game imported from Britain. Indeed, nearly a century earlier, newspaper reports in the Carolinas had made reference to golf, or at least to golf clubs. However, there is little indication that the game as we know it was actually played, and these newspaper accounts vanished after 1811.

We were a nation of spectators, not participants. Horse racing and prizefighting were constantly in the papers, with Maud S. the outstanding trotter of the day and the bare-knuckled John L. Sullivan putting up his dukes against all comers. Baseball was on the rise, and in 1888 the American Association pennant went, for the fourth straight time, to the St. Louis Browns, with the New York Giants taking the National Association title.

The average guy got his only thrills and spills from cycling. At the Centennial Exposition in Philadelphia in 1876, the country had been introduced to the high-wheel bicycle, and many men were riding them. But only men, since no woman in skirts could hope to mount the wheel. The fact was, in 1888 there was no vehicle—either literal or figurative—for mass recreation. Indeed, in the pages of that February 22 issue of the *Tribune* the hottest sports news was a riveting account of the twelfth annual Westminster Kennel Club Show. Without question, America and its people were more sedentary during the 1880s than at any time before or since.

Ah, but this lost weekend was coming to an end. In 1888 the United States stood on the threshold of the greatest era of expansion and development in its history. In Menlo Park, New Jersey, Thomas Edison had perfected his light bulb, and alternating current had begun to bring electric power into homes everywhere. In Detroit, Henry Ford was producing the

BY GEORGE PEPER

an American Passion

first of his automobiles, and in Dayton, Ohio, Orville and Wilbur Wright had turned their bicycle repair shop into the world's first hangar. During the Gay Nineties, we would brighten our homes, lighten our loads, and heighten our expectations. High civilization was coming to America, and with it would come what Andrew Carnegie called "the indispensable adjunct of high civilization," golf.

It came via two transplanted Scotsmen, Robert Lockhart and John Reid. Lockhart was a New York linen merchant and a friend of Reid, a resident of Yonkers and manager of the J.L. Mott Iron Works at Mott Haven. The two had been schoolmates in Dunfermline, a quiet manufacturing town five miles above Scotland's Firth of Forth.

Lockhart's business took him back and forth to his home soil frequently, and he invariably returned with unusual gifts for his friends, often for Reid. On one occasion, he had actually brought back *tennis racquets and balls,* and the two men had built a court on Reid's front lawn and formed a small club. For whatever reason, this effort failed to stimulate much interest.

However, in the late summer of 1887 Lockhart's Scottish visit included an excursion into Fife and the Royal Burgh of St. Andrews, the cradle of golf. At the shop of Old Tom Morris, resident professional for the Royal and Ancient Golf Club of St. Andrews and a four-time British Open champion, Lockhart ordered six clubs and two dozen gutta-percha balls. The clubs, handmade by Old Tom himself, included three woods (a driver, a brassie or 2-wood, and a spoon or 3-wood) and three irons (a cleek or long iron, a sand iron, and a putter). They cost between $2.00 and $2.50 each. (Similar clubs today can fetch two *thousand* dollars and more from collectors.)

Lockhart had learned the game as a youth on the links at Musselburgh, and although he was not an avid practitioner,

he was reasonably able and knew the basic rules. When the equipment arrived, late in the fall of 1887, before sending it to Reid, he put it quickly to a test.

Stories abound about the circumstances of that day. Some historians claim that Lockhart was arrested for committing golf in a public place and that Reid bailed him out. However, H.B. Martin in his *Fifty Years of American Golf* seems to have the most reliable account, a first-hand recollection from Lockhart's son Sydney:

> One bright Sunday morning, father, my brother Leslie, and myself went up to a place on the river which is now Riverside Drive. It was not a wilderness by any means, as I recall there was a mounted policeman near the spot father selected as a teeing ground.
>
> Father teed up the first little white ball and, selecting one of the long wooden clubs, dispatched it far down the meadow. He tried all the clubs and then we boys were permitted to drive some balls too. One of father's shots came dangerously close to taking the ear off an iceman, but the policeman did not arrest my father, and merely smiled. Later the cop asked if he could hit one of those balls and naturally my father was more than pleased that he was so friendly. The officer got down off his horse and went through the motions of teeing up, aping father in waggling and squaring off to the ball and other preliminaries. Then he let go and hit a beauty straight down the field which went fully as far as any that father had hit. Being greatly encouraged and proud of his natural ability at a game that involved a ball and stick, he tried again. This time he missed the ball completely and then in rapid succession he missed the little globe three more times; so with a look of disgust on his face he mounted his horse and rode away.

Having concluded his test, Lockhart passed the batons to his friend Reid. In so doing, the soft-spoken merchant drifted

The par three 16th at St. Andrew's today, part of a major redesign by Jack Nicklaus.

into the background of golf history while his compatriot Reid assumed the mantle, "Father of American Golf." In 1923, however, a friend of both men recalled Lockhart as "the introducer of the game of golf in this country" while Reid became "the missionary who so ably carried on its perpetuation."

A mid-winter thaw, coinciding with the presidential birthday, afforded Reid and his cronies their initial opportunity. Bright and early, the six men reconnoitered on the pasture just across the street from Reid's home on Lake Avenue in Yonkers. Three rudimentary holes were laid out, the first of them beginning at the top of a hill. Since the group had just the six clubs, it was decided that only two men would use them, passing the clubs back and forth. The game was thus played by John Reid and John B. Upham. The four others present were Henry O. Tallmadge, who lived next door to the pasture, Harry Holbrook, another neighbor, Kingman H. Putnam, and Alexander P.W. Kinnan. All six became instant converts.

The experiment was successful, but short-lived, because on March 12 the notorious "Blizzard of '88" dumped over three feet of snow on the New York area, putting golf's progress on hold for several weeks. Once the pasture was clear and the weather mild, however, the cohorts were back, this time with enough clubs and balls for all of them to play. Indeed, it soon became apparent that the three short holes in the pasture were inadequate territory to withstand the assaults of everyone. A decision was made to move the enterprise around the corner to a thirty-acre meadow at the northeast corner of Broadway and Shonnard Place, owned by the local butcher, John C. Shotts, a thrifty German who had bought the property as an investment. The group never asked permission, they simply appropriated the land, but Shotts, knowing Reid & Co. were some of his best customers, chose not to complain.

In their new surroundings, the little group played with a happy perseverance that withstood a torrent of ridicule and condemnation from their uninitiated neighbors. Many a passerby would lean across Shotts's fence to observe with bemusement the strange band of men, clad in their old hobnail shoes, faded suits, and battered derbies, ritually swatting and following little white balls around the yard.

The man who literally brought the game—or at least the implements—to America, Robert Lockhart. He imported six clubs and two dozen gutta-percha balls for his friend John Reid from Old Tom Morris's shop in St. Andrews, Scotland.

James II feared the obsession would result in diminished time for practicing the military skill of archery. In 1457—the first recorded reference to the game—Parliament decreed that "the Fute-ball and Golf be utterly cryit downe, and nocht usit."

However, regal opposition had little effect on Scottish golfers, and the game took firm hold in that country. Similarly, clerical admonition did nothing to deter the intrepid little band of men in Yonkers. Quite the contrary, it helped to bring them permanently and officially together.

On November 14, 1888, five of the players finished their round on Shotts's meadow and repaired to the home of John Reid, who had arranged a dinner of "particular significance." Reid's guests were Harry Holbrook, Kingman H. Putnam,

Horace Hutchinson, the fine English golfer who was also the game's first true essayist, chronicled the beginning of golf in his own country with observations that applied equally to the fledglings of Yonkers:

> If you announced yourself a golfer, people stared at you. What did it mean? Oh yes! That Scotch game—like hockey, was it not or like polo? Did you play it on horseback? . . . In general people had never seen the weapons before, and asked you, with an apology for their inquisitiveness, what their use could be. . . . Or if people did know a little of the game, then their regards were no longer curious but pitiful, as who would say, "See the poor looney—is he not a sad sight?" It grew common to regard golf as a harmless form of imbecility, holding towards it much the same attitude that the general mind has towards a grown man with a butterfly net and a taste for entomology.

But since Reid and his men played golf religiously every Sunday, the local clergy was not amused. The pulpit bemoaned the fact that a game could entice church members away from the weekly service and predicted that anyone who indulged in these nefarious rites of pasture would almost certainly make the acquaintance of "His Satanic Majesty."

The clerics' reaction harkened back to the very beginnings of the game. In the fifteenth century, Scotsmen apparently gave themselves up so completely to the gods of golf that King

The father of American golf, John Reid, was a transplanted Scotsman who founded the St. Andrew's Golf Club in Yonkers, New York, in 1888. Two identical "originals" of this oil painting hang in the United States Golf Association (USGA) Museum in Far Hills, New Jersey, and in the current St. Andrew's clubhouse in Hastings, New York.

The first photograph of golf in America, taken in November of 1888 in butcher Shotts's cow pasture near John Reid's home. John B. Upham is putting on the first green as Reid (foreground) waits to play. At left are fellow clubmembers Harry Holbrook and Alexander P. W. Kinnan, along with America's first caddies, Warren and Fred Holbrook.

Henry O. Tallmadge, and John B. Upham. The purpose of the meeting was to devise ways and means of perpetuating their play on the pastureland course. Reid thought this could be best accomplished by forming a club that could provide funds for maintenance while cementing the comradeship that had evolved among the handful of golf lovers.

The minutes of that meeting indicate that the first order of business was to select officers. John Reid was unanimously elected president, John Upham was elected secretary and treasurer, and the others made up the "Board of Managers." At Reid's suggestion, the club was named St. Andrew's (with an apostrophe) in the hope that the name might inspire interest in America as effectively as had its namesake St. Andrews (no apostrophe) in Scotland.

It was resolved that Reid and Upham would develop a set of rules and regulations for the club. Finally, just before adjournment, a toast was proposed and drunk to the man who had introduced them to the game, Robert Lockhart. To honor him more officially, the club then elected Lockhart its first member. Gilbert Turner, a gentleman from Brooklyn who had made frequent trips to the Yonkers course and shown great enthusiasm for golf, was elected the second active member. The meeting then adjourned to a festive supper during which the future prosperity of the club was toasted.

The handful of simple resolutions, duly recorded in the Minute Book of the Club, constitutes the "Magna Carta" of American golf. It is this day—November 14, 1888—that historians agree with virtual unanimity is the official beginning of golf in the United States.

At that moment, St. Andrew's was the only golf club in America. Five years later, a handful of others would join it. Ten years after that, American golf would be spreading like wildfire. By the turn of the century, the number of golf clubs would reach one thousand.

Golf at St. Andrew's in 1888 was unquestionably the same game we play today, but undeniably more primitive. The layout on the butcher's meadow was hilly, the "fairways" were as long as our modern rough, and a footpath wound through the property. The greens actually were not green at all, at least not after a few months of play, as constant tramping wore them to bare dust. The cups were cut by scooping a hole with the blade of a cleek. Three-foot-high stakes, topped with numbered metal plates, served as the flagsticks.

There were no golf bags, and the first caddies, Warren and Fred Holbrook, sons of member Harry Holbrook, carried the clubs on their shoulders. They were paid twenty-five cents for each round (and with a novice player those rounds could sometimes last half a day). Each member owned a half dozen or so Scottish-made cleeks and distinguished his from others by painting a colored stripe on the shaft just below the grip. Most players carried only two guttie balls, the favored brand being the Eclipse, which cost thirty-five cents. Reid helped everyone keep their clubs in good condition by turning over repair jobs to one of the carpenters in his ironworks.

The first clubhouse was a table set up in the backyard of Theodore Fitch, whose home adjoined the pasture. And

Two cartoons by H.B. Martin provide a good deal of valuable information about the Apple Tree Gang and their golf course.

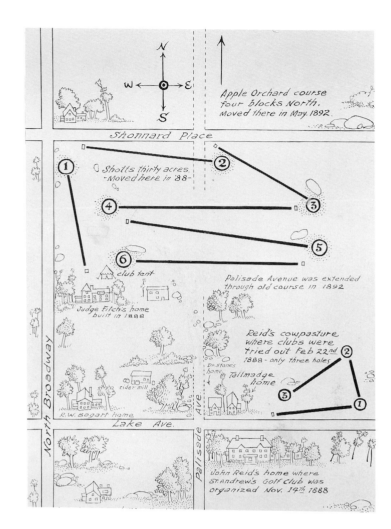

even that table was a bit crude, a couple of boards supported by two empty barrels. Under the table were tubs of ice and water, constituting the first nineteenth hole. The establishment was tended by one of Reid's black employees who doubled as America's first course superintendent, cutting the fairways and doing odd jobs with assistance from Tallmadge's gardener. Later, the club quarters expanded to the dignity of a tent.

Six more members joined the Saints that first year, bringing the total to thirteen, and that is the size it remained for four years. Expansion, of both the club and its playing facilities, was discussed from time to time, but on each occasion it was staunchly opposed by Reid, a strict conservative. However, when the Yonkers city fathers decided to extend Palisade Avenue through Shotts's meadow, a move had to be made.

In April 1892, the club relocated four blocks north to a thirty-four-acre apple orchard on the Weston estate. It was a scenic piece of property, set on a hill that sloped severely toward the valley below. A panoramic view from the top of the hill included the Hudson River and the Palisades in New Jersey.

The course was designed in a day. Without so much as cutting a single apple tree limb, Reid and his men threaded their holes through the arbor. The result was a six-hole layout of 1,500 yards, steeply banked and studded at every turn with fruit-bearing obstructions.

It was here that the group became known as the Apple Tree Gang, the moniker referring to one tree in particular, which was situated near the first tee and final green and which served as a combination locker room and nineteenth

Above:
Part of the original minutes of the first meeting of the St. Andrew's Golf Club, held in John Reid's home on the evening of November 14, 1888.

Left:
The actual apple tree as it appeared in 1922. Only two branches remain: One hangs in the St. Andrew's clubhouse in Hastings, the other at the Royal and Ancient Golf Club of St. Andrews in Scotland.

Opposite above:
The nineteenth hole of the St. Andrew's Golf Club in 1892 was an apple tree. The members hung their coats, lunches, and a wicker demijohn containing several pints of Scotland's other gift to the world in its branches. A wide wooden bench girding the trunk could accommodate most of the thirteen members of the Apple Tree Gang.

Opposite below:
The final home of the St. Andrew's Golf Club at Mt. Hope, on a hill near Hastings, New York.

Right:
John Reid on the first tee at Grey Oaks. Note the spats, knickers, natty plaid shirt, and bow tie, not to mention the baseball grip and the wide "ten-minutes-to-two" stance.

Below:
The course at Grey Oaks was not particularly long or tight, but it featured unusually daunting obstacles—stone walls crossing seven of the nine holes.

Bottom:
An early newspaper review of the Grey Oaks course included this photograph of the first green with its imposing hazard, a bunker banked by a six-foot-high prism of turf.

Top:
The St. Andrews (Scotland) swing was adopted by one and all, complete with severely crooked left elbow, as demonstrated here by John Upham. By this time (1894), golf bags were in use, although five or six clubs still constituted a privileged player's set. The dress code was starchy, and hats—of every variety—were de rigueur.

Above:
John Reid essaying a ticklish putt at the ninth hole at Grey Oaks while a keenly interested Robert Lockhart observes from behind. The other players include, at left, H. Moffat, J. C. Ten Eyck, John B. Upham, C. F. McKim, Henry O. Tallmadge, and to the right of the caddies, Messrs. S. Tucker and Harry Holbrook.

The handsome clubhouse at Shinnecock Hills.

hole. In its branches the members hung their coats, their lunch baskets, and a wicker demijohn containing several pints of Scotland's *other* gift to the world. A wide wooden seat encircling the trunk served as the club's lounge.

The tree no longer stands, but one of its branches hangs in the current St. Andrew's clubhouse, and another is in the Royal and Ancient Golf Club at St. Andrews, Scotland, a gift to it in 1923. It was accepted for the club by Edward, Prince of Wales (later King Edward VIII before his abdication), the captain of the Royal and Ancient at that time.

So imposing were the apple trees that initiates to the game of golf assumed them to be integral to any reputable course. In his book, *Scotland's Gift—Golf,* Charles Blair Macdonald includes a story from a Judge O'Brien, who, having niblicked his way through his first round of golf (at St. Andrew's), made a visit, in 1894, to Shinnecock Hills Golf Club on the comparatively barren, windblown turf of Eastern Long Island. Seeing that course for the first time, the judge declared with full confidence that it "was not a golf course at all . . . because it had no apple trees over which to loft and play."

Once settled in their new and roomier location, the club started a membership drive, swelling to twenty by the end of the year.

The game was growing in other New York neighborhoods as well, and by 1894 there were clubs at Shinnecock and Meadow Brook on Long Island, Richmond on Staten Island, Ardsley, Knollwood, Rye, and White Plains in Westchester, Greenwich in Connecticut, and Lakewood, Paterson, Montclair, Morris County, New Brunswick, and Baltusrol across the Hudson in New Jersey.

Each of these clubs had nine holes, putting the Apple Tree Gang to shame. When some of the new members saw the elaborate clubhouse that Shinnecock's members had erected, a movement began within St. Andrew's to upgrade the facilities.

The progressives won out. In 1894, the club took possession of the Odell Farm at Grey Oaks, a hundred-acre tract three miles northeast of the apple orchard on the Sawmill River Road.

At last America's first club had a clubhouse—a haunted one. It seems that at one time the farm was used as a boarding-house for workers who were doing construction on a nearby aqueduct, and one of the workers died in the house, presumably a violent death. Ghosts, it was alleged, had made things so uncomfortable for tenants that it was impossible to keep the property rented for any great length of time.

Several members outside the clubhouse at Grey Oaks. The porch was a popular gathering place; besides, the house was rumored to be haunted.

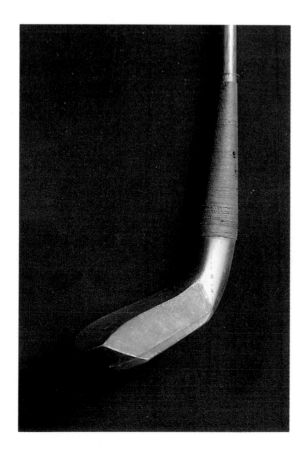

Above:
The USGA Museum contains this gavel carved from the wood of the original apple tree and used for many years at meetings of the St. Andrew's club.

Left:
John Reid's driver. Note the longish nose, heavy soleplate, and thick neck. The hickory shaft was about a foot longer than the drivers of today.

William Howard Taft was among the most avid of America's golfing presidents.

Undaunted, the St. Andrew's stalwarts moved in on May 11, ousting the resident apparitions with their own indomitable spirit of progress. Again they laid out a golf course—this one a nine-hole design of some 2,382 yards, took two days to create. A diverting feature was that every hole except two had a stone wall traversing its fairway.

A new formality came with the new quarters as the tattered togs of the cow pasture days gave way to the golf attire of the turn of the century—scarlet coats. The coats had been worn at many of the early Scottish and English clubs and had been adopted by Shinnecock, Newport, Brookline, and others. At St. Andrew's the coat was adorned with brass buttons and complemented by a blue-checked waistcoat, winged-collar shirt, pearl gray hat with blue and white band, gray knickers, hose of Scotch plaid, and gray gaiters. A silver cross, the symbol of St. Andrew's, adorned the collar of the coat. This attire was all the rage for a few years, then vanished completely as the layers of wool impeded the practical necessity of striking the ball, particularly in the summer months.

But St. Andrew's put several red coats of paint on the old Grey Oaks clubhouse, and members began joining the new club in droves. In a short time, the count was well over a hundred and included such names as H. P. Auchincloss, Oliver Harriman, Jordan L. Mott, Charles Schwab, Stanford White, Henry Taft, and Andrew Carnegie. New members and old took to their modern course with a vengeance, some starting play at five in the morning and going continuously until seven at night. Tournaments were held constantly, and a special division was created for players who had been at the game less than two years.

Golf was catching on, not only at St. Andrew's but across the country, particularly with the monied classes. In 1894, the *New York Times* society pages carried the observations of a non-golfer on the new sport:

> Society is as prone to fads as are the sparks to fly upward. And the latest in outdoor fads is golf. Tennis, archery and polo have each had their turn, and golf is

The members of St. Andrew's were a jovial group, and their meetings always ended in song. John Reid started the tradition by singing Scottish ballads, and in later years the members wrote their own songs. The lyrics for this one came from the pen of sportswriter Grantland Rice, an avid golfer in the 1920s and 1930s.

now coming in to replace them in the fickle minds of the Four Hundred.

Without being as violent as tennis or polo, the ancient Scottish game furnishes more exercise than either archery or croquet and seems to find favor with those lovers of outdoor sports who are too stout, too old or too lazy to enjoy any of the severer games.

And, on December 27, 1895, the *Times* gave the game its crowning accolade:

> In the history of American field sports there can be found no outdoor pastime that developed and attained such popularity in such a relatively short period of time as the game of golf.

With dozens of fine golf courses and distinguished clubs springing up all across the country, the members of St. Andrew's were justifiably proud—and embarrassed. Once again, they were being outpaced. Most of the new clubs were building full eighteen-hole courses, twice the size and opulence of the facilities at Grey Oaks.

In 1897, after three years at the Odell Farm, the members approved a bond issue and purchased, for $65,000, 160 acres of densely wooded land, a couple of miles farther up the valley, again alongside the Sawmill River Road. The cost of designing and building the new course was a then-exorbitant $1,500 (today, it would be well over a million).

An attractive but modest clubhouse was designed at a cost of $65,000. This expense proved to be little burden after Andrew Carnegie personally signed a mortgage for $50,000.

Carnegie loved his new club and, in fact, built himself a weekend cottage on the property, just north of the clubhouse, so that he could be near the game he so enjoyed. With a stone foundation and solid steel shutters, the house was designed to protect the steel baron from the volatile union workers with whom he was in constant dispute. Carnegie spent many days at the club, but always hurried home before dark, afraid of being kidnapped.

He was a rabid though middling golfer, and on the day he sold the Carnegie Steel Corporation to U.S. Steel for $250 million, he played the course and triumphantly parred its fifth hole for the first time. Later that day, as he pulled up in front of J.P. Morgan's bank, a friend came up, and obviously aware of the major business transaction at hand, said, "I've been hearing great things about you," at which point Carnegie stared in amazement and said, "How did you know I had a par on the fifth today?"

That fifth hole featured a drop from the tee to the fairway of nearly 250 feet, and other holes played uphill, downhill, and sidehill in various bends and breaks. The original course measured over five thousand yards, and according to one appraisal there was "hardly a hole that can be said to come under the category of 'levellers,' and good long driving [was] consequently essential for a low score." Ninety years later, despite several modifications, more than a thousand added yards, and a major redesign by Jack Nicklaus, the Mt. Hope course retains much of the original flavor.

The new course was more closely maintained than any of its progenitors, as the club invested in the services of a manager, a steward, and even a golf professional. Samuel Tucker, a young Scottish lad, began teaching the members and repairing their clubs. He was soon joined by his brother Willie. Willie had a major hand in constructing the course (to Henry Tallmadge's design) and served as the club's first greenkeeper. Later, he became one of the country's better golf course designers, crafting, among many others, the original course at Maidstone on Long Island and the Woodstock course in Vermont. Tucker was also a turfgrass expert, and he developed and sodded the first surfaces at both Yankee Stadium and the West Side Tennis Club at Forest Hills.

Perhaps the most valuable of the club's early employees were the horses, which did double duty, pulling the machinery that sculpted and then maintained the course and also pulling the conveyances that brought members to the club. Unlike the previous sites, Mt. Hope was a tough place to reach, set five miles north of Yonkers on the top of a long, steep hill. Even the Yonkers members resorted to trolleys and trains, which deposited them at the Chauncey Station. There, the club's four-horse stagecoach and three-horse bus were waiting.

When the train pulled into the station, golfers jockeyed for position near the door, and when the door opened the rush was on to scramble into the first conveyance to leave, so as to get ahead of the crowd.

On the way to the club, matches and wagers were made, generally a ball a hole. By this time Silvertown balls were the favorites, costing 50 cents each. Up the steep, stony road to the club, the horses struggled to pull their heavy loads. Invariably, the younger members would alight and walk behind to give the animals a break, then hop back on just before the final hundred yards or so, downhill to the first tee.

Once at the club, the St. Andrew's golfers made a day of it, most of them playing thirty-six holes, then gathering at the nineteenth. At last, after nine years of wandering, the Apple Tree Gang had found a proper and comfortable home.

Toward the end of that first year at Mt. Hope, John Reid retired as president of the club. American golf was then only a decade old. But it was burgeoning. Within the next decade, this country would have more golf courses—over 2,000—than the rest of the world combined. Britain's Harry Vardon would make a grand promotional tour, showing Americans just how well the game could be played, and a man named Coburn Haskell would introduce a new rubber ball that would bring two-hundred-yard drives within Everyman's reach.

Golf swiftly became synonymous with the good life in America, as millions of people began learning it and loving it. One of them was William Howard Taft.

In 1908, at a dinner commemorating the twentieth anniversary of the St. Andrew's Golf Club, Taft, then President-elect of the United States, was the featured speaker and made these remarks:

> When I learn that your club—the oldest in the country—is only twenty years old, and realize that I have been playing golf since 1896, I am surprised. I would, in respect to any other matter, feel very much discouraged at having attained in so long a time so little excellence. But golf is different from other games. Pope's lines have a greater application to it than to any other sport I know: "Hope springs eternal in the human breast; Man never is, but always will be, blest."

One hundred years after John Reid and the Apple Tree Gang, hope springs in the breast of twenty million American golfers who are blest to usher the game into its second century.

As the game of golf caught on, courses—both private and public—sprang up throughout the country. By 1900, America had more than a thousand places to play, and most of them were crowded.

Within three years after St. Andrew's was formed, other clubs were springing up simultaneously and independently in other parts of the country. William K. Vanderbilt and some associates formed Shinnecock Hills in Southampton, New York, after watching the young Scottish professional Willie Dunn at the French resort of Biarritz. Florence Boit, a young woman who had learned to play in Pau, in the French Pyrénées, introduced the game to influential Bostonians. At the same time, Charles Blair Macdonald was awakening the Midwest. Macdonald had learned the game as a student at St. Andrews University in Scotland and had known both Old Tom and Young Tom Morris, David Strath, Jimmy Anderson, Andrew Kirkaldy, and Bob Martin, all but Strath British Open champions. In the early 1890s, Macdonald helped organize the Chicago Golf Club.

At about the same time, golf was introduced to Newport, Rhode Island. Tuxedo Park, New York, and Meadow Brook, on Long Island, had nine-hole courses by 1893, and clubs were organizing in Philadelphia, Baltimore, and Washington. Each club conducted tournaments and other affairs independently, and inevitably two clubs became rivals.

At its roots, golf is a competitive game, and at their roots, Americans are a competitive people. Since it seemed important to find the nation's best players, both Newport and St. Andrew's arranged to hold national amateur championships. On a windy morning in September 1894, twenty men set out from the first tee at Newport in a stroke-play tournament, but they were a sorry lot of mostly novice golfers. As their scores mounted at a terrifying rate they began dropping out, sometimes one by one, often in whole lots. When the day ended, eight men had survived the thirty-six holes—four turns around a crude nine-hole course—and only three of those

America's first clubhouse, Shinnecock Hills in Southampton, New York, was designed by Stanford White in 1892. The club hosted the second U.S. Open in 1896 and the eighty-sixth in 1986.

had scored under 200. William G. Lawrence, a Newport member, shot 188 and beat Macdonald by a stroke.

Macdonald was annoyed. He considered himself the best golfer in America and felt he would have won except for a shot that settled close to one of the stone walls running through the course, an improper hazard in his view. No matter—he had a chance to redeem himself a month later at St. Andrew's in a match-play tournament, which Macdonald considered a more proper method of determining a champion. Twenty-eight men entered. Once again, Macdonald was in the thick of it, but again he was not good enough, losing to Laurence B. Stoddard, a St. Andrew's member.

The two tournaments settled nothing, but they caused enough controversy to convince two powerful and persuasive

Champions the Game

men that the game needed a central authority. Disturbed at a situation he perceived as anarchy, Lawrence Curtis, who had influenced a frugal board of governors to spend fifty dollars for nine holes at The Country Club in Brookline, Massachusetts, spoke to Henry O. Tallmadge, one of the five men who had organized St. Andrew's. They agreed Tallmadge should invite representatives of various clubs to form a central body with the authority to conduct national championships and otherwise further the interests of the game.

On December 22, 1894, over dinner at the Calumet Club, on the corner of Fifth Avenue and Twenty-ninth Street in New York City, men representing St. Andrew's, Newport, Shinnecock Hills, The Country Club, and the Chicago Golf Club created the United States Golf Association (USGA). Theodore A. Havemeyer of Newport was its first president. For nearly a century, the USGA has been the bond that has held the game together.

The association's original aims were to establish and enforce uniformity in the rules of play, to establish a uniform system of handicapping, to establish its executive committee as a court of reference and final authority in matters of controversy, and above all "to decide on what links the Amateur and Open Championships shall be played."

It was easy in the early years. From 1895 through 1897, both championships were played at the same time and over the same course. The U.S. Amateur covered three days of match play the first year and, as the fields grew, took four the next two. The U.S. Open, then only thirty-six holes, was played in one day. The USGA took the first Amateur and Open Championships under its aegis to the Newport Golf Club, a nine-hole course that bordered the Atlantic Ocean. Frustrated in those first two amateur championships, Mac-

donald finally broke through. In bright, clear, but blustery weather, he won five matches, the closest by 5 and 3, and set a record score for the final that still stands, defeating Charles Sands of St. Andrew's, a man who had only recently taken up the game, by 12 and 11.

For a variety of reasons, Macdonald's winning the Amateur was considered more significant than Horace Rawlins's winning the Open, played the day after the Amateur final. The Amateur was for sportsmen, men who played the game primarily for the fun of it, whereas the Open was primarily for professionals, acknowledged as the better golfers but belonging in another, lower social stratum. Professionals were usually a rough, crude band, mostly from Britain, who spoke dialects difficult to understand, laced with vulgar, back-alley expressions, and they drank, sometimes heavily.

Although he tried many more times, Macdonald never won again. Indeed, he never again advanced beyond the

Chicago Golf Club, one of the five charter members of the USGA and site of the first eighteen-hole course in America. The club was founded, and the course designed, by Charles Blair Macdonald.

This print, titled The First Amateur Golf Championship Held in America, *shows C. B. Macdonald driving during the final match against Laurence Stoddard at St. Andrew's. John Reid, pipe in hand, is at left.*

Above:
Lawrence Curtis, a Bostonian who convinced fellow members of The Country Club in Brookline, Massachusetts, to spend fifty dollars for a nine-hole golf course.

Left:
Henry O. Tallmadge, one of the original St. Andrew's members, became the USGA's first secretary. The white cross on his lapel is the St. Andrews symbol in both Scotland and the United States.

Theodore Havemeyer (straw hat) and sons putting on the third green at
Newport. Havemeyer was the first president of the USGA.

Above:
C. B. Macdonald receiving the trophy for his victory in the first U.S.
Amateur Championship, a decisive 12-and-11 triumph over Charles
Sands. Theodore Havemeyer presented the trophy on the veranda of the
Newport clubhouse.

Left:
Arguably the stepfather of American golf, autocratic C. B. Macdonald
brought the game west to Chicago, designed several top-notch courses
and helped found the USGA. This painting, taken from the frontispiece
of his book, Scotland's Gift—Golf, shows the author on the National
Golf Links, his seminal design on the eastern tip of Long Island, New
York.

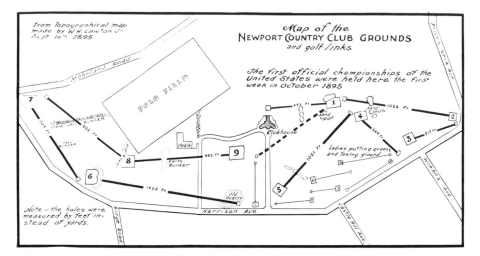

The Newport course as it was laid out in 1894, nine holes measuring a total of 8,120 feet. Hazards included sand pots, an earth bunker, an old quarry, and a stone wall.

The opulent exterior of the Newport Golf Club in Rhode Island, site of the first unofficial amateur championship in 1894, won by William G. Lawrence with a thirty-six-hole score of 188. C. B. Macdonald finished second by a stroke but a year later came back to Newport and won the first official U.S. Amateur.

semifinals, but the championship remained in the family for two more seasons. H. J. Whigham, Macdonald's son-in-law, won in 1896 and 1897. These were the last times the Amateur and Open were played together. The Open was extended to seventy-two holes in 1898 and played at a separate course.

At a time when Willie Anderson, a dour and melancholy Scot, was winning four Open Championships (1901, 1903, 1904, 1905) and was acknowledged as the best golfer in the country, Walter Travis was America's first golf hero. A native of Australia, he taught himself to play the game, labored for a year until he became a deadly putter, then won the U.S. Amateur in 1900, 1901, and 1903.

Travis became an influential and occasionally a controversial figure in the game, winning the British Amateur at Sandwich, England, in 1904 using a new model putter with the shaft set forward of the heel. Brought before the Royal and Ancient (R&A) Golf Club of St. Andrews, Scotland, it was banned because of its unusual design, driving the first wedge between the USGA and its older sibling, the R&A.

By then the USGA had established its right to regulate equipment by refusing to allow one Richard Peters to putt with a pool cue in the first Amateur Championship, and forces within the organization were working to move the association away from the R&A. At his election as USGA president in 1901, R. H. Robertson warned against being

"held down by precedent and tradition. . . . Do not let us be afraid of innovation. . . . Nothing can come to America . . . without becoming Americanized."

Even though it was banned in Britain, Travis's Schenectady putter was declared to conform with the rules in the United States.

Travis founded *The American Golfer* magazine in 1909. Perhaps because he was an amateur, or because the public demanded it, the Amateur Championship was given more coverage than the Open Championship. In its first year, *The American Golfer* devoted seventeen pages to Robert Gardner's Amateur victory and only nine to George Sargent's record 290 in the Open. In 1914, Walter Hagen rated six pages in *The Golfers' Magazine* for winning the Open, and Francis Ouimet rated ten pages for winning the Amateur. The trend continued through the 1920s and into the 1930s, when the great golf magazines died in the desperate economic conditions of the Depression. In 1926, *The American Golfer* gave Bobby Jones six pages for winning the Open but eight for losing to George Von Elm in the Amateur final. By the mid-thirties, the ratio was nine for the Amateur, eight for the

Open. Not until after World War II and the exploding interest in professional golf, fed by the great heroes of the day—the Ben Hogans, Sam Sneads, Byron Nelsons, Cary Middlecoffs, and Lloyd Mangrums—did press coverage of professional tournaments catch, then pass, the amateurs.

Some of the early amateurs played the game at least as well as the professionals, and an occasional few played better. Three of the four U.S. Opens from 1913 through 1916 were won by amateurs. Francis Ouimet, the twenty-year-old son of a French-Canadian mailman, won the 1913 Open in what is still considered among the most significant golf tournaments ever played. Jerry Travers, an absolute wizard with a putter, won in 1915, and then Chick Evans, one of the finest ball strikers but worst putters who ever lived, won in 1916, the last Open before the United States entered World War I.

Even though John McDermott, a teen-age professional, had become the first native American to win the Open, in 1911, he is largely forgotten while the memory of Ouimet's championship lives on. The tension of the 1913 Open had been building for months, principally because Harry Vardon, the great English golfer, who by then had won five British

From left to right:

H. J. Whigham, son-in-law of C. B. Macdonald, kept the U.S. Amateur trophy in the family with victories in 1896 and 1897.

Scotsman Willie Anderson won the U.S. Open in 1901, 1903, 1904, and 1905, and was acknowledged as the best player in the country during that period.

Walter Travis, a native of Australia, was America's first golf hero. Self-taught, and a deadly putter, he won the U.S. Amateur in 1900, 1901, and 1903.

Jerry Travers, winner of five U.S. Amateur Championships, is one of only five amateurs to win the U.S. Open.

On a damp, cool afternoon, Francis Ouimet set American golf on fire.
This was the scene at the final hole as the champion surveyed his putt.
His score of 72 beat Harry Vardon by five strokes, Ted Ray by six.

Opens, was on his second American tour (he had come over in 1900 and won the Open) and had entered again. As he and Ted Ray, his partner on the tour, won match after match, it seemed inevitable that one of them would win at The Country Club, by now expanded to eighteen holes. On a rainy September day, both Vardon and Ray stumbled to 79s in the fourth round and stood by while Ouimet tied them at 304. Next day, in more drenching rain, Vardon and Ray, apparently at nerves' end, played tentative, shabby golf, and shot respective scores of 77 and 78 while Francis calmly shot 72.

Ouimet was a hero. He won the Amateur the following season, but then, within a few years, he was stripped of his amateur status because he had worked for a sporting goods

manufacturer who sold golf equipment. Nothing lasts forever, though. He was reinstated when he entered the army in World War I, and he played on or served as captain of the American team in eleven Walker Cup Matches, a competition played every other year between amateurs from the United States on one side and from Great Britain and Ireland on the other.

The effect of Ouimet's Open victory was enormous. Two of Britain's greatest players had been beaten badly by a young American amateur. Britons were about to lose their dominance, and the game was spreading. About 350,000 Americans were playing golf at the time Ouimet astonished the world; within the next decade, two million were playing.

Other factors were at work. The wound-rubber ball had replaced the old gutta-percha ball in the first years of the century, and by 1910 a patent had been taken on the steel shaft. Both were to have enormous effects. The new ball flew farther, made scoring easier, and, therefore, made the game more enjoyable to play. With steel shafts, clubs could be mass-produced in large factories cheaper, quicker, and in more quantity than the original wooden shafts, which often were shaped by hand.

In spite of these obvious benefits—perhaps because of them—steel shafts were not accepted immediately. The USGA held off approving them on courses until 1926, the Royal and Ancient until 1929. This was the second split between the USGA and the R&A over equipment. In another matter, though, they acted together.

Since the beginning, golf balls had come in differing sizes and weights. In the gutta-percha days, Harry Vardon played with a ball 1.7 inches in diameter, and some early wound balls had been 1.71 inches and 1.72 ounces. Anybody could do anything with a ball; no rules applied. Before an R&A medal tournament played during a raging October gale in the nineteenth century, Maitland Dougal, one of the club's better golfers, drilled a hole in his gutta-percha ball, stuffed it with buckshot to hold it low in the wind, slogged around in 112 and finished second.

Manufacturers had been producing balls that flew farther and farther, and courses were playing shorter and shorter. Attempting to control distance, the USGA and the Royal and Ancient acted together in 1921 and set uniform standards. The ball could weigh no more than 1.62 ounces and measure no less than 1.62 inches in diameter. The agreement lasted ten years, until the USGA broke once more with the R&A, lowered the approved weight to 1.55 ounces and increased the size to 1.68 inches. The new ball was a failure. It was so light the wind tossed it about in flight, and a putted

ball quickly lost momentum and would not hold its line. The weight was increased to 1.62 ounces again in 1932, but the diameter remained at 1.68 inches. It has stayed constant ever since, and within the last fifteen years has become the standard size ball throughout the world. The Royal and Ancient announced in 1987 that the old 1.62-inch ball no longer could be played in its championships, and would be phased out completely in 1990.

During this next decade of change and expansion, the master of the game was an amateur—Robert Tyre ("Bobby") Jones, Jr., a young Georgian with a fluid, flowing swing, a charming manner, and an unconquerable will to win. From 1923 through 1930, he set standards that have never been approached. In those eight seasons, he won four U.S. Opens, three British Opens, five U.S. Amateurs, and one British Amateur. Through the same period he finished second in four other Opens, twice losing playoffs, and lost in the final of one U.S. Amateur (he also went to the 1919 final). He retired from competitive golf in November 1930 after winning the U.S. and British Opens and the U.S. and British Amateurs in the same year, the most compelling accomplishment the game has ever known. He was so much better than anyone else that Bobby Cruickshank, an old friend and rival, sent $500 to his father-in-law in Britain to place a bet with a bookmaker at 120–1 odds that Jones would win all four. Cruickshank collected $60,000.

Nothing was easy, though; Jones struggled for every championship he won. Perhaps his first Open was the most exhausting. With one hole to play at the Inwood Country Club, across Jamaica Bay from where New York's John F. Kennedy Airport stands today, Jones had the Open in his hand. Needing only a bogey five to win, he pulled a 3-wood onto the tee of another hole, played a tentative pitch into a bunker, and made 6. Cruickshank, an immigrant Scot who had fought in World War I, tied him. Jones redeemed himself the next day for what he considered a cowardly finish by playing one of the most memorable shots in the game's lore—a 190-yard mid-iron from a sandy lie in the right rough, across a pond set tight against the front of the green, to within six feet of the hole. Cruickshank, meanwhile, was making 6. This was Jones's first national championship; he would win thirteen.

Jones ruled at a time when Americans surpassed the British as the world's best golfers. The inaugural Walker Cup Match was played in 1922, and in the thirty-one matches played through 1987, the United States has won twenty-eight, lost two, and halved one. Four years after the first match, Jess Sweetser, a member of the American Walker Cup team, became the first native-born American to win the British

Opposite, above left:
Charles E. ("Chick") Evans, Jr., in 1916 became the first player to win both the U.S. Amateur and the U.S. Open in the same year. Only Bobby Jones would duplicate the feat.

Opposite, above right:
Even as a fourteen-year-old boy in his first U.S. Amateur, Bobby Jones showed the form and demeanor of a champion.

Opposite, below:
The clubhouse at The Country Club, site of the U.S. Open in 1913, 1963, and 1988. It was one of the five charter members of the USGA and the scene of Francis Ouimet's momentous upset of Harry Vardon and Ted Ray in 1913.

September, 1930   13

FROM MERION

TO MERION

Jones to Make Greatest Stand Over the Course That Saw His First Start

By GRANTLAND RICE

Here we see Bobby Jones, as he will appear in the Amateur Championship at Merion late in September, at the finish of a drive. This picture has been selected for comparison with the one which accompanies the article on the preceding page, which tells something of his first start at Merion in 1916

FOURTEEN years ago in Philadelphia, I was sitting at breakfast one morning with a somewhat chunky, ruddy-faced youth of fourteen, who was extremely anxious to get away and get out to Merion. He was to play his first match in a national golf championship, and his opponent was E. M. Byers, ex-amateur champion and a hard-fighting match player, who was no set-up for any one.

The youth's name was Bobby Jones. He wanted to get out more than an hour ahead and he was as restless as a young colt. He was full of nervous energy, and yet, in some way, he was not nervous. He was merely keen for action.

It was at Merion that Bobby Jones suddenly flashed on the golf world and the nation and the universe at large. He gave a great exhibition in that first stand. Although only fourteen years old, he was hitting out drives beyond the two hundred and fifty-yard mark, and ramming long irons and short pitches up to the pin. I know on the last nine against Frank Dyer he had a 4 for a 31.

It was at Merion in 1924 that Bobby Jones won his first amateur championship. He needed eight years after his dazzling start to break down the barrier at match play. And now, fourteen years after his début, he comes again to Merion in September with a record of twelve national and international titles, and the chance to set a new mark in golf by winning his fourth major title in one summer's campaign.

Jones and Merion

So Bobby Jones and Merion have become historic together. Their traditions have become interwoven. Together they have become part of golf history. Bobby Jones can look back on Merion with the happiest of all golf memories—his championship start and later his first amateur championship. And now he comes to the same battle field hoping to set a record that has never been approached and that may never be equalled again in golf.

What about Bobby Jones' fourth title for 1930? What should the odds be against him? What is his chance? Who in the field has the better chance to head him off?

It gets down largely, if not entirely, to those two eighteen-hole matches on Wednesday after the qualifying rounds. These are the two tough patches in his fourth charge.

(Continued on page 52)

Above:
Bobby Jones and his trusted hickory-shafted putter, Calamity Jane, were virtually unbeatable in the major championships of the late 1920s.

Left:
On the eve of the 1930 U.S. Amateur—Jones's fourth and final leg of the Grand Slam—Grantland Rice wrote this piece for The American Golfer.

Opposite above:
In an era of popular champion athletes, Jones was the most loved and revered of them all. Typically, his gallery was larger than those of the rest of the field combined.

Opposite below:
The first Walker Cup teams, for the 1922 matches between Great Britain and the United States, played at the National Golf Links in Southampton, New York. The United States won, 8 to 4.

Amateur, and a few weeks later Jones won the British Open. Walter Hagen already had won in 1922 and 1924, and within the next four years, both he and Bobby would win twice again.

Jones was the world's best golfer in an era when the rewards of professional golf were not so imposing as they became later, and the best amateurs—at least those who could make a

Left:
Jess Sweetser, a U.S. Amateur champion and the first American to win the British Amateur (1926).

Below:
Lawson Little with the U.S. Amateur trophy. During 1934 and 1935 he accomplished a feat that not even the great Bobby Jones could perform—he won the British and U.S. Amateur championships back-to-back.

Bottom:
Nebraskan Johnny Goodman is the last amateur to win the U.S. Open (1933). He also won the U.S. Amateur in 1937.

comfortable living in business—tended to remain amateurs: Sweetser, Ouimet, Evans, Max Marston, George Von Elm, Jesse Guilford, Jack Neville, Roland MacKenzie, and Bob Gardner. Some not so well off stuck it out as well. Johnny Goodman, a short, blond Nebraskan, rode a cattle car from Omaha to California to play in the 1929 Amateur, then defeated Jones in the first round. Four years later, he held a collapsing fourth round together and nipped Ralph Guldahl by one stroke. He waited another four years, then won the Amateur.

In any other climate Goodman might have been considered the best amateur in the game, the successor to Bobby Jones, but this was not an ordinary time. After he defeated Jones in the 1929 Amateur, Goodman was eliminated in turn by Lawson Little, the nineteen-year-old son of an army officer posted to the Presidio in San Francisco. Blocky, broad-shouldered, and powerful, with a thick mane of dark, curly, and unruly hair, Little dominated amateur golf as not even Jones had done. During 1934 and 1935, he won thirty-one consecutive matches at the highest level of international

competition. Besides his foursomes and singles in the 1934 Walker Cup Match, Little won the United States and British Amateur Championships in 1934 and won again the following year. Not even Jones had done that. Thirty-two years later, in 1967, Bob Dickson, an American, won both in the same year.

Little gave up amateur golf in 1936, and in 1940 won the U.S. Open. Caught in the Great Depression, others had gone before him—Jerry Travers's brokerage business had gone bad, and he booked exhibitions; George Von Elm claimed he did not feel qualified to call himself a professional, but he accepted a check for $750 when he lost a playoff to Billy Burke in the 1931 Open.

As the 1930s were ending, the USGA and the Royal and Ancient grew increasingly concerned over two matters of equipment. Throughout most of his career, Harry Vardon had carried six clubs, Chick Evans carried seven, and Jones fifteen. The variety of clubs grew alarmingly during the next few years. At the peak of his career, Little carried thirty-one, and most tournament golfers carried from twenty to twenty-five. It was common to carry two or three putters—one for fast, one for slow, one for medium-speed greens—maybe two drivers, some trouble clubs, like chippers, and perhaps a putting cleek to use for long putts over bumpy greens.

Concerned that the game was being changed by the specialty clubs and feeling tournaments should be won by the player with the best swing, not the man with an infinite supply of clubs specially designed to fit every conceivable situation, the USGA imposed a limit of fourteen clubs in 1938; the R&A followed in 1939.

The ball had been causing more concern than the clubs. With improving technology manufacturers had added more muscle and made the ball go farther. Recognizing that even those courses built in the 1920s could become obsolete, the USGA in 1942 imposed a limit on the ball's initial velocity, designed to control how far it would fly.

As the game spread, entries to the Amateur and Open Championships increased. Where thirty-two men had played in the first Amateur in 1895, the field had climbed to 120 in 1898, to 217 in 1910, to 583 in 1913, and to 1,118 in 1936. It dropped off in the years remaining before World War II, and fell to 637 when Marvin (Bud) Ward won the 1941 Amateur Championship, the last until the USGA revived all its championships in 1946.

The U.S. Open was growing as well, although not quite as fast. Where the Amateur field had passed one hundred in 1898, the Open waited until 1912, when the field leaped from seventy-nine the previous year to 131. After that the rise was steady. The field reached 265 in 1920, the year

The original U.S. Amateur trophy, donated by Theodore Havemeyer in 1895. It was the perpetual trophy until 1925, when it was destroyed in a fire at the East Lake Country Club while in the possession of Bobby Jones.

Bobby Jones played for the first time. Two years later, it jumped to 323, then to 360 in 1923. Clearly that many entrants could not play in the Open itself; instead, every entrant played thirty-six holes of qualifying at the site to determine the final field.

Until 1923, the qualifying process had taken two days. With an entry of 360, qualifying had to be spread over four days. This was too awkward. In 1924, the USGA organized regional qualifying rounds at Worcester, Massachusetts, and Oak Park, Illinois. Forty players qualified from each site; with the championship proper played at thirty-six holes on each of two days, only eighty men could be accommodated. The process established, it expanded over the years. As the entry climbed above two thousand, a second round of thirty-six holes was established in 1959, and by the late 1980s, with it approaching six thousand, qualifying rounds were played at

The U.S. Open champion's medal, won by James Foulis in 1896 at Shinnecock Hills.

about sixty-five sites in May, reducing the original entry to six hundred, then another at usually thirteen sites in early June, establishing the final field of about 150 (the number varies from time to time, because of special exemptions).

The USGA made another change in 1926, extending the U.S. Open to three days. Under the new format, 150 starters played eighteen holes on each of the first two days, and the fifty low scorers and ties played thirty-six holes on the third day. The Amateur had gone through some alterations, too. Thirty-two men went into match play until 1925, when the USGA experimented with a different format: after thirty-six holes of stroke play, sixteen men played thirty-six-hole matches. At the finish, Jones won over Watts Gunn, the only time members of the same club met in the Amateur final. Experiments continued. The final field was expanded to 210 in 1947 and eventually reduced to sixty-four in 1964, and the championship converted to seventy-two holes of stroke play in 1965, and back to match play again in 1973.

Meantime, the Open continued to grow as well. As the entry climbed, so also did prize money. The original $150 for 1895 had grown to $1,745 for the 1919 championship, the first after World War I, then to $5,000 for 1924, with $1,000 going to the winner, and to $6,000 in 1937. It remained at that level through 1941, the last before World War II.

In the years immediately before war broke out in Europe, Sam Snead had emerged, and Byron Nelson became the greatest player of the day. Snead was both a glorious and a tragic figure; he won everything but the U.S. Open. Joining the tour in early 1937, he won the Bing Crosby National Pro-Am, then a minor thirty-six-hole interlude, the Nassau, Miami, and Oakland Opens, and by June was favored to win the first U.S. Open he had ever entered. When he shot 283, only a stroke above the year-old record, he looked like the winner, but Ralph Guldahl played the last nine at the Oakland Hills Country Club, near Detroit, in 34 and beat Snead by two strokes, with 281.

In the Open two years later, Snead came to the seventy-second hole of the Philadelphia Country Club needing only a par five to win, but went from one bunker to another, took three putts and staggered to an eight. Byron Nelson won, beating Craig Wood and Denny Shute in a playoff. This was the only Open Nelson was to win; he was at his peak during the war years and retired after the 1946 championship, burned out from the years of intense competition in tournaments that for the most part paid money only to the top fifteen or twenty men.

With such scant pickings, the good amateurs held on to their jobs—those who needed them—and played among themselves. The same men tended to show up for the Amateur year after year, and they were good. There was Willie Turnesa, who recovered so well from Oakmont's furrowed bunkers in defeating Pat Abbott, a public parks golfer, by 8 and 7, in the 1938 Amateur final that he was named Willie the Wedge; Dick Chapman of Winged Foot Golf Club in Mamaroneck, New York, who is still the only man to have won at his home course, in 1940; and Bud Ward, who won twice, in 1939 and 1941.

The war over, the once moribund economy returning to the euphoric days of the twenties and Americans finding more leisure time on their hands, golf went into another of its periodic expansions. At the end of the war, the country had 4,817 courses. Within the next twenty-five years, the number had grown to ten thousand. More and more people were playing. Where two million had been playing in the middle 1920s, more than four million were playing by 1950, five million by 1960, and eleven million by 1970.

The reasons for such growth were complex. Some could be

traced to the additional leisure time available to blue-collar as well as white-collar workers, and some, of course, to heroes who focused attention on the game. While Nelson was about to retire, Snead was still around and still winning everything but the U.S. Open. In 1948, Ben Hogan became the new hero when he won the U.S. Open by shooting a record score of 276. Less than eight months later, on a foggy morning in early February 1949, a bus that was passing other cars on a two-lane road in western Texas smashed head-on into Hogan's car. He was injured so badly he didn't play another tournament until January 1950, then completed his comeback by winning the Open in a playoff at Merion Golf Club, near Philadelphia. His legs wrapped with elastic bandages from his ankles to his crotch, Hogan could barely drag himself around the course. Driving from the twelfth tee during the fourth round, his legs locked and he almost fell. He struggled to reach a friend, hung on to his shoulder, and said, "My God, I don't think I can finish."

But he did, spanking a glorious 1-iron onto the home green and making the par four that forced a playoff with Lloyd Mangrum and George Fazio. The next day he shot 69, Mangrum 73, and Fazio 75. He won again the next year at Oakland Hills, perhaps the Open's most severe course ever, improving his score every day. Until the fourth round, it had

The finest player never to win a U.S. Open Championship, Sam Snead. On several occasions he came agonizingly close. In this photograph, Ben Hogan is standing behind him, Lawson Little kneels at right.

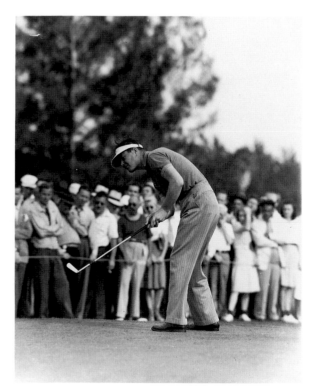

The 1939 U.S. Open champion, Byron Nelson, who won in a playoff over Craig Wood and Denny Shute. Snead had needed a closing par five to win that Open but ran into bunker trouble and took eight.

Willie ("the Wedge") Turnesa tamed the bunkers of Oakmont Country Club in the 1938 U.S. Amateur and won his final match 8 and 7.

Severely injured after his car collided with a bus in February 1949, Ben Hogan was widely assumed to be finished as a professional. He fought back and, incredibly, won the 1950 U.S. Open at Merion Golf Club, Ardmore, Pennsylvania.

Scottish golf came to America complete with the stymie, and "lofting the stymie" was an essential shot until 1951, when it was officially banned by the USGA. Today, golfers simply mark the intervening ball. Here Ted Ray demonstrates how to negotiate a stymie.

yielded no scores lower than 70, but after saying on the first tee, "I'm going to burn it up," Hogan blistered the second nine with a 32, shot 67, and won his third Open in four years. Two years later, in 1953, he won his fourth, finishing at 283 at Oakmont and beating Snead by six strokes. Only Willie Anderson, from the early 1900s, and Bobby Jones had won as many. He was the greatest striker of the ball who ever lived, and there was no reason to think he would not win a fifth Open. He seemed to have it at Olympic in San Francisco in 1955, but Jack Fleck birdied two of the last three holes to tie him, then shot 69 in the playoff and won by three strokes.

In the nearly sixty years the game had been organized in the United States, the USGA's rules of play had drifted apart from the rules of the R&A. The two organizations differed on the penalties for out-of-bounds, for an unplayable ball, and for a ball in a lateral water hazard. Meeting in St. Andrews in 1951, negotiating committees compromised their differences and established a single code for the game throughout the world. Along the way, the stymie was lost.

As Hogan ruled professional golf, amateur golf was dominated by Harvie Ward, a blond, curly-haired North Carolinian who had a three-quarters backswing, played deadly irons and putted like a dream. He became not merely the best amateur of his time, but a threat to win any tournament he

entered. He won the 1952 British Amateur, defeating Frank Stranahan, another outstanding golfer, 6 and 5 in the final, and then led the 1955 U.S. Open after thirty-six holes. Playing the eighth hole, his tee shot became lodged in the upper branches of a cypress tree and never came to ground. Ward finished seventh. Three months later he demolished Bill Hyndman by 9 and 8 in the U.S. Amateur, and repeated the next year, defeating Chuck Kocsis, 5 and 4. Ward was at the peak of his game. No amateur had won the Open since Goodman in 1933, but Ward could have, he was that good. Within a year, though, he lost his amateur status for accepting expense money from his employer to play golf, a violation of the USGA's stringent code that was designed to draw a clear line between amateurs and professionals. It has become more liberal than it had been, but the USGA insists on maintaining that distinction.

By then Dwight Eisenhower, a devoted and enthusiastic golfer, had become president. USGA agronomists helped install a putting green on the White House lawn, and he visited Augusta National annually for a ritual round with The Masters winner.

In two of the biggest boosts the game ever had, television discovered golf, and Arnold Palmer joined the tour three months after winning the 1954 U.S. Amateur. The times

The clubhouse of the Royal and Ancient Golf Club of St. Andrews, Scotland. Together, the R&A and the USGA set policy with regard to the Rules of Golf.

were changing. Where the tour had played for $411,000 in 1946, $782,000 was at stake in 1955. Within three years, purses topped $1 million. As prize money rose, the lure of professional golf grew stronger, and many of the best amateurs turned to the tour.

Nevertheless, some of the older players who had become established in business remained amateurs—Willie Turnesa had won again in 1948, Charley Coe in 1949, and Jack Westland in 1952—but Gene Littler, the 1953 Amateur champion, had turned professional, and Palmer followed him.

Palmer and television were made for each other. Highly photogenic, with an expressive face that projected all his emotions, Palmer was a daring, aggressive golfer who knew only one way to play: attack. From 1958 through 1964, he dominated the game, winning four Masters Tournaments, two British Opens, and in his finest hour, the 1960 U.S.

Open. Seven strokes behind with eighteen holes to play, Palmer drove the first green and birdied, made five more over the next six holes, bogeyed the eighth and played the first nine in 30. He shot 65 and won, with 280 for seventy-two holes.

As Palmer holed his final putt and flung his visor to the sky, Ben Hogan sat in the locker room and said, "I just played thirty-six holes with a kid who should have won this thing by ten strokes." Instead, Jack Nicklaus, then only twenty years old, had finished second, two strokes behind Palmer.

The 1960 U.S. Open was a rare moment. In Nicklaus it gave us a glimpse of the future, in Palmer a close look at the present, and in Hogan a glance into the past. Any one of those three men could have won; indeed, any one of the three should have won. No one played those last thirty-six holes—all in one day then—as well as Hogan. Paired with Nicklaus, he hit the first thirty-four greens in regulation, but he was

Right:
During the mid-fifties Harvie Ward was one of the finest players—amateur or professional—in America, winning the U.S. Amateur Championship back-to-back in 1955 and 1956 and the British Amateur in 1952.

Below:
President Dwight Eisenhower's devotion to the game helped spur golf's greatest boom during the 1950s and 1960s.

forty-seven by then, and his putting was so bad he was only four under par for the day. Normally a prudent golfer who seldom took risks, Hogan felt he needed one more birdie to win, and the seventeenth, a par five, offered the best chance. He gambled and attacked the hole, set at the front of the green close to a narrow stream. His shot was short; the ball hit the far bank and fell into the stream. He bogeyed, lost three strokes on the eighteenth and fell to ninth, four strokes behind Palmer. Two pars would have tied. Then past the time when normal men could rise to the great occasion, Hogan never threatened to win another.

Palmer grew into the biggest attraction the game has known and remained a threat for fifteen more years. But he never won another U.S. Open. Two years after he reached the zenith of his career, Nicklaus beat him in a playoff for the 1962 Open at Oakmont and changed the face of the game. He, not Palmer, became the game's leading player.

For a time, it seemed Nicklaus could become the first amateur since 1933 to win the Open. He had finished second to Palmer in 1960, then fourth to Gene Littler in 1961. He had won the U.S. Amateur twice, first in 1959 by defeating Charley Coe in a classic match at the Broadmoor Golf Club in Colorado Springs that ended on the thirty-sixth hole, where, with both men under par and the match all square,

Coe's recovery from heavy grass behind the green failed to drop by half a turn of the ball, and then Nicklaus holed from eight feet. He won again, at Pebble Beach Golf Links in California, two years later.

Throughout the time when Nicklaus ruled the amateurs, he had strong rivals. Coe was still around and still dangerous (he nearly won The Masters in 1961), Deane Beman had won the Amateur in 1960, and Ward, Billy Joe Patton, Bill Hyndman, Bill Campbell, Ed Tutwiler, and the Canadian Gary Cowan remained dedicated amateurs. Nicklaus seemed to be. Turning down a number of scholarship offers, he paid his way at Ohio State University and talked about joining his father in the family pharmacy business (they owned three stores). Instead, he joined the tour in December 1961. Six months later he won the U.S. Open.

With Nicklaus no longer around, Beman, a short, tough, crew-cut insurance broker, succeeded him as the game's leading amateur. Perhaps the best wedge player and most reliable putter in the game, professional or amateur, Beman won again in 1963. After the Amateur format was changed to stroke play in 1965, he tied Cowan for first place in 1966, then lost the playoff. One year later, Beman joined the tour.

Oddly enough, in Beman's first Open as a professional, another amateur held the lead going into the last round. At

A dedicated amateur, Bill Campbell won the U.S. Amateur in 1964. He went on to become president of the USGA and captain of the Royal and Ancient Golf Club of St. Andrews.

A decade before he became commissioner of the PGA Tour, Deane Beman was winning first amateur, then professional events. His wedge play and putting were the envy of most golfers, and his haircut was the envy of most greenkeepers.

The rivalry of the 1960s, and perhaps of all time—Arnold Palmer and Jack Nicklaus.

Top:
At Baltusrol Golf Club in 1967, Nicklaus and Palmer battled it out, with Nicklaus winning the U. S. Open on a record seventy-two-hole total of 275 and Palmer the runner-up.

Above:
One of the greatest shots in U. S. Open history, Tom Watson's pitch for birdie two at the seventeenth hole of Pebble Beach in 1982. With another birdie on eighteen, he edged Jack Nicklaus by two strokes.

Top:
The ninth and eighteenth greens at Winged Foot West, Mamaroneck, New York, a stern examination in putting and bunker play.

Above:
The course at Inverness Country Club in Toledo, Ohio, concludes with this short but devilish par four. Ted Ray won the first Open held here, in 1920.

Right:
The monstrous 630-yard seventeenth hole at Baltusrol Golf Club in Springfield, New Jersey, site of a record six U.S. Opens.

The seventh at Pebble Beach Golf Links in California, perhaps the longest, hardest 107 yards in championship golf. The course ranks third on the list in "GOLF Magazine's 100 Greatest Courses in the World."

Baltusrol in 1967, Marty Fleckman, a twenty-three-year-old college student from Texas, led by a stroke over Nicklaus, Palmer, and Billy Casper, but he drove over a fence on the second, shot 80, and fell out of the chase. Beman hung in close, but in the end, Nicklaus and Palmer had the championship to themselves. Battles between Nicklaus and Palmer were sure to attract big and noisy galleries. They cheered mainly for Palmer and carried banners and signs urging him on. They were no help. Playing exquisitely precise golf, Nicklaus gradually pulled away and ended the round with a stunning 1-iron onto the seventy-second green and rolled a twenty-foot putt into the center of the hole. He shot 65 and broke the Open record, with 275.

This was Nicklaus's second Open. Five years later, in 1972, after losing a playoff to Lee Trevino at Merion in 1971, he won his third, shooting 290, five over par, at Pebble Beach.

Although Pebble Beach had been the site of three Amateur championships, this was its first Open. Unlike the

R&A, the USGA has not established a firm rotation of courses for the U.S. Open. While six Opens had been played at Oakmont and Baltusrol through the 1980s, five at Oakland Hills, and four at Inverness in Toledo, Ohio, Merion, and Winged Foot in suburban New York, new courses are brought in occasionally. Not all return, but others cry out to be used again. Pebble Beach could be the best Open course ever, and Shinnecock Hills the next best, even though the 1986 championship was its first since 1896.

With three Opens won, Nicklaus hungered for a fourth, so he could join Willie Anderson, Jones, and Hogan. For a time it seemed he would not make it as the championship went to a series of journeyman golfers—Johnny Miller, Hale Irwin, Hubert Green, Lou Graham, Jerry Pate, and Andy North.

By 1980, Nicklaus had passed forty and had not won a tournament of any kind in two years, but he was back at Baltusrol, where he had set the record thirteen years earlier, and once again he was on form. Missing a putt from inside

*Merion Golf Club, site of Bobby Jones's first U. S. Amateur (1916) and
his crowning victory in the Grand Slam (1930).*

five feet on the home green that would have given him 62 in
the opening round, he came to the seventy-first hole two
strokes ahead of the Japanese golfer Isao Aoki, made two
stunning birdies on the last two holes, closed with 68, and
not only beat Aoki by two strokes, but once again lowered the
Open record, to 272. Nicklaus had his fourth Open.

As Hogan had tried so hard and so long for that fifth Open
that would have set him apart, Nicklaus kept on trying, too,
and with the championship at Pebble Beach once again in
1982, it seemed he might have won it when Tom Watson first
bogeyed the sixteenth hole, the seventieth of the championship, to fall into a tie with Nicklaus, who had already finished, then missed the seventeenth green, hooking his iron
into heavy rough close by.

Facing a struggle to make a par three, Watson told his
caddie he was going to hole the shot, then lobbed the ball
onto the green and into the cup for a birdie two while
Nicklaus watched on a television set in the scorer's tent.

Ahead by one now, Watson added another birdie on the
eighteenth, shooting 282 and beating Nicklaus by two
strokes.

Meanwhile, as the professional tour grew—total prize
money had reached $15 million in 1982 and would top $25
million within five more years—the likelihood diminished
that an Amateur champion would repeat; young men were
coming out of colleges trained to look to the tour, and they
used the U.S. Amateur as a step toward their goal. Some of
them were very good—Steve Melnyk, Lanny Wadkins, Craig
Stadler, Jerry Pate, John Cook, Mark O'Meara, and Hal
Sutton. Still, a solid corps of amateurs remained, men like
Vinny Giles, Jim Holtgrieve, and Bob Lewis, who had a brief
fling on the tour but couldn't putt well enough to last.

Above all, though, there was Jay Sigel, a dark, somber
Philadelphian with a slow, deliberate backswing and enormous controlled power, who holed every putt he ever looked
at. In 1982 and 1983, as he approached forty, he became the

Jay Sigel in 1983 became the first player since Harvie Ward to win the U.S. Amateur in successive years.

Dubbed "The Monster" by Ben Hogan in 1951, Oakland Hills Country Club in Birmingham, Michigan, has intimidated the contestants in five U.S. Opens. This is the par four 16th hole.

first to win the U.S. Amateur in successive years since Harvie Ward. He won the 1987 Mid-Amateur Championship and has played in six successive Walker Cup Matches through 1987.

As any golfer passes forty, the competitive fires that drive him burn with diminishing fury, and he eventually gives way to younger, hungrier men. Although the number of first-class dedicated amateurs grows smaller under the lure of more than $25 million in prize money on the tour, they are still around, and others will join them. The entry to the Amateur Championship increases every year, passing four thousand in 1986. As the world struggles ahead toward the twenty-first century, we know that more than twenty-five million people from all over the world play the game, and that it continues to attract converts. In the 1980s it returned to China after having been banned following the 1949 revolution, and even as the countries around the Persian Gulf were threatened by war, the small nation of Dubai announced that an all-grass golf course was under construction.

Amateur golf will continue to thrive. It is, after all, the base of the game.

Chapter
THREE Th

The story of the golf professionals of America in the first hundred years is the story of three triumphs: over the British pros, the American amateurs, and disregard and poverty. In its early years in this country, the profession had nowhere to go but up: the local pro was just another tradesman working around the club. Even Walter Hagen, the first truly renowned American pro, gave tennis and ice-skating as well as golf lessons as part of his duties as an assistant pro in Rochester, New York.

But Hagen comes later in the story, really. All the earliest pay-for-play practitioners of golf in the United States were Scottish or English. A standing joke of the era was the availability of a club pro's job for anyone coming off the boat with a sufficiently thick brogue. That accent was deemed the best qualification of all, so closely was the new game associated with Scotland. A first name of "Willie" helped, too. Willie Dunn, who designed the first course at Shinnecock Hills (Southampton, New York), came from Westward Ho! by way of Biarritz, France; Willie Campbell arrived at The Country Club in Brookline, Massachusetts, from Musselburgh; Willie Anderson, the dominant turn-of-the-century player, with four U.S. Open titles in five years, was a transplant from North Berwick; and Willie Smith, winner of the U.S. Open in 1899, journeyed from Carnoustie to Midlothian outside Chicago. Carnoustie was an astoundingly prolific incubator; by 1925, more than 250 men had emigrated from this tiny Scottish town to jobs as golf professionals at American clubs.

Likewise, all of the winners of the U.S. Open came from Great Britain until 1911, when John McDermott won the seventeenth edition of the Open at the Chicago Golf Club. It is not known who the first American pro was—the man who gave a lesson for a fee or demonstrated the new game before a paying crowd—but it can be acknowledged that McDermott was the first "native" professional of real distinction. Indeed, McDermott successfully defended his national championship title the following year in Buffalo, New York. However, McDermott and everyone else knew that the best Scottish players—the best players, in other words—were not usually around for the American national championship. *Theirs* was the more important tournament.

At least it was until 1913, when McDermott hoped to tie Anderson's record of three straight U.S. Open titles. In that year, Harry Vardon, the most famous of the British golfers, the man with the beautiful swing in an era of less-than-beautiful swings, would take a break from his transcontinental promotional tour (twenty thousand miles worth, according to one account; eleven-year-old Bobby Jones watched a Vardon exhibition in Atlanta) to play in the Open at The Country Club in Brookline, outside Boston. Also in the tournament was Ted Ray, Vardon's trusty sidekick with the large girth. Each man played the game with a pipe in his mouth. Golf in America was still a minor sport, but among those who cared about the game, the 1913 Open Championship was thus considered the first real test of the prowess of American professionals. This feeling was somewhat in the air in Great Britain, too: the *Times of London* sent over Bernard Darwin, Charles's grandson and the most famous golf writer of the day (there were no golf writers at all in this country; the papers sent out whoever was handy).

Along with defending champion McDermott, Americans Mike Brady and Tommy McNamara were given the best

Professionals — A Threefold Triumph

chance of hoisting the flag. Another young player, named Walter Hagen, arrived on the scene unknown and untouted but boasting that he would help McDermott teach those Brits a thing or two. Also unknown and untouted was one Francis Ouimet, a mere twenty years old but playing on his home course. Ouimet won, handily defeating Vardon and Ray in a playoff. The triumph over the best of the Brits was the most significant victory in the brief history of golf in this country, not the least because Ouimet was an amateur, a salesman of sporting goods for a Boston firm. Ironically, this amateur's victory splashed the professionals' game onto the front pages, where it has stayed ever since. The U.S. Open was held at The Country Club in 1963 to celebrate the fiftieth anniversary of Ouimet's triumph and again in 1988 on the seventy-fifth anniversary.

A year after winning the U.S. Open, Ouimet won the most important championship in America, the U.S. Amateur. To put it bluntly: some of the amateurs back then were as good as the pros, or better. One of the amateurs certainly was as good as the pros—much better. But Bobby Jones is another chapter in the story.

Only one professional was remotely in the same class as Jones: Walter Hagen. Hagen's boasting before the 1913 Open was not entirely empty: He finished a surprising fourth in the tournament, and he won the following year. Hagen was sometimes wild off the tee, sometimes wild from the fairway, and sometimes wild off the golf course, too. The Haig made the game look hard, and that's one of the reasons he was able to infuse a tame sport with rabid fan enthusiasm. He was the first pro who pulled this off, accomplishing for his era what Arnold Palmer later did for the televised game. Frank Beard,

a journeyman pro of the modern era, was correct when he quipped, "I should tithe twenty-five cents of every dollar I make to Arnie," but Gene Sarazen made that tribute first, decades earlier, when he said, "Whenever a tournament professional stretches a fat winning check between his fingers he should give silent thanks to Walter Hagen."

In many respects Hagen was the opposite of his gentlemanly peer Bobby Jones, but he had what Jones had and what the pro ranks needed: charisma. (Hagen is commonly given credit for "inventing" the huge golf bag that is now standard equipment on the PGA Tour.) Like all of the early pros, he was a man of the people—the son of a blacksmith—but he had loftier preferences. "I don't want to be a millionaire," he quipped. "I just want to *live* like one." Hagen is sometimes credited with being the first athlete who earned a million dollars during his career, including unofficial money. In two decades, he won eleven major championships (two U.S. and four British Opens and five PGA Championships), about sixty other titles, and played in some 1,500 exhibitions (on some tours he would play one a day for weeks until he dropped from fatigue and his manager took mercy on him). His breakneck pace was the only way to win a million back then: a winning purse was worth a thousand dollars or less, with rare exceptions: Three events in Florida in 1921 offered a combined purse of $8,500. Hagen's prize for winning the 1919 Open was five hundred dollars and a gold medal, with only twelve other players picking up checks.

Hagen had a much bigger payday in 1926 when he trounced Jones in a widely publicized seventy-two-hole battle of the titans played over two layouts in Florida. Hagen won, 11 and 10, and collected the entire $7,500 purse. (Because

Top:
The first pros were barely distinguishable from their caddies. Clad in the bow tie is Willie Anderson, winner of three consecutive U.S. Opens, in 1903, 1904, and 1905. He has his arm around the man who ended his streak with a victory in 1906, Alex Smith.

Above:
The first American-born player to win the U.S. Open, John McDermott was the victor in 1911 at the Chicago Golf Club.

Right:
Willie Dunn, runner-up to Horace Rawlins in the first U.S. Open, had a hand in designing the course at Shinnecock Hills in Southampton, New York.

In 1913, two of the finest swings in America were British imports, belonging to Harry Vardon (left) and Ted Ray. Still, they were not good enough to beat Francis Ouimet at Brookline, Massachusetts.

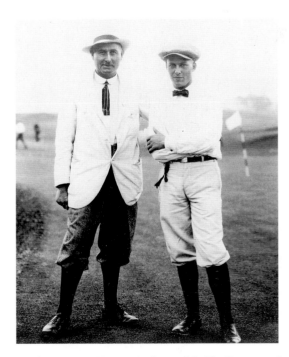

Ouimet, the twenty-year-old amateur, stunned the two pros as well as the rest of the world of golf with his convincing playoff victory at The Country Club. A year later he won the U.S. Amateur Championship.

The greats of two eras—Harry Vardon and Bobby Jones—at Inverness Country Club in Toledo, Ohio, for the 1920 U.S. Open. Vardon finished second, Jones eighth.

Above:
A reflection of the disregard for the early pros was the fact that Fred Herd, the U.S. Open champion in 1898, was required to put up security for the trophy while he held it for a year.

Opposite above:
Occasionally wild off the tee, occasionally wild off the golf course, Walter Hagen ("the Haig") was the first pro with certified charisma. Flashy cars were part of his standard equipment.

Opposite, below left:
The Haig was a match for anyone, including the Duke and Duchess of Windsor.

Opposite, below right:
Sir Walter crusaded successfully on behalf of his fellow pros, winning access to the country club clubhouses.

Jones was an amateur, Hagen would have collected even had he lost.) Things had come a long way from 1895, when two imported British pros, Willie Park and Willie Dunn, played what might have been the first big-time match on these shores: three games, two hundred dollars apiece, winner take all. (That was a big purse, indeed, before the turn of the century. That the combatants were from overseas didn't lessen the significance of that first major professional golf event in the United States: There was more money on this side of the Atlantic, and this money would eventually establish the dominance of American professional golf worldwide. When worldwide money for golf began to catch up in the 1970s, so did the worldwide game.)

There was no pro tour as such for the first two or three decades of the century. The early tournaments were solo affairs, promoted by the owners of winter resorts in Florida, Texas, and California, who quickly learned that the presence of some "name" players would attract paying clientele (two players made an exhibition; a dozen made a tournament). Matters have not changed much since that day, and some of the longest-running tournaments on the modern PGA Tour have their origins in the old days.

The early tour wasn't much, and neither were the pros who played it. Decades were required for the pros to shed a second-class status, an attitude adopted by the ruling gentry in America under the influence, apparently, of their brethren in Great Britain. Even the famous visitor Harry Vardon was required to take his meals *elsewhere* during his tours of American golf clubs. Fred Herd, U.S. Open champion in 1898, was required to put up security for the trophy that would be his for one year—or so the story goes. It was not until 1920 at the Inverness Country Club in Toledo, Ohio, that pros were extended the full privileges of the club. (Three years later, at Troon in Scotland, the governing body of golf in Britain, the Royal and Ancient, opened its doors to Walter Hagen—or tried to. Miffed at his and the other pros' treatment in Britain, Hagen repaired, instead, to the local pub that had been his headquarters for the week. And the stories are true that Hagen more than once used his limousine as his locker at the British Open.)

Club pros in the early days in the United States often were placed in their positions by brokers who acquired the franchise and paid the professional a straight salary, maybe twenty-five dollars a week. In short, professional golf was not much of a way to make a living for all but a few campaigners like Walter Hagen or Gene Sarazen. Even in 1940, Jimmy Demaret, who had won six straight events, including The Masters, had to return to his club job in Texas for fear of losing it because of absenteeism.

The first true championship dedicated to professional golfers *only*—no amateurs allowed—was the PGA Championship of 1916. The idea for the tournament, and the national organization to go with it, is credited to Rodman Wanamaker, a Philadelphia department store heir who had the foresight to see the direction in which the game was heading. He established a purse of $2,500, and Jim Barnes won the match-play format that featured thirty-one players, almost all of them from the Eastern United States. The tournament was a success but with one major qualification: any tournament that excluded Bobby Jones was a champion-

Left:
In 1916, Rodman Wanamaker, heir to the department store fortune, founded a tournament for professionals and a national organization to go with it, the Professional Golfers Association (PGA) of America.

Below:
The first American Ryder Cup team, victors over the British squad at Worcester Country Club, Worcester, Massachusetts, in 1927. Back row, left to right: Johnny Golden, Joe Turnesa, Johnny Farrell, Al Watrous. Foreground: Leo Diegel, Bill Mehlhorn, Captain Walter Hagen, Al Espinosa, and Gene Sarazen. The 9½ to 2½ drubbing marked the beginning of American supremacy in world professional golf.

ship of somewhat tainted value. Walter Hagen completely dominated the PGA in the 1920s, and good for him, but he simply was not beating the best in order to do it.

In 1922, Hagen became the first *American* to win the *British* Open. (Jock Hutchison, the winner of the British Open the year before, was considered an American player, but he was born in St. Andrews, Scotland.) Hagen's triumph signaled that the American pro game finally had arrived as an equal to the British standard. When Hagen was joined by Gene Sarazen and other American pros in beating the British in the first official Ryder Cup Matches in 1927, a sound 9½ to 2½ drubbing in Worcester, Massachusetts, the American pro game established a hegemony it has not relinquished yet.

Right:
The first man to win the modern Grand Slam, Gene Sarazen rose from the caddie ranks to become one of the game's best loved—and best dressed—champions.

Below:
There was no formal pro tour in the early years, but top players such as Gene Sarazen and Walter Hagen found ways to entertain the fans and earn a few extra dollars.

Above left:
The first PGA Championship, a match-play event that attracted only thirty-one players, was won by lanky Jim Barnes at Siwanoy Country Club in Bronxville, New York. After a two-year hiatus for World War I, Barnes won the second PGA in 1919.

Above right:
Leo Diegel "Diegeling." With his unique elbows-out putting style, the two-time PGA champion added a new verb to the instruction lexicon.

Left:
The Silver Scot, Tommy Armour, with his 1931 British Open trophy. He also won the U.S. Open (1927) and PGA Championship (1930) before going on to a successful career as a teaching pro in Florida.

Opposite, above left:
One of the few players to win consecutive U.S. Opens was Ralph Guldahl (1937–38), whose backswing was longer than his career. All eleven of his victories came between 1936 and 1939.

Opposite, above right:
A happy Denny Shute with his wife, moments after his victory over Jimmy Thomson (left) in the 1936 PGA Championship. He won it again in 1937, the last man to score back-to-back victories in that championship.

Opposite below:
Loaded with personality and talent to match, Jimmy Demaret was one of the most popular champions of the 1940s and 1950s.

Not until Jones retired did the pro game become *the* game at the highest level of competition. Jones's niblick (9-iron) to the green on the eleventh hole at Merion Cricket Club outside Philadelphia to win the U.S. Amateur, the last leg of the Grand Slam (the three other events were the U.S. and British Opens and the British Amateur) in 1930, was the truly final shot of the amateur era, even though three years later, Johnny Goodman won the U.S. Open as an amateur. It has not happened since and is not likely to.

Strangely enough, the pro game immediately suffered a decade-long decline in the thirties. For one thing, everyone missed Bobby Jones. For another, no charismatic pro came along to inherit the mantle of the Haig, who was fading. Pros such as Tommy Armour, Olin Dutra, Leo Diegel, Ralph Guldahl, Paul Runyan, and Denny Shute won multiple major titles. The colorful little man who had changed his name from Sarazeni was active and winning golf tournaments, but Gene Sarazen could not carry the load alone, even with the incredible double eagle on the fifteenth hole at The Masters in 1935. That shot secured Bobby Jones's year-old invitational a place in the fans' imagination and, soon enough, status as one of the four majors in the new era of professional golf. (Its status was acquired before the PGA Championship

In 1934, Bobby Jones unveiled the Augusta National Golf Club in Augusta, Georgia, and invited his friends on the pro tour to his first tournament. The Masters was born.

earned it, mainly because the match-play format of the PGA was deemed outmoded, since it could produce "fluky" winners. The PGA went to medal play in 1958.)

As the tour waited for its next big drawing card, it worked to establish an organizational base. In 1930, the Professional Golfers Association (PGA) hired its first full-time tournament organizer. Soon, Fred Corcoran joined the tour as a full-time ramrod and introduced golf to the public relations era. In 1936, tour purses totaled about $100,000. Horton Smith, the leading money winner that year, earned $7,682. Ten years later, purses totaled more than $400,000, and leading money winner Byron Nelson won almost $40,000 in war bonds.

The dearth of great players and/or personalities following Jones's retirement did not last long. In 1937, Sam Snead, a mountaineer or hillbilly or farm boy from West Virginia (it

Bobby Jones holing out at the eighteenth (now the ninth) hole in the second round of the first Masters.

Everyone appeared on time for this photograph of the first Masters field. Everyone, that is, except the Haig, whose larger-than-life image was later added to the far left end of the back row.

Bobby Jones and Walter Hagen were paired in round three. Here the host tees off at the first hole (number ten on the current course) while Hagen, his ball already teed up, waits to play.

Sam Snead's talents on a golf course were boundless and were not limited to striking the ball.

Bobby Jones relaxing at his tournament with three men who were perennial contenders. Jimmy Demaret won three Masters, Byron Nelson and Ben Hogan two each.

didn't matter which; he was colorful), awed the writers on the West Coast with his prodigious drives, beautiful swing, and slow drawl. When "Sneed" (a common misspelling) won in Oakland, he was an overnight sensation. The neophyte tour publicity machine made sure of that. The following year, Snead (properly spelled) led the money list. Two years later, in 1940, another Texan named Ben Hogan won his first pro event and led the money list.

Bantam Ben Hogan, Slammin' Sammy Snead, and Lord Byron Nelson were America's own triumvirate to match the original "Great Triumvirate" of Vardon, Ray, and J.H. Taylor, forty years earlier. Add in Jimmy Demaret, and the tour had a collection of great talent and interesting personalities that would propel it through the war years and into the age of television.

The modern era of professional golf started in earnest when everyone returned from the war. A new level of play went along with the new, great players. The game the pros played was marked by longer drives, because steel shafts were standard equipment, and these shafts were more lenient than hickory had been. The game of sweet swinging was replaced by hard hitting. Ben Hogan swung at the ball with all his might, especially in his earlier (and less productive) years. Also, the art of clubmaking had perfected the matched set of irons. Long gone were the days of a ragtag bag of niblicks and cleeks, much less the days when a Harry Vardon played par golf with half a dozen clubs. Before the United States Golf Association (USGA) instituted the fourteen-club maximum in 1938, some pros (or their caddies, to be precise) were toting several dozen sticks.

Longer drives and more accurate irons meant shorter, more makeable putts, so it is no contradiction that putting rather than shotmaking emerged as the key to the power game, and that is the way it is today on the PGA Tour.

Consider the better maintenance standards of golf courses, and it is easy to understand why scores plummeted. Even without the stiff competition, which would have been offered by his missing comrades, Nelson's record in 1945 of a 68.33 scoring average for 120 rounds, when he won eleven tournaments in a row, exemplified the low-scoring prowess of the new game, as played by any of the triumvirate and a handful of other top performers.

When Hogan returned to golf late in 1945, he proceeded to win five tournaments in the summer and fall. Snead won six tournaments late in the year. Nelson semi-retired after the following year's campaign, which was billed as a shootout between him and Hogan—final verdict: a draw—and thus Hogan and Snead were left to dominate the game for the next half decade. Not even the almost-fatal car crash in 1949

In 1953, Ben Hogan did what no man had ever done—he won The Masters, U.S. Open, and British Open in a single year. New York City gave him a tickertape parade. Horton Smith (at left), then president of the PGA, went along for the ride.

could derail Hogan's phenomenal performance in that period. He returned to the tour less than a year after the accident to play the best golf of his life. In 1953, he had a year equal to Bobby Jones's in 1930. Hogan won the U.S. and British Opens and The Masters. He passed up the PGA Championship on the grounds that his legs could not stand up to the torture of seven rounds of golf over five days of match play.

That also was the year of the first televised golf extravaganza, the self-designated World Championship at Tam O'Shanter outside Chicago. The event was dreamed up by

George S. May, often referred to as golf's P. T. Barnum, and it was May's luck that the tournament was highlighted by the second most famous shot in the history of the American game up to that point, after Sarazen's double eagle. At Tam O'Shanter, Lew Worsham holed out with a wedge from about a hundred yards to win the incredible first prize of $25,000 (plus a contract for twenty-five exhibitions at $1,000 each). It was a fitting introduction to the "new" televised game that would reshape professional golf. Two years later, Arnold Palmer won his first professional tournament, the Canadian Open.

Opposite:
These oil paintings of (clockwise from left) Walter Hagen, Gene Sarazen, Ben Hogan, and Byron Nelson are exhibited in the United States Golf Association (USGA) Museum in Far Hills, New Jersey.

Above left:
The classic finish that was his trademark even in his later years. At age sixty-seven Snead shot sixty-seven, then sixty-six in the 1979 Quad Cities Open, the only man ever to equal or better his age in a tour event.

Above right:
Ben Hogan made only one appearance in Britain, played only one golf course, but that was enough. He tamed rugged Carnoustie and won by four strokes.

Right:
Arguably the first big-time golf promoter, George S. May created the Tam O'Shanter event in 1941 with a total purse nearly twice as big as any other on the tour. By 1954, first prize was $50,000, and May paid it to Bob Toski.

It was in 1953 also that golf's purses topped the half-million-dollar mark; five years later, the one-million barrier was broken. There has been no stopping them. Credit television and golf's great luck that along with the new medium came a personality perfectly suited to it. Palmer came across like gangbusters on TV. It made millions off him, and he made millions off television.

Pros learned to exploit their new status as celebrities, signing contracts for any and all golf-related products and services. This was a booming but not by any means a new exploitation: Harry Vardon's stateside tour in 1900 was sponsored by A.G. Spalding and Bros. as a promotion for its Vardon Flyer ball.

The money also brought in the major celebrity golfers, and vice versa. The Palm Springs Desert Classic in 1960 was one

Hogan's last opportunity to win a record fifth U.S. Open ended in 1960 at this creek fronting the seventeenth green at Cherry Hills Country Club outside Denver, Colorado.

An exultant Arnold Palmer, having come from seven strokes back to win the 1960 Open, hurls his visor to the delighted crowd.

of the early celebrity extravaganzas, the super pro-ams which are among the most popular events on the tour today. But the biggest celebrities of all were the pros themselves. When Bobby Jones remarked at The Masters that Nicklaus played a game that Jones wasn't familiar with, he was referring to the Golden Bear's powerful play, but he also could have been talking about the wealth and celebrity that a great pro could aspire to in this Golden Age of golf. Whether or not Walter Hagen was, indeed, the first of the golfing millionaires, he has been followed by nearly one hundred professionals who have earned a bona fide one million dollars in official money on the tour, not to mention unofficial and off-the-course earnings.

And looming over the boom of the last three decades has been Jack Nicklaus, who horned in on the Palmer era so early that Palmer never had a true era of his own. Nicklaus outlasted Palmer, Gary Player, Johnny Miller, Lee Trevino, Tom Weiskopf, and Tom Watson—all of them. His remarkable statistics do not need repeating. Money—five million dollars officially—is the least of it. The simplest way to put it might be this: Nicklaus has won more tournaments and many more *major* tournaments against much better competition over a longer period of time than any other player in the history of the game. His career is a fitting "conclusion" to the first hundred years of the game in America.

Golf—amateur and professional—is now safe and sound on these shores, but it has not always been easy or pretty. It was not until 1961 that the "Caucasian only" clause was stricken from the PGA by-laws, and no black man was invited to The Masters until 1975.

The money has created problems, too. As the game of the touring pros became the focus of big-time golf, the PGA, the pros' own organization, divided into two camps, the club and teaching pros, who make up the bulk of the membership on the one side, and the touring pros, who garner most of the publicity, and, with the advent of television, most of the revenue for the PGA through the television contract for the championship, on the other. The tour pros believed that the television money should go to them exclusively, or close to it. PGA officials balked. In 1966, the players first uttered serious warnings of mutiny after the PGA nixed a Frank Sinatra tournament in Palm Springs on the grounds that it would diminish the support for the popular Bob Hope Classic. The decision cost the touring pros a $200,000 purse. The following year, just weeks before the PGA Championship at Columbine Country Club in Denver, they threatened to boycott unless PGA officials reached a television contract acceptable to the players. A cool-down period was used to save the tournament, but in 1968 a group of the leading pros, including Jack Nicklaus, announced the formation of a separate tour group, the American Professional Golfers, with plans for establishing their own tour in 1969. Regular tour sponsors vacillated in their loyalties. ABC, the network holding the contract for the 1969 PGA Championship at Dayton, Ohio, told the PGA it would break the agreement if the stars were not present. Dayton officials also said they

would cancel. Arnold Palmer remained neutral. Finally, a new PGA president, Leo Fraser, realized the gravity of the situation and worked out an agreement with the players, the most significant long-term aspect of which was the creation of the autonomous Tournament Players Division within the PGA structure, with Joseph C. Dey as its first commissioner.

In 1974, the touring pros staged their own event, the Tournament Players Championship, won by Jack Nicklaus. Now the tournament (renamed The Players Championship) is nominated as a fifth major, a designation that will happen, if at all, by some quiet, unofficial "vote" of media and fans. In that year, the players rebelled against the new PGA Tour Commissioner Deane Beman's plan for a super tour, which would have required the attendance of all the top players at a

Jack Nicklaus sinking the twenty-three-foot putt that won the 1967 U.S. Open at Baltusrol Golf Club in Springfield, New Jersey, with a record score of 275. Arnold Palmer, the runner-up, stands at the side. As much as any tournament, this one symbolized the transition from the Palmer era to the Nicklaus era.

large number of designated tournaments. The players refused to relinquish their status as independent contractors.

A pleasant problem created by all of the new money was competition for places on the tour. In 1965, the tour had to hold its first qualifying tournament. The "winners" of this 108-hole marathon were then eligible to compete on Mondays for positions in the field at any given tournament. A hundred players might be trying to qualify for ten spots in the field. Those were the days of the "rabbits." Perhaps perversely, the golf pros took pride in the fierce competition on the tour and the possibility of little or no money at the end of a week's work. They enthusiastically compared their entrepreneurial status with the pampered life of the salaried pros in the team sports. They also noted that, no matter how

Left:
Jack Nicklaus's record of twenty major championships, won over a twenty-seven-year span, is a mark that will probably never be approached.

Below:
Nicklaus applies the final touch to his victory in the 1972 U.S. Open at Pebble Beach Golf Links, Pebble Beach, California. Nicklaus, who had also won the U.S. Amateur at Pebble, is the only player ever to win both titles on the same course.

much money they earned on the golf course, it was far less than the straight salaries earned by the baseball stars.

Then that spirit of free enterprise changed, too, and, again, money was the reason. There was so much money on tour by the late seventies, with dozens of players earning six figures on the course and as much or more off the course, that some of the journeymen in the ranks began to cast about for a way to see more of this money trickle down to them. The solution to the "problem" was the "all-exempt tour" that went into effect in 1983, the format in which players in various categories automatically qualify for almost all tour events. One of those categories was the top-125 finishers in the preceding year's money list. The old format had granted automatic places in a field to only the top-60 money winners and the players who had made the cut the previous week;

Right:
Although physically small, South Africa's Gary Player had enormous determination and used it to win scores of tournaments worldwide, including the four major championships.

Below:
The Masters did not invite a black competitor until 1975, when Lee Elder broke the barrier.

thus, some less popular tournaments had room for dozens of Monday qualifiers.

Doubling the number of automatic exemptions makes life on tour much easier for the second echelon of players, but also makes it more difficult for young players just out of the tour qualifying school to break in. Some observers now believe that the all-exempt tour has had a much greater impact on the tour than was initially anticipated. They argue that the automatic exemptions, combined with purses in which the winning share is $100,000 or more, have created a generation of get-rich-quick professionals, aggressive players who disdain the long haul, one-week and one-year wonders who cash in when they are hot, then disappear.

But the fans do not want a new winner every week or a new star every year. They want a few big stars, year after year. The critics of the all-exempt tour wonder whether enduring stars can emerge under the new system. The statistics are not heartening in this regard. In the decade following World War II, the first decade of the modern era, the leading pro averaged seven victories a year. In the following decade, 5.3 victories. Then 5.3 again, then 6.0. But no one has won more than four events since 1979.

More money and more talent have created fewer stars. The last of the great Watson years was 1983. Since then, the game has been not so much dominated as populated by a glut of near-superstars. Names like Ray Floyd, Hale Irwin, Tom Kite, Calvin Peete, Curtis Strange, Larry Nelson, Lanny Wadkins, and Ben Crenshaw have had the almost-right stuff, while the American tour has suffered a strong challenge from the pros of Great Britain, Europe, and all parts East. Since its inception in 1986, the Sony World Ranking system, designed to compare professionals among the United States, European, Asian, and Australian tours, has been led exclusively by foreign players such as Australia's Greg Norman, Spain's Seve Ballesteros, Bernhard Langer of West Germany, Tommy Nakajima of Japan, and Ian Woosnam of Wales. The British/European team has won the past two Ryder Cup Matches against America, an unprecedented achievement, including a solid victory in 1987 on American soil, the first in the sixty-year history of the competition. Since Watson's last British Open in 1983, the string of champions in that event has been Ballesteros (1984), Scotland's Sandy Lyle (1985), Norman (1986), and England's Nick Faldo (1987).

But Arnold Palmer is still a star—on the Senior PGA

Opposite left:
The golden boy of the mid-1970s, Johnny Miller. When he was "on," he was unbeatable, as at Oakmont in 1973, when he closed with a 63 to win the U.S. Open.

Opposite right:
Talented, tempestuous Tom Weiskopf. Living and working in the shadow of fellow Ohioan Jack Nicklaus, he used one of history's sweetest swings to win fifteen tournaments, a British Open, and more than $2 million.

Below left:
Unquestionably the best player of the post-Nicklaus era, Tom Watson was the tour's leading money winner for four years in a row.

Below right:
One of the game's most durable competitors, Ray Floyd joined the PGA Tour in 1963 at age twenty. Since then, he has won The Masters, the U.S. Open, the PGA Championship (twice), and competed on six Ryder Cup teams.

Tour. That separate circuit for professionals over fifty is the most significant development in the game in the last few decades. Officially born in 1980, with two events, it actually began two years earlier with the first Legends of Golf tournament in Austin, Texas. The popularity of that team competition first made tour officials aware of the commercial prospects for seniors-only tournaments. The 1988 version of the senior tour featured thirty-five events and purses totaling almost $10 million, and the prospects for the seniors seem solid, as more of the stars of the sixties and seventies begin to qualify. Nicklaus and Lee Trevino will be eligible in 1990 and intend to play—Trevino, full time.

On the golf course, the last two decades have been the Nicklaus era. Off the course, the Beman era. Beman, a former insurance broker as well as pro golfer with four titles to his credit, has overseen the growth of the senior tour, the funding of a player retirement plan, and the move by the tour into a variety of businesses and marketing enterprises. The tour listed thirty-two official licensees in its 1988 guide. The most visible and important of Beman-era enterprises is the stadium golf concept at the Tournament Players Clubs (TPC), of which there are now twelve around the country.

Top:
*Golf becomes almost an art form when it is played by Seve Ballesteros,
generally agreed to be the most naturally gifted of today's players.*

Above:
*Australia's Greg Norman reached peak form in 1986, winning ten
tournaments worldwide, including the British Open, and leading the
four major championships going into the final round.*

Right:
Quietly, unobtrusively, Curtis Strange has become one of the most productive players of the modern era. He was GOLF Magazine's Player of the Year in both 1985 and 1987.

Below left:
Two of the most popular professionals of the modern era, Ben Crenshaw and Spain's Seve Ballesteros. The occasion here is Crenshaw's 1984 Masters victory. Ballesteros, the 1983 champion, helps him don the traditional green jacket.

Below center:
"Mr. Consistency," Tom Kite, is the only player on the PGA Tour to have won a tournament in every year from 1981 to 1987.

Below right:
Quick-swinging Lanny Wadkins is respected as one of the game's toughest competitors. Every shot he hits is an aggressive one.

Top:
(Clockwise from top left) Miller Barber, Billy Casper, Gene Littler, and Chi Chi Rodriguez—four players who had success on the regular tour, then went on to bigger money on the senior circuit.

Above:
One of the most photogenic players, Lee Trevino entertained the galleries and won tournaments for twenty years. He now does television commentary while looking forward to playing on the Senior PGA Tour.

After a major rift arose between the PGA of America and the playing pros, the Tournament Players Division was created and Joseph C. Dey became its first commissioner.

Deane Beman, a former insurance broker/amateur golfer/pro golfer, who, as PGA Tour commissioner, has changed the face of pro golf, raising total purses from $8 million dollars in 1975 to nearly $30 million in 1988.

Beman's brainstorm, the first Tournament Players Club course at Sawgrass, owned by the tour and designed to test the players while catering to the spectators.

Ten of these courses host official or unofficial tour events, but in the other fifty-one weeks of the year, they are resort courses open to the public. The layouts have proved popular with spectators at the tournaments and with amateur golfers.

In the early, hand-to-mouth days of the tour, most of the tournaments were played on resort and public layouts. That tour slowly gave way to tournaments played mostly at private clubs. Now with the advent of the TPC courses, the golf the pros play is once again brought closer to the game of the average golfer. The pros still play a different game, of course, but on some of the same courses as the amateurs. That's about all their game has in common with the game of the amateurs in America who, in the early days, beat the pros on the golf course and then refused them admission to the clubhouse. Those tables are turned: The pros always win, and the locker room during tournament week is off limits to the members.

When Robert Lockhart returned from a business trip to Britain in 1887 carrying three woods, two irons, a putter, and two dozen gutta-percha balls for his friend John Reid, it was Mrs. John Reid who made room for them. And when Reid and his friends gathered to formalize their friendly association on a November evening in 1888, it was over dinner at Reid's home in Yonkers, New York, a dinner undoubtedly overseen by the mistress of the house. Furthermore, the dinner was a success. Afterward, Mr. Reid, a Scottish immigrant, was induced to entertain his guests by singing "Scots Wa Hae," with encores. But the one thing the pioneering Mrs. Reid was *not* was America's first golf widow. On March 30, 1889, she teamed with John B. Upham in the first mixed-foursome played on the St. Andrews six-hole course, and beat her husband and a Miss Carrie Law.

The three new sports that preceded golf in post-Civil War America were baseball, bicycling, and lawn tennis. Baseball, the spectator sport, was a man's game; but bicycling and tennis were pastimes at which women were more than decorative adjuncts. The bicycle-built-for-two moved women out of the Victorian parlor and into the sunshine, and tennis kept them there. By the time golf took hold in America in the 1890s, women were ready to play. For precedent they could point to the Ladies' Green at St. Andrew's, Scotland, a course that was little more than a glorified putting green, but which had existed at least as early as 1875.

The Shinnecock Hills Golf Club in Southampton, New York, opened in 1891. By 1893, the wives of the members had convinced their husbands to create a separate nine-hole course for them. Where the men could not be persuaded to share, women created their own courses. In Morristown, New Jersey, a group of female golfers organized a club, built a seven-hole course, and opened it for play in the spring of 1894. In October that year, they held their first tournament,

Two years after the founding of the Shinnecock Hills Golf Club, Southampton, New York, in 1893, wives of the members persuaded their husbands to provide a separate nine-hole course for ladies only.

won by Annie Howland Ford, who shot 48–46—94 to win by a margin of fourteen strokes. That first tournament at Morris County was a social if not an athletic milestone. The *New York Sun* reported, "As soon as the game was over all hands adjourned to the clubhouse for tea and gossip and to discuss in particular the popular new creation—the golfing cloak. The next day the men were permitted to hold a tournament, and they bettered substantially the remarkable low scores made by the women golfers."

Meanwhile, in Boston, Florence Boit had returned from France to spend the summer of 1892 with her aunt and uncle, Mr. and Mrs. Arthur Hunnewell of Wellesley. While visiting Pau in the south of France, site of the first golf course on the

man's — and Lady's — Game

BY SARAH BALLARD

Continent, Boit had learned the rudiments of the game. She returned to America with her golf clubs in tow. Boit's description of the game and her demonstrations of the clubs' use interested her uncle sufficiently that, with his brother-in-law whose property adjoined his own, he laid out a seven-hole course. In the fall of that year, Hunnewell invited several of his friends to try the game. Among those was Lawrence Curtis, like Hunnewell a member of The Country Club in Brookline, Massachusetts. The Country Club had been established ten years earlier to provide "a comfortable clubhouse for the use of members with their families, a simple restaurant, bedrooms, bowling alley, lawn tennis, a racing track, etc.: also to have race meetings occasionally and music in the afternoon." After little more than a month's exposure to Florence Boit's new game, Curtis saw to it that The Country Club added golf to its roster of activities.

Had enthusiasm for golf grown less rapidly among clubmen of the nineties than it did, women might have remained fairly represented on the early courses. But crowding set in early, and the women were frequently the ones forced to make room. In 1899, The Country Club course was expanded to eighteen holes, but at the same time the club forbade women the use of the course on Saturdays, holidays, and before 2:00 P.M. on weekdays. Earlier, in 1895, the men who had financed the establishment of Morris County, the first women's golf club, and had been given membership and voting rights in return, took the club back. They voted in an all-male slate of officers, but when they offered Annie Howland Ford an "honorary presidency" she declined, which makes it clear the coup was not bloodless.

Shinnecock Hills abandoned the ladies' course; the first women's course west of the Alleghenies, King's Daughters in Evanston, Illinois, was swallowed up; and Saegkill, a women's club founded by Mrs. Reid and her friends when St. Andrew's barred women altogether, was taken over by male golfers. Only the Women's National in Glen Cove, New York, created in 1924, escaped confiscation until 1941, when it merged with the Creek Club.

If American women golfers were handicapped in their early efforts to master the game by the territorial imperatives of their male counterparts, they were further hampered by the fashions to which they were slaves. Wide-brimmed straw hats, starched leg-of-mutton sleeves, corseted waistlines, and graceful ankle-length skirts that drifted charmingly in the slightest breeze were enchanting subjects for the illustrators of the day, but they must have been infuriating to their victims. Joyce Wethered, England's greatest woman player,

The intrepid women golfers of the Morris County (New Jersey) Country Club. In 1894, they founded their own club and built their own seven-hole course.

once described a device called a "Miss Higgins," "a band of some elastic material intended to slip over the knees as a preliminary to putting." Wethered also pointed out that the game's cardinal rule, "Keep your eye on the ball," was irritating advice "when any glimpse of the ball, quite apart from swinging, was a matter of extreme uncertainty."

In spite of adversity, the hardiest of the women golfers persevered. In 1895, they held the Women's Amateur Championship at the Meadow Brook Club in Hempstead, New York. It was a one-day, eighteen-hole affair, with lunch between the nines. Thirteen women competed for a silver pitcher, but the occasion was of greater significance than their scores. Mrs. C. S. Brown of Shinnecock Hills won with a 132. Annie Howland Ford finished tied for eighth with 161.

The next year, the Women's Amateur was held again. By this time the scoring and the event were much improved. A visiting Scot, Robert Cox of Edinburgh, who had helped lay out the Morris County course in 1894, donated a graceful, thistle-topped, silver loving cup, the trophy that is still in competition, on the condition that the tournament be held at Morris County. The United States Golf Association (USGA), which was a year old at the time, agreed. A notice was put out to member clubs announcing a "Women's Championship Golf Competition for the championship of the United States, open to all women golfers belonging to the clubs which are members of the United States Golf Association."

Mrs. C. S. Brown chose not to defend her title, which was just as well, since, in the medal round, Beatrix Hoyt, also of Shinnecock Hills, shot a 95, lowering Mrs. Brown's eighteen-hole score by thirty-seven strokes. In the final, Hoyt, who was sixteen, beat Mrs. Arthur Turnure, 2 and 1, for the first of her

An early feminine fairway foray. The player seems to be watching the birdie more closely than the ball. Note the raised, grassless teeing area with the ball perched on a pinch of dirt. (Tees, as we know them, were not invented until 1920.) Note also the gloves on both the right and left hands of the waiting player.

three consecutive titles. Possibly even more amazing than Hoyt's score were the number and enthusiasm of the spectators for the final match. They required restraint behind a rope.

In 1899, the championship was played in Philadelphia for the first time, at the Bala course of the Philadelphia Country Club. The runner-up that year was the pride of the Huntingdon Valley club, Mrs. Caleb Fox, who had reared a family before she took up golf. Margaret Fox was already thirty-nine in 1899, yet she continued to compete for the next twenty-six

Right:
Straw hats and close-fitting jackets were the early American ladies' golf attire.

Full-fingered gloves saved wear and tear on milady's hands.

Neither rain nor snow nor constricting garments could stay the lady golfer from her appointed round. Note—as early as 1900—a colored ball.

ADVICE TO CADDIES.

Above:
The above was captioned: "Advice to Caddies: You will save time by keeping your eye on the ball, not on the player."

Opposite above:
Mrs. C. S. Brown of Shinnecock Hills, winner of the first women's national championship in 1895. With an eighteen-hole score of 132, she topped the dozen other players in the field.

Opposite below:
In 1896, Beatrix Hoyt's medal round of 95 lowered Mrs. Brown's record by thirty-seven strokes. Miss Hoyt went on to win the second championship at match play, then repeated in each of the next two years.

years. She retired in 1925 after her twenty-second Women's Amateur, never having won but having been medalist, co-medalist, and three times semifinalist.

Women's golf grew and prospered in Philadelphia as nowhere else. A Women's Golf Association was formed as early as 1897, and Women's Interclub matches have been held from that day forward. The Merion Cricket Club in Haverford, later the Merion Golf Club of Ardmore, produced some of the great players of the early years of the American game. One was Frances Canby ("Pansy") Griscom, who had played in the 1896 championship at Morris County and won the 1900 title at Shinnecock Hills. She played for Merion in the first Philadelphia Interclub matches and in every subsequent series through 1924. She also drove a Red Cross ambulance in World War I, and is thought to have been the first woman in Philadelphia to own and drive an automobile. In 1965, at the hundredth birthday celebration of the Merion Cricket Club, Pansy Griscom returned to the club the silver cup its officers had given her when she became Merion's first amateur champion in 1900.

In 1909, the Women's Amateur was held at Merion (Cricket, not Golf) a second time. The winner was Dorothy Iona Campbell, a native of North Berwick, Scotland, who was that year's British Ladies champion. The next year Campbell, now living in Canada, acquired the Canadian title in addition to the British and American titles, making her not only the first double winner in women's golf, but its first triple winner. She was a slip of a girl when she appeared on the American scene in a wide-brimmed boater and a high, stiff collar, but she looked at the camera then just as she did for the rest of her life—directly, eye-to-lens, as if to say she was interested and ready, at any moment, to be amused. She became a Merion institution, and when her record was totted up for the ages, she was said to have won 750 tournaments, among them three American titles, two British titles, and three Canadian titles.

World War I and the immediate postwar years were dominated by Alexa Stirling, a childhood golfing companion of Bobby Jones, from Atlanta. Both were pupils of Stewart Maiden, a celebrated Scottish-born teaching professional. Alexa was a fragile-looking girl of seventeen with long curls when she played in her first Women's Amateur in 1914 at the Nassau Country Club in Glen Cove, New York. That year she lost in the first round of match play, but the next year she survived to the semifinals, and, in 1916, she won the first of her three consecutive titles.

During the war, when all USGA championships were suspended, Alexa and Bobby Jones played in an exhibition match for the benefit of the Red Cross at the Wannamoisett

Above:
In Philadelphia, golf became an integral part of Main Line society. Here the ladies are welcomed after a round at the Philadelphia Country Club.

Left:
Merion's finest, Frances ("Pansy") Griscom won the U.S. Women's Amateur in 1900.

Opposite, above left:
In 1910, Dorothy Iona Campbell won the amateur championships of the United States, Great Britain, and Canada. In all, she is said to have won 750 tournaments.

Opposite, above right:
Alexa Stirling, who learned the game along with Bobby Jones, won three consecutive U.S. Women's Amateurs from 1916 to 1918.

Opposite below:
As golf became fashionable, it appeared in advertisements for everything from cruisewear to cigarettes.

Club in Rhode Island, where one of the spectators was a tall, athletic fifteen-year-old girl from Providence who before long was to blossom into America's first great female player. Until she was introduced to golf by her father, Glenna Collett had been a swimmer, a diver, and a baseball player on her brother's team. Watching Alexa Stirling on a summer afternoon in 1918 inspired Collett to become a golfer, which she did with the encouragement of her athletic father and the guidance of another transplanted Scot, Alex Smith. Smith then was the pro at Shennecossett in New London, Connecticut, in the summer and Belleair, on the west coast of Florida, in the winter. Collett was a promising golfer from the start, but it was 1922 before she won the first of her six Amateur Championships. Throughout the twenties, however, she was the preeminent American woman player. Predictably, newspaper writers called her "the female Bobby Jones." Like Jones, Collett traveled to Britain to compete, but unlike Jones she never was able to add the British Ladies to her collection of titles, although she tried four times between 1925 and 1930. Twice she was eliminated by England's greatest player, Joyce Wethered.

Top left:
Glenna Collett Vare dominated women's golf during the 1920s and 1930s, winning six amateur titles and countless other championships.

Above left:
Helen Hicks, the 1931 U.S. Women's Amateur champion, was one of the first to turn professional. Note the wooden shafts on her fifteen clubs.

Top right:
Virginia Van Wie, a delicate young woman who took up golf for her health, became Glenna Vare's archrival in the mid-1930s.

Above right:
Glenna Collett Vare's last victory in the U.S. Women's Amateur was over seventeen-year-old Patty Berg. Three years later, Berg won the title, turned professional, and went on to become one of the legends of the game.

Out for a stroll on the links, seven of the game's greatest players of a half century ago. From left, Jean Bauer, Isabel Ogilvie, Jane Cothran Jameson, Kathryn Hemphill, Patty Berg, Helen Dettweiler, and Marion McDougall.

With her marriage in 1931 Collett, now Mrs. Edwin H. Vare, Jr., competed less frequently, but in 1935, having borne two children, she returned to win the last of her six championships.

Glenna Collett Vare threw a long shadow over women's golf through the twenties, but her triumphal progress was by no means unopposed. An expanding corps of fine female players had come to the game in a new, postwar mood of liberation, their swings unfettered by restrictive clothing and their competitive spirits freed, to an unprecedented degree, of societal restraints. Mary Kimball Browne, who upset Collett in the semifinals of the 1924 championship, was a prewar tennis champion, who two weeks earlier had made it to the semifinals of the national tennis championships. A few years later, Browne accompanied France's incomparable Suzanne Lenglen on her professional tennis tour of the United States.

In 1925, when the championship moved west of the Mississippi for the first time, to the St. Louis Country Club, Collett beat the former Alexa Stirling, now Mrs. W. G. Frazer of Toronto, 9 and 8 in the final, but only after her opponent had set a new scoring record of 77 in the medal round.

In the late twenties, Glenna Collett's principal rival was Virginia ("Gino") Van Wie, a delicate young woman from Onwentsia Golf Club near Chicago who had taken up golf for the sake of her health. In their first meeting in the Amateur Collett routed Van Wie 13 and 12 in the thirty-six-hole final, but later, with Collett married and playing less, Van Wie took the upper hand, winning the title in 1932, 1933, and 1934.

Glenna Collett Vare's last championship in 1935 actually marked the beginning of a new era. Her opponent in the final at the Interlachen Country Club in Minneapolis was Patty Berg, a freckle-faced, seventeen-year-old local golfer. Three years later, Berg won the title; two years after that, she turned professional, going to work promoting the products of the Wilson Sporting Goods Company. Berg was not the first American woman champion to turn professional—Helen Hicks, who won in 1931, also went to work for Wilson—but Berg is the surviving link between the pre-World War II age of the amateur and the postwar rise of the professional. It was she who, along with later Women's Amateur champions Betty Jameson (1939 and 1940), Babe Zaharias (1946), Louise Suggs (1947), and seven other women professionals met in Wichita, Kansas, in 1949 to charter the Ladies Professional Golf Association (LPGA), with 1950 as its official founding date. The Wichita meeting set in motion an organization that has grown, by fits, starts, and, finally, million-dollar leaps, into the vehicle that provides frequent competition for women golfers at the highest level.

Open competitions, in which professionals could compete for prize money alongside amateurs, were virtually nonexistent in the 1930s. The few that did exist, such as the

The Babe. Mildred Didrikson Zaharias, an Olympic gold medalist in track and field, took up the game and quickly mastered it. Her natural athletic talents enabled her to hit tee shots that sailed almost as far as those of the male pros.

Women's Western Open, begun in 1930, offered prize money that would hardly have covered the winner's train fare. In 1939, when Helen Dettweiler, who eventually became a celebrated teacher, won the Western, she received no cash prize at all, only a silver bowl. In 1941, the total purse available to women professionals in American golf was five hundred dollars.

Forming a professional organization for female golfers, even in 1949, was a shot in the dark. An earlier effort, the Women's Professional Golfers Association (WPGA), had struggled along for a few years and had staged three Open Championships, but its failure to attract either financial backing or an affiliation with the men's professional tour spelled an early doom.

What the fledgling LPGA had that the WPGA did not was Mildred Didrikson Zaharias. Babe, as she was always known, had been a national celebrity since the 1932 Olympic Games in Los Angeles when, as a raw-boned twenty-one-

year-old from Beaumont, Texas, she had won two gold medals and a silver in track and field events. There was nothing Babe could not do and do well. After the Olympics, having been declared a professional by the Amateur Athletic Union, Babe earned her living in a variety of bizarre ways—barnstorming with the bearded House of David baseball team or with her own basketball team, the All-Americans, or appearing on vaudeville stages running on a treadmill and playing her harmonica. (She was good at that, too.)

Meanwhile, with encouragement from sportswriter Grantland Rice, Babe was becoming a golfer, hitting a thousand balls a day whenever her schedule allowed. Her first important tournament was the 1935 Texas Women's Amateur at the River Oaks Country Club in Houston, which she won, only to be barred from all further amateur competition on the grounds that if she was a professional in the eyes of the AAU, she was a professional golfer as well.

From 1935 until 1940, when she requested reinstatement as an amateur, Babe played the two or three tournaments open to professionals each year, endorsed Wilson golf equipment, and, one summer, toured with Gene Sarazen playing exhibitions. After a three-year purification period, during which she mastered tennis and bowling, Babe was reinstated as an amateur by the USGA. She celebrated by shooting 70–67 in a thirty-six-hole charity match against Clara Callender, the California champion. In 1944 and 1945, in spite of the difficulty of civilian travel in wartime, she got herself to Indianapolis for the Women's Western Open and won that too. In 1946, with golf's tournament schedule returning to postwar normality, Babe was playing the best golf of her life. She won seventeen straight tournaments in one year, including the U.S. Women's Amateur and the British Ladies.

In 1947 Babe turned pro again. She acquired the services of Fred Corcoran, a well-known agent who also handled Sam Snead and Ted Williams, and she signed with Wilson for $100,000 a year. She was making money, but what she needed even more was competition and an audience. It was primarily to meet and exploit those needs that Corcoran and Wilson agreed to assist at the birth of the LPGA. At a meeting in 1949 at the Venetian Hotel in Miami with Patty Berg and Babe and George Zaharias, Corcoran agreed to stage manage the tour, and Wilson to pay the bills.

Babe Zaharias was not the greatest female golfer who ever lived. Her swing was not a model, and she gave something away on the tees because she so much liked to astonish the galleries with the enormous distance of her drives. She played to her audiences, and she hated to lose, both traits leading her to excesses that made enemies of some of her colleagues, but she was a personality made to order for a professional sport in

During the early days of the LPGA, Patty Berg and Babe Zaharias took home most of the trophies.

Babe Zaharias and Ben Hogan in 1951 just after they won the men's and women's World Championships at Tam O'Shanter. Babe's first prize was $2,100, Hogan's, $12,500.

its infancy. Patty Berg once said, "Sometimes I find myself leaning back in a chair thinking about Babe and I have to smile. With Babe there was never a dull moment. Her tremendous enthusiasm for golf and life was contagious. Even the galleries felt good when Babe was around."

Betsy Rawls, who played the tour from 1951 to 1975, then served the LPGA as its tournament director for six years, said of Babe, "She was the most physically talented woman I've ever seen, and if she had started golf at an earlier age she would have been sensational."

Through the 1950s and well into the 1960s, women's professional golf remained a hand-to-mouth business. Players supplemented their prize money with clinics and exhibitions, those of them who could, and as the scattered tournaments that made up the schedule grew into a tour, they traveled

Above:
Betsy Rawls played the Ladies Professional Golf Association (LPGA) Tour for a quarter century (1951–75), winning fifty-five events, then served as the association's tournament director for six years.

Left:
Babe Zaharias driving in the Women's Weathervane Open Golf Tourney on May 10, 1952.

from place to place by car, sharing expenses and living out of their trunks. They set up their own courses, distributed their own prize money, and, when the tournament was over, they got on the phone and publicized their own accomplishments. Their real rewards were independence and a career in golf.

Seven of the first twelve U.S. Women's Open champions were former Amateur champions who had turned professional—Patty Berg (one), Betty Jameson (one), Babe Zaharias (three), and Louise Suggs (two). The logical inference from these figures is that the best golf was now being played among the professionals. But the professional life was not for everyone. Some excellent players continued to compete in the amateur ranks. Foremost among them for more than a decade were JoAnne Gunderson Carner and Anne Quast Sander. Between 1956 and 1968, those two Seattle area champions batted the Women's Amateur back and forth like a shuttlecock. Carner won in 1957, 1960, 1962, 1966, and 1968 and was runner-up in 1956 and 1964. Sander won in 1958, 1961, 1963 and was runner-up in 1965 and 1968.

Louise Suggs, one of the founding members of the LPGA and winner of fifty titles, was one of four players inducted into the LPGA Hall of Fame in 1951.

Anne Quast Sander won three U.S. Women's Amateurs and was runner-up twice between 1958 and 1968. She also knew how to scramble out of trouble, even if it meant backhanding the ball with her putter.

Their long rivalry was especially interesting because it was a match-up of opposites. Carner was a strong, long-hitting athlete in the mold of Zaharias, a fun-loving competitor who was at ease with galleries. Sander was an intense, high-strung golfer whose nerves sometimes got the better of her, but whose will and finesse more than made up for what she lacked in power. Sander has remained an amateur; in 1980, while living abroad, she won the British Ladies. Carner turned professional in 1970, when she was thirty, and since then has won two Women's Opens, forty-two tournaments, and more than $2 million.

An early milestone on the LPGA's road to respectability occurred in 1953 when the USGA took over conduct of the Women's Open. As keeper of the flame lit by Mrs. C. S. Brown with her 132 in 1895, the USGA could do no less. With the change in stewardship, however, Open courses became tougher. The year before the USGA took over, Louise Suggs won a second Open title at the Bala Golf Club in Philadelphia with a 70–69–70–75—284, the lowest sev-

Catherine Lacoste of France, the only amateur since 1946 to win the U.S. Open (1967).

JoAnne Carner won five U.S. Women's Amateur titles, then turned pro and went on to win more than forty events.

enty-two-hole score ever recorded by a woman in a major tournament. But the Bala course was only 5,460 yards long, and par was sixty-nine. Under the auspices of the USGA, the first competition was held at The Country Club of Rochester (New York)—6,417 yards with a par of seventy-four. Betsy Rawls and Jackie Pung of Hawaii tied at 302, and Rawls won in an eighteen-hole playoff. The event still attracted more amateurs than it did professionals, but the low amateur's score that year was thirteen strokes off the pace. In fact, only once since 1946 has an amateur won the Women's Open, that being Catherine Lacoste of France in 1967. Lacoste was the daughter of France's famous tennis player of the twenties, René Lacoste, and of Thion de la Chaume, the British Ladies golf champion of 1927. Catherine Lacoste also won the Women's Amateur two years later.

With the death of Babe Zaharias of cancer in 1956, the era of the pioneers ended, although the hardships attendant to establishing a place in the sun and in the public imagination for female professional athletes continued. The emergence of Mary Kathryn ("Mickey") Wright in the late 1950s, however, made life a little easier for all. As one of her contemporaries said, "Mickey got the outside world to take a second look at women golfers and when they looked they discovered the rest of us."

Mickey Wright was reared in San Diego and attended Stanford for one year. She was a tall woman with an engaging manner who combined a beautiful swing with great distance from the tees. She had started playing golf when she was

Generally agreed to be the possessor of the best swing in women's golf history, Mickey Wright used it to good advantage. Between 1959 and 1968 she averaged almost eight victories a year; in 1963 alone, she won thirteen of the thirty-two events on the women's tour.

eleven, and at seventeen she won the USGA Girls' Junior Championship. In 1954 she was low amateur in the Women's Open. In the same year, Wright left college, and a year later joined the LPGA Tour. In 1958, when she was twenty-three, she won the first of four Women's Opens.

It is a personal tribute to Mickey Wright that her colleagues thought so highly of her, since for several years she was taking bread from their mouths every time she entered a tournament. In 1963, she won thirteen of the tour's thirty-two events (40.6 percent) and earned $31,269, which at 1988 levels would be just under $1 million. Between 1959 and 1968, she averaged almost eight victories a year, and for five straight seasons (1960–1964), she won the Vare Trophy for low scoring average. Singlehandedly she overcame the reluctance of the sporting press to cover women's golf, and, as

the press was won over, so was the public. Ten thousand golf fans showed up at Baltusrol in Springfield, New Jersey, to watch her win the 1961 Open. Her 72–80–69–72—293 on Baltusrol's par-seventy-two lower course beat Betsy Rawls by six strokes; her final round has been called "nearly flawless." On Baltusrol's four par-five holes, she was seven under par for the tournament.

After 1969, Wright played only occasionally, but in 1973 she returned to take the Colgate–Dinah Shore tournament, whose winner's purse alone was worth more than she had made in all but her four best years.

International golf for women had its origin in a group, organized by Pansy Griscom of Philadelphia in 1905, which traveled to England to play in the British Ladies Championship. Eight prominent American players of the day made the trip, among them Harriot and Margaret Curtis, sisters from Boston, who later won four American championships between them. In 1927, the Curtis sisters donated a trophy "to stimulate friendly rivalry among the women golfers of many lands," and in 1932 the first biennial Curtis Cup matches between amateur teams from Great Britain and the United States were played in Wentworth, England. Since then, the Curtis Cup has been the crown jewel of women's international amateur competition, at least from the colonial perspective. Although British teams won in 1952 and 1956, United States amateurs held a thirteen-match winning streak until they were defeated in 1986.

The LPGA's purses increased from $600,000 in 1970 to $4 million in 1979. The reasons, simply stated, were corporate sponsorship, television, Title IX, and Nancy Lopez, not necessarily in that order. The first major corporation to see advertising potential in women's golf was Sears, Roebuck & Company, which sponsored a $100,000 event in Port St. Lucie, Florida, for a few years. However, it was David R. Foster, chairman of the giant Colgate-Palmolive empire, who was the first visionary. Foster threw his weight and his budget behind first golf and later half a dozen other women's sports on the theory that they gave better value for his promotional dollar than did the higher-priced men's sports. Furthermore, as a manufacturer of dozens of household products, Foster figured that endorsements by women for women would be useful.

Eventually, Foster's beneficence toward the LPGA extended far beyond practical considerations. He fully intended to give women's golf credibility equal to men's. For a start, he created the Dinah Shore-Colgate Palmolive Winners Circle tournament in the desert near Palm Springs, California, and turned it into a lavish, week-long party, which attracted to its pro-am the same mix of CEOs and Hollywood celebrities who regularly showed up for the Bing Crosby and Bob Hope events on the men's tour. As long as Foster remained the head of Colgate, the LPGA had a godfather; by the time he was replaced, and Colgate withdrew from sports sponsorship, the LPGA had Nancy Lopez, its first bona fide charismatic champion of the television era.

Nancy Marie Lopez was born January 6, 1957, a little over three months after Babe Zaharias died. She grew up in Roswell, New Mexico, the daughter of Mexican-American parents who played golf on Roswell's municipal course. Her father, Domingo Lopez, known in Roswell as Sunday, owned a small auto body repair shop. When Domingo shook a stranger's hand, he would apologize for his own, which was callused and hardened by the chemicals he used in his work. Her mother, Marina, was, well, motherly. Nancy was their adored youngest child, the others being grown and gone. Domingo was the only teacher Nancy ever had, and what he knew of swing techniques he learned from reading instruction articles in golf magazines.

Once it became clear that Nancy had the knack and the interest, Domingo devoted his life and all his limited resources to giving her what she needed to become a golfer. When her youthful interest flagged, he would invent games and offer her small daily rewards. What Domingo could not give his daughter was access to Roswell's country club course, out of bounds to Roswellians of Mexican descent. Nancy earned her way onto that and other country club courses by winning everything in sight, starting at twelve with the New Mexico Women's Amateur. Afterward, though, she always returned to the flat, arid terrain of the municipal course. In spite of a swing that the experts said was suspect, Nancy won the U.S. Girls' Junior Championship when she was fifteen, the same year she won the New Mexico Women's Amateur for the third time and the Western Junior for the first of three times.

By the mid-seventies, the effects of Title IX legislation, enacted in 1972, were being felt in colleges and universities. Under threat of federal funds being withheld from institutions that discriminated against women in any area, women's athletic teams were springing up where none had existed before, and athletic departments began to compete for the services of talented female athletes. Thanks to Title IX, Lopez went to the University of Tulsa on a full golf scholarship. Although she left school at the end of her sophomore year to turn professional, she did gain two extra years of seasoning in amateur tournaments. During that period, she won the Women's Collegiate Championship, finished tied for second in the Women's Open, and played on the winning 1976 Curtis Cup and Women's World Amateur teams.

Harriot and Margaret Curtis, two sisters from Boston, in 1927 donated the Curtis Cup "to stimulate friendly rivalry among the women golfers of many lands."

When Lopez began playing the tour in the waning months of 1977, she was well-known in golf circles and unknown elsewhere. Within a year, she had played golf with a president of the United States, and her face had been on the cover of the *New York Times Magazine*. Lopez's rookie year was phenomenal. She won two tournaments early on the schedule, and then, beginning in May, she won the next five events she entered, including the LPGA Championship. That tournament was played at the Jack Nicklaus Golf Center in Cincinnati, at 6,312 yards, one of the longest the women play, yet rookie Lopez shot a thirteen-under-par 275 to beat her old junior rival, Amy Alcott, by six strokes. Before the year was out, Lopez had won nine tournaments, lowered the LPGA record for seasonal scoring average, and earned more prize money than any rookie golfer ever had, male or female.

Lopez is now married to baseball player Ray Knight and has two young children. In ten years as a pro, she has bettered every record she set that first year, except winning five tournaments in a row. She has not been able to repeat that feat, but neither has anyone else. The only prize that has eluded Lopez so far is the U.S. Women's Open.

A gauge of the growth of the LPGA in the 1980s is that in 1981 Kathy Whitworth became the first woman to reach $1 million in career prize money, and in 1986 Pat Bradley was the first to win $2 million. Whitworth, a Texan who joined the tour in 1958, had to wait four years to win her first tournament, but in the ensuing twenty years she passed Mickey Wright's record of eighty-two victories and since has added six more. Bradley, who once considered a career as a ski instructor, is not so much a late bloomer as a hardy perennial. She has played in nearly four hundred LPGA tournaments and finished in the top ten in more than half of them.

A century has passed since Mrs. John Reid made space in a Yonkers closet for Mr. Reid's new toys. Making space for women in a game with masculine traditions already centuries old has been more difficult. Where opportunity has been denied, women golfers have created their own, with the result that today nearly half of all golfers entering the game are women. In its hundredth year, American golf is close to being a truly *All*-American game.

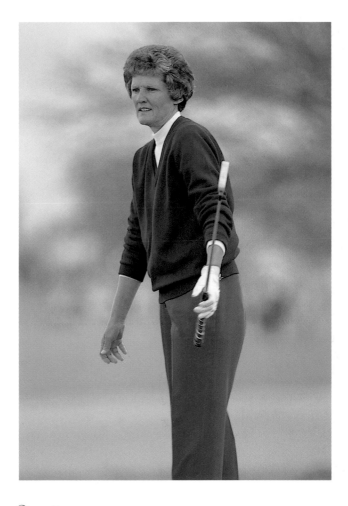

Opposite:
Nancy Lopez won nine tournaments, including five in a row, in her rookie year and attracted new attention to the LPGA Tour.

Above:
Kathy Whitworth has more official tour victories—eighty-eight—than any other professional, male or female, and was LPGA Player of the Year seven out of eight times between 1966 and 1973.

Above right:
In 1986, Pat Bradley won five events, finished runner-up six times, and became the first player to pass the $2-million mark in career earnings.

Right:
Jan Stephenson has become one of the LPGA's most popular players.

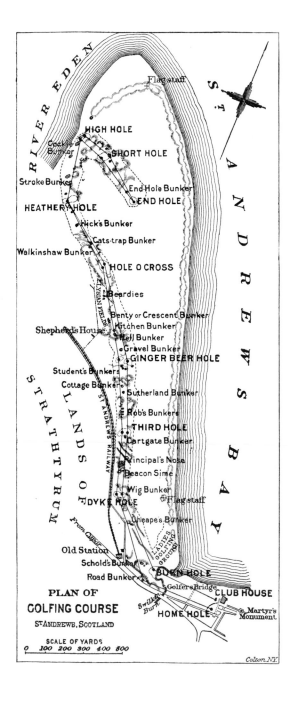

PLAN OF
COLFING COURSE
St ANDREWS, SCOTLAND

SCALE OF YARDS
0   100 200 300 400 500

Colton.N.Y.

In Scotland, where the game of golf evolved, natural forces and grazing sheep were the first golf architects, carving hazards from the sandy, links terrain. The early players had only to choose the fairest patches of turf on which to hole out and the most reasonable and interesting route of play between holes. In America, the early courses had to be laid out on land provided not by nature but on sites selected by players. From the beginning, the American version of the game has required some sort of golf course architecture.

Understanding the history of American golf architecture means first appreciating two opposing forces that have guided its development: a yearning for tradition in an environment of changing standards. From that day in 1888 when John Reid and his friends named their golf club St. Andrew's, golf in America has sought to preserve the traditions of the Scottish game, and golf architects have attempted to build holes that possess similar challenges to those of the links. But at the same time, golf architects have struggled to maintain an integrity of design as improvements in golf equipment and course conditioning have made the game easier to play. The first hundred years of American golf course architecture have been marked by a handful of milestone courses of ever-increasing severity.

Whatever John Reid knew of playing golf, he apparently did not much concern himself about modern notions of classic golf architecture—providing a variety of interesting holes of all lengths, routing the course to encounter the wind from all quarters, minimizing blind holes, and adapting the course to the natural terrain. In its early years, the St.

The place where golf began, St. Andrews, Scotland. Designed by nature and maintained largely by grazing sheep, the Old Course remains a classic of thinking man's golf. This map shows the narrow loop design of the course and includes the names of many of its treacherous bunkers.

Course of Architecture

BY TOM DOAK

Andrew's club moved from cow pasture to apple orchard to farm; but even in its fourth incarnation, Henry Tallmadge, one of the founding members, recalled years later that "it took the greater part of two days to lay out the new course, but it was well worth the time spent on it." Indeed, the annual upkeep in the budget amounted to $1,020, including the ground man's salary.

Most of the approximately one thousand courses in turn-of-the-century America were of similar, uninspired design, staked out in a few hours by club members or, more likely, immigrant Scottish golf professionals hired for a design fee of twenty-five dollars. The most prolific of the early architects was Tom Bendelow, who toured the country under the auspices of A. G. Spalding and Bros., which had a secondary interest in the development of golf courses: providing clubs and balls to new players. Despite their rudimentary design, these courses helped popularize golf, and it should be remembered that many future great players (and course designers) learned the game on courses of similar pedigree.

Thankfully, though, a handful of golfers in the United States had higher aspirations: Willie Dunn, who had emigrated from Musselburgh, Scotland, to lay out a twelve-hole course for the Shinnecock Hills Golf Club in Southampton, New York; Charles Blair Macdonald, who laid out the first eighteen-hole course in the United States at the Chicago Golf Club in 1895; and Herbert C. Leeds, an accomplished, self-taught golfer, who laid out probably the best turn-of-the-century course in America, the Myopia Hunt Club in Hamilton, Massachusetts. The strength of the Myopia's layout derived from the placement of its hazards: they presented difficulties for the better players (Leeds often marked the spot where an accomplished visitor's poor drive had come to rest and built a bunker there afterward) while leaving the weaker members an open, if narrow, path to the hole.

Myopia's dogleg fourth hole, approximately 390 yards long, typifies Leeds's wonderful design. A marsh in the inside corner of the dogleg and the severe tilt of the green create a formidable challenge, but the tilt of the approach to the green around the front bunkers allows weaker players to bounce in even the longest of approaches if the sidehill roll of the fairway is judged correctly. Holes such as this one made Myopia a popular venue of early U.S. Open Championships (four prior to 1910), and have kept the course interesting and enjoyable for the members right to the present with a minimum of adjustments.

Before the turn of the century, American golf still suffered from an inferiority complex in relation to the British version. Around the same time that the landmark victories of Walter Travis and Francis Ouimet made a mark for American players, American golf architecture also began making strides. America's first milestone course was the Oakmont Country Club outside Pittsburgh, founded in 1903 by Henry and William Fownes, whose philosophy of design was stated emphatically: "A poorly played shot . . . should be a shot irrevocably lost." Since William Fownes's standard of what constituted a well-played shot was very high (he was U.S. Amateur champion in 1910), his Oakmont layout was an extreme test of golf. In its heyday, the Oakmont eighteen included narrow fairways, about 220 bunkers (each raked in furrows since the clay subsoil prevented Fownes from digging them very deep), twenty-one drainage ditches, sharply tilted greens maintained at breakneck speed, and more length than any course of its day, because Fownes anticipated the acceptance of the livelier Haskell ball. Oakmont spawned a wave of early courses that imitated its penal philosophy.

Other designers turned back to study the great British links. Walter Travis himself became involved in the redesign of the Garden City Golf Club, a Devereux Emmet layout on

The eighteenth hole at Shinnecock Hills in Southampton, New York. Originally a twelve-hole layout, it was arguably the first top-notch course in America.

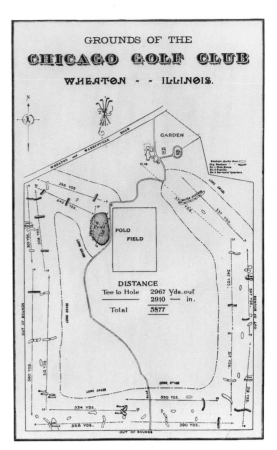

The Chicago Golf Club, designed by Charles Blair Macdonald in 1895, was America's first eighteen-hole course.

The fourth hole at Myopia Hunt Club (Hamilton, Massachusetts), a cleverly crafted par four. Although well bunkered, it allows for a bounce-on approach to the right of the green. Myopia was the site of four U.S. Opens before 1910.

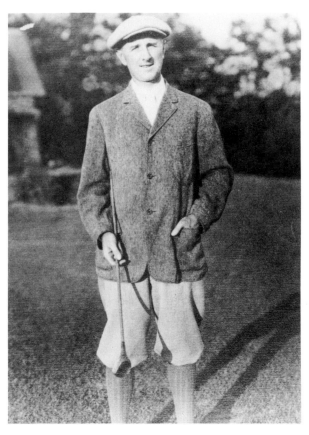

William Fownes, 1910 amateur champion and co-designer (with his father Henry) of Oakmont Country Club (near Pittsburgh), America's first revolutionary course.

The original Oakmont course included about 220 bunkers, the most notorious of which were the "church pews."

Oakmont's church pews are as daunting today as they were eighty-five years ago.

The sixteenth hole at Merion East in Ardmore, Pennsylvania, a par four where the approach must be played directly over a quarry. Hugh Wilson designed the course after members of the Merion Cricket Club sent him to study the classic layouts of Scotland.

Long Island, adding fairway pot bunkers and recontouring some greens to closely emulate the challenges of the best British links. In fact, Travis's revised eighteenth hole at Garden City was closely based on the famous eleventh on the Old Course at St. Andrews, Scotland. Meanwhile, the Merion Cricket Club, near Philadelphia, sent young member Hugh Wilson on a six-month trip to study the famous links and gather ideas for the club's new golf course. Though Wilson shied away from direct imitation of the great British holes, his grasp of the concepts of classic golf course design shines in his work. Merion East, virtually from its opening, has been regarded as one of America's premier courses.

The inspiration for the efforts of Travis and Wilson, though, was provided by Charles Blair Macdonald. By the turn of the century, Macdonald's career as a competitive amateur golfer was past, and he began to think more and more of golf architecture as his calling. His experiences at St. Andrews and other courses overseas had convinced him that, although America had a handful of good courses, it still had none to match the best of the links courses. Beginning in the summer of 1902, Macdonald journeyed abroad several times to survey and study the best links holes. At the same time, he began searching the Eastern seaboard for a site on which to build "a classical golf course, one which would eventually compare favorably with the championship links abroad, and serve as an incentive to the elevation of the game in America." By 1911, Macdonald's National Golf Links of America, in Southampton, New York, was complete.

The National received instant acclaim from both American and foreign players as one of the great courses in the world. Everything about the course was carefully conceived and constructed to the highest standard. The sophistication of the design was rivaled only by the Old Course at St. Andrews, with each hole featuring an impressive array of hazards and contours, but cunningly laid out to offer a safe alternate route to the green for the weak or those lacking confidence in their games. Although a great number of hazards lurked to punish the failed shot, careful, tactical planning could help any player succeed. Indeed, it was Macdonald's goal to create a course without a weak link among the eighteen holes, a standard that even the great British links failed to equal.

To succeed in his lofty aims, Macdonald also had to elevate the standards of construction of the day. Unlike John Reid's two-day layout in 1894, Macdonald spent two years in the actual construction of The National, moving tons of earth if necessary to adapt the Long Island terrain to his design. Moreover, to ensure that the upkeep of the course remained at the same high standard as the design, he spent a great deal of time cultivating grasses for the fairways, greens, and roughs, and a great deal of money developing an artificial irrigation system for the greens.

To this day, The National remains a wonder for the student of golf architecture, but its "weaknesses" belie the difficulty of maintaining shot values across seventy-five years of technology. Improvements in golf equipment, which have shortened other courses, have been partly balanced out by modern fairway irrigation, which has taken much of the bone out of the ground. Errant tee shots now come lazily to rest on sidehill lies, instead of careening through the wide fairways into the fairway bunkers that Macdonald crafted so patiently. The blind shots that Macdonald incorporated into the second and third holes, which were all the rage in Britain at the turn of the century, are considered outdated in modern architectural thinking. Despite the changes, The National retains the unique character that places it on the upper rung of courses.

No sooner was The National finished, however, than it became overshadowed by another new course east of Philadelphia in the New Jersey pine barrens: Pine Valley Golf Club. Pine Valley was the brainchild of Philadelphia hotel owner George Crump, an avid golfer who became obsessed with the idea of constructing the finest, hardest course in the golfing world. Crump was assisted in routing the course by the English designer H. S. Colt, and in devising strategy for the holes by several friends who were making their first forays into design, including A. W. Tillinghast, William Flynn, and George C. Thomas, Jr. But Crump himself was responsible for the grand scale of the course, which sets it apart from

Two of Pine Valley's earliest assailants pause at the tee of the fifth hole, a 226-yard shot over water to a severely bunkered, heavily contoured, plateau green. Known as the hole where "only God can make a three," it has continued to give golfers pause for three-quarters of a century.

The par-three fourteenth hole at Pine Valley, about 1920. Carved from New Jersey's pine barrens, the course was—and is—the ultimate in target golf. Wayward shots meet with disastrous consequences.

Top:
The National Golf Links of America, C. B. Macdonald's homage to the links courses of Scotland, met with instant acclaim when it opened in 1911. Although short by today's standards, it still puts a premium on careful shot-planning. This is the view from the fifteenth tee.

Above:
Number ten at Pine Valley is a short iron on a calm day, but the serenity ends quickly if the tee shot should catch the cavernous right-front bunker.

Right:
Careful placement is important on the tee shot to Merion's short ninth hole, where the smallish green is protected by both water and sand.

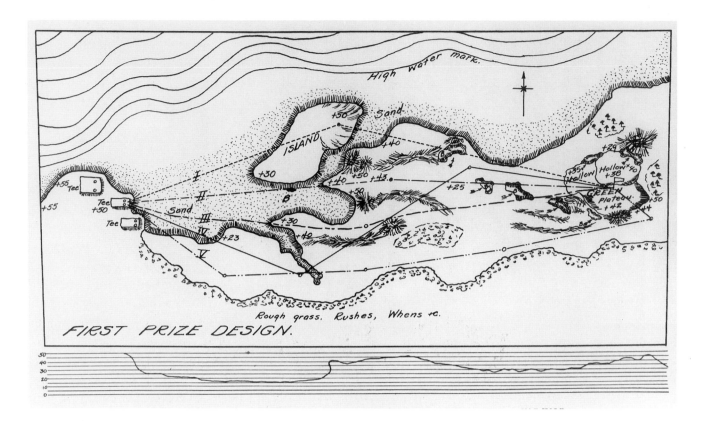

When C. B. Macdonald undertook the design of the Lido Golf Club on the south shore of Long Island in 1914, a British magazine ran a contest to design the eighteenth hole. This is the winning entry, which came from a doctor named Alister Mackenzie. In the 1920s, Mackenzie would achieve architectural fame of his own. By 1950, however, the Lido, hailed widely after its completion, would run into financial trouble and be forced out of existence.

any other in the world. Every target area (fairway or green) is set off by the sand and scrub that characterizes the region, effectively forcing players to proceed around the course from one island to the next, with disastrous consequences for the wayward shot. This concept severely penalized the beginning player. For the better player, each hole retained an intense, strategic interest, with the landing areas and greens carefully positioned and proportioned to the shots required. Other designers, including Donald Ross and Macdonald, declared Pine Valley to be unquestionably the finest in America, and astoundingly, it has remained that way. The 1987 edition of *GOLF* Magazine's "100 Greatest Courses in the World" placed Pine Valley in the No. 1 position.

But instead of emulating Pine Valley's penal qualities, other architects recognized that Crump's was a unique project, impossible to surpass for grandeur and unfit for service to the average golfer. Pine Valley discouraged imitations and

emphasized the need for less strenuous layouts. In the historical timeline of golf architecture, several other courses have performed a similar function.

One other course of this generation deserves mention as an example of the advanced ingenuity of early designers and as a solemn reminder of the precarious existence of even the best clubs and courses. In 1914, C.B. Macdonald was commissioned to build on the south shore of Long Island his second masterpiece, the Lido Golf Club. Occupying flat to marshy land on the narrow strand between the Atlantic Ocean and the intracoastal waterway (Reynolds Channel), the Lido was an enormous undertaking because its developer gave Macdonald a free hand to construct whatever ideal contours he conceived by dredging and filling from the channel. An English magazine even held a competition to design an ideal finishing hole for the course. It was won by a doctor and architectural enthusiast named Alister Mackenzie, who would himself leap to the forefront of the design business in the 1920s. By that time, Macdonald's Lido Golf Club was completed and so highly regarded that only Pine Valley and The National were considered in its peer group. But within thirty years, financial trouble among the members forced the Lido out of existence.

With courses such as Pine Valley and The National serving as models of quality design, combined with the economic and

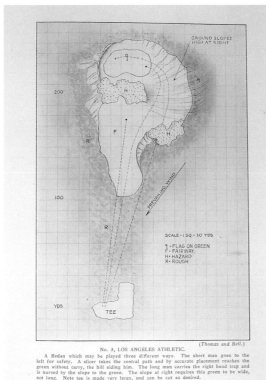

No. 3, LOS ANGELES ATHLETIC.   *(Thomas and Bell.)*

A Redan which may be played three different ways. The short man goes to the left for safety. A slicer takes the central path and by accurate placement reaches the green without carry, the hill aiding him. The long man carries the right hand trap and is nursed by the slope to the green. The slope at right requires this green to be wide, not long. Note tee is made very large, and can be cut as desired.

An illustration from George C. Thomas, Jr.,'s treatise, Golf Architecture in America—Its Strategy and Construction. *Books such as this one helped to spread knowledge and contributed to the Golden Age of course design in the 1920s.*

The earliest American courses were built with the help of good old-fashioned horsepower. This was the scene during the construction at Pinehurst in North Carolina.

social boom of the postwar years, the decade of the twenties was perhaps the capstone of golf course architecture in America: more of the highly regarded courses in America today were built between 1920 and 1929 than in any *two* decades before or since. The contributing factors to this Golden Age include the following:

1. The science of golf course construction had made great strides by the start of the decade, particularly in turfgrass research, because of the foundation of the United States Golf Association (USGA) Green Section in 1920.

2. The architects of the decade were less antagonistic than those in the modern era. Many, in fact, pursued the trade more as an avocation than for profit. Some wrote books detailing their philosophies of design (such as Dr. Mackenzie's *Golf Architecture*, Robert Hunter's *The Links*, and George C. Thomas, Jr.'s *Golf Architecture in America*), and most freely exchanged ideas, not surprising, since many designers had been golf companions in the previous decade.

3. The painstaking methods of course construction compelled designers to ponder every delicate contour. Grading changes for shaping bunkers and contouring putting greens were achieved with the help of old-fashioned horsepower. Teams of horses dragged scraper pans that could be adjusted by an operator to cut and fill to exact specifications. Architect Robert Trent Jones recalls the contouring of a typical green that took seven teams of horses one week.

4. The architects of the twenties had the good fortune to work with some of the finest terrain ever made available to designers, as the popularity of the game and society in general spread from the Eastern seaboard across the country. From Pebble Beach and Cypress Point in the West, to Seminole and the Upper Cascades in the East, the Golden Age advanced because of golden opportunities.

5. Finally, it is possible that, from today's perspective, the courses of the twenties appear particularly alluring because modern improvements in equipment have made the average player the equal of the accomplished twenties player, for whom designers targeted their

The par-three seventh hole at San Francisco, one of A.W. Tillinghast's first courses (1915) and, in the view of many, his finest.

For George C. Thomas, golf architecture was a hobby, but he pursued it with the expertise of a professional. This is the seventeenth green at one of his classics, Riviera in Pacific Palisades, California.

A. W. Tillinghast, designer of Winged Foot (West), Baltusrol (Lower), Quaker Ridge, San Francisco, Baltimore (Five Farms), Brook Hollow, and Somerset Hills, all ranked among "GOLF Magazine's 100 Greatest Courses in the World."

Donald Ross, putting on a sand green near his office in Pinehurst. Ross turned out more than a hundred courses over a ten-year period.

layouts. If golf club and golf ball technology is allowed to continue unchecked for another twenty years, the courses of the 1920s may fall out of favor, and the next generation of courses will be cherished classics.

Six prominent designers were especially busy in the United States during the decade of the twenties. Charles Blair Macdonald still was very active, at St. Louis, Yale, and the revamped Chicago Golf Club (Macdonald's assistant, Seth Raynor, designed fine courses such as Camargo and Shoreacres on the side). A. W. Tillinghast, another American who had learned the game during an extended visit to St. Andrews, turned out a stunning number of championship-quality courses, including the two-course complexes at Winged Foot and Baltusrol, twenty-seven holes at Ridgewood Country Club, and eighteens at Baltimore Country Club, Quaker Ridge, and Brook Hollow. William Flynn, a Philadelphia protégé of Hugh Wilson who carried on his legacy after Wilson's premature death, produced such gems as Cherry Hills, Upper Cascades, the Philadelphia Country Club, and the revised layouts for The Country Club and Shinnecock Hills with engineer Howard Toomey. George C. Thomas, Jr., another Philadelphian, moved to southern California in 1919, conveniently providing him an open market to practice his new hobby of golf course design at Los Angeles Country Club, Bel Air, and Riviera. In 1927 he published his classic treatise, *Golf Architecture in America—Its Strategy and Construction.*

Donald Ross, an immigrant Scot from Dornoch, was the most prolific architect of all and perhaps the most representative of the style of the times as well. From his office in Pinehurst, North Carolina (the site of his masterpiece, Pinehurst No. 2), Ross turned out more than a hundred courses in the decade. Several of his designs consisted of no more than a course routing, based on topographical maps his clients had submitted, leaving it up to the club in question to find a competent construction supervisor; still, Ross felt that providing the routing was getting the client off to a good start. Some projects, though, received more attention if the client was lucky enough to have one of Ross's close assistants or Ross himself on site during construction. A few of Ross's

Raised, contoured greens and spacious bunkers characterized the Ross courses, as reflected in the sixteenth hole of Pinehurst No. 2.

better-known layouts from this period include The Country Club of Birmingham, Alabama; Seminole Golf Club, North Palm Beach, Florida; Salem Country Club, Peabody, Massachusetts; Northland Country Club, Duluth, Minnesota; Plainfield Country Club, New Jersey; Oak Hill, Rochester, New York; and Wannamoisset Country Club, Rumford, Rhode Island. These courses featured the classic small, raised, contoured greens and carefully placed bunkers that characterize the Ross look and perhaps the entire Golden Age.

The sixth and final prominent designer of the 1920s was Alister Mackenzie. Mackenzie's output in the United States was limited by his efforts overseas, which in this decade alone included work in Ireland, Uruguay, New Zealand, and Australia (most notably the Royal Melbourne club, currently ranked sixth in the world by *GOLF Magazine*). But in the late twenties, Mackenzie found time to create two California projects, Cypress Point in Carmel and Pasatiempo in Santa Cruz, which vaulted him to prominence in America. Cypress

Point, a dazzling layout through the forest and along the cliff tops of the Monterey Peninsula, is well known as one of this country's classic courses, but in the history of course design, its greatest influence was in attracting the attention of Bobby Jones, who played the layout several times after being upset in the first round of the 1929 U.S. Amateur Championship at Pebble Beach. Jones's admiration for Cypress Point led him to choose Mackenzie to assist with the design of a pet project for his friends, the Augusta National Golf Club.

It was the Augusta National that revolutionized strategic course design in America. Unlike Oakmont, The National, or Pine Valley, which depended heavily on fairway hazards to provide strategic interest, Augusta had few bunkers or other hazards to indicate the correct line of play or trap errant shots. Jones and Mackenzie wanted only to ensure that the poorly planned or executed shot would leave the player in an extremely difficult position from which to reach his or her next objective. This they achieved by carefully conceiving greens and pin positions that could be safely approached from only one angle. The rest of the Augusta National appeared wide open, with nearly eighty acres of fairways and just twenty-two bunkers to begin with.

Yet, in practice, rare is the great course that does not include a considerable overlap of the penal, strategic, and heroic philosophies of design. The most famous stretch of the Augusta National, holes eleven through thirteen (christened the Amen Corner by golf writer Herbert Warren Wind), illustrates the point.

The eleventh, a 445-yard two-shotter, is a classic example of the strategic philosophy. Its key hazard is a modest-size pond to the left of the slick green, compounded by a pronounced right-to-left slope of the ground on the approach. Recovery from it requires an exceedingly difficult downhill chip toward the pond. (This is the shot Larry Mize holed to win the 1987 Masters in sudden death.) Players driving down the left can aim their approaches away from the pond to the fat of the green; from the right side of the fairway, the player can angle past the pond at a tough left-hand pin position.

Left:
Alister Mackenzie during a round at the Old Course at St. Andrews, Scotland. Few architects have had a greater influence on design.

Below:
The short but treacherous par-four ninth hole at Cypress Point, Alister Mackenzie's masterpiece on the Monterey Peninsula.

Above:
Bobby Jones in his role as architect, amid dozens of the trees hewn during the clearing stage of construction of the Augusta National Golf Club, Augusta, Georgia.

Right:
The strategic, penal, and heroic schools of architecture merge at Augusta's Amen Corner. At the eleventh hole, a generous fairway but a tightly guarded green reflect the strategic philosophy.

The designers saw no need to bunker the landing area for the drive; each player is given the chance to play the approach as it best suits him, provided he plans and executes his drive accordingly.

Augusta's twelfth hole, at 155 yards, by contrast, gives the player little choice but to confront its difficulties head-on. The short pitch across Rae's Creek to a sliver of green set at an angle to the line of play with bunkers front and rear places the utmost premium on correct judgment of distance. Yet swirling winds in this low corner of the property add an element of chance to club selection. The margin for error is so slight that even the best players in the world prefer to play to the safer

Augusta's twelfth hole, a par three played into swirling winds toward a shallow green, is penal architecture at its best.

left side of the green, regardless of the location of the pin. However, in architectural theory it is generally held that a short hole is the most appropriate place for a penal touch, since every player is given the benefit of a perfect lie for his approach. Even on the shortest two-shotters, some allowance must be made for those who have driven badly.

Finally, the thirteenth hole, a 465-yard par five, represents the third "school" of design—the heroic. A player with the daring and skill to bring off a drawn tee shot around the corner of this dogleg left, guarded by a swift-flowing creek, followed by a long second across the creek as it slashes in front of the green, may gain a stroke over an opponent who opts for the safer three-shot route to the green. It is interesting to note, however, that were this hole called a par four instead of a par five (as the USGA would no doubt insist of a 465-yard hole in an Open Championship), players would condemn it as a penal hole simply because the scorecard would oblige them to attempt the difficult approach.

The year 1935 drew great attention to the contrasting styles of course design. In April, Gene Sarazen's famous double eagle on the fifteenth hole in the final round of The Masters focused nationwide interest on the Augusta National course. Barely two months later, Sam Parks, Jr., won the U.S. Open Championship at Oakmont at the height of its difficulty, being the only player in the field to break three hundred for the four rounds. Competitors, writers, and architects agreed that the Augusta style of design provided more enjoyment for a greater number of players.

The golf world had a long time to ponder its preference. Between the start of the Depression in 1930 and the end of World War II, more clubs went broke and disappeared than new ones were built to replace them. Some architects, prominent among them A.W. Tillinghast, made a living during this period by streamlining courses to reduce maintenance costs—mostly by eliminating extraneous bunkers in keeping with the new, strategic style of architecture. Others, includ-

The par-five thirteenth hole at Augusta beckons a long shot over Rae's Creek from anyone who wants to get home in two. Such is the stuff of the heroic school.

ing a young designer fresh out of Cornell University, Robert Trent Jones, built public courses as part of the Works Progress Administration (WPA) programs.

Classic architecture did not disappear completely. In fact, several outstanding courses were built in odd corners of the country during the thirties: John Bredemus's Colonial Country Club in Fort Worth, Texas; William Flynn's revised layout at Shinnecock Hills; Alister Mackenzie's Crystal Downs in northern Michigan; and Perry Maxwell's original nine holes at Prairie Dunes in Kansas. Any of these courses might have started a revolution in design. Instead, with the exception of Colonial, they languished in obscurity for decades.

During the long lull, the business of golf architecture underwent drastic changes. Heavy earthmoving machinery had evolved dramatically from the prewar era, allowing courses to be constructed faster than previously possible and affording designers the prerogative of moving large volumes of dirt to overcome serious deficiencies in the natural terrain,

eliminating the blind shot as a routing problem. By the early 1950s, automatic irrigation for the entire course created a golf boom in the Southern states that previously had difficulty establishing playable turf. Riding maintenance equipment allowed courses to be maintained more cheaply, but the sizes of greens, tees, and bunkers had to be enlarged to accommodate the wide turning radii of the new machinery. And the burgeoning population brought new demands for golf, much of it integrated with the simultaneous housing boom. The rationale for building a golf course had changed: most projects in the modern generation were built to profit from the surrounding land development rather than because the land was suited for golf.

The most revolutionary change—the development of air and auto travel—allowed designers to move quickly from job to job checking the progress of the work. As most of the leading architects of the Golden Age had died between 1930 and 1948, the field became wide open for several young designers to corner the market on the design of new courses and the revision of fine prewar layouts. Into the breach stepped two designers who would dominate the profession during the fifties and early sixties, Robert Trent Jones and Dick Wilson.

Trent Jones, whose middle name became common usage to distinguish him from the legendary golfer Robert Tyre ("Bobby") Jones, Jr., had trained himself specifically for the profession of golf architecture in the graduate schools at Cornell University and had served as an apprentice and later a partner to Stanley Thompson, who had designed nearly all of Canada's outstanding courses a generation earlier. Jones's style of design was greatly influenced by Thompson and Mackenzie and particularly by the Augusta National, on which he helped the other Bob Jones with some major modifications after the war.

While Trent Jones designed many prominent resort layouts, his most influential work was on courses that would host major tournaments, getting maximum television exposure. From 1951 to 1956, four of the six courses hosting the U.S. Open (Oakland Hills, Baltusrol, Olympic, and Oak Hill) were revamped by Jones to strengthen them against the improvements in equipment, course conditioning, and play. Trent Jones's solution was to pinch the fairways down to twenty-five to thirty yards in the landing areas, with either stringent fairway bunkers (as at Oakland Hills) or punitive rough (as at Olympic). The results of his work at Oakland Hills were especially dramatic: two rounds under par were returned in the entire seventy-two-hole tournament, and the architect was regarded by many (except the players) as a hero. Trent Jones thus became the first golf architect whose name was a selling point in the marketing of a course, a phenomenon that led to greater recognition and higher fees for those at the top of the profession.

Dick Wilson, an engineer who had apprenticed under William Flynn, was Trent Jones's greatest contemporary rival. His style differed considerably from Trent Jones's, but the basics fit in with the new American mode: long tees for flexibility, fairly big greens, wide fairways, and perhaps a slightly more stringent bunkering around (especially in front of) the greens. Wilson, however, conducted business very differently from Jones. Having been brought up in the construction end of the business, he considered on-site supervision essential, so he worked on only a handful of projects at a time, concentrating them within the same area to reduce his travel schedule. A few of Wilson's early courses are spread across the country, including Meadow Brook on Long Island, Laurel Valley in Pennsylvania, La Costa in California, and Cog Hill outside Chicago. But the bulk of Wilson's best work

Robert Trent Jones, the most prolific designer in history, adapted Augusta National's expansive style to courses around the world.

can be found in southern Florida, where he produced Bay Hill, Doral, J.D.M. Country Club, and arguably his masterpiece, Pine Tree Golf Club, within a four-year period. These courses featured much water, as much out of the necessity of draining the low-lying Florida land as for strategic value. Wilson died in 1965, at the peak of his popularity, leaving his assistants, Joe Lee and Bob Von Hagge, to carry on his practice.

Overall, though, the products of this period of design are considered somewhat disappointing today. Hundreds of new courses were turned out every year, to a fairly high standard of construction, by an increasing number of accomplished professional designers. Most of them lacked individuality, relying too heavily on length to make them challenging. One sometimes wishes that more amateurs had become involved in the business of design: surely there would have been some lunatic layouts, but possibly also one inspired course in the

Stringent fairway bunkering is characteristic of Trent Jones's redesign work, as here at Oakland Hills Country Club, Birmingham, Michigan.

tradition of George Crump's Pine Valley or Jack Neville's Pebble Beach.

The straw that broke the back of the ultralong school of design occurred in the mid-sixties when two American courses, The International Golf Course in Massachusetts and Dub's Dread in Kansas, extended their back tees to eight thousand yards. The necessarily larger fairway areas and bigger greens also entailed ever-greater maintenance costs. The shock of these two courses was enormous. Like Pine Valley two generations before, designers realized that, although these courses provided a championship test, they were not proper models for the majority of courses.

The two men most responsible for changing course design to the style called "modern" in 1988 first worked together in the late 1960s. Pete Dye was an accomplished amateur golfer who dabbled in course design one summer and never went back to his old business; Jack Nicklaus was a young profes-

sional at the top of his game and showing an interest in course design. Their milestone was the Harbour Town Golf Links in South Carolina, a tight layout winding through the live oaks and along a marsh, which measured only 6,600 yards but proved challenging enough for the professionals, including Nicklaus, who had assisted on the design and hit countless balls in the dirt to test the shot values of the layout. Dye used railroad-tie bulkheads to form the boundary between greens and water or to set off bunkers as he had seen on early Scottish courses. A combination of various grasses of different textures demarking fairway, green, bunker face, and rough added the final artistic touch that set the course apart from those of the previous generation.

Harbour Town was not Dye's first top-notch course: three years earlier, he had completed The Golf Club outside Nicklaus's hometown of Columbus, Ohio, which opened to outstanding reviews. But the exclusive nature of The Golf Club

prevented it from drawing attention. In the modern era, television has to be involved in any design revolution. When Arnold Palmer won the inaugural Heritage Classic, Harbour Town was almost instantly named one of America's top ten courses.

Jack Nicklaus made the next major breakthrough in 1974 with his Muirfield Village layout. Recruiting British land planner and golf architect Desmond Muirhead to help him with the routing of the golf course in relation to the development, Nicklaus planned his "home" layout in minute detail, with certain holes on the layout suggestive of holes Nicklaus

admired throughout the world, as Bobby Jones had done at Augusta. Since he also hoped to attract a PGA Tour event to his course, Nicklaus included spectator mounds around the greens on many holes. Muirfield Village also met with instant acclaim. Nicklaus was praised as a designer for his perfectionist approach to ensuring that all the hazards on the course were completely visible from the tees and landing areas, even if great volumes of earth had to be moved to do it.

Between them, Nicklaus and Dye came to dominate the golf course design business in the last half of the seventies and in the eighties. Other designers built noteworthy courses—

particularly Robert Trent Jones, the bulk of whose work in this era was confined to Europe; Jones's two sons, Rees and Robert, Jr., who established practices of their own around 1970; and George and Tom Fazio, who did graceful work, from Butler National in Chicago to Jupiter Hills, Florida, to Wild Dunes, South Carolina. (The Fazios also were called on to revise several old championship courses, such as Donald Ross's Oak Hill and Inverness, in preparation for upcoming championship events. Their changes renewed debate over whether the original handiwork of the masters' courses or the shot value of their courses should be preserved.) Nicklaus's

success in the profession also paved the way for other leading players to enter the golf course design business, usually in conjunction with an established designer or construction supervisor. Still, it was the designs of Dye and Nicklaus that attracted the greatest attention, loudest praise, and sharpest criticism, and eventually the most imitation. By the mid-eighties, for better or worse, it was tough to find a designer who did not display a railroad-tie or rock bulkhead along the edge of a water hazard, or who did not require a huge construction budget to complete the design. Even the St. Andrews' Golf Club, which had been at home in Yonkers since 1897, underwent a $2-million facelift at the hands of Nicklaus, who incorporated a new condominium development into the design.

The last milestone course of golf's first hundred years in America, however, belonged to Pete Dye's Tournament Players Club (TPC) at Sawgrass, Florida, founded in 1979 by PGA Tour Commissioner Deane Beman as the new home of the tour and the site of its own championship event. Reclaimed from a swamp south of Jacksonville Beach, Dye's layout tested every facet of the professionals' games, including their patience and response to pressure. In some respects, the TPC resembles an obstacle course, with difficult, "unreceptive" greens and water in play on virtually every hole, most notably at the par-three seventeenth, whose green is an island tethered to shore by a narrow causeway, designed to ensure that even the biggest of leads would not allow a player to limp home. While players criticized the tortuous nature of

the test, galleries marveled at the mammoth spectator mounds dredged from the many lakes and canals, which allowed tremendous views of the action for a larger audience than previously possible.

The success of the Tournament Players Club from the fans' point of view prompted the tour to franchise a chain of similar stadium courses for the sites of a dozen tour events by 1988, amid great controversy from some corners that the courses were not necessarily of tournament quality and that they were all too similar, favoring a certain class of player. More than anything else, though, the courses have suffered from the success of Dye's model at Sawgrass, which led the tour to expand the chain too rapidly, while other designers were still under the influence of Dye's style. The latest model, the stadium course at PGA West in La Quinta, California (opened in 1986 and designed again by Dye), has been so universally criticized for its severity that it is unclear whether

The fourteenth hole at Nicklaus's Muirfield Village (Dublin, Ohio), host to the annual Memorial Tournament and to the 1987 Ryder Cup matches.

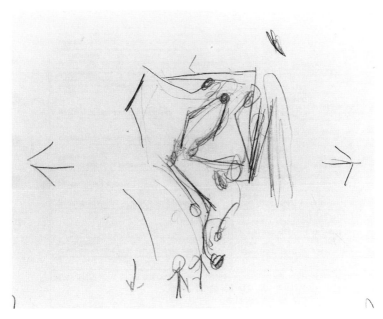

The first "design" of the Tournament Players Course (TPC) at Sawgrass, as sketched on a restaurant placemat by Pete Dye. The original of this sketch hangs in Deane Beman's home.

Number eleven at the TPC offers an interesting twist—alternative fairways to the left and right of the large waste bunkers that nearly encircle the green.

Above:
The ninth at Pete Dye's PGA West, La Quinta, California. The most severe and innovative of his designs to date, its place in the history of golf architecture is still uncertain.

Left:
The TPC at Sawgrass was designed with gallery viewing in mind, such as here at the island seventeenth, a hole that quickly became one of the most famous in golf.

its place in the history of course design will be as an innovator like TPC/Sawgrass, as a pariah like The International, or as a classic like Pine Valley.

Whatever the case, one can only hope that future advances in the manufacture of golf balls and clubs do not become so overpowering that they destroy the challenges of the great golf courses from the first century of American design, since the great variety of playing fields sets golf apart from other sporting endeavors. Only through their preservation may the history and further development of the art and science that is golf architecture be understood.

Chapter SIX

Players of the

EDITED BY

<table>
<tr><td>

Decade

ROBIN McMILLAN

</td><td>

ORIGINAL PAINTINGS BY WALT SPITZMILLER

</td></tr>
</table>

CHARLES BLAIR MACDONALD
1888–1897

One of the finest of the early players, Charles Blair Macdonald earns the nod as the best of decade not merely for his playing accomplishments (he won the first U.S. Amateur Championship in 1895) but for his role in bringing the game to this country, for his zealous belief in its rules and traditions, and for his achievements as a golf course architect.

Macdonald had an enviable introduction to golf. The son of a wealthy Chicagoan, he journeyed to St. Andrews, Scotland, in August 1872, at the age of sixteen to study at the university. He was entrusted to the care of his grandfather who resided there. The day after Macdonald arrived, he was taken to the shop of Old Tom Morris (a four-time winner of the British Open Championship). Macdonald's grandfather bought the youngster several golf clubs and arranged for a locker in Morris's shop because juniors were not permitted inside the Royal and Ancient clubhouse. Macdonald was soon spending every spare moment playing the fabled links or in Morris's shop, listening to the top golfers of the day, including Morris and his sons, among them Young Tom, himself winner of four consecutive British Opens.

America was devoid of golf courses when Macdonald returned in 1874, so he made do playing on business trips to Britain. In 1892, Macdonald was asked to lay out a few holes on a friend's estate in Chicago. They were met with enthusiasm, and he soon designed nine holes, then an additional nine in the nearby town of Belmont for members of the Chicago Golf Club. In 1895, the Chicago Golf Club moved to a new, Macdonald-designed, eighteen-hole course in Wheaton, Illinois. These two courses are recognized as the first eighteen-hole layouts in America.

Besides a passion for the game, Macdonald brought home the conviction that the true way to play the game was the Scottish way, and strictly by the rules, preferably the original thirteen that dated back to 1754. This single-mindedness was aided by Macdonald's commanding presence; he was broad-shouldered, mustached, well-spoken, and humorless.

There is no doubt that Macdonald numbered among the best players—amateur or professional—in America. Notable among the professionals who had ventured from Scotland across the Atlantic to preach golf to the uninitiated was Willie Dunn, originally from Musselburgh, who had been invited to lay out a course at Shinnecock Hills in Southampton, New York, for a group of wealthy American businessmen. Another well-known player of the day was John Reid, the founder of the St. Andrew's Golf Club in Yonkers, New York, who has been celebrated more for his devotion to the game than his aptitude. Enough players were around to fill out a small field of a national amateur tournament, held at Newport (Rhode Island) Golf Club in September 1894.

Macdonald was the favorite, but the course was not to his liking, which contributed to his losing by a stroke over thirty-six holes, 188 to 189, to William G. Lawrence of the Newport club. In his memoirs, *Scotland's Gift—Golf,* all Macdonald says, after reporting the score, is, "I can recall that the tournament was extremely interesting, and the club's committee did everything to make the competitors happy."

Not happy enough, apparently, for Macdonald protested that a stone wall, which cost him two strokes the final day, was not a legitimate hazard under the Rules of Golf, and, therefore, the championship should be voided. He also protested that a proper championship should not be played at medal, as this one was, but at match play.

Hoping to calm the waters, the St. Andrew's Club held a second amateur championship, at match play, the following month. Macdonald managed to better Lawrence in the semifinals but, after halving the eighteen-hole final, lost on the first playoff hole to Laurence Stoddard of the host club. This time Macdonald argued that the result was invalid because one club may not undertake to run a national tournament.

Although in both cases Macdonald's complaints were largely self-serving, they did help point out the need for a national governing body. In 1894, the United States Golf Association (USGA) was established. When this body organized an amateur championship at the Newport Golf Club the following year, Macdonald won it—his only major title—handily, defeating Charles Sands, a neophyte golfer of three months, 12 and 11, over a thirty-six hole final.

Macdonald's lasting reputation, ultimately, is not as a player but as an architect. His finest creation is the National Golf Links of America (opened in 1911) in Southampton, New York, regarded as the first great course in America. In his travels, Macdonald had acquired maps and drawings of the best holes on the finest courses in Britain, which he used as models for several holes at The National. This course revolutionized golf-course architecture in this country and around the world. Macdonald's other designs include Bermuda's Mid-Ocean Club (1924), the Yale University course (1926) in New Haven, Connecticut, and the Old White course (1914) at the Greenbrier resort in West Virginia.

WILLIE ANDERSON
1898–1907

Many fine British golfers emigrated to America around the turn of the century—Jock Hutchison, Willie Dunn, Alex Smith were but three—but none of them performed as well as Willie Anderson. The young Scot's four U.S. Open Championship victories have been equaled by only Bobby Jones, Ben Hogan, and Jack Nicklaus. Three of Anderson's wins arrived consecutively, which never has been equaled. Anderson also placed second in the U.S. Open once, third once, fourth twice, and fifth three times and was a four-time winner of the Western Open, the other significant tournament for professionals at that time.

Anderson was born in North Berwick, on the southeast coast of Scotland, in 1878. The son of the local greenkeeper, Tom Anderson, Sr., Willie was a constant figure on the North Berwick links. Although he never actually caddied, Anderson kindled his competitive spirit by playing in caddie tournaments.

Across the Atlantic, golf was in its explosive infancy. Along with the golf boom came opportunities for work. In 1895, the Anderson family emigrated, Willie taking work at the Misquamicut Golf Club in Watch Hill, Rhode Island. Two years later at the U.S. Open at the Chicago Golf Club, the nineteen-year-old Anderson gave notice that he was to become the dominant player of the day.

With the tournament in its final stages, Anderson's total of 163 appeared to be enough for the victory. Only the Englishman, Joe Lloyd, had any chance of catching Anderson. Even then, Lloyd would have to summon from somewhere a three on the long (465-yard) final hole to avoid a playoff. Incredibly, Lloyd crushed a huge drive, followed by a brassie (2-wood) to eight feet. He holed the putt, and as quick as that, Anderson was runner-up.

Anderson was unperturbed. He knew that he had youth on his side and that such an experience under pressure could only improve his technique. Right he was. Four years later, in 1901, at the Myopia Hunt Club in South Hamilton, Massachusetts, Anderson won his first U.S. Open.

This one, too, almost slipped away. Alex Smith, a gregarious Scot who, some said surprisingly, became a sound friend to the dour Anderson on and off the course, had to birdie the final hole to better Anderson's total of 331 (the Open had gone to seventy-two holes in 1898). Like Lloyd, Smith reached the green in two, but this time the winning putt stopped short. Anderson defeated Smith the following day in the Open's first playoff, 85 to 86.

If the scores seem high—indeed, no player has won the Open with more than 331 strokes—it was because the pros of the day steadfastly resisted changing from the gutta-percha ball to the rubber-cored Haskell model. When Anderson next won the Open in 1903, there was nary a golfer who had not been enchanted by the Haskell's extra distance. This eventually led to Anderson finding another place in the record books: he is the only golfer to have won the U.S. Open using both types of ball.

He also is the golfer who has come closest to winning the Open on his home turf. Anderson held ten different club jobs over the somewhat nomadic fourteen years he lived in America. One post was at Baltusrol Golf Club in Springfield, New Jersey (others included Apawamis in Rye, New York, and Onwentsia in Lake Forest, Illinois). Anderson had departed Baltusrol by the time it hosted the 1903 U.S. Open, but he believed his knowledge of the course would give him an edge on the field, and it did. Anderson's five-stroke lead at the halfway mark remains a record (since equalled). After three

rounds, Anderson led by six, but then he collapsed in the last round with an 82, allowing David Brown, another Scot, to catch him. Again the Open went to a playoff. Anderson won, 82 to 84.

A year later, it was Anderson's turn to play catch-up, at the Glen View Club in Golf, Illinois. After opening rounds of 75–78–78, he trailed yet another transplanted Scot, Fred McKenzie, by two. This time, Anderson's final round of 72 was outstanding. He covered the final eight holes in thirty swipes. The 72 was a record, as was his total of 303.

Anderson's last U.S. Open title (1905) may have been the most satisfying. It took a drawn-out, head-to-head tussle with Alex Smith (who was to win two U.S. Opens—in 1906 and 1910). Anderson trailed Smith by five strokes at the halfway mark and by one stroke with eighteen holes to play. Although Smith shot an 80—his third of the championship—Anderson managed a 77. The one blemish on an otherwise excellent performance: Anderson's total of 314 is the highest since the demise of the gutta-percha ball.

Anderson was not a graceful golfer by modern standards. He employed an exceedingly flat swing plane, swiveled his hips on the backswing and bent his left arm. Yet the style produced success. Although Anderson maintained that his best weapon was the mashie (5-iron), most people were impressed by his prodigious driving. Anderson also was an extremely accurate shotmaker. One famous story tells of how Gene Sarazen was practicing bunker shots at a tournament when he asked Bill Robinson, a former pro, if Anderson could have played as well from bunkers. "Get out of them?" Robinson replied. "He was never in them."

Anderson garnered much admiration from his fellow golfers but went largely unappreciated by the public. But then, a solemn demeanor, which characterizes many champion golfers—Ben Hogan and Tom Watson are two modern examples—has never lent itself to public relations. However, as Smith would attest, Anderson was a likable man and was deeply disappointed that the public misunderstood him.

By his late twenties, Anderson was in poor health. Like many pros of his day, he drank heavily. In October 1910, Anderson conducted a series of thirty-six-hole exhibition matches in and around Pittsburgh. The matches proved exhausting. After the final contest—Anderson and Gil Nicholls dueled William Fownes, the U.S. Amateur champion, and Eben Byers, the 1906 Amateur champion, to the final hole, where they lost—Anderson almost collapsed from the strain. Two weeks later at home in Philadelphia, Anderson died. Official cause of death: arteriosclerosis, or hardening of the arteries. Public perception: Willie Anderson drank himself to death.

FRANCIS OUIMET
1908–1917

Golf in America in 1913 held to a common pattern: The gentry played at a few exclusive clubs; the best players were British; and the common man looked on in bewilderment. A wiry, twenty-year-old amateur named Francis Ouimet changed all that.

No one looked for Ouimet in the opening field of the 1913 U.S. Open Championship at The Country Club in Ouimet's hometown of Brookline, Massachusetts. Harry Vardon, five-time British Open champion and victor in the only previous U.S. Open he had entered (1900), and Ted Ray, the reigning British Open champion, came into the U.S. Open having completed a whirlwind tour of the United States, in which they had won every exhibition but one. The man who had broken the British monopoly of the Open, John McDermott, also was at The Country Club, looking for his third consecutive U.S. Open title. McDermott seemed to be America's only hope of stemming the strong British tide again (although a young pro named Walter Hagen traveled from Rochester, New York, to bolster the forces).

Among the amateurs the USGA officials had rounded up to fill out the field was Ouimet. He had grown up playing on a makeshift course behind the family's small house, directly across from The Country Club. Even though Ouimet was a Massachusetts Amateur champion and had regular employment in a local sporting-goods store, Ouimet caddied at the private club for a few cents, sneaking on in the dawn hours to play a few holes before his loop. Three times before 1913 he had tried to qualify for the U.S. Amateur; three times he had failed. Just weeks prior to his Open entry, he had qualified for the Amateur but had lost to eventual champion Jerry Travers in the second round. In the Open, Ouimet expected only to catch a glimpse of Vardon and Ray in action.

To the surprise of all, including himself, Ouimet was enjoying more than a glimpse by the end of the third round. He was tied with the famous pair for the lead. Then, early in his final round, Ouimet heard that both men had finished with 79s. Ouimet saw his chance. But on the 140-yard tenth hole, Ouimet duffed his drive, put the approach to eight feet, and three-putted. A bogey at the twelfth meant Ouimet would have to play The Country Club's final six holes in two under to *tie*—no small feat, considering the equipment and course conditions of the day. But he did. Ouimet chipped in from thirty feet on thirteen for birdie and curled in a birdie putt from fifteen feet on seventeen while negotiating eighteen in par. The championship went to a playoff.

On a rained-soaked course the next day, the threesome matched 38s on the front nine. Ouimet took the lead for good when the visiting Brits three-putted the tenth. Vardon still was within a stroke of Ouimet on the seventeenth tee, and gambled by trying in vain to cut the dogleg of the 360-yard par four but could manage only a bogey. Ouimet played safely down the middle, put a 4-iron to fifteen feet and sank the putt for an insurmountable lead. The new hero parred in for a 72 to Vardon's 77 and Ray's 78.

An American had won the Open before, but McDermott had not had to contend with Vardon. Ouimet was gracious in victory. "Naturally, it was my hope to win out," he told a partisan crowd. "I simply tried my best to keep this cup from going to our friends across the water. I am very glad to have been the agency for keeping the cup in America."

Despite his success, Ouimet never turned pro, coveting instead the U.S. Amateur title, which he won the following year and in 1931. In the years that followed, Ouimet won the 1914 French Amateur, the 1932 Massachusetts Open, and five more Massachusetts Amateur Championships.

Ouimet served the game valiantly in many capacities outside competition. He represented the United States on eight straight Walker Cup teams from 1922–34, and acted as non-playing captain in 1936, 1938, 1947, and 1949. He served for many years on the USGA executive committee and in other posts within the administrative body of the game. In 1951, the British appointed Ouimet the first non-British captain of the Royal and Ancient Golf Club of St. Andrews. Ouimet was an original inductee to the PGA Hall of Fame in 1940 and into the World Golf Hall of Fame in 1974.

To the American public, Ouimet's Open victory meant more than any piece of silverware. He changed the game's image forever. Statistics support this: In 1913, 350,000 Americans played golf. By 1923, there were more than two million golfers.

His was a triumph for the masses.

WALTER HAGEN
1918–1927

Walter Hagen was one of golf's most colorful figures, its first true professional, and among its greatest shotmakers. From 1914 through 1931, Hagen won two U.S. Opens, four British Opens, the Canadian and French Opens once each, and captained the Ryder Cup team from 1927 to 1939.

Hagen's greatest achievements came in the PGA Championship, which he virtually owned in the 1920s. He appeared in six finals, winning five, including four in a row from 1924–27, when he won twenty-two consecutive matches. (He won again in 1921 and placed second in 1923.)

Victories and statistics are only part of the Hagen mystique. He was a showman and a shotmaker, a blacksmith's son from Rochester, New York, who epitomized the go-for-broke, playboy style of the day. He won unheard-of amounts of money and spent nearly every penny, and he brought to the game a mental toughness never seen before, a sense of psychology and public relations that kept him the people's champion whether he won or lost.

Hagen's first showing was in the 1913 U.S. Open, when he finished tied for fourth behind the young American Francis Ouimet and Britishers Harry Vardon and Ted Ray. At the time, Hagen was a twenty-year-old assistant pro, a virtual nobody, but he was damn sure of himself. Entering the clubhouse of The Country Club in Brookline, Massachusetts, he marched up to defending Open champion John McDermott and said, "I'm W.C. Hagen from Rochester and I've come to help you boys take care of Vardon and Ray."

The next year, Hagen won the Open at Midlothian Country Club outside Chicago, but this victory was just a taste of things to come. Hagen needed a little maturing first and did not show his real stuff until 1919, when he took his second U.S. Open title. By then, he had quit the club job, determined to make it solely as a player. Hagen was the first to prove that could be done, parlaying his victories into endorsements, exhibitions, and other money-making opportunities. He also was one of the first to fight for the rights of professional golfers, by demanding access to clubhouses and locker rooms.

Hagen's style of play was an unusual mix of swaying and lunging into the ball; he was frequently wild off the tee. But this aggressive approach, and its sometimes disastrous results, only endeared the Haig to fans all the more. They came out wherever he played. They wanted to see the flashy clothes, the bravado—he would stand on the first tee and say for all to hear, "I wonder who's going to take second"—and his magnificent recoveries from trouble. Despite, or because of, his spraying off the tee, Hagen had to be a master of trouble play. He thought he could get out of anything, and he usually did, before sinking the saving putt, regardless of the distance or the enormity of the situation.

As brilliant a short-game stylist and putter as he was, Hagen was first and foremost a great thinker. He philosophized that he was bound to hit a few bad shots a round, so why worry about them? Along with amazing control over his own mind, he could cast spells over the minds of his

opponents: they always were wondering what he would do next, how he would beat them.

The final round of the 1926 PGA Championship pitted Hagen against Leo Diegel, who had had the misfortune to lose many times to Hagen. Early in the match, Hagen conceded several short putts to Diegel, who gratefully took them. On one of the final holes, Diegel faced a putt of fewer than two feet. He looked for the nod from Hagen, who ignored him. Diegel suddenly was worried: if Hagen would not concede, there had to be something tricky about the putt. Diegel scrutinized it, nervously set up—and missed. Hagen won the match 5 and 3.

Such ploys were Hagen's stock in trade. He regularly underclubbed approach shots to entice an opponent to do the same. Hagen knew his short game was good enough to get down in two, while the other guy rarely could. It is no wonder Hagen dominated the early PGA Championships. His styles of play and mind games were perfect in the one-on-one cauldron of match play.

Some of Hagen's finest matches pitted him against Gene Sarazen. The Squire beat Hagen for the PGA title in 1923, and they played many exhibition matches, including a two-day, seventy-two-hole match over two courses in 1922. Despite Hagen's ploys, Sarazen held on to win 3 and 2; several hours later, Sarazen underwent an emergency appendectomy.

As for Hagen, he was still to win four straight PGA Championships and many other prizes. Among them was a series of unofficial "World Championship Matches," in which he trounced Cyril Walker 17 and 16 over thirty-six holes in 1924; dealt Bobby Jones the worst defeat of his career, 12 and 11, in 1926; and beat Johnny Farrell three matches out of five in 1928. In 1927, Hagen evened the score against Sarazen, bettering him in an exhibition 9 and 8.

Hagen retired from golf in the mid-thirties, the good life having claimed the fine touch so necessary to his game. He spent his twilight years on his lakeside estate in northern Michigan, regaling visiting friends with tales of his days as America's top golfer.

BOBBY JONES
1928–1937

Robert Tyre ("Bobby") Jones, Jr., played six tournaments in 1930 and won five; the first two—the Savannah Open, in which he finished second, and the Southeastern Open, which he won by thirteen strokes—were merely tune-ups for the four to follow. Jones had set his sights on the year's four

major tournaments: the U.S. and British Open and Amateur Championships. No one before had come close to winning this Grand Slam, but Jones did it that year and with relatively little trouble. His slam is one of the greatest accomplishments in sports, but forms only part of the Jones legend.

Bobby Jones played tournament golf for only a short time, entering his first important event, the 1916 U.S. Amateur, at age fourteen and retiring shortly after completing the Grand Slam at age twenty-eight. But his record is a litany of excellence. In that span he won twenty-three of the fifty-two tournaments he entered. Beginning with the 1916 U.S. Amateur, Jones played in twenty-seven majors and won thirteen (although none before the 1923 U.S. Open). From 1924–30, Jones entered the U.S. Amateur seven times, won five of them and was runner-up in one other. In the U.S. Opens between 1922–30, Jones posted four victories, finished second twice and lost twice in playoffs. He played in four British Opens and won three of them.

What makes these statistics even more impressive is that Jones played his entire career as an amateur and for only a few months of the year. He spent the rest of his time either as a student—first studying engineering at Georgia Tech, then literature at Harvard, later law at Emory—or as a lawyer in his native Atlanta.

Jones learned the game by imitating, then working with, Stewart Maiden, the pro at East Lake Country Club in Atlanta. Jones's graceful, controlled swing is perhaps the most flawless ever—it had "a touch of poetry," noted golf writer Bernard Darwin—but was just one component in a game that included a hair-trigger temper and a mental block against winning that characterized what Jones's friend and confidant O. B. Keeler called the "seven lean years"—1916–23. With hard work and determination, his trademarks on and off the course, Jones overcame these obstacles and broke through in 1923, taking the U.S. Open at Inwood Country Club in New York.

Now Jones was all but unstoppable. During the "seven fat years," he concentrated on the majors, defeating the best golfers—amateur and professional—on both sides of the Atlantic. All the while Jones was respected by his rivals and modest about his own achievements. He was also a stickler for the Rules. In the 1925 U.S. Open, Jones claimed his ball moved after address and, despite USGA protests, demanded a one-stroke penalty. The extra stroke put Jones in a playoff with Scottish player Willie Macfarlane, which Jones lost.

Jones's quest for the Grand Slam began with a trip first to Royal St. George's, in Britain, for the Walker Cup, where he won both matches he contested, and then north to St. Andrews for the British Amateur, which proved to be the toughest challenge of the year. His fourth-round match against defending champion Cyril Tolley, who was playing on his home course, was a classic. In strong winds, the two men battled back and forth, and Jones had to sink an eight-foot putt on the eighteenth hole to force a playoff. On the first extra hole, Jones was on in two, a stroke up on Tolley, then laid a stymie (in which one golfer leaves his ball between his opponent's ball and the hole, a practice now illegal), to close him out.

In the sixth round, against fellow American Jimmy Johnston, Jones had to hole another eight-foot putt on the last hole to avoid extra holes; that afternoon in the semifinals, Jones was two down to George Voigt, yet another American player, with five to play, but rallied to win 1 up. The final against Roger Wethered was anticlimactic. Jones had bettered Wethered by 9 and 8 in a Walker Cup singles match a few days earlier. This time, Jones won 7 and 6.

The British Open at Hoylake (Royal Liverpool) proved an easier campaign. Although Jones had played better, he managed to lead from start to finish and break the seventy-two-hole course record by ten.

Back at home, the U.S. Open went to Interlachen Country Club in Minneapolis and weather as hot as Jones had known. (Jones perspired so much that at one point he could not untie his necktie; Keeler had to cut it off with a knife.) But Jones was just as hot in the first three rounds, shooting 71, 73, and 68 for a five-shot lead. Although he finished with a mediocre 75, the score went unchallenged, and Jones won by two, also becoming the first man to break par for seventy-two holes (his 287 being one under) in the championship.

In the U.S. Amateur Championship at Merion Cricket Club outside Philadelphia, Jones was never down to an opponent, winning each match handily. On the twenty-ninth hole of the thirty-six-hole final, he defeated Eugene Homans from New Jersey and completed the Grand Slam.

Having realized his dream, Jones officially retired from competitive golf a few weeks after Merion. He continued to contribute to the game. He made a series of short instructional films called *How I Play Golf* that introduced thousands to the game. He wrote a nationally syndicated column and a few books, most notably *Down the Fairway* with Keeler and *Golf Is My Game,* and appeared on the radio. Jones became a director and advisor to Spalding, the sporting-goods manufacturer, in 1931 and helped design a set of clubs—the first flanged models—that was a best-seller for decades.

Perhaps Jones's most lasting monument is Augusta National, the course he designed with Scottish architect Alister Mackenzie in Augusta, Georgia, and the site of The Masters, the tournament Jones created. Jones continued to play in The

health. He died in 1971, leaving a game that was far richer for his having played it.

BYRON NELSON
1938–1947

The closest mankind has come to a golfing machine was Byron Nelson. Wind him up, and Iron Byron won golf tournaments: eighteen in 1945, including eleven in a row, with a scoring average of 68.33, an all-time low. Even Nelson admitted twenty-five years later that the streak "isn't really very believable." (The next best streak is four in a row by Jack Burke, Jr., in 1952.)

Nelson was playing on a different level than his peers. "I had this wonderful momentum going," he said, "and I didn't seem to have to worry about anything or think about anything. Everything I hit went pretty much where I wanted it to go. I was almost in a trance."

Nelson had already established himself as one of the best, most consistent players in the game by 1945. He was one of the straightest drivers ever—so straight that it was said of Nelson, as it had been of Harry Vardon and others, that he was at a disadvantage playing thirty-six holes in one day because he would drive into the divots taken in the first eighteen. Nelson also was a fine iron player, operating with such monotonous ease that his rounds seemed tedious. Not that he played conservatively; Nelson never feared to attack the pin. He simply seldom missed a shot.

Nelson's career is difficult to assess by numbers alone. He won fifty-four tour events, ranking fifth all-time, but could have won more had he not retired to his ranch in Texas in 1946 at age thirty-four, playing only occasionally thereafter. He won five major championships, but that figure also might have been higher. He played only once in the British Open and the U.S. Open was not held during Nelson's peak years, 1942–45, because of World War II. In addition, the PGA Championship was canceled in 1943, as was The Masters, from 1943 to 1945.

On the other hand, competition was weaker in those seasons. Many professionals had gone into the services. (Nelson was rejected because of a blood disorder.) But the fields in 1945 were better than is commonly perceived. Sam Snead had been released from the navy the previous fall, and Nelson's other main rival, Ben Hogan, returned midway through the season. (Nelson, Snead, and Hogan formed a great triumvirate in the decade of 1938–47: Nelson won

forty-six tournaments while Snead and Hogan won forty each. Nelson captured four majors, Snead two, Hogan one.)

Nelson was born in Fort Worth, Texas, in 1912. He and Hogan both picked up the game as caddies at the Glen Garden Country Club. Nelson learned primarily from watching other golfers. Through constant experimentation, he developed a swing that was trustworthy but unique in its day. Instead of hitting against a straight left side, Nelson employed a more lateral shift, driving the legs firmly through the ball. Although this style rid him of the hook he had acquired upon changing from hickory to steel shafts, it temporarily burdened him with a new problem—an occasional shank.

The kinks had been ironed out by the time Nelson hit the winter tour in 1933–34. He managed to break even in 1935, earning an invitation to The Masters. Two years later, Nelson won at Augusta National for his first major title by making up six shots on Ralph Guldahl over the final stretch.

More major titles followed: the 1939 U.S. Open at the Philadelphia Country Club, where Nelson defeated Craig Wood and Denny Shute in a playoff; the 1940 PGA Championship at the Hershey Country Club in Pennsylvania, where he beat Sam Snead 1 up in the final; the 1942 Masters, where he defeated Hogan, 69–70, in a playoff; and the 1945 PGA Championship at Morraine Country Club in Dayton, Ohio, where former baseball player Sam Byrd was Nelson's final victim. In all, Nelson reached the final in five out of the six PGA Championships between 1939 and 1945, finishing second three times.

Tournament play was suspended in 1943, and when it resumed the next year, Nelson and Jug McSpaden, the Gold Dust Twins, dominated the tour, Nelson leading with eight victories. Nelson's scoring average that year was 69.67, but the "little black book," in which he tracked his play, revealed, "I found two things. I chipped poorly too many times and played too many careless shots. I didn't concentrate hard enough."

Nelson improved his concentration in 1945, made a slight adjustment in his stance on chip shots, and was off to the races. From March 11 through August 4, he won all outings while shooting a final-round mean of 66.67. When the streak was broken (Nelson placed fourth as amateur Fred Haas won in Memphis), Nelson retaliated by waltzing home by ten shots the following week. He capped the year by shooting 259 at Seattle to win by thirteen and then winning by eight at Glen Garden. Not once all year did Nelson fail to total par or lower.

The pressure of the winning streak did not bother Nelson's play, yet it caught up with him off the course. When he visited the Mayo Clinic that July because of gastrointestinal problems: "They told me I was more tense than I should have been . . . I couldn't get the game out of my mind," he said later. Those problems, the wear of travel, and the feeling that he had "reached all the goals I ever wanted to reach" led him to retire in August 1946.

Nelson did emerge from his ranch in Texas to play select tournaments over the next five years, scoring his last American victory in the 1951 Bing Crosby Pro-Am (he won the French Open in 1955). He has remained involved with the game, working for a time as a commentator on golf telecasts and tutoring several tour players, including Tom Watson.

PATTY BERG
1938–1947

In the fall of 1938, Patty Berg won the U.S. Women's Amateur Championship and began a decade in which this feisty, freckled fireplug from Minneapolis set women's golf on a course for greatness.

Berg had challenged in vain for the title three times previously. As the 1935 Minnesota State champion at age seventeen, she had lost to Glenna Collett Vare in the final by 3 and 2 (and gave Vare a record sixth U.S. Women's Amateur title). The following year, even though Berg had won five tournaments in twelve starts, she reached only the quarterfinals. In 1937, Berg again finished as runner-up, this time to Estelle Lawson Page, by 7 and 6. But 1938 was different. Berg had two Curtis Cup appearances (1936 as well as earlier in 1938) behind her, and had the momentum of winning ten of the thirteen events she entered that year. Displaying a gritty style opponents would learn to fear in the ensuing years, Berg beat Page in the final by 6 and 5, one-putting seven of thirteen greens in the eighteen-hole match at the Westmoreland Country Club in Wilmette, Illinois.

Because of her sparkling record that year, which included the second of seven Titleholders Championships (once a women's major tournament), the Associated Press dubbed Berg Woman Athlete of the Year. It was the first of three such awards Berg would win, the others coming in 1943 and 1955.

Later in the fall of 1938, Berg enrolled at the University of Minnesota, where she took business courses each morning, practiced golf each afternoon and studied each night. The following spring, she started the golf season quickly with six victories, including a second Titleholders, but an appendix operation that summer prevented her from defending her Amateur title. The year took a further turn for the worse when Berg's mother died on Christmas Day.

Seizing the opportunity to help out financially at home, Berg turned professional in 1940 and was signed to an endorsement contract by Wilson Sporting Goods Company, which she still represents. She then toured the country conducting instruction clinics and staging exhibitions under the company banner. The meager schedule for professional golf tournaments for women comprised three events that carried a total purse of $500.

Not until the following year did Berg win her first professional title, the 1941 Women's Western Open (another major championship of that era). That joy was short-lived. In December, the day after Pearl Harbor, tragedy again struck. Berg was involved in a car crash that fractured her knee in three places. To compound the agony, the cast was incorrectly set, and the knee had to be rebroken. Berg's rehabilitation stretched on for eighteen months.

Throughout the ordeal, Berg's thoughts focused solely on her comeback. At the 1943 Western Open, she made a triumphant re-entry, winning the qualifying medal and then the title after being three down to Dorothy Kirby with six holes to play.

Following service in the Marine Corps Reserves during World War II, Berg resumed play in 1946. That season brought four more victories, including her only U.S. Open Championship. She defeated Betty Jameson by 5 and 6 in the final (1946 was the only year the event was contested at match play). Berg won three times in 1947; in 1948, she added three more victories, including a fourth Titleholders and a third Western Open.

All this was no small wonder for this small wonder—a tiny (five foot one) but powerful woman of Irish and Norwegian descent. Growing up in Minneapolis, where Berg was born in 1918, she took on an early toughness by participating in various sports with the neighborhood boys. In grammar school, Berg quarterbacked the "50th Street Tigers," a football team that featured tackle Bud Wilkinson, who went on to become a University of Oklahoma and NFL coach.

Football eventually gave way to golf, the passion of Berg's father. Herman Berg's hobby was to film the great players of the day—Bobby Jones, Walter Hagen, and Gene Sarazen—and then to study and learn from their swings. He encouraged his daughter to do the same and cut down four clubs for her from an old set. By the age of fifteen, Patty had become committed to the game. At sixteen, she won the Minneapolis City Championship, which earned Berg her first full set of clubs: five woods and ten irons.

The equipment served Berg well over the ensuing years, but Berg served the game even better. In the spring of 1949, when the future of women's professional golf looked dim—the four-year-old Women's Professional Golfers Association (WPGA) tour was facing its demise—Berg met with Babe and George Zaharias and Fred Corcoran at the Venetian Hotel in Miami, Florida, to found the Ladies Professional Golf Association (LPGA). Wilson served as the sponsor; Corcoran, Babe Zaharias's manager, was named tournament manager. Berg became the first president (1949–52) of the fledgling association. Later that year, the LPGA charter members were named: Berg, Zaharias, Jameson, Betty Mims Danoff, Helen Dettweiler, and Helen Hicks.

Berg was not content simply to administrate; she maintained a powerful playing presence on the women's tour. She won three times in 1949 and four times in 1950. After a fourth Western Open title and one other title in 1951, she became one of four charter inductees to the Women's Golf Hall of Fame (renamed the LPGA Hall of Fame in 1967), a vehicle created during Berg's presidency to add credibility to the women's tour.

Berg amassed a record fifteen major championships in all—one U.S. Open, seven Titleholders, and seven Western Opens—the last being the 1958 Western at age forty. She won eighty-four titles (twenty-nine amateur, fifty-five professional) and was one of the first thirteen inductees into the World Golf Hall of Fame in 1974. She received the Bob Jones Award, the USGA's highest honor, in 1963. Finally, in 1979, the LPGA recognized Berg's impact on golf when it created the Patty Berg Award for diplomacy, sportsmanship, goodwill, and contributions to the game.

BEN HOGAN
1948–1957

Ben Hogan liked to eliminate the risk in golf. While practice and preparation were necessary evils to other pros, to Hogan they were no more than steps in his personal quest for perfection. Hogan beat balls until his hands ached. In practice rounds, he would pick the course apart, square inch by square inch, deciding on the best routes to play each hole. Then, when the battle was on, he would execute his plan with the mechanical precision of a robot, isolating himself from any possible distraction, leaving nothing to chance. "Management," Hogan always said, "is 80 percent of winning."

This monkish devotion to perfection may have taken the human element out of the game, but it paid off for the monk. Between 1948 and 1957, Hogan won four U.S. Opens (Willie Anderson, Bobby Jones, and Jack Nicklaus are the only other golfers to have done so), two Masters, one British

Open, and a second PGA Championship, his first having come in 1946. In 1953, Hogan captured three legs of the modern slam, missing only the PGA Championship in which he chose not to play. No one since has come as close. He finished in the top ten in sixteen consecutive U.S. Opens through 1960 and in fourteen consecutive Masters through 1956. That he achieved much of this after facing death in a terrifying car crash is testament to the man's steel will.

Hogan was born of Irish stock in Texas in 1912 (ironically in a town named Dublin). His father, who was the village blacksmith, died when Hogan was ten, whereupon his mother moved the family northeast to Fort Worth, where Hogan took up the game as a caddie at the Glen Garden Country Club.

Hogan showed little promise when he turned pro at nineteen, principally because of a hook he seemed unable to repair. Nonetheless, he joined the tour in 1931 and went broke. He tried again in 1933 and again went broke. Finally, after three years of solid practice, Hogan scraped out a meager living on the 1937 circuit and over the next two years.

Hogan broke through in 1940 by winning four tournaments, the Vardon Trophy for low scoring average, and the money list. The following year, Hogan won another five events, another Vardon Trophy, and the money list again. Then World War II intervened. Hogan won six times in 1942 (and finished second behind Byron Nelson in The Masters), but beyond that no official records were kept. That year, he joined the Army Air Corps.

When Hogan returned to the tour in 1945, he had some catching up to do. Nelson already had won The Masters twice (1937 and 1942), the PGA Championship twice (1940 and 1945), and the U.S. Open (1939). The other fine players of Hogan's era also had cracked the major market. Jimmy Demaret had won The Masters in 1940, Sam Snead the PGA Championship in 1942.

By this time Hogan had rid himself of his hook. While still swinging hard through the ball with a full extension of his right arm, he now rolled the face of the club open on the backswing. Then, as he neared the top of the swing, he curled his left wrist closed. (He later sold this "secret" to *Life* magazine for a reported $20,000.) From hammering low draws, Hogan went to hitting crisp, accurate fades. He remained vulnerable only on the greens but solved that problem by hitting close to the hole. Hogan's game took off.

He won five times in the remainder of the 1945 season. In 1946, he took the PGA Championship, twelve other events and led the money list. He won seven events in 1947 (although Demaret won more money), then in 1948 Hogan took his first U.S. Open, at the Riviera Country Club in Los

Angeles, while setting a seventy-two-hole Open record of 276. (Jack Nicklaus set the current record of 272 in 1980.) Hogan won a total of eleven tournaments that year and the Vardon and the money list yet again. It looked like nothing could stop him.

A transcontinental bus almost did.

On a foggy morning in February 1949, while Hogan was driving with his wife Valerie from a tournament in Phoenix, Arizona, back to Fort Worth, a bus suddenly appeared in the same lane, speeding straight toward them. Hogan instinctively threw himself over his wife to protect her. He suffered a double fracture of his pelvis, a fractured collarbone, broken right ribs, and a broken ankle. After waiting an hour and a half for an ambulance, Hogan was driven 150 miles to a hospital in El Paso. There, blood clots began to form in his legs. His life was in doubt.

But Hogan's strength in any venture always had been his steely determination, the quality that drove him to practice so hard and to analyze every part of his game. Hogan recovered, entered the U.S. Open that year but was too weak to play. He did make the trip to Britain as non-playing captain of the 1949 Ryder Cup team.

Early in 1950, he entered the Los Angeles Open at Riviera in Los Angeles to test whether his body and mind could endure four rounds of competition. The experiment ended with Hogan tied for first with Snead, who won the playoff.

Come summer, Hogan hobbled into the U.S. Open at Merion outside Philadelphia. After two rounds, he lay fifth and faced a final thirty-six holes on Saturday. Many doubted that Hogan, who was playing with his legs bandaged up, could survive. In the morning, he returned a 72 and lay two shots behind leader Lloyd Mangrum. Hogan could not even pick the ball from the cup, the pain had grown so unbearable, never mind walk. Somehow he managed a 74 to force a playoff with Mangrum and George Fazio. The pair was no match for Hogan on Sunday. His 69 beat Mangrum by four and Fazio by six, and he had his second U.S. Open.

Hogan defended his title the following year at Oakland Hills, whose tight fairways and treacherously bunkered greens some pros considered unbeatable. Hogan was not one of them. When his final-round 67 clinched a third Open title, he commented, "I'm glad I brought this course, this monster, to its knees."

Hogan did not win a major in 1952, but he made up for the drought in 1953, which he calls "my greatest year in golf." First, he sliced five strokes off The Masters scoring record with a 274 (since lowered to 271 by Nicklaus and Raymond Floyd) and won by five. Next, he won the U.S. Open at Oakmont Country Club outside Pittsburgh by six strokes, leading in every round. Hogan then decided to join the immortal Americans who had won the British Open before him—among them Bobby Jones, Walter Hagen, and Gene Sarazen. He traveled to Carnoustie and, after sharing the third-round lead, executed an almost perfect 68 to leave the field four strokes in his wake.

That was Hogan's only appearance in the British Open and was his last major victory (but twice he finished within two strokes of a fifth U.S. Open title and he finished second in the 1954 and 1955 Masters). As the 1950s faded into the 1960s, Hogan's putting all but disappeared. "My nerves are shot," he admitted. By the mid-sixties, he had retired into virtual seclusion in Fort Worth, still taking time to pound balls on the range when not supervising the Ben Hogan equipment company.

Hogan, whose feats can be compared only with those of Jones and Nicklaus, undoubtedly was one of the greatest golfers ever. But along with the meticulous talent came a cold, uncompromising surliness. The galleries who crowded to watch him did so not because of his charisma. The machine at work was simply a sight worth seeing.

Some people took Hogan's taciturnity in stride, particularly his close friend and frequent foursome partner Jimmy Demaret. Asked to corroborate Hogan's renown for absolute silence on the course, Demaret concurred but deftly summed up Hogan's mastery of the game. "When I play with him," Demaret said, "he speaks to me on every green. He turns to me and says, 'You're away.'"

BABE ZAHARIAS
1948–1957

Mildred Didrikson Zaharias was one of the greatest women golfers of all time, and almost certainly the greatest woman athlete. Pursuing a successful career in athletics—and on the stage—Zaharias took up golf seriously just before she turned twenty. In a career that spanned two decades, Zaharias won nearly everything a woman player could win, and was instrumental in the founding of the Ladies Professional Golf Association (LPGA).

Zaharias died tragically of cancer in 1956 after a prolonged illness, yet she remains the finest player of the decade 1948–1957. During that time, Zaharias won three U.S. Women's Open titles among a total of thirty-one professional titles and reigned as the leading money winner from 1948 to 1951.

Zaharias was a tomboy growing up in Beaumont, Texas (she was born in nearby Port Arthur), after World War I. She earned her nickname, Babe, because as a schoolgirl she hit home runs with the frequency of Babe Ruth. She was a match for any boy in any sport.

Zaharias entered the 1932 National Amateur Athletic Union track meet and Olympic trials. Sponsored by the Dallas, Texas, insurance company for which she worked, Zaharias entered eight of the ten events held, winning the eighty-meter hurdles, baseball throw, shot put, broad jump, and javelin. She also tied for first in the high jump and placed fourth in the discus—all in one afternoon. Along the way, she set three world records and, competing alone, won the *team* competition.

Zaharias's next stop was the 1932 Olympic Games in Los Angeles, where she took gold medals in the eighty-meter hurdles and javelin. She would have shared the gold in the high jump had she not been disqualified for using the "western roll" (a technique later legalized). Having thus stood women's amateur sports on its ear, Zaharias accepted an invitation from sportswriter Grantland Rice to play golf the following day. Picking up clubs for the first time in more than a year, Zaharias toured Brentwood Country Club in Santa Monica in under 100, forging a 43 on the back nine, including two wood shots into the wind to the fringe of the 523-yard, par-five seventeenth hole. A star was born.

For a number of years thereafter, Zaharias was something of a curiosity, tap-dancing and playing the harmonica in vaudeville (for $3,500 a week), then stepping out on an exhibition golf tour with Gene Sarazen. Crowds thronged to watch this woman crush a ball 250 yards and more. After marrying professional wrestler George Zaharias in 1938, she settled down and decided to concentrate on her golf game, particularly on those aspects that required finesse. She sought out Tommy Armour, a leading teacher of the day, and practiced until her hands bled.

The Babe performed in many exhibitions during World War II and won a number of tournaments, including the Women's Western Open three years running, from 1943 to 1945. During most of that time, Zaharias played as a professional, but she regained her amateur status in 1944, which left her free to pursue the crown jewels of women's golf, the American and British amateur titles.

In 1946, the U.S. Women's Amateur was contested over the Southern Hills Country Club in Tulsa, Oklahoma. Zaharias was never down to an opponent in the entire tournament and beat Clara Callender Sherman of California, by 11 and 9, in the thirty-six-hole final.

In the years 1946 and 1947, Zaharias transformed herself into a victory machine, winning seventeen consecutive events. She went after the 1947 British Ladies Champion-

ship, the only major British title that had yet to be captured by an American. Playing over the Gullane Number One course near Edinburgh, Scotland, Zaharias beguiled the crowds with her prodigious hitting and easy manner. Zaharias lost only four holes in the first six rounds and won the title by 5 and 4 from Jacqueline Gordon. Soon after returning home, Zaharias again turned professional, signing a $300,000 contract to make short golf films.

As might be expected, Zaharias's total tournament earnings between 1948 and 1951 amounted to less than $40,000; the bulk of her earnings came from exhibitions. She would entertain baseball crowds before games by elegantly hitting and fielding baseballs, then rapid-firing long golf shots. It paid well—$500 a night—but like the tours with Sarazen a decade earlier, it was not exactly golf.

Her tournament performances most certainly were golf. In 1948, Zaharias won three of eight events, including the U.S. Women's Open, then two of seven the following year. In 1950, the Babe won her second Open, plus five of nine other events. The women's tour expanded to fourteen tournaments in 1951—Babe won seven. She won four times in 1952 before undergoing the first of several operations for cancer. Amazingly, Zaharias returned to the fray in 1954, winning five times, including a third U.S. Women's Open in which she led the field by twelve strokes. In 1955, the Babe won twice early in the season but became too ill to continue.

ARNOLD PALMER
1958–1967

In the 1950s, Arnold Palmer changed the face of golf as America had come to know it. For several years, the game had been missing a 24-carat marquee star such as Ben Hogan, Byron Nelson, or Sam Snead. With television an exciting new arena for the game, golf needed a figure with whom America could identify, someone who could take golf out of the country club and into the living room; a blue-collar boy next door, a Babe Ruth—a Superman.

Arnold Palmer turned out to be all of these.

There were other great players in the Palmer era. A powerful, burly youth named Jack Nicklaus arrived on the scene. South African Gary Player became, with Palmer and Nicklaus, the third part of golf's Big Three, winning all over the world. Billy Casper quietly stacked up the laurels. Doug Sanders was as colorful as Palmer if not as successful.

But Palmer played a different game from his peers: Palmer played hard. He would take a difficult course and crash headfirst into it until it collapsed. One sportswriter noted how Palmer, breaking through the galleries to the tee and hitching up his pants (his trademark), looked for all the world like a prizefighter climbing into the ring. Oh, there were plenty of golfers who could make a ball dance whatever steps they desired. Palmer simply whacked it into the hole until no holes were left to play.

If one of Palmer's hell-for-leather, risk-laden strategies turned into a blunder, so what? Palmer's emotion would flow, his handsome, chiseled features would bleed despair. His legions of fans—Arnie's Army, as they were called—would suffer along with him. That was part of the Palmer charisma. In victory, he was immortal. In failure, merely human.

Born in 1929, Palmer was introduced to the game three years later by his father, Deacon, first the greenkeeper at Latrobe Country Club in western Pennsylvania and then, when the Depression dictated cutbacks, also the club professional. During his boyhood, Palmer was not permitted to mix with the members but was allowed to play the course at certain times. Out of school, he spent hours on the practice range.

From the start, Palmer swung hard. That was Deacon's doing. The father figured tempo and balance would come later, which they did. But swinging from the heels can turn the club over too early, producing a hook. Palmer prevented this fault by pushing an almost rigid right arm through and beyond the hitting area. He was a long and accurate driver, a proficient iron player, and he always putted as though he had money in his pocket.

After a successful stint as a college golfer (three-time Atlantic Coast Conference champion while at Wake Forest) and as an amateur (1954 U.S. Amateur champion), Palmer turned pro. It took him a year to win his first PGA Tour event, the 1955 Canadian Open. In 1956, Palmer won two events. In 1957, four. The following year, Palmer embarked on an astonishing string of major championship results. Between 1958 and 1964, he won seven of the twenty-five majors he competed in and finished in the top ten on twelve other occasions. In the decade 1958–67, Palmer won forty-four tour events (plus two British Opens and one Australian Open) and led the money list four times. On July 21, 1968, Palmer became the first golfer to reach $1 million in career earnings. Because of that achievement, the annual leading money winner on tour takes home the Arnold Palmer Award. (Palmer could take credit for his wealth. When he joined the tour in 1954, purses totaled $600,819. With the interest Palmer created, they almost quadrupled over the next ten years.) Finally, Palmer has won the Vardon Trophy for low scoring average four times.

The achievement that symbolized for good the Palmer *modus operandi* came at the 1960 U.S. Open at Cherry Hills

Country Club outside Denver, Colorado. Seven shots behind leader Mike Souchak with the final, afternoon round to play (at the time, the Open played thirty-six holes on Saturday), Palmer struck up a brief, now-famous conversation with Bob Drum, his acquaintance and sometime amanuensis who covered golf for the *Pittsburgh Press*.

"What would happen if I shot a 65?" Palmer asked as he sat over a hamburger in the Cherry Hills grill room.

"Nothing," Drum replied. "You're out of it."

Palmer was enraged. "The hell I am," he roared. "A 65 would give me 280, and 280 is the kind of score that usually wins the Open."

At that, Palmer rose from the table, stomped off to the course, drove the green of the par-four first hole, fired six birdies over the first seven holes and came home with his 65 and the championship.

Palmer's four Masters victories (only Jack Nicklaus has won more) came in a not-as-dramatic but nevertheless impressive fashion. In 1958, he scraped by only a stroke better than Doug Ford and Fred Hawkins. In 1960, he birdied the last two holes to snatch the green jacket from Ken Venturi; in 1962, he won in a playoff with Gary Player and Dow Finsterwald, despite being three strokes off the lead with nine holes to play; and in 1964, he sauntered home six strokes clear of the pack.

All this success recruited thousands more fans for the Army, but Palmer's legions were not restricted to America. In the sixties, the British, too, fell hopelessly in love with Palmer, as he resuscitated their venerated but financially ailing Open. When Palmer attended the 1960 event at St. Andrews, Scotland, he finished second to Kel Nagle, the Australian, and that was enough to entice him back. The following year, Palmer won amid a maelstrom at Royal Birkdale; then at Troon in 1962, he left the nearest finisher six strokes back, the third-place competitor twelve back. All the while, Palmer cruised along smiling and shooting the breeze with the crowds.

Palmer's success was not confined to the golf course. With the help of business manager Mark McCormack—now president of the vast International Management Group sporting conglomerate—Palmer parlayed his personality into a business empire worth millions. These days, while playing a moderate schedule on the Senior PGA Tour, he has businesses ranging from the Pro Group equipment manufacturing company to the operation of the Bay Hill and Isleworth golf clubs in Orlando, Florida.

Palmer still draws an impressive Army wherever he plays, but he will be best remembered for his accomplishments and his style of play between 1958 and 1967. For years to come,

whenever a golfer—anyone, anyplace in the world—tries to pull off a shot that seems impossible, no matter whether he succeeds or not, someone will ask, "Who do you think you are? Arnold Palmer?"

MICKEY WRIGHT
1958–1967

Women's golf metamorphosed from a curiosity into a serious professional sport in the mid-fifties, powered in large part by the achievements of Mickey Wright. The willowy blonde from San Diego matched the prodigious prowess of Babe Zaharias with the consistency of the top male players and set new standards in the women's game. Between 1955 and 1973, Wright recorded eighty-two wins and set many LPGA records, including thirteen victories in a single year, 1963.

Mary Kathryn Wright's father had expected the new baby to be a boy and had already picked out the name Michael. He imbued "Mickey" with a love of sports and introduced her to golf when she was eleven. By thirteen, Wright could score in the high 80s. In 1950, she made the finals of the U.S. Girls' Junior Championship, and in 1952, she won it. The next year, Wright enrolled at Stanford University to study psychology, but dropped out after a year to pursue golf.

Wright's father bankrolled her in 1954, when she won the World and All-American Amateurs, reached the final of the U.S. Women's Amateur, and finished fourth and was leading amateur in the U.S. Women's Open. In November 1954, Wright turned professional. In her first event, the 1955 L.A. Open, she won $450, finished in the top ten, and knew she had made the right step.

But it took some seasoning for everything to come together. Early in 1956, the LPGA fined Wright $150 for "saying some things I shouldn't have." Wright's first professional victory, the Jacksonville Open, came later that year. Having savored the taste of victory, there was no stopping her. Although Wright began her career playing in the shadow of the same great players who had helped her adjust to life on tour—notably Patty Berg, Louise Suggs, and Betsy Rawls—in no time Wright was outplaying them.

The domination began in 1958 when Wright won five tournaments, including the LPGA Championship and U.S. Women's Open, which made her the first woman to win two majors in the same year. She won the Open again in 1959 to become the first back-to-back winner, and in 1961, Wright captured three majors—the U.S. Open, the LPGA Championship, and the now-defunct Titleholders Cham-

pionship—a feat as yet unmatched. Other accomplishments included a fourth U.S. Open title in 1963, LPGA Championship titles in 1960 and 1964, another Titleholders in 1962, and three Western Opens (another defunct major). Wright won seventy-two events in all between 1958 and 1967 and thirteen majors, more than any other woman.

Wright was the first woman to have her swing favorably compared with that of the best men players; she wasted no motion and generated far more power than any other woman could muster. Wright regularly reached par fives in two and could hit approaches with mid-irons when her peers had to opt for fairway woods.

If there was a single weak link in Wright's game, it was her short game. But even then, she could summon the talent when the need arose. The 1964 U.S. Women's Open was played at the San Diego Country Club, in Wright's hometown. Her parents and countless friends came out to watch the three-day event that culminated with a grueling thirty-six-hole final day, and witnessed Wright getting up and down from a tough downhill lie in a greenside trap on the seventy-second hole to tie Ruth Jessen. Wright won the ensuing playoff by two strokes.

Although Wright's eighty-two victories run second to Kathy Whitworth's eighty-eight in the LPGA record book, Wright has set a few marks of her own. She twice won four consecutive events, and her 62 in the first round of the 1964 Tall City Open in Midland, Texas, still shares the LPGA's low for eighteen holes. She topped the money list from 1961–64, won at least once a year for fourteen years (1956 through 1969), and won the Vare Trophy for low scoring average five straight seasons (1960–64). In 1963, Wright was utterly spectacular, winning thirteen of the thirty-two LPGA tournaments, better than 40 percent. (It is estimated that the $31,269 she won that year would be worth more than $800,000 today.)

Wright also was a leader of the young LPGA Tour, serving in a number of capacities, including president and treasurer. But it was a personal struggle for her to take command and act as a spokeswoman for the fledgling organization. She was painfully shy, and only constant exposure to speechmaking, radio and television appearances, and other public-relations responsibilities rid her of inhibitions.

Wright returned to school in the mid-1960s, studying math at Southern Methodist University in Dallas, then left to concentrate on managing her stock portfolio. Yet, although she played less on tour as of 1966, Wright won another sixteen tournaments by the end of 1969.

Wright was suffering from a number of health problems by then. A nerve disorder in her left foot forced her to wear tennis shoes on the golf course. She had been battling ulcers since the mid-sixties, and having crisscrossed the country for more than a decade, was tired of the travel and had a severe aversion to flying. Wright made occasional appearances in the early seventies, notching her final win at the prestigious Colgate-Dinah Shore tournament in 1973. In 1979, she played well enough to make the five-way playoff for the Coca-Cola Classic, eventually won by Nancy Lopez.

Wright saw the LPGA Tour attain respectability and set a fine example with her outstanding play and devotion to the LPGA cause. She was inducted into the LPGA Hall of Fame in 1964. She lives on a golf course in Port St. Lucie, Florida, but, although she will sometimes venture out to practice, she seldom plays an entire round.

JACK NICKLAUS 1968–1977

Jack Nicklaus has won almost everything there is to win in golf. As an amateur, he won the NCAA collegiate title (when with Ohio State University), two U.S. Amateurs, and played on the winning 1959 Walker Cup team. Since turning professional in 1961, Nicklaus has won eighteen major championships (five more than his nearest rival, Bobby Jones), including six Masters, five PGA Championships, four U.S. Opens, and three British Opens. Nicklaus won his first major (as a professional) in 1962, his most recent in 1986. He has won fifty-six PGA tournaments, fifteen foreign events (other than the British Open), has played on six winning World Cup teams and on five victorious Ryder Cup squads (as well as captaining the winning 1983 Ryder Cup team and participating in the 1969 Ryder Cup Matches, which were tied). He has been PGA Player of the Year five times and has won at least one tournament a year for seventeen years (1962–78). He has led the money list eight times, won at least $100,000 in twenty-three campaigns, at least $200,000 in twelve; although Nicklaus was "only" the third pro to pass the $1-million mark in career earnings, he was the first to win $2 million, $3 million, $4 million. Had he played enough rounds per year to qualify for the Vardon Trophy for low scoring average, Nicklaus would have won that honor eight times.

So why has this golfer for all seasons been chosen Player of the Decade for only 1968 to 1977?

Because not only was Nicklaus at his most dominant in this period, he also convinced those who considered him little more than the overweight, crew-cut nemesis of Arnold Pal-

mer that, as the Golden Bear, he was the best golfer in the world, bar none—and very possibly the best ever.

The man who recognized Nicklaus's extraordinary skills before anyone else was Jack Grout. Nicklaus was ten years old when he joined Grout's classes at Scioto Country Club in Columbus, Ohio, where Charlie Nicklaus, Jack's father, was a member. The stocky youngster was a fast learner and was strong, so Grout paid him extra attention, tutoring him rigorously in the fundamentals. Keep the head still, he told Nicklaus; make a full arc; work on your balance; hit down on the ball; keep your weight back. Grout taught Nicklaus to hit a high ball with a left-to-right trajectory, even though his pupil hit naturally the other way. Grout reasoned that the fade was easier to control than the draw and that a youngster with Nicklaus's strength—which would surely grow—had distance to spare. These remain the trademarks of the Nicklaus game, and Grout remains Nicklaus's teacher.

Nicklaus first qualified for the U.S. Open as a seventeen-year-old and missed the cut. After finishing forty-first in 1958 and again missing the cut in 1959, Nicklaus fired a 282 in the 1960 U.S. Open at Cherry Hills Country Club outside Denver, Colorado, to finish second, two strokes adrift of Palmer. Nicklaus's score remains an Open record for an amateur.

Nicklaus caught up with Palmer soon after turning pro when he beat him in a playoff in the 1962 U.S. Open at Oakmont Country Club in Oakmont, Pennsylvania. From that time on, Palmer and Nicklaus have retained respect for each other—if always competitive—and eventually became good friends. But Arnie's Army wanted none of that. They resented this youth outdriving, outputting, and outscoring their idol and adopted malicious measures to distract him. They would scream on Nicklaus's backswing, whistle while he putted or brandish massive banners blaring "Over here, Fat Boy!" or "Hit it here, Jack."

Such treatment hurt Nicklaus, but not his game. He had won twenty-five tournaments by the end of 1967, including seven professional majors. The last of these was the 1967 Open at Baltusrol Golf Club in Springfield, New Jersey, where Nicklaus's 275 shaved a stroke off Ben Hogan's Open record, which had stood for nineteen years, and beat Palmer, who finished second, by four strokes. As Robert Sommers notes in his book, *The U.S. Open: Golf's Ultimate Challenge*, "we were clearly into a new era."

For the next ten years, golf fans witnessed a different Jack Nicklaus. He lost his crew cut, let his hair down if you will, lost a hunk of weight and a little distance off the tee and charismatically turned a staunch anti-Jack public into some of his most ardent fans.

This decade also marked an amazing run of success. Nicklaus won seven of the forty majors he contested and posted another twenty-five top-ten finishes. He also won thirty-one PGA events, five of his money titles, and four of his Player-of-the-Year awards.

The significant victories? The 1973 PGA Championship at Canterbury Golf Club in Cleveland, Ohio, finally pushed Nicklaus past Bobby Jones's record of thirteen majors (including those won as an amateur). Nicklaus took the 1972 Masters and U.S. Open and came within two strokes of winning that year's British Open. And who can forget the 1975 Masters when Nicklaus, Johnny Miller, and Tom Weiskopf swapped and dropped the lead on the final day until Nicklaus rolled in a treacherous forty-foot birdie putt on Augusta National's sixteenth hole to seal the win.

In this decade Nicklaus also branched out into golf course architecture, working initially with Pete Dye and Desmond Muirhead, later creating his own design company. Today Nicklaus is one of the world's most prolific and sought-after architects. Like Palmer before him, Nicklaus has created a business empire (Golden Bear, Inc.).

But the legacy Nicklaus ultimately leaves the game will not only be his numbers, his talent as an architect, or his ability to raise, with wife Barbara, a family of five children who saw more of their father than do the children of the average pen pusher. It will be his uncanny ability to produce the vital shot at the vital moment. Never did this come home so clearly as in the 1986 Masters when Nicklaus tamed the back nine at Augusta National in a record-equaling thirty strokes and swept to a record-breaking sixth green jacket.

Exactly twenty-one years earlier, when Nicklaus won a second Masters and set the tournament's seventy-two-hole scoring record, Bobby Jones had marveled, "Jack is playing an entirely different game—a game with which I am not familiar."

Well, Nicklaus always has been a cut above the rest.

KATHY WHITWORTH 1968–1977

Kathy Whitworth's career on the LPGA Tour has spanned several eras. When she joined in 1958, the typical tournament purse totaled around $5,000 and the ladies toiled in relative obscurity. By her second decade, 1968 to 1977, the women's tour had grown, but soon suffered a period of stagnation followed by growth again. This growth became an explosion, and Whitworth was still playing in the 1980s when

purses had soared into the $500,000 range and many tournaments aired on national television.

What the eras had in common, however, was that Whitworth won in all of them. In fact, Whitworth has won more tournaments (eighty-eight) than any player, man or woman.

For her first victory in 1962, Whitworth collected $1,300. For her eighty-eighth victory, she earned $30,000. The latter is more than Whitworth made in all of 1965, when she led the money list with $28,658, but although she is glad to see the LPGA grow in prestige and affluence, Whitworth always has held the playing to be as important as the prize. "I find joy and fulfillment in swinging a golf club that is difficult to describe in words," she said in 1967. "All I know is that this feeling never leaves me when I have a golf club in my hands."

The years 1965 through 1973 were especially fulfilling for Whitworth in that she led the money list every year but 1969, in which she ranked second. She also was LPGA Player of the Year and won the Vare Trophy for low scoring average seven times each. Whitworth won eight tournaments in each of 1963, 1965, 1966, and 1967, and ten in 1968.

Whitworth always has been an accurate player while hitting the ball adequately long, and has been one of the better putters among the women. In her prime, she seldom went through a slump because she had supreme confidence in her mechanics. "Some of the girls start to tinker with their grip or address position or something else as soon as they hit a few bad shots," she once said. "I've come to regard making the slightest change in my regular manner of playing a very serious matter."

Whitworth has withstood remarkably talented competition. Mickey Wright ruled the roost when Whitworth came along, and Betsy Rawls and Louise Suggs were still forces. In the mid-sixties, however, Whitworth moved to the head of a new generation, a group that also included Carol Mann and Sandra Haynie. Between 1968 and 1977, Whitworth recorded forty-three victories, Mann won twenty-eight times, and Haynie twenty-six. Also successful in this period were Judy Rankin, who posted twenty-four wins and, in 1976, became the first woman to earn over $100,000 in a year, and the dominant amateur JoAnne Carner, who turned pro in 1970 and had won nineteen times by the end of 1977.

Whitworth was born in Monahans, Texas, but grew up in Jal, New Mexico, a small town near the Texas border. While still attending high school, she won the 1957 and 1958 New Mexico Women's Amateur Championships. She attended college for one semester, but finding she preferred golf clubs to schoolbooks, Whitworth opted for a try at the pro tour.

It seemed like a questionable decision. Whitworth earned only $1,217 in 1959, barely improving in 1960 and 1961.

She almost walked out in her third year. "I shot an 89 in Jacksonville and just came unraveled," she later recalled. "But my family convinced me I should go on back, that they'd still love me if I made it or not."

Whitworth never put them to the test. She won twice in 1962, her second victory by one shot over Wright. By 1963, only Wright was winning more often.

Whitworth won LPGA Championships in 1967, 1971, and 1975. But just as Sam Snead—the winningest player on the men's tour with eighty-four victories—has never won the U.S. Open, so the U.S. Women's Open has eluded Whitworth.

And just as with Snead, the lack of an Open is only a small blemish on an amazing record. Whitworth won at least one tournament in seventeen consecutive years (1962–78), an LPGA record—actually winning more than one in all but three of those years. In 1969, she tied Wright's record by winning four consecutive tournaments.

Whitworth last led the money list in 1973, but remained in the top twelve for the next four years. When she toiled winless throughout 1979 and 1980, Whitworth seemed destined for a career total of eighty victories—two short of Wright's record eighty-two. But having corrected a swing flaw with the help of long-time teacher Harvey Penick, Whitworth won eight tournaments over the next five years to surpass both Wright and Snead. In 1981, Whitworth became the first woman player to reach $1 million in career earnings—an unthinkable total when she started out on tour.

Along the way, Whitworth received many honors. She was the Associated Press Women's Athlete of the Year in 1965 and 1967, was inducted into the World Golf Hall of Fame (1982), LPGA Hall of Fame (1975), and Women's Sports Foundation Hall of Fame (1981), and in 1985 received the Golf Writers Association of America's William Richardson Award for outstanding contributions to golf.

TOM WATSON
1978–1987

Tom Watson's greatest moment, his chip on the seventeenth hole of the 1982 U.S. Open at Pebble Beach, California, tells much about the choice of Watson as the Player of the Decade for 1978–87. His magnificent wedge shot from deep rough left of the green gave him a birdie, a one-stroke lead over Jack Nicklaus, and propelled Watson to his first Open title.

Few players of his, or any, era have been more proficient at escaping unscathed from seemingly impossible positions. Either on or around the greens, Watson seems to be a natural, but that is not altogether true. The chip-in also shows another aspect of Watson's supremacy: his work ethic. He is willing to pay the price to make himself a great player. "I've practiced that shot for hours, days, months, years," he said later. He has spent as much time laboring on the rest of his game. Finally, it was fitting that Watson should come from behind to better Nicklaus. Watson has written his most memorable chapters in the game's history by winning three epic battles against the Golden Bear.

The pair waged the first two in 1977 at The Masters and British Open. Despite his victory in the 1975 British Open, Watson had become notorious for losing tournaments; the 1974 and 1975 U.S. Opens and several tour events had slipped from his grasp, and in the month before the 1977 Masters, he had squandered two third-round leads.

So Watson was facing defeat once more as he led The Masters through three rounds. In the final round, Nicklaus charged home with a 66, but Watson immediately responded with a 67 that included a tie-breaking birdie on the seventeenth hole. He won by two.

Three months later, both men fought one of the greatest duels ever, in the British Open. They matched scores of 68–70–65 through three rounds at Turnberry before Watson birdied four of the last six holes for a 65 and a one-shot victory. The third-place finisher languished another ten strokes back.

No more was Watson labeled a choker. "I don't blame the press for those choker stories," he said later, admitting, "I walk too quickly, swing too quickly, and breathe too quickly under pressure." Watson, often betrayed by wild driving, also was not totally confident in his swing in his early years on tour. The Masters victory was a turning point. "Most important, it told me I had a swing I could rely on under pressure."

If the question remained whether Watson would be a one-year wonder, he answered by winning twenty-five tour events between 1978 and 1987, more than double anyone else. After leading the money list, being named PGA Player of the Year, and winning the Vardon Trophy for low scoring average in 1977, Watson added money titles in 1978, 1979, 1980, and 1984, top-player honors in each of those years, plus 1982, and the Vardon Trophy in 1978 and 1979. He won five major championships in this decade: three more British Opens (1980, 1982, and 1983), one U.S. Open (1982), and another Masters (1981).

Nicklaus remained on the scene; he and Seve Ballesteros each won four majors in those ten years. Calvin Peete ran second to Watson in tour victories with twelve during the decade; Ray Floyd (eleven victories) and Fuzzy Zoeller (ten) each claimed two majors. But Watson was the best.

Watson has stirred galleries more with his play than his personality. He rarely speaks on the course, either with his playing partners or the spectators behind the ropes, although he does show emotion. Ever since being introduced to golf by his father at age six in his native Kansas City, Missouri, Watson has been drawn to the game because, as he explained many years later, "the beauty of golf stems from the fact that success, as well as failure, comes from within."

Watson learned the fundamentals as a youngster in group lessons at the Kansas City Country Club. He went on to win the Missouri State Amateur four times but made little impression nationally as an amateur. Not until his senior year at Stanford University, where he earned a degree in psychology, did Watson decide to pursue a pro golf career. That was a wise choice. Through 1987, his sixteenth year on tour, Watson had won almost $4.8 million, second only to Jack Nicklaus.

Watson turned thirty-eight years old in September 1987 and finished the year with thirty-two tour victories and eight major titles to his credit. Although lacking the PGA Championship to complete a career grand slam, his place as one of the all-time greats is secure. Watson holds three of the lowest winning totals in British Open history (268 at Turnberry in 1977, 271 at Muirfield in 1980, and 275 at Birkdale in 1983), and his five British titles rank second to Harry Vardon's six. Only four players (Jack Nicklaus, Walter Hagen, Ben Hogan, and Gary Player) have won more professional majors, and only Nicklaus, with eight, has led the tour money list more times than Watson's five.

Nancy Lopez
1978–1987

On a Sunday evening in Sarasota, Florida, in February 1978, Nancy Lopez played the par-five final hole at the Bent Tree Country Club the old-fashioned way: she parred it; three to the green, two putts. She later headed for the press room, where she picked up a telephone. As she spoke, Lopez's normally incandescent smile darkened, tears ran down her cheeks, and her voice cracked. But she was not unhappy.

"Daddy," she said softly. "I won."

The seduction by Nancy Lopez had begun.

So it went for the next two years when Lopez won sixteen more tournaments, including five in a row, and hoisted women's golf out of agate type into headlines across the

country. *Time, Newsweek,* Johnny Carson fawned over her. NBC-TV cut into its Saturday *baseball* telecasts in the heat of Lopez's winning streak to report on her progress. The public jumped on the bandwagon, too. Lopez remembers strolling down Fifth Avenue in Manhattan when a stranger yelled, "Keep it going, Nancy!" across four lanes of rush-hour traffic.

She kept it going. Lopez's success rate may have calmed down, but for the past decade she has been far and away the biggest draw in women's golf.

Her father, Domingo, and her mother, Marina—who died suddenly not long before the Sarasota tournament and to whom Lopez dedicated that first victory—can take much of the credit for their daughter's rise. Her father donated her first club, an old 4-wood; and when the eight-year-old Lopez began knocking around the local muni in Roswell, New Mexico, to which the family had moved from Torrance, California, soon after Lopez was born, it was her mother's Patty Berg clubs that she swung. And it is said that Lopez came by her remarkable ability to judge distance on the golf course from sighting deer for her father on hunting trips. Most important, the parents put their weight behind the youngster's career, spending their savings on equipment or on traveling with their daughter to tournaments.

By the age of twelve, Lopez had won the New Mexico Amateur and was the first girl to play on her all-male high school team. Around this time, Domingo suspected that his daughter's swing held a myriad of mistakes. He contacted Lee Trevino and asked him to take a look at a backswing that looped on its way to the top, where the club face remained tightly shut. "As long as her swing works," said Trevino, "use it. When it stops working, change it."

Except for minor adjustments to her grip and tempo, Lopez still uses that swing and remains one of the LPGA's longest drivers, most accurate iron players and, with JoAnne Carner, the best at escaping trouble. And she has yet to see a putt she does not like. "Her swing belongs to her and her alone," noted veteran golfer Kathy Whitworth in 1979. "It's the same with [Arnold] Palmer and [Jack] Nicklaus. Their swings aren't perfect, but look what they've done."

Lopez took two U.S. Junior Girls' titles, in 1972 and 1974, and tied for second in the 1975 U.S. Women's Open as an amateur. She turned pro in mid-1977, abandoning a college career at Tulsa University in which she won fourteen of eighteen events, and finished second in her first money event, the U.S. Women's Open. She also finished second in her first two LPGA events, the Colgate European Open and, the following week, the Long Island Classic.

Then, in 1978, Lopez's world went into warp speed. She won the Bent Tree Classic at Sarasota and the Sunstar Classic the following week. Nine weeks later, she ran off with the Baltimore Classic, then, in a row, the Coca-Cola Classic, the Kent Golden Lights, the LPGA Championship (her first major) by *six* strokes, and the Bankers Trust Classic.

She added the Colgate European and Far East Opens by the end of a season in which she took home an LPGA record $189,813—more than any rookie, male or female, before her—Player-of-the-Year and Rookie-of-the-Year honors, and the Vare Trophy for low scoring average (71.76).

The following year, Lopez won eight times, her worst finish a tie for thirteenth, and won the money list, Player-of-the-Year, and Vare honors again.

Her life soon returned to more mortal proportions. Lopez won twelve tournaments over the next five seasons and became the fifth LPGA pro to top $1 million in career earnings, yet she won neither the money list nor the Vare Trophy. Worse, her marriage to Tim Melton, a Cincinnati sportscaster she had married in 1979 on her twenty-second birthday, disintegrated.

But no one forgot about Lopez. She still guaranteed lucrative gate receipts and still beamed like a little girl when she was playing well. So when she climbed back to the top in 1985 with a daughter (she now has two) and a new husband (baseball player Ray Knight) in tow, the golf world smiled along with her. That year, Lopez took five events, including the LPGA Championship, which she won by eight strokes, and the Henredon, in which her twenty under par and twenty-five birdies set LPGA records. She also set a new money record with $416,472 and took the Vare Trophy with an average of 70.73, another record.

What was missing, however, was a niche in the LPGA Hall of Fame. With one major under her belt, Lopez needed thirty-five victories and ten-years' membership in the LPGA. In February 1987, she secured the vital win—at Sarasota. By July, she had served her time. Lopez was inducted into the Hall of Fame at a ceremony in New York City, where she took the podium, alternating smiles with tears. Onstage with her was her family, including Domingo, and if you looked ever so closely you saw his daughter's lips move.

"Daddy," she was saying softly, "I *did* it."

If the mists of time obscure the true origin of golf, as Andrew Lang rather romantically suggested, the reason is simple: printing had not yet been invented. Mr. Gutenberg, playing out of Mainz, Germany, did not unveil his movable type until 1456, just one year before the game was banned in Scotland.

The now famous Acts of (Scottish) Parliament, which banned the game, were passed, successively, in 1457, 1471, and 1491 by King James II, James III, and James IV, respectively, of Scotland. The Acts could not be described as the work of golf writers. They were, however, the first known references in print to the game of golf.

Evidence of media reports on the game in America may be said to have begun with an advertisement that appeared in *Rivington's Royal Gazette,* published in 1779 in New York City. It stated: "The Season for the pleasant and healthy Exercise now advancing, Gentlemen may be furnished with excellent Clubs and the veritable Caledonian balls by enquiring at the Printer's." The ad presumably was inserted to catch the eyes of Scottish troops then stationed in the city. It is a happy thought to contemplate braw Scottish laddies baffing the ball up Broadway. It was, of course, more than a century later before the game became established in this country.

When golf was formally introduced into the United States with the formation of the St. Andrew's Golf Club, the media of the day—newspapers and magazines—did not pay too much attention. Indeed, some of the early reports on golf were completely erroneous. On February 24, 1889, one article appeared in the *Philadelphia Times.* It was such a masterpiece of misinformation that it was reprinted and read with much hilarity in Edinburgh in an April issue the same year of the *Edinburgh Evening Dispatch:*

. . . [Golf] is . . . a most aristocratic exercise, for no man can play . . . who has not a servant at hand to assist him. . . . When the word has been given to start [the player] bats his ball as accurately as possible to the next hole, which may be either one hundred or five hundred yards distant. As soon as it is started in the air he runs forward in the direction which the ball has taken, and his servant, who is called a "caddy," runs after him with all the other nine tools in his arms. . . . The one who gets his ball in the hole at which they began first, wins the game.

In addition to the guffaws it produced in Scotland, the article is a mystery to golf historians. It appeared, apparently, on the same day in a St. Louis newspaper, and today amateur golf historians still are trying to figure out how the same article could have appeared in two newspapers eight hundred miles from each other and before the invention of teletype.

The first *informed* article to appear in America was written by W. E. Morris and published in *The Century Illustrated Monthly* in 1892. It was titled "The Apotheosis of Golf." Two years later, *The Ladies' Home Journal* ran a full-page article that included several delightful illustrations and the precious line, "a gallant gentleman will not cheat a woman and a woman at all worthy of consideration will not cheat anyone at all."

The increased popularity of the game almost forced the media to recognize golf's impact upon American society. However, the newspaper editors had a problem deciding where to put this game: in the society pages, the sports pages, or the business pages. Nor did tournament officials know where to put the people who reported on the game. The man

Chroniclers

assigned to a golf event was not welcomed enthusiastically, and even if accepted, he was left on his own to find out what was going on. This attitude on the part of officials lasted into the 1930s.

Today, the once lowly ink-stained wretches are treated a bit more civilly. An air-conditioned pressroom, replete with electric typewriters, touch-tone telephones, a computerized scorekeeping system, and a buffet of tempting proportions, serves the scribe as he sits at his assigned desk and gazes—not over far-distant hills—but at a closed-circuit television monitor and a hole-by-hole summary of the action posted in front of his glazed eyes. Unlike his early predecessors, he no longer needs to hike over five miles of undulating ground while following a favorite and completely missing the exploits of the other players who are ripping the course apart. Instead, the action is transmitted to him.

Golf events were local news until 1894, when the first (and abortive) attempt was made to hold a national championship at Newport, Rhode Island. The event was reported in the *New York Sun* by Hugh Louis Fitzpatrick, who is now presumed to be playing on heavenly fairways and wearing a large button proclaiming him to be "the first American golf writer." It may be a specious claim, but it is all his.

However, others were making their mark. P. C. Pulver wrote on golf for the *New York Advertiser* and went on to report on the game for another twenty-five years. He became the editor of *The American Golf Guide and Yearbook* in 1916, which included a summary of the preceding year's play and a state-by-state list of clubs in the country. Pulver edited the book for many years and was later succeeded by others. His books, difficult to find today, are a treasure for anyone seeking information about golf in the early days of the game in this country.

The next early writer probably was H. J. ("Jim") Whigham. He had the good sense to be born an Englishman, and having learned how to play golf at Cambridge, he became a newspaper reporter. His London paper sent him to Chicago in 1893 to report on the Chicago Exposition. In that city, he inevitably met with Charles Blair Macdonald, the strong-willed architect who was instrumental in helping to spread the game in this country. Whigham wooed and won Macdonald's daughter, worked as a reporter for the *Chicago Tribune,* and was a good enough golfer himself to win the U.S. Amateur Championship in 1896 and 1897.

In that same last gasp of the nineteenth century, the first American golf magazines began to appear. The first, titled simply *Golf,* began in 1897 and was edited by Josiah Newman, a native Englishman. Some years later, he wrote, "For many years I made the unusual editorial rule of inviting the press to copy freely any article that appeared in 'Golf.' It will be easily understood that in the early days the American newspaper writers possessed but little golfing lore. . . . Today, the American golfer is usually better informed on the history and traditions of the game than many an English golfer."

Newman returned to England in the early years of the century and was succeeded by W. G. van Tassell Sutphen, truly a name of impressive structure. The magazine became the official publication of the USGA, the Western Golf Association, and other sectional golf associations. The contributors invariably wrote under pseudonyms, which further impede any attempts to identify them.

One of the first magazine covers to feature golf, this 1897 issue of Harper's Weekly showed the work of famed sporting artist A. B. Frost. Note the long-nosed woods and the pinch of sand used to tee the ball.

A year later, this posterlike Harper's cover poked fun at the "red coats" posing among the ploughfields. In the right background, a gentleman tees the ball for his lady.

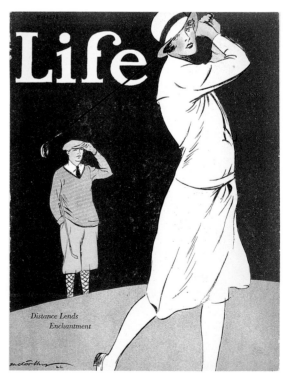

As women became more involved in the game, magazine editors found fodder for amusing art. The magazine's title, Liberty, is particularly appropriate to this illustration.

Golf also became a popular and colorful cover subject for general interest magazines such as this early version of Life.

Whereas the early golf writers were consigned to a dark, damp hut, today's pressrooms are air-conditioned, catered, and equipped with computerized score-reporting systems.

H.B. Martin, a writer and illustrator for the New York Globe, included this cartoon in a 1916 column. It depicts a charity match at Siwanoy pitting Chick Evans and Jerry Travers against Jim Barnes and Walter Hagen.

As the game grew, so did the number and variety of golf advertisements appearing in the journals of the day.

The first truly knowledgeable golf writer, and arguably still the best, Bernard Darwin. His essayistic columns were works of art, and today his books are collector's items. He was also no mean player.

Golf was the lead story in Boston on the morning after the 1913 U.S. Open Championship. Francis Ouimet's victory was the beginning of increased coverage everywhere.

At about the same time, other American publishers with an eye to a rising market were entering the field. In the first decade of the new century (and alphabetically) were published: *The American Golfer*; the aforementioned *Golf*; *Golf and Lawn Tennis* (originally, *American Lawn Tennis*); *The Golfer*, which started out as *Outdoors, a Magazine of Country Life*; *The Golfers' Magazine*; *Golfing* and *Gulf Coast Golfer* (out of Houston, Texas). Even the staid *American Cricketer*, which had been published in Philadelphia since the 1870s, began to add pages on golf as the game grew in the Quaker City.

There are a few scattered records, as the years eased into the pre- and post-World War I era, of writers who now understood the game and could write intelligently about it.

It was in this period that Bernard Darwin in England began to write columns about the game that are still held as models of golf reporting. In this country, O.B. Keeler in Atlanta; Paul Gallico, Innis Brown, and Grantland Rice in New York; Joe David in Chicago; and Hay Chapman in San Francisco were natural successors to those earlier—and mostly anonymous—reporters on the game.

The victory of Francis Ouimet, a then unknown amateur golfer, in Brookline, Massachusetts, in the 1913 U.S. Open is popularly supposed to have sparked a great burst of enthusiasm for the game of golf in this country, but there is little

Grantland Rice loved the game and played reasonably well. A close friend of Bobby Jones, Rice helped to establish The Masters and was a member of the Augusta National Golf Club.

evidence that it became front-page news other than in Ouimet's hometown.

The *New York Times* headlined its article (on the sports pages) "Ouimet, World's Golf Champion." There was no byline. The story began, "Another name was added to America's list of victors in international sports here today when Francis Ouimet, which for the benefit of the uninitiated is pronounced 'we-met,' a youthful local amateur, won the nineteenth open championship of the United States Golf Association."

It was about the time of Ouimet's win (immediate pre-World War I) that film entered the media scene. If the medium was not of any great maturity at that date, it should be noted that in 1915 an enthusiastic golfer could rent a film of the day's golfing greats for sixty dollars. At that time and place, it was an exorbitant figure, and few took advantage of the offer.

As America entered the Roaring Twenties, the game of golf boomed. Some pundits said it was spurred by Ouimet's win in the U.S. Open. Others, perhaps more practical, cited the business surge of "the long weekend," as Darwin so deliciously described that period between the two great wars.

Whatever the reason, businessmen began to take Saturday afternoons off, and in seeking diversion, they joined the new golf and country clubs that were springing up rapidly. News-

papers, still the prime medium in spreading the word, published the results of weekend competitions, and the duffer who shot 136—with the right handicap—saw his name in the Monday morning paper.

One of the features of golf coverage in the twenties was the "syndicated column," which appeared in newspapers under the name of a recognized authority but which was usually written by an anonymous golf writer. These were designed to help the hapless hacker reduce his handicap from twenty-three to eighteen, and a number of highly respected names were guilty of the charade. Chick Evans, the fine amateur from Chicago; Chester Horton, a respected professional in Detroit; A.J. Morrison, who vigorously promoted the game in his columns and on the vaudeville circuit, wrote columns that appeared weekly in the papers. Toward the end of the decade, Bobby Jones wrote a weekly column for Bell Syndication, which was later reprinted in booklet form and is today a collector's item.

Grantland Rice's column, "The Sportlight," was not syndicated until 1930. He was one of the outstanding golf journalists from 1910 through the 1930s. He loved the game and played it reasonably well, which is unusual for a golf writer. Rice also was a skilled writer, given to poetry, and he could string words on gossamer threads. For years he worked for the *New York Tribune*.

Rice's verse, perhaps more Edgar A. Guest than John Masefield, was without classic construction, but it was unstudied in its simplicity and its appeal to Rice's readers. The following lines appeared in a 1911 edition of the *New York Mail* and were later put to music by the members of the St. Andrew's Club, who sang the song at their club dinners:

KEEP YOUR EYE ON THE BALL

Boy, if the phone should ring
   Or anyone should call;
Whisper that it's Spring,
   To come again next Fall.
Say I have a date on a certain tee,
   Where my friends, the sand traps, wait in glee;
Tell them the "doc" has ordered me
   To keep my eye on the ball.

Boy if they wish to know
   Where I shall haunt the scene;
Tell them to leave and go
   Out by the ancient green.
Tell them to look where the traps are deep
   And the sand flies up in a powdered heap,
And out of the depths loud curses creep
   To the flash of a niblic sheen.

Then if the boss should sigh
   Or for my presence seek,
Tell him the truth, don't lie;
   Say that my will was weak
For what is a job to a brassie shot
   That whistles away to an untrapped spot?
Or the thrill of a well cut mashie shot
   Or the sweep of a burnished cleek?

Rice was to become instrumental in establishing The Masters Tournament as one of the premier events of the year and may well have been the only golf writer to become a member of that distinguished club.

More and more sections of the country were taking to the game, and the guy who owned the hardware store or the local egg merchant was enjoying the prosperity of the postwar boom. Among the messages received by the newly affluent was "you should learn to play golf." Not just the men but the women as well.

The surge of interest made golf the subject of everything from sheet music to cartoons. One of the latter revealed two women lounging on the clubhouse lawn overlooking the first tee. "Would you like to learn the game?" asked the first. The second replied, "No, I learned yesterday."

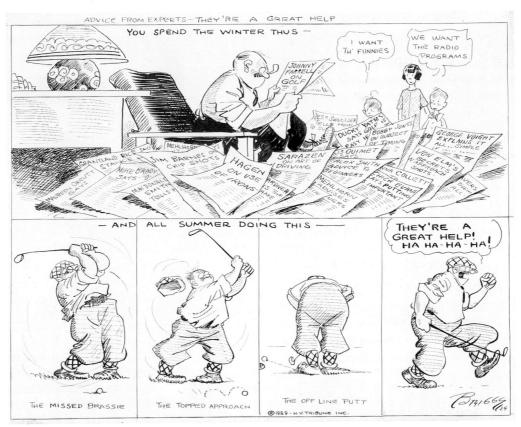

This 1929 cartoon by Briggs is not only amusing but informative. A close look at the headlines in the newspapers reveals a roster of the era's champions, both male and female.

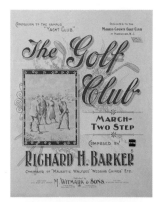

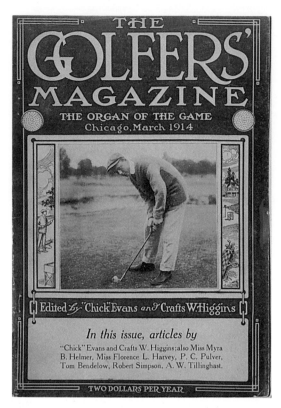

As the game boomed, it manifested itself in several forms, not the least of which was sheet music. Numerous waltzes, marches, and two-steps were named after, or dedicated to, golf clubs and associations.

One of the earliest magazines was The Golfers' Magazine, *a Chicago-based publication co-edited for a time by Chick Evans.*

Inspired by this spread of the game, magazines such as *The New Yorker, The Saturday Evening Post,* and *Collier's* began featuring golf on their covers. In this same period magazines devoted almost exclusively to the game—*10,000 Lakes Golfer and Outdoor Magazine, The Bridle and Golfer, Canadian Golfer, Chicago Golfer, Fairways,* and *Golfdom*—started publication, the last-named by the remarkable Graffis brothers.

It is not quite true that Herb and Joe Graffis started the Chicago Fire, but they did burn the candle at both ends in promoting the game in Chicago and across the country. Their pioneering efforts are legendary. *Golfdom* was started to fill the need the two brothers saw for a magazine that could provide the club professional and greenkeeper with news and information that would help them do their jobs more effectively, more efficiently, and ultimately, to raise their respective jobs to greater importance in the minds of the members.

Later the Graffises were to establish the magazine *Golfing,* which was distributed free to any golfer who would pick up a copy. Still later, they came up with the concept of the National Golf Foundation to promote "the game of a lifetime," and that organization today is a powerful force in spreading the game and providing important services both to individuals and golf organizations.

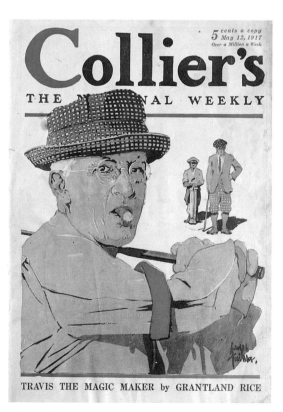

Collier's frequently featured golf on the cover. This one shows Walter Travis.

APRIL - 1933

Golfing

PLAYBOY · NO GOLD IN MY RAINBOW · PARDON ME
ANYTHING CAN HAPPEN · SIMPLIFYING GOOD GOLF

Golfing, *one of several golf journalistic brainstorms by Chicago entrepreneurs Herb and Joe Graffis.*

The American Golfer, *founded in 1909, was first edited by Walter J. Travis, then by Grantland Rice.*

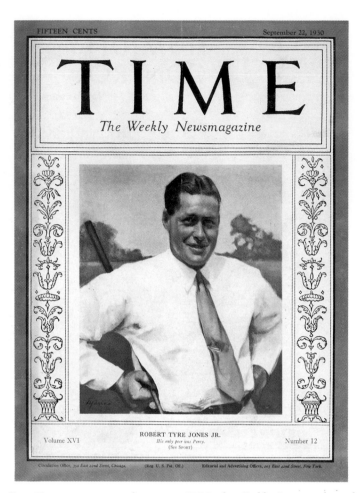

Even Time *magazine took notice in 1930 when Bobby Jones undertook the "impregnable quadrilateral."*

Three truly great golf magazines of the "between-the-wars-period" were *Golf Illustrated*, *The Golfers' Magazine*, and *The American Golfer*.

The Golfers' Magazine was a Chicago-based publication that began life in 1902 and later was co-edited by Chick Evans. *The American Golfer* started in 1907 and was first edited by the great Australian-born American champion Walter J. Travis. When Travis retired, his place was taken by Grantland Rice, later to move to *Golf Illustrated*. *Golf Illustrated* was founded in 1914. Its full title at the time was *Golf Illustrated and Outdoor America*, simplified in 1923 to the first two words. In 1935, the heart of the Great Depression, it merged with *The American Golfer* in an attempt to save both from failure; sadly, the attempt failed, and by 1936, it (they) stopped publication.

Each of these monthly magazines was printed on quality paper, carried numerous illustrations, and sought out the finest golf writers for contributions. Regrettably, the Depression cut them down, as golfers began to concentrate on bringing home the bacon instead of banging home the birdies.

The final and brightest light of that glorious decade of the twenties was Bobby Jones's victories in the "impregnable quadrilateral"—that most descriptive but almost unpronounceable phrase created by a golf writer named George Trevor.

Today's tremendously successful Professional Golfers Association (PGA) Tour was born in this same period, and you can bet a golf writer was involved. In 1922, Jack O'Brien, a sportswriter for a San Antonio newspaper, was scratching his head trying to figure out an angle for promoting the charms of his native city when he came up with the idea of inviting some of the snow-bound pros to play in sunny San Antone. O'Brien convinced a few local Texans to put up some money, and a total purse of $5,000 was raised. Bob Macdonald from Chicago won the first Texas Open.

The idea caught on, and in the next few years, various sunbelt cities began to invite the pros to play. The Los Angeles Open began in 1926, and soon after, Pasadena and

Bobby Jones was a fine writer himself, but his career was ably chronicled by his close friend, O.B. Keeler (right).

Oakland came aboard. St. Petersburg, Miami, and Daytona Beach soon saw the wisdom of reporting to northern newspapers that "sun-drenched galleries were following the play of nattily dressed professional golfers in their shirt-sleeves. No sweaters, no wind-breakers, never an overcoat." The tour was on its way, and those insidious newspaper reports were greatly responsible.

If it is difficult to pin down the origin of golf five centuries back, it is just as difficult to trace the history of golf coverage by radio, which cannot be much more than, say, sixty years ago.

Ted Husing was one of the first to offer reports from the golf course, and it is a matter of record that Bill Stern, usually assisted by Harry Nash, a golf reporter for the *Newark News,* also broadcast golf reports. There is little evidence that any of these reports were blow-by-blow. Supposedly the majority of such broadcasts were summations of a day's play.

In England, Henry Longhurst attempted to report on the action but ran into difficulties. In the late thirties, he was sent out on the course with two engineers: One carried a luggage-sized transmitter on his back, and the other carried a heavy load of batteries. Longhurst soon discovered that he could not be too close to the action because his voice would disturb the players, and when he retired to a discreet distance on a nearby hill, he was too far away to see what was going on.

Radio had problems in trying to cover golf, and the weekend hacker went to the newspaper for his satisfaction.

Darsie L. Darsie was in Los Angeles and had a name that only fun-loving parents could have given a kid. Hay Chapman was still in San Francisco; Charlie Bartlett and Harry Brown were in Chicago; Frank McCracken was in Philadelphia; and Bill Richardson, Innis Brown, and H. B. Martin wrote lovingly of the game in New York. Al Laney, during a misspent youth in Paris, covered the international golf scene (which in the thirties meant Great Britain), and a young cub reporter, Joe Dey, followed the game for the *Evening Bulletin* in Philadelphia. Joe was later to become Joseph C. Dey, Jr., a major figure in the development of the game, when in 1943

Radio broadcasts posed a predicament for the announcer: Move in too close and he bothered the players, move too far away and he could not see what was going on.

By the 1940s, golf was a common subject on the newsreels in movie theaters. This short subject on the Gold Dust Twins (Byron Nelson and Jug McSpaden) was narrated by "famous NBC sports announcer Bill Stern."

he accepted the position of executive secretary—later to become executive director—of the United States Golf Association. Joe, who has remained human despite all the honors thrust upon him, still likes to remember those days when he "covered" golf.

Golf magazines continued to be born and to die. Some of them had problems in establishing an identity: *10,000 Lakes Golfer and Outdoor Magazine* began life as *Northwest Life*, changed to *Amateur Golfer and Outdoor Magazine*, and finally became *Golfer and Sportsman*. *Kansas City Golfer* began in 1924, changed its title to *Western Golfer*, and in 1927, gave up the ghost.

It is generally accepted by golf historians, although perhaps not by the Augusta National Golf Club, that The Masters Tournament was created by the media. The circumstances of its beginning and the habits of sportswriters were coincidental and fortuitous.

It was beautifully timed, at its inception, to take place when the golf professionals were winding up their "winter tour" in Florida and the baseball writers, who often doubled

as golf writers, were wending their way back north from baseball's spring training.

Encouraged by O. B. Keeler (Atlanta, Georgia) and Grantland Rice (a member), sportswriters such as Bill Richardson of the *New York Times* and Alan Gould of the Associated Press stopped off in Augusta, Georgia, to see and report on the happy meeting of Bobby Jones and his friends. It is equally important to emphasize the great regard these writers had for Jones and their willingness—even desire—to help him make the tournament a success.

One other important ingredient was Clifford Roberts, the guiding genius of the event, who had the good sense to treat writers as welcome guests. They responded by sending glowing reports of the beauty of the Augusta course and the pleasant atmosphere that pervaded the tournament.

New stars in media were beginning to twinkle, and two of them were destined to become important personalities in the ever-spreading world of golf. Bob Harlow and Fred Corcoran both started out in Boston. Harlow was a sportswriter in that city and was hired as a public relations man for Pinehurst,

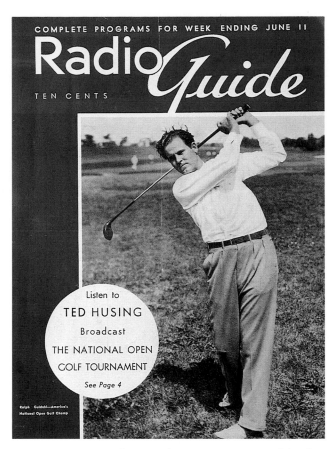

The U.S. Open Championship was cover material for the
June 11, 1938, issue of Radio Guide.

Another of the fine early writers, Innis Brown chronicled
the game for the New York Sun.

Al Laney was one of the first to cover golf
on an international scale.

Bob Harlow at the offices of Golf World, *the weekly magazine he founded in 1947. It is still in existence today.*

North Carolina, in 1935. In addition to those duties, he took on the task of setting up a schedule of tournaments for the budding professional tour. That same year, he purchased the *Pinehurst Outlook,* the local weekly newspaper, and under his direction that newspaper is said to have published more golf news than any other newspaper in the country. He would also establish, in 1947, the weekly magazine *Golf World,* which was quickly embraced by golf enthusiasts all over the country who wanted to know more about the game as it was played in the rest of the world, not just locally. If you were peculiar enough to want to know who won the Spanish Open or the Montana Amateur or the Kansas City Invitational, you found it in *Golf World.*

Fred Corcoran did not have a newspaper background unless, as is quite possible, he sold them on the streets of Boston. Through a series of circumstances that can only be described as a combination of luck, talent, and Irish charm, Fred became a force in golf. He was an official scorer for USGA championships, he ran the PGA Tour for a number of years, he is the father of the Ladies Professional Golf Associa-

tion (LPGA) Tour, and, perhaps to his shame, he was behind the formation of the Golf Writers Association of America. He loved golf with a passion, could not play it a lick, and if there is a special corner in heaven for the golf media, he probably presides over the table.

And certainly among the others present at that table are Kerr Petrie, a transplanted Scot from Carnoustie; Maury Fitzgerald of Washington; Red Smith of, successively, St. Louis, Philadelphia, and New York. Smith, we are told, never really liked golf, but it is testimony to his journalistic skill that he could write so well about it.

The wartime period (1941–46) was a difficult one for golf in America and around the world. The game was encouraged by the government as a recreation and a method of raising funds, and stars such as Bob Hope and Bing Crosby toured the country doing exhibitions for war bonds. But still the clubs and the courses suffered: the first from diminishing membership as the young men were taken into the services; the latter from a lack of funds and manpower to maintain them.

In 1946, as the world returned to normal, a group of golf writers convened at the PGA Championship, held in Portland, Oregon, and made history. Led by a Bostonian who claimed he could not write, and a golf writer from Chicago who could not play golf (Fred Corcoran and Charlie Bartlett, respectively), the group organized the Golf Writers Association of America. O.B. Keeler, Grantland Rice, Kerr Petrie, Herb and Joe Graffis, and Russ Newland, the AP wire man out of San Francisco, were the ringleaders, and probably out of spite for their Eastern employers, they elected Newland president.

In that same immediate postwar period, audio and video were bouncing back from five years of standing still. The electronic wizards who had helped to win the war went back to inventing new and more sophisticated ways of using the air waves—improving the equipment, making it lighter and more portable, more sensitive to carrying the voice and able to transmit a picture over miles of open country. Despite the improvements, television transmission had some way to go. The early golf shows were filmed rather than "live," so that movie theaters could provide most of the coverage.

If one went to the local Bijou back in the thirties, the ten cent admission fee bought enough to keep you there all night. Pathé News or Fox Movietone News or any one of several other newsreels ran first. If the golf fan was lucky, one of them might show Bobby Jones winning another national championship. (It might be noted, parenthetically, that very few main features have been made about golf. One of the first was *Follow Thru,* which, perhaps strangely, had been a successful Broadway play. Many years later, Katharine Hepburn and Spencer Tracy starred in *Pat and Mike,* which featured some of the early women professionals such as Babe Zaharias and Helen Dettweiler. One more was *Follow the Sun,* starring Glenn Ford, which was a reasonable copy of Ben Hogan's life. (It might be added that, although Hepburn and Ford knew which end of the club to hold, in the Hogan film Ben himself played most of the shots.)

After renouncing his amateur standing in the early thirties, Bobby Jones was paid a princely sum to film a series of short features, which remain classic golf films. Usually about ten minutes in length, they showed Jones in the company of such Hollywood stars as W.C. Fields, Joe E. Brown, Harold

Fred Corcoran (left) helped to found the Ladies Professional Golf Association (LPGA) and the Golf Writers Association of America. He also ran the Professional Golfers Association (PGA) Tour for a time and was close to every major player from Gene Sarazen to Jack Nicklaus.

Above:
During the early 1940s, Bob Hope and Bing Crosby, avid and accomplished golfers, played exhibition matches to raise money for war bonds.

Left:
Herb Graffis's contributions to the game ran so broad and deep that in 1977 he was inducted into the World Golf Hall of Fame, one of the first to be included under the category of "Distinguished Service."

Opposite above:
Full-length feature films on golf are rare, but Ben Hogan's life story, Follow the Sun, made the big time. It starred Glenn Ford and Anne Baxter as Ben and Valerie. Ford did the talking, but all the swing sequences were Hogan's.

Opposite below:
Soon after his retirement in 1930, Bobby Jones made a series of short-subject movies co-starring various Hollywood personalities. This one, titled The Putter, featured comedian Joe E. Brown. In this scene, the smiling Brown has just plucked his ball out of the cup after making a hole-in-one.

Charlie Bartlett introduced golf statistics in his coverage for the Chicago Tribune.

In the early days, as today, golf was the toughest sport to cover, involving dozens of technicians and miles of electric cables.

Lloyd, Guy Kibbee, and others. These films have been preserved, fortunately, and the USGA has a complete file of them in its outstanding museum and library in Far Hills, New Jersey.

Another successful series of short-subject films was produced by RKO-Pathé and director Joe Walsh under the title *Sportscopes*. Walsh filmed these at various locations around the country from 1938 to the late 1940s. In capturing some of the better players of the day on film (Ben Hogan, Sam Snead, Lloyd Mangrum, and others), Walsh bequeathed a record of the greats that otherwise would have been lost. Among these films were two featuring Joe Kirkwood, the great trick-shot artist. In them, Kirkwood's ball was placed in situations that required him to perform his magic. In film, of course, the director had the option of retakes, and although no one knows how many retakes Kirkwood may have needed, the finished film was magic.

In this period, also, old writers re-emerged and new ones debuted. The USGA, which had gone for a couple of decades without an official publication, resumed publishing *Golf Journal,* which happily continues to this day. Fred Corcoran was finding new (and sometimes strange) places for the growing PGA Tour to play, and the *Chicago Tribune's* Charlie Bartlett was convinced that golf fans were as interested in statistics as baseball fans. He began to work on a golf box score, in which he would summarize the number of fairways hit, the greens

hit in regulation, and the number of putts taken. To his sorrow, no one seemed to pay much attention.

Assuming that Charlie now sits in a heavenly clubhouse, next to Grantland Rice and O.B. Keeler and opposite Corcoran, he must be smiling as new members join the table and report that in 1980, the PGA began to accumulate such statistics and pay awesome sums to the players who are the yearly winners in each of the various categories.

Bright and talented newcomers joined the corps of writers who kept the golf troops at home informed. Among these were Herbert Warren Wind, Charles Price, John Ross, John May, Fred Byrod, the improbable Waxo Green, and a fresh-faced kid from west Texas, Dan Jenkins. Always lurking in a corner were Herb and Joe Graffis.

The still-growing electronic media—radio and television—were trying to figure out how to reduce 150 acres of golf course to a six-inch television screen or, on radio, to eliminate the noise of wind blowing through a microphone sounding like the 20th-Century Limited driving down the home stretch between Elkhart and Chicago.

In those early days, producers quickly determined that elevation was necessary to get the cameras and the announcers looking over the crowd and down on the action. Early movie cameras—and later television cameras—were placed on the roof of a station wagon or truck. The first television coverage of the U.S. Open was in 1947 in St.

The first attempts at television coverage took some imagination. The floating camera at left was perched on a scaffold, propelled by truck, and camouflaged by a blanket of tree branches.

Louis. Station KSD-TV backed its truck up to the eighteenth green and aimed the camera onto it. The picture was beamed to the six hundred sets that made up the entire market in St. Louis, and in mentioning the innovation, one writer offered the opinion that most of those six hundred sets were in saloons.

There were millions of radios in the country, but trying to describe a golf match on that medium was difficult. In both 1947 and 1948, the PGA tried to sell the "radio rights" to its championship and could find no buyers. Harry Wismer, another of the pioneer sports reporters on radio, described the action, but if the PGA got any publicity out of it, they certainly did not make much money.

One radio story that can be confirmed is quite unusual. Dave Garroway, who was later to become a very popular television personality, once described a golf match in which he was one of the players. Garroway, then in Chicago, was a fine player, good enough to qualify several times for the U.S. Amateur. On this occasion, he was playing a match against Lawson Little at Tam O'Shanter outside Chicago and, accompanied by a technician (who presumably held the microphone while Garroway hit his shot), offered a shot-by-shot account of the match.

Televised golf struck it rich on a quiet Sunday afternoon in August 1953. It happened this way. A golfer named Lew Worsham sank an improbable wedge shot on the seventy-second hole of an improbable tournament, which its promoter, George S. May of Chicago, billed as "the World Championship." With that shot Worsham won the tournament and the then improbable sum of $50,000. The incident—or, more properly, accident—was watched by the first national television audience and created headlines in newspapers across the country.

We are told by a veteran newspaper golf writer that Harry Wismer was the announcer in the television tower overlooking that eighteenth green at Tam O'Shanter and that, as Harry was often known to do, he had just turned the microphone over to a guest who was, in this case, Jimmy Demaret, one of the great golfers of the day. Demaret was always comfortable behind a microphone—whether to croon a Cole Porter tune or describe a golf shot—and he confirmed, as the audience watched, that Worsham had studied the shot, selected a wedge, settled into his address, and made his swing. There was perhaps a five-second silence as the camera followed the flight of the ball, which bounced onto the green and ran inexorably into the cup. The silence was broken by Demaret's first words since the ball had been hit: "Well, I'll be god damned, he sank it!"

In 1957, Peter DeMet, a young entrepreneur in Chicago, conceived the idea of matching two professional golfers in a head-to-head match with the winner to be challenged the following week. The American Broadcasting Company

Jack Burke and Arnold Palmer joined the crew for this 1958 photograph during the making of an episode of "All-Star Golf," the first serious attempt at a golf television show.

(ABC) bought the idea. Over the winter, the series "All-Star Golf" was telecast from four to five in the evening, every Saturday for twenty-six weeks. Prize money for the entire series was $80,000. One sure sign of its success was that the show was renewed for the following year.

Two years later, the National Broadcasting Company (NBC) added to the fun for the home viewer. Its show was also a "king-of-the-hill" concept for a total purse of $171,000 and called, perhaps immodestly, "World Championship Golf."

In this new "busting-at-the-seams" decade, the 1950s, another economic boom was in full flower. Along with more jobs and higher incomes, more diversion time was available. Golf satisfied the need of many who wished to use that time with sports activity. The media was not slow in recognizing the need and the wish.

Newspaper coverage of the expanding PGA Tour increased, and on the "funny pages" a cartoon strip was introduced: "MacDivot" followed the fortunes of a prototypical

professional who looked an awful lot like Tommy Armour. Perhaps by accident, each day's strip contained a little golf tip on how to play the game better.

In the magazine field, in 1951 three young men in Chicago put out a "throw-away" magazine they called *Golf Digest*. Later in the same decade, *GOLF Magazine* began publication with Charles Price as editor. Today those two monthlies are the dominant magazines on the national scene, each reaching more than two million readers with every issue. Even *The New Yorker*, sophisticated and dedicated to the proposition that life did not exist west of the Hudson River, covered the game with a delightful column titled "Tee Time," and it is to the joy of many golf fans today that the magazine, which started a sporting department in 1962, carries Herbert Warren Wind's masterful reports each year of The Masters, the U.S. Open, and when Wind can talk the editors into it, his coverage of the British Open.

Wind is today considered by many to be the doyen of American golf writers. A lifetime lover of the game, Wind graduated from Yale in 1937. Unable to find a job in the heart of the Depression, he went to study at Oxford University in England where, presumably, he learned to write English. He learned wonderfully well.

After service in the army, he joined the staff of *The New Yorker,* and when *Sports Illustrated* magazine started in 1954, he became its golf editor. Not too many years later, he returned to *The New Yorker,* where he has remained.

Television continued to make an impact in the early sixties, and more Americans were buying television sets. One show in particular created greater interest in golf: the Shell Oil Company's "Wonderful World of Golf." The show was created by Fred Raphael (who in 1979 came up with the now-popular "Legends of Golf" senior tournament). Raphael's basic formula was simple: take two professionals to a great course somewhere in the world and give the winner a little more money than the loser. In the first year, the show featured courses in eleven different countries. Before it ended in 1970, almost two hundred fine golfers had played ninety-two matches in fifty-eight countries. Many American golfers had never seen a golf course anywhere other than their own country and perhaps Great Britain. The Shell show, with, successively, Gene Sarazen, George Walsh, and Jimmy Demaret describing the play, revealed that golf was a worldwide

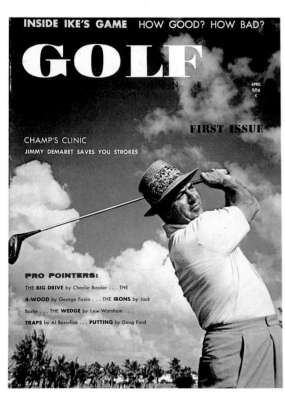

GOLF Magazine *began publication in 1959. Its monthly circulation today is nearly one million. Sam Snead graced the cover of the first issue.*

game and that American golfers were not necessarily the only men and women who could play it well.

In the same year that the Shell show was introduced (1962), another "World" was born. The World Series of Golf now is a standard stop on the tour. Originally, the show was conceived as a television special by Walter Schwimmer, who had been involved in the distribution of the earlier "All-Star Golf" on ABC-TV.

Schwimmer came up with the capital idea of matching the winners of the four major tournaments (The Masters, U.S. and British Opens, PGA Championship), and in that particular year his idea had some popular merit, for the winners of those tournaments were three in number—Jack Nicklaus, Arnold Palmer, and Gary Player, already billed as the "Big Three." One can only wonder whether Schwimmer would have come up with the same idea had the winners of those tournaments been, that year, Claude Harmon, Neil Coles, George Fazio, and Walter Burkemo. In any case, the concept caught the fancy of the golf-viewing public. Still, if it once was perceived by PGA officials as a season-ending championship, it is today one more event in a long and seemingly unending series of televised tournaments presented on the three major networks—ABC, CBS, and NBC—as well as on the cable systems ESPN and USA.

Golf on television has come a very long way since those early, primitive days when a camera was stuck up on the roof of a station wagon. So have the costs of producing such a show. Reports indicate that as much as $150,000 may have been spent covering a tournament in those early days. Today, that cost may be multiplied by six, eight, or ten. The Masters was first shown nationally in 1956, with six cameras covering the final four holes. By 1984, all eighteen holes were covered by more than thirty cameras, and the telecast was beamed to the other side of the world where avid Japanese golf fans stayed up until the day *before* to watch the winner.

Color television made golf more popular than ever. In 1966, The Masters was televised in color for the first time. Producer and director Frank Chirkinian was not slow to seize the beautiful opportunity of directing his cameras to linger lovingly over the azaleas and dogwood that marked golf's rite of spring.

That same year, Henry Longhurst came to America to attend the Carling Open. While there, he was invited to mount one of the television towers to comment on the unfolding golfing scene. Longhurst immediately made an indelible impression upon the viewing public by doing two things that a proper television announcer never did. He actually described one particularly bad shot as "particularly bad" and he remained silent when he felt he had nothing to say.

Gene Sarazen and Jimmy Demaret brought color to the telecasts of Shell's popular "Wonderful World of Golf."

Chirkinian, who was directing that event, hired Longhurst to come over the following year to sit at the sixteenth hole at Augusta, where he presided for many years. One of the annual delights for the golf fan up north, knowing he could not get a ticket to The Masters, was Chirkinian's opening shot of a trembling dogwood leaf set against Longhurst's silence at sixteen.

In the years that followed, others came along to establish themselves. Pat Summerall, a former professional football player, has proved his worth as a skilled anchor on the eighteenth tower of any CBS-TV golf event; Steve Melnyk, a gifted amateur golfer who did not find the same success as a professional, turned out to be gifted and gracious in interviewing winners and losers. Lee Trevino delivers one-liners with much the same élan he exhibited when bantering with his gallery. And Dave Marr, Bob Rosburg, Ken Venturi, Bob Goalby, Ed Sneed, Judy Rankin, and Marlene Floyd all offer insights as they describe shots for their respective networks, insights they acquired as fine players on the tour "yesterday."

The networks also have employed some men for the gorgeous resonance of their voices, not necessarily for their skill with a golf club. These include Charley Jones, Vin Scully, Jack Whitaker, and a North Carolinian by way of England, Ben Wright. They may "top 'em" with the worst but they can lyrically describe a golf shot with the best.

Inevitably, radio has suffered. Today, radio "reports" from the golf course are primarily updates on the progress of a tournament. Normally, radio reports cover only tournaments being played in the station's listening area. The only exceptions are occasionally the four major championships.

John Derr is another of the few great "voices" who made the transition from radio to television and one of the few who knew the difference between a driver and a wedge. He described The Masters on both radio and television and may well have been the only announcer in history who has described the U.S. Open while perched in a tree.

During the past two decades, newspapers have cut down on the amount of space they devote to local golf, and this has had a devastating effect. At one time, the Monday morning paper would run several columns on the tournaments that had taken place at local golf and country clubs over the weekend. A guy who had won second low net at his club's member-guest could make a feature out of it at Monday lunch. Today, his name is impossible to find. The PGA Tour may get some space. The local and state championships get almost nothing.

If golf writers today struggle to get their golden prose into their papers' pages, they are rewarded with more substantial accolades than were the old-timers. Some three decades ago, together with the Golf Writers Association, the MacGregor Golf Company instituted awards for the best writing in three categories of the newspaper medium: news, features, and columns, and one overall category of magazine. A number of fine writers have won these annual awards, including Thomas Boswell, Ross Goodner, Ron Green, Greg Larson, Jim Murray, Gary Nuhn, and Blackie Sherrod.

Today, the coverage of golf on television is more comprehensive, innovative, and fascinating. With the advent of lighter, more portable equipment, the development of videotape and attendant machinery, which enables a director to replay a shot within seconds after it was struck, the director becomes a choreographer whose show rivals a dance production by Busby Berkeley or Bob Fosse.

The pictures are magnificent but do not always capture the emotion, which a golf writer can capture. Most people remember Tom Watson's dramatic wedge shot on the seventy-first hole of the 1982 U.S. Open at Pebble Beach or perhaps Fuzzy Zoeller's grand gesture in waving, prematurely as it developed, the white flag of surrender at Winged Foot in 1984. No picture, however, could have conveyed the emotion of the moment when Bobby Jones accepted, in 1958, the citizenship of St. Andrews. That, too, was a dramatic event in golf history, and it was preserved forever for those who love golf by Herbert Warren Wind.

So each of these media has its place in reporting and recording golf history. We listeners and readers and viewers are fortunate, for as the fine English golf writer Patrick Smartt once observed, "A game gets the writers it deserves." The game of golf has always deserved the best.

One of many tree houses provided for photographers at The Masters.

A fine player, and an even finer writer, Henry Longhurst concluded his career by ascending the tower to cover The Masters and other events for CBS-TV.

Modern television coverage spares little expense in providing a bird's-eye view.

Before John Reid and friends could play their pioneering game of golf on Washington's Birthday, 1888, they had to have the necessary equipment. Because golf was virtually nonexistent in America at the time, the paraphernalia had to be imported. It came, of course, from Scotland. The "Old Grey Town" of St. Andrews was not only the cradle of golf, it was the crucible of golf equipment.

Reid obviously had been planning this golf outing for some time, for he had requested a fellow Scot, Robert Lockhart, a linen merchant, to bring back clubs and balls from a trip he was making home in 1887. In St. Andrews, Lockhart purchased six clubs—a driver, a brassie (equivalent to a 2-wood), spoon (3-wood), cleek (long iron), sand iron, and putter—and two dozen gutta-percha balls from the shop of Old Tom Morris, a leading clubmaker (or cleekmaker, as they were called) and a four-time winner of the British Open.

The clubs and balls had been handmade in Morris's shop. Although the Industrial Revolution had begun more than 125 years before, golf equipment in 1887 was crafted by hand, as it had been for four centuries. Within a decade, fueled in large part by the acceptance and subsequent growth of the game in America, the manufacture of golf equipment would leave the shop and move into the factory.

The story of golf equipment begins in the fifteenth century with the feather-filled ball. The "feathery" was constructed from strips of leather, two to four per ball, stitched together to form a pouch, soaked in water and alum, then tightly stuffed with goose or chicken feathers. As the ball dried, the feathers expanded and the leather contracted, forming a pellet that remained playable until it split, usually from wetness or from a bladed iron shot.

The feathery was a durable product until it got wet or was hit clumsily with an iron, when it would split open. Each ball was stuffed by hand with a top-hat full of feathers; a good worker could turn out three or four a day.

The clubs of the feathery period had long, thin, shallow heads and were formed of hard woods such as thorn and apple. Shafts were commonly made of ash and wrapped at the end with soft sheepskin, forming a grip. Iron clubs were rare because they tended to damage, rather than propel, the ball.

Around 1848, featheries were replaced by balls made of gutta percha, a rubberlike sap imported from India into Britain. The gutta revolutionized the game: they were easier to make, less expensive, lasted longer, flew farther and rolled truer on the greens. These improvements brought many new players to the game. Because the ball flew farther, holes had to be longer, and because there were more players, courses had to be roomier and have more holes.

Hickory Cleeks Metal Woods

BY JAMES A. FRANK

The harder, more resilient gutta-percha ball also brought about changes in clubs. Wooden heads became shorter and squatter and were constructed of slightly softer woods such as beech, sometimes with leather inserts in the face. Hickory shafts replaced ash. Irons, used only as a last resort to extricate the feathery from wheel ruts and other hazards, became more popular. The gutta-percha ball withstood contact with irons, and players like Young Tom Morris (son of the clubmaker and himself the winner of four successive British Open titles) quickly exploited the new metal clubs.

Golfers began to notice that the nicks and scratches the irons made in the surface of the ball actually improved its aerodynamic performance. Soon, balls were hammered deliberately, causing patterns to appear. Metal molds formed (and reformed) gutta percha, increased and standardized construction, and patterns were scored directly into the molds.

In the 1880s, clubmaking was a skilled profession in Scotland. Wooden heads were cut from blocks, filed and formed, then treated with a mixture of oil and varnish. By the 1890s, clubmakers were experimenting with inserts and "bulge," a slight convex shaping of the clubface that made for straighter shots.

Irons were hand-forged from a bar of iron that was heated, shaped with a hammer, polished, and fitted with a socket for a hickory shaft, which was trimmed to fit and held in place by a rivet. Grips were fashioned from a layer of cloth covered by strips of untanned leather wound around the end of the shaft and tacked in place. Both ends of the grip were wrapped with twine that was then shellacked.

The production of irons advanced with "drop-forging" in the 1890s. Instead of a man hammering out each iron head by hand on an anvil, a mechanical hammer stamped heated iron bars into shape faster and more uniformly. About this time, Scottish cleekmakers started stamping clubs with their names or marks; extra symbols sometimes were applied for the retailer or professional who would be selling the wares. Initials, arrows, crests, and other identifying marks were used. One of the most famous was the three-feathered plume of Forgan and Sons of St. Andrews, indicating that the family was clubmaker to the Prince of Wales. (When the prince became King Edward VII in 1901, Forgan's stamp changed to a crown.)

Gutta percha, a tree sap that was molded into balls, was black, so early balls were painted white. As the color wore off with use, golfers could buy special paint and make touch-ups themselves.

Beginning in the early 1890s, a number of enterprising Scottish pros made the passage to America and set up shop, giving lessons, laying out golf courses, and making clubs either from imported parts or ones they fashioned themselves. About the same time, a number of American companies, using more modern manufacturing techniques, entered the scene.

First was A.G. Spalding and Bros. of New York. Albert Goodwill Spalding had been a pitcher for the Boston Red Stockings and Chicago White Sox between 1871 and 1878. In those days, ballplayers often constructed their own equipment, and Spalding made his own baseballs. He was successful both as ballmaker and pitcher, becoming the first two-hundred-game winner. He retired in 1876 and, with his brother James, began a sports equipment company.

In 1892, Julian Curtiss, a Spalding director, visited Britain, returning with more than $500 worth of clubs and balls from Scottish cleekmakers. This purchase shocked the other directors, who did not think the company could ever sell that much golf equipment. In time, Spalding recognized the potential of the American golf market and began importing heads from Scotland and assembling them in America.

Spalding is recognized as the first company in the United States to assemble and sell clubs; the company's claim of offering the first American-made club in 1894 is more difficult to prove. But there is little doubt that Spalding pioneered the drop-forging process and manufactured the first American-made golf ball, a gutta percha, in 1898.

In 1899, James Spalding saw Harry Vardon win his third British Open title and afterward offered him a contract worth the then unprecedented sum of nine hundred pounds (the Open prize had been only thirty pounds) for a series of exhibition tours in America the following year. The tours would promote Spalding's new gutta-percha ball, the Vardon Flyer.

While Vardon was in the United States, he won the 1900 U.S. Open. His exhibitions attracted thousands of curious onlookers who soon tried the game. But the Flyer was not as successful, because about the time it was introduced, golf-ball technology took a giant step forward, leaving the gutta percha behind.

Other American companies began producing golf equipment just before the turn of the century. Bridgeport Gun Implement Company of Bridgeport, Connecticut, had manufactured firearms before turning to clubs, probably around 1897. Willie Dunn, one of the first Scottish pros to come to America, and his nephew, John Duncan Dunn, worked for BGI for a short time as designer and manager, respectively. BGI sold a novel Dunn-designed "one-piece" wood, a single piece of hickory head to shaft.

In 1898, Dunn worked for Crawford, McGregor and Canby, forerunner of MacGregor Golf. The firm began as the Dayton Last Company, a manufacturer of shoe lasts formed by the Crawford brothers, Archibald and Ziba, in the 1820s. In 1895, Edward Canby, who had recently bought into the company, visited Britain, where he was exposed to golf. Company history is cloudy, but it is believed that while there he met John McGregor, a former Scottish clubmaker. McGregor supposedly returned to the United States with Canby, bought into the company and introduced his partner, C.H. Crawford, to the game.

Below left:

Two turn-of-the-century gutta-percha balls. The ridged "Faroid" had to be teed a special way, hence the instruction "This End Up." Molding the cover allowed unusual designs, such as the one on the aptly named Willie Dunn's Stars and Stripes. The Dunns were a prominent Scottish golfing clan; Willie, Jr., was one of the first pros to leave his homeland for the United States.

Bottom left:

Gutta-percha balls were malleable enough to allow changing the patterning on their covers. The raised bramble pattern became popular in the early 1900s after it was shown to offer more control than other alternatives. Also pictured is half a gutta-percha mold, this one for creating a ball with a smooth cover.

Below right:

One of the first iron-headed clubs, this track, or rut, iron was made in Scotland in the mid-1800s. Its small head was used for extricating the ball from ruts, cart tracks, and other areas below the surface.

Above left:
Robert Simpson of Carnoustie, Scotland, was one of six golfing brothers (another, Jack, won the 1884 British Open). He started the family clubmaking concern in the mid-1880s. The man in the jacket (front row, far right) is Ally Simpson, Robert's son. This photograph probably was taken around 1910.

Above rightl:
Albert Goodwill Spalding, a successful major-league pitcher in the 1870s, formed A. G. Spalding and Bros. in 1876 to manufacture baseballs. By the 1890s, the firm was producing golf equipment; it was responsible for the first American-made club (around 1894) and ball (1898).

Folklore has it that Crawford broke a driver during a round and gave the club to George Mattern, chief engineer in the plant, for repair. Mattern fashioned a new head out of a block of persimmon, a hardwood used to make children's shoe lasts. In 1897, the company entered the wood-head manufacturing business, turning them out on the same copying lathes that made lasts.

Besides baseballs, firearms, and shoe lasts, golf-equipment manufacture in America evolved from buggy whips. William Burke of Newark, Ohio, sold hickory to buggy-whip makers at the end of the nineteenth century. Burke prophetically realized that buggies and whips soon would be outdated by "horseless carriages," and in 1903, he began producing hickory golf shafts. By 1910, the Burke Golf Company was making complete golf clubs.

The 1890s will be remembered for other advancements in golf equipment. In 1894, Englishman Thomas A. Horsburgh patented a steel shaft made from a solid-steel rod. Horsburgh had trouble convincing pros to use his shafts, and the idea vanished for more than twenty years until Allan Lard, an independently wealthy golf enthusiast, experimented with perforated steel shafts in 1913. Not until the mid-twenties

would production methods allow the manufacture of an acceptable steel shaft.

Probably the single greatest advancement in the history of golf equipment can be traced to 1898. The product was the wound-rubber ball, created by Coburn Haskell, a wealthy entrepreneur and not-too-distinguished golfer from Cleveland, Ohio. His idea was simple enough: Instead of a solid mass of material, such as gutta percha, Haskell wound a continuous rubber thread around a small, solid, rubber ball and wrapped the whole mass in a gutta-percha cover. With the assistance of Bertram G. Work, an engineer with the B.F. Goodrich Rubber Company in Akron, Ohio, Haskell built his ball, which flew a longer distance than any available.

Surprisingly, the Haskell ball did not catch on immediately. It certainly flew and rolled farther than the gutta, but it tended to sail off line. The Bounding Billies, as they were soon dubbed, were hard to control around and on the greens until, the story is told, James Foulis, the professional at the Chicago Golf Club and winner of the 1896 U.S. Open, unknowingly put a gutta-percha-covered Haskell into a ball press that produced a raised, bramble pattern. This ball did not play like the others Foulis was using: It traveled a long

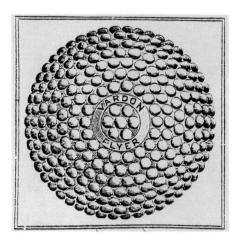

Above:
Spalding introduced the Vardon Flyer, a gutta-percha ball with a bramble-patterned cover, in 1899. The next year, the company brought the ball's namesake, the great English golfer Harry Vardon, to the United States for a series of exhibition matches to promote the ball. While in America, Vardon won the U.S. Open.

way, and he could control it. Only after cutting it open did Foulis realize it was a Haskell; from then on, the bramble was the pattern of choice.

Other pros remained unconvinced. Haskell supposedly sent some samples to English golfer J.H. Taylor, who would become the first five-time British Open winner and one of the "Great Triumvirate" (with Harry Vardon and James Braid) that dominated golf in the early 1900s. Haskell hoped Taylor would use the new ball in the 1900 U.S. Open, but Taylor stuck with gutta percha (and finished second to Vardon). Soon after the Open, it is said, Taylor teed up a Haskell on the opening hole at Rockaway Hunting Club on Long Island. Never a long hitter, he figured the group on the green about 250 yards away was safe. His drive rolled up to the players as they were holing out.

In 1901, Walter Travis played the Haskell ball to win a second, consecutive U.S. Amateur. But the final factor in the Haskell's ascendance seems to have been its victory in the 1902 British Open captured by Sandy Herd. Wrote Englishman Horace Hutchinson in 1903, "We accept the American invention, as Britons will, of course, with grumbling, but with gratitude down in our hearts."

As with the feathery and gutta-percha balls before it, the Haskell demanded alterations in clubs. The softer wound ball needed a harder wood, and persimmon fit the bill (followed by the laminated heads that would appear in the 1940s), fitted with hard inserts. Irons were made larger to give the livelier ball more time on the clubface, which improved. The quest for control also led to scoring iron faces with deep grooves meant to impart spin.

Once the Haskell was accepted, advances in golf balls came fast and furious. As quickly as Spalding failed with the Vardon Flyer, it introduced a rubber ball, the Wizard, in 1903. Soon thereafter, Spalding developed a cover made of balata, a natural rubber that adhered more securely than gutta percha to the rubber windings inside the ball and that was easier to control. In 1905, Spalding came out with the first true "white" balls: rather than black material painted white, these started with a white cover.

Other companies experimented with the rubber ball's core. The Kempshall Golf Ball Company replaced the solid-rubber

Left:
As golf equipment proliferated, so did its attendant accessories. The golf bag made its first appearance in England in 1891. The first ball "pickups," forerunners of the shag bag, were patented in the early 1890s, as were gadgets such as the tethered practice ball, hand-held ball cleaner, and adjustable-headed club. The practice putting mat was patented in the United States in 1906, wooden tees were introduced in 1920, and this advertisement for the Frisk Auto Caddy appeared in 1923.

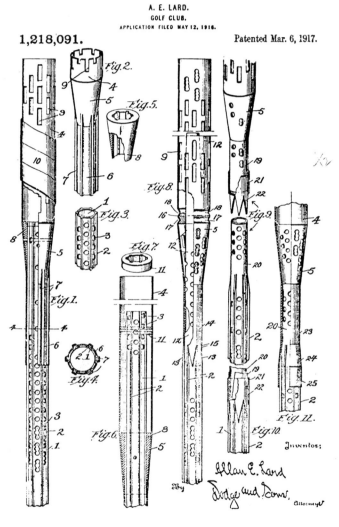

A. E. LARD.
GOLF CLUB.
APPLICATION FILED MAY 12, 1916.

1,218,091.

Patented Mar. 6, 1917.

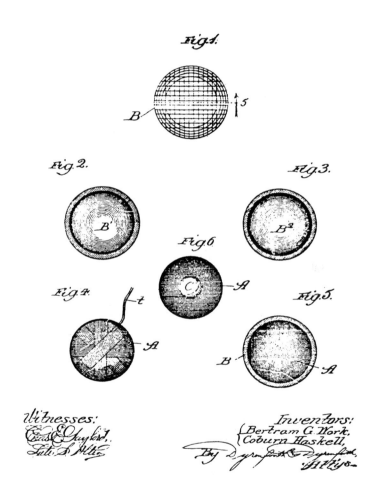

Above:
Experiments with steel shafts began around 1910. Inventor Allan Lard hoped that perforating the shaft would help lessen its weight. When tested, perforated shafts tended to whistle, and they were not taken very seriously.

Top:
A Haskell ball with the original cross-hatched cover and half a gutta-percha ball-press mold.

Above:
The patent for the original Haskell ball, filed by Coburn Haskell, a wealthy Cleveland entrepreneur (and a high handicapper), and Bertram G. Work, an engineer with the B. F. Goodrich Rubber Company. Goodrich had exclusive rights to manufacture the ball during the original patent.

Above:
The two basic methods of wood-head construction are lamination (top) and solid-block persimmon (above). The lamination process was invented in the 1940s and involves building a block of wood by gluing together thin sheets of maple, then turning the head from the block on a lathe. Persimmon clubheads, turned from a single block of persimmon, have been popular since the late 1890s; they are not as durable as laminated heads but are preferred by many players for their feel and beauty.

Below:
Evolution of the golf ball. The feathery (far left), a small sack of leather stuffed with goose or chicken feathers, was played from the 1400s until the mid-1800s, when it was replaced by the one-piece, molded gutta percha (second from left). The three-piece Haskell ball (second from right), which appeared in 1898, revolutionized the game: A small rubber center wrapped with rubber windings and sheathed in a gutta-percha cover, the Haskell was the first ball to mix distance and control. Introduced in the late 1960s, the two-piece ball (far right), a solid mass inside a tough, synthetic cover, sacrificed control for distance but was an immediate success.

core with a small, rubber sac filled with water on the theory that the less resistance at impact, the better. In the years that followed, other companies tested sacs loaded with mixtures combining water with lead, zinc oxide, glue, glycerin, even tapioca. (Modern hollow-core balls mix water with salts for a little extra weight.)

Another area open to improvement was cover design. While the bramble sold on the early Haskells, further study showed that indentations, rather than bumps, made for more consistent club-ball contact and flight. In 1905, Englishman William Taylor received a patent on a dimpled cover, a virtual reverse of the bramble. Spalding bought the American rights, and, by 1930, the dimple was king.

The original wound-rubber balls were light and large, about 1.55 ounces and 1.71 inches in diameter. No regulations governed ball size and weight, so manufacturers tried various combinations looking for the longest, straightest flight. A heavier core was popular for a time, then both size and weight dropped, so in 1915, when Haskell's original patent expired, 1.62 ounces and 1.63 inches in diameter were roughly standard.

Once the patent ended, competitors mushroomed. Just as development of the gutta-percha ball threatened courses, so did the wide variety of rubber balls suddenly available. In 1920, the United States Golf Association (USGA) and the Royal and Ancient (R&A) Golf Club of St. Andrews, Scotland, the two recognized governing bodies of golf, jointly agreed on ball-size restrictions. As of May 1, 1921, balls used in their competitions could no longer weigh more than 1.62 ounces or measure less than 1.62 inches.

Over the next decade, the USGA experimented with different limits. In 1923, the association stated that a ball could weigh no more than 1.55 ounces while measuring no less than 1.68 inches. This "balloon ball" came into play in the United States in 1931, but proved too light to hold a line while in flight or on the green; it was gone after one year. The new rules in 1932 read 1.62 ounces and 1.68 inches, standards that still apply today. The British held to the original

The finest golfer never to make a par, Iron Byron is the stalwart of the USGA's golf equipment testing facilities.

1.62/1.62 all along, but as America came to dominate the game, the smaller ball fell out of favor.

Ball size has not been the only concern of the ruling bodies. In 1942, the USGA, which had become the leader in matters of equipment, introduced the Initial Velocity Standard, which says a ball's velocity at impact cannot be greater than 250 feet per second (measured by USGA machines under laboratory conditions). In 1976, the Overall Distance Standard limited the distance a ball could travel to 280 yards

(plus 6 percent tolerance) when hit by the USGA's mechanical golfer, Iron Byron. And in 1983, the Symmetry Standard mandated that a ball "must fly the same distance, same height, and remain in flight for the same length of time no matter how the ball is placed on the tee."

In 1921, Scotsman Jock Hutchison, one of the leading British players in the years before World War I, won his country's Open using the deeply slotted irons that had become popular with the advent of the wound-rubber ball. In

Grooves and other markings on iron faces made their first appearance in the 1890s; before that, faces were smooth. Once golfers realized that grooves helped them control the ball, they tried numerous patterns and sizes. Deep, wide grooves appeared around 1914; they were banned in 1925.

In 1927, the True Temper Corporation, which had experience making steel fishing rods, patented a method of making steel tubes with "steps," places on the tube where it stepped down to a narrower diameter, allowing more speed, more control, and lighter weight while creating a more uniform and concentrically shaped shaft. The USGA allowed steel shafts as of 1926, the R&A in 1929, and golf equipment took another big step forward.

It took less than ten years for steel shafts to unseat hickory. In 1930, Bobby Jones won the Grand Slam—capturing the U.S. and British Open and Amateur Championships—using hickory-shafted clubs. The next year, steel won its first major tournament, the U.S. Open, when Billy Burke beat George Von Elm in a two-day playoff at the Inverness Club in Toledo, Ohio. The last major won with hickory was the 1936 U.S. Amateur, by Johnny Fischer at Garden City Golf Club in New York.

fact, face markings were a recent innovation. Early irons had smooth faces, which were roughened as the result of caddies wiping away rust with emery cloth; players noticed that the roughening improved spin and control on their shots. The first deliberate face markings were punched dots, which appeared in the 1890s. By 1910, smooth-faced irons were hard to find, and the most popular scoring patterns were dots, grooves (such as are found today), and dashes. Deep-grooved irons, such as Hutchison used to win the British Open, were introduced around 1914 and then banned in 1925, largely in reaction to his victory.

A.F. Knight, an amateur golfer from Schenectady, New York, made two contributions to golf equipment. The first was the center-shafted Schenectady putter he invented around 1901, used by Walter J. Travis to win the 1904 British Amateur Championship. In 1910, the R&A banned center-shafted putters, helping to ensure the Schenectady's success in America, where it remained legal. Also in 1910, Knight obtained a patent for a seamed, tubular, steel golf shaft. Hickory had been the choice in shaft material since the era of the gutta-percha ball, but it was whippy, that is, it twisted during the swing, making accurate shotmaking difficult, and it varied markedly in performance from one shaft to the next.

Interest in steel picked up again in the early twenties when Horton Manufacturing of Bristol, Connecticut, used Knight's patent to produce a seamed, copper-plated, steel shaft. Steel shafts were illegal under USGA and R&A regulations, but MacGregor, Spalding, and a few other companies offered clubs fitted with them.

Walter J. Travis, three-time holder of the U.S. Amateur title, with the center-shafted Schenectady putter he used while winning the 1904 British Amateur. In 1910, the Royal and Ancient Golf Club of St. Andrews (R&A) banned "mallet-headed implements" such as the Schenectady; the ruling stood until 1951. In the meantime, the Schenectady remained legal in the United States.

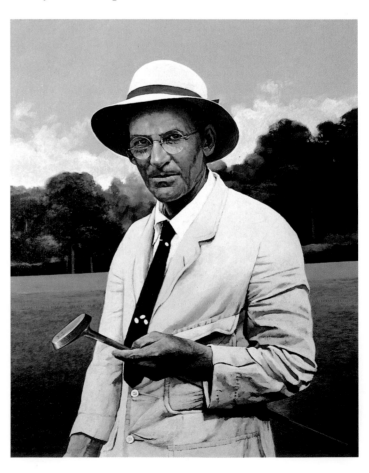

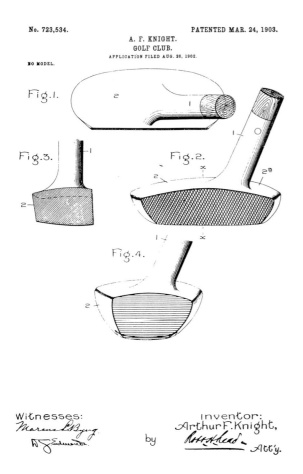

No. 723,534. PATENTED MAR. 24, 1903.
A. F. KNIGHT.
GOLF CLUB.
APPLICATION FILED AUG. 26, 1902.

NO MODEL.

Fig.1.

Fig.3.

Fig.2.

Fig.4.

Witnesses: *Marena L. Byng* *W. J. Edmonton.*

Inventor: Arthur F. Knight, by *Rottstead* Att'y.

The patent for A. F. Knight's Schenectady putter shows how the shaft attached to the center of the head, instead of at the heel, which is what the R&A decreed was the only permissible design.

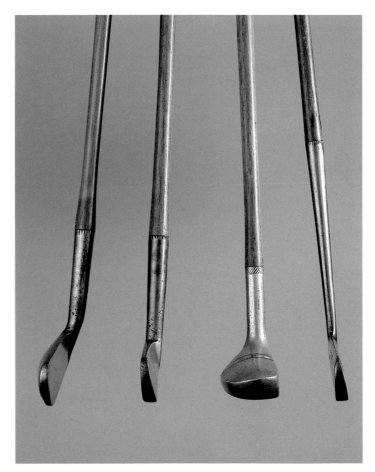

Before the fourteen-club limit was adopted in 1938, players could carry as many "tools" in the bag as they liked, so they often toted a variety of putters for the different green conditions they would encounter in a round. This standard putter (left), popular before 1920, was used on greens of average speed. The "putting cleek" (second from left), common from the 1880s through the early 1900s, had more loft than normal; it was used for bumpy greens when the ball might have settled into a slight depression and needed to be popped up before rolling. The mallet putter (second from right), circa 1930s, was heavier than normal and thought to be advantageous on slow greens. The extra-thin, long-hosel putter (right) from the 1920s was used for fast greens.

While hickory hung on and steel made inroads, many manufacturers offered clubs with a choice of the two. Steel shafts came in a variety of colors and finishes, including a wood-grain look for players who did not want it known that they had abandoned hickory. But steel eventually won out and remains the standard today despite the brief bursts of enthusiasm for fiberglass shafts in the fifties and aluminum shafts in the sixties. Today, graphite and other strong, lightweight, composite materials are winning converts, but steel continues its dominance.

Acceptance of steel shafts in the thirties had ramifications other than the demise of hickory. First was the concept of the "matched set," allowing a golfer to buy a collection of clubs with similar specifications rather than individual pieces. The more exacting tolerances available with steel meant that clubs could be manufactured and matched more precisely regarding flex, weight, and feel. Once upon a time, the clubmaker or consumer would match clubs by taking sandpaper to the hickory shafts and rubbing away until the different sticks felt alike.

With the advent of steel, equipment manufacturers also started selling sets of clubs that promised a tool for every predicament. The USGA put a stop to that in 1938, adopting the rule that limited the number of clubs a player could use in a round to fourteen. The R&A followed suit in 1939.

When matched sets came in, calling clubs by name went out. The driver was always the driver, followed by the brassie (2-wood), spoon (3), cleek (4), and baffy (5). In the irons, there was the driving iron (1), mid-iron (2), mid-mashie (3), mashie-iron (4), mashie (5), spade mashie (6), mashie niblick (7), pitching niblick (8), and niblick (9). Starting in the thirties, they were numbers—1-iron, 2-iron, and 3-irons. In the 1850s, Scotsman Allan Robertson, the greatest player

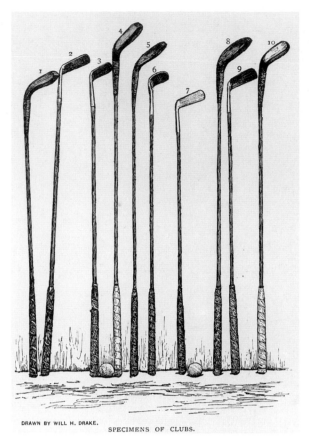

DRAWN BY WILL H. DRAKE.

SPECIMENS OF CLUBS.

Above:

When American golf began, a full set of clubs included: (1) wooden putter; (2) cleek; (3) mashie; (4) driver; (5) short spoon; (6) niblick; (7) iron putter; (8) long spoon; (9) sand iron; (10) brassie.

Above right:

Golf boomed in America in the 1920s and became more accessible to the masses—as did better, mass-produced equipment. Along with a catalogue, ruler, score book, and general introduction to the game, MacGregor here offered to send interested parties a pamphlet for "laying out a new course."

of his day, had named his clubs Sir Robert Peel and The Doctor. Willie Park, Jr., winner of the 1887 and 1889 British Opens, called his wooden putter Old Pawky. Jones's putter was the famous Calamity Jane. Players did not see fit to personify a 5-iron, and some of golf's glamour vanished.

Golf boomed after World War I, fueled by the play of Walter Hagen, Gene Sarazen, and, of course, Bobby Jones. Spalding and MacGregor continued to lead the pack of manufacturers, introducing matched sets, steel shafts, and improved balls. Other companies entered the market: Hillerich and Bradsby, famous for Louisville Slugger baseball bats, began producing woods in 1916; Hagen became the first player in the clubmaking field, opening the Walter Hagen Golf Company in 1922; Nat Rosasco started Northwestern Golf in the basement of his Chicago home in 1929.

Another new company was Wilson Sporting Goods, which had its roots in a turn-of-the-century Chicago meatpacking firm that branched out by turning animal entrails into tennis-racquet strings. During the twenties, Wilson grew by buying up smaller companies, including some that made golf equipment. In the thirties and forties, Wilson was responsible for a number of innovations, including "gooseneck" (offset-hosel) irons, Strata-Bloc laminated-maple wood heads, and improvements in the weighting of irons so more weight was behind a club's "sweet spot."

Wilson also pioneered the advisory staff, hiring prominent golf personalities to test, evaluate, and make recommendations on equipment. The first member of the Wilson staff was Gene Sarazen, who signed on in 1924. Over the years, he was joined by Sam Snead, Lloyd Mangrum, Helen Hicks, Patty Berg, and Babe Zaharias. Another great who signed on was Walter Hagen, whose club company was acquired by Wilson in 1944

When the Depression hit, golf suffered along with the rest of the country. Some firms struggled, many vanished, but others prospered, and a few new ones entered the marketplace.

After Bobby Jones retired from competitive golf in 1930, he signed on as an advisor (and member of the board) for

Spalding, an association that helped keep the company solvent during hard times thanks to Jones's autograph-model clubs.

Titleist, today the country's largest seller of golf balls, began in 1932 in a dentist's office. Phil Young, a good amateur golfer and owner of a rubber-parts company, was frustrated by the erratic performance of the balls he used, so with a golfing buddy (and dentist), he x-rayed the balls and found centers that were out-of-round and of varying size. Young and a fellow engineer devised a method of making wound-rubber balls with consistently round centers, launching the company.

In 1934, MacGregor signed Tommy Armour, pro at Chicago's Medinah Country Club, to its advisory staff. Armour brought with him a young assistant pro named Toney Penna. In the ensuing years, Armour's name, backed by Penna's designs, helped make MacGregor the premier clubmaker with instant classics such as Silver Scot irons, Eye-O-Matic woods, and the Ironmaster putter. Penna's compact, muscleback MT (for MacGregor Tourney) irons, introduced in 1949, probably are the most imitated clubs in history. MacGregor also created its own staff of touring pros, including at one time or another Armour, Byron Nelson, Louise Suggs, Ben Hogan, and Jimmy Demaret, to name a few.

The 1930s witnessed another equipment innovation, the creation of a new club, the sand wedge. In January 1931, the USGA and R&A banned "concave wedges," heavy clubs with a big flange and a concave face designed to "shovel" the ball out of the sand. Bobby Jones had used such a club to win the British Open at Hoylake in 1930, the third leg of the Grand Slam.

Credit for the development of the modern sand wedge goes to Gene Sarazen. During the winter of 1931, the Squire, who was familiar with the concave wedge, was learning to fly when he noticed that lowering a plane's tail flaps made the nose rise. He thought that principle could apply to sand play: lower the tail of the club below the leading edge to help it cut through the sand and thrust the ball up into the air. He experimented by applying solder to the back of standard niblicks, filing them down, adding more solder and testing the results in a bunker on the golf course behind his Florida home.

It took more than six months, but when he was done, Sarazen had a club he could use out of the sand, for short, punch approaches, from the rough, and over hazards. It debuted at the 1932 British Open at the Prince's course in England; Sarazen won handily, playing superbly from the sand. Wilson introduced Sarazen's "R99" sand wedge in 1934, and the golfer's bag had a new weapon.

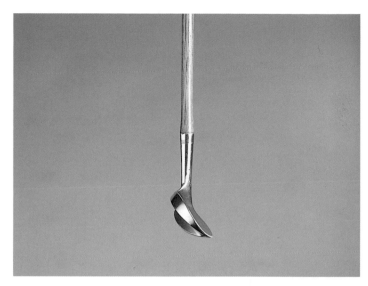

Before they were banned by the United States Golf Association (USGA) and R&A in 1931, concave wedges, such as the one shown here, were designed to shovel the ball out of the sand.

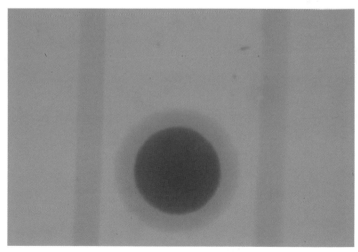

Starting with the Haskell, the three-piece, or wound ball, became the sphere of choice. But rudimentary manufacturing methods often resulted in cores that were neither uniform nor centered. In 1932, an amateur golfer named Phil Young x-rayed some balls in a dentist's office. When he noticed the deformities, he set out to make a ball with a perfectly round, properly positioned core. The company he founded, Titleist, is the country's leading seller of golf balls.

In 1931, the year the concave wedge was made illegal, Gene Sarazen transformed an ordinary niblick into a heavy-flanged club for blasting out of traps. The club helped Sarazen win the 1932 British Open, and copies were put on the market the next year. Here Sarazen admires one of the wedges, which he donated to the USGA for a collection of clubs used by winners of U.S. national championships.

Golf all but stopped for the duration of World War II. Rubber was rationed, so golf balls had to be reprocessed and recycled. Most factories were converted to the war effort. Titleist, for example, applied its expertise with rubber to the manufacture of gas masks for Allied troops, while Mac-Gregor's Dayton, Ohio, factory turned out parachute packs, safety belts, and other air force gear.

Immediately after the war, the country went crazy for golf. Men home from the war wanted to enjoy their leisure time. In the fifties, President Eisenhower played whenever he could, making golf almost a national sport. But because so few clubs had been produced during the war, demand far exceeded supply. Golf-equipment manufacturers geared up again and prospered; new companies multiplied.

The small Hansberger Tool and Die Company that started in Chicago in 1946 became Sportsmans Golf in 1950, grew steadily, and became Ram Golf in 1967. A manufacturer of clubs and balls, Ram in 1967 produced the first commercially available ball covered with DuPont's tough-to-cut synthetic material, Surlyn. The Hansbergers also made the famous George Low putters in the fifties and sixties.

Ben Hogan entered the clubmaking field in 1953 with the stated intention of building the finest clubs possible. Hogan was involved in virtually every part of the business, from designing to marketing. The company was ready to ship its first clubs in summer 1954, when Hogan looked at the finished product, decided it wasn't up to his standards and ordered more than $100,000 worth of merchandise scrapped; the first clubs that met Hogan's approval sold later that year.

Arnold Palmer, who as a player almost single-handedly pulled golf into the 1960s, introduced a line of clubs in 1964 after finishing a ten-year endorsement contract with Wilson. Produced for Palmer by Pro Golf/First Flight, the clubs were among the first to offer the new, lighter-weight aluminum shafts that burst on the scene, proved too weak to stand repeated play, and vanished. Today, Palmer still is associated with First Flight's descendant, the sports conglomerate Pro-Group.

Well into the sixties, forging remained the method of manufacturing irons. Automation and mechanization had improved quantity and quality since the days of the Scottish cleekmakers, but irons still were made by pounding heated metal into shape; this resulted in most of a club's weight being concentrated behind a small area of the face, which became the sweet spot. A small hitting area was fine for the skilled player who made consistent contact with the ball. But the less able player had trouble with forged irons, spraying the ball every which way.

In the early part of the decade, a number of small West Coast companies that supplied precision parts to the aerospace industry tried making golf equipment. The process they used, known as investment casting, called for pouring molten metal into molds. Casting changed the look and playability of irons.

At the turn of the century, designers had tried spreading a clubhead's weight out toward its toe, but rudimentary production techniques made the idea unworkable. With casting, weight could be redistributed merely by changing the mold. One design moved mass away from the center of the club out to its edges, creating a cavity on the back side. Cavity-backed, or perimeter-weighted, clubs featured an expanded sweet spot that helped compensate for imperfect contact. Investment casting ushered in a new generation of golf equipment and, like earlier innovations, made golf more enjoyable for many new players.

Among the early investment-cast clubmakers were Bob Mader at Confidence Golf; John Riley and Carl Ross at Lynx; and Karsten Solheim, who started in the early sixties casting putters in his garage and later created Ping clubs. By the early seventies, investment-cast woods were being made by Riley for Pinseeker and Phil Skrovonsky and Gary Adams for Taylor Made. Within a decade, metal woods were an accepted and profitable product for nearly every major equip-

Among the professionals who entered the club-making field have been Walter Hagen, Tommy Armour, and Arnold Palmer. Ben Hogan started the company that bears his name in 1953, devoting himself to building the best product possible and taking an active interest in the company, specifically club design. Here he oversees the drilling of iron hosels (the sockets into which the shafts are inserted).

ment company, even gaining popularity on the women's and men's professional tours.

Golfers today can choose among many models of forged and investment-cast irons and among woods made of wood or metal. The latest innovations are clubheads and shafts made of composite materials such as graphite and boron; leading the way with large expenditures in research and development are Japanese clubmakers, notably Daiwa, Yamaha, Mizuno, Yonex, and Bridgestone, plus smaller companies specializing in component parts. Other materials currently in vogue include beryllium copper and ceramics for clubheads and titanium for shafts.

Experimentation affected golf balls, too. Well into the sixties, the preeminent design was the wound-rubber, or three-piece (core, windings, cover), ball, a direct descendant of the Haskell. Advances in technology had led to improvements in cover materials and windings, but they only made a good product better. In the sixties and again in the seventies, a one-piece ball was marketed, updating an idea that can be traced back to the gutta percha of the mid-1800s but that never took off.

In 1968, Spalding unveiled the two-piece ball, a solid mass wrapped in a cover made of Surlyn. The Top-Flite, as Spalding called it, won quick acceptance thanks to its longer distance. The few extra yards came at the expense of control and feel: The harder, synthetic cover did not take spin as willingly as the softer balata, and better players and old-timers did not like the harder feel of the two-piece at impact. But distance plus a hard-to-cut cover proved an unbeatable combination, and two-piece balls teamed well with the new, investment-cast clubs.

Two- and three-piece balls kept improving. New synthetic cover materials (such as Spalding's Zinthane) play and feel more like the softer, faster-spinning balata. More dimples squeezed onto the cover yield more control or more distance, depending on the company making the claim. At the beginning of this decade, most golf balls had fewer than 350 dimples; today, 400- and 500-dimple balls, mixing depressions of different sizes and arranged in numerous geometric patterns, are available. Variations in dimple patterns affect ball flight, particularly trajectory.

After a century of golf in America, what passes for acceptable equipment in 1988 includes the traditional designs of the past plus whatever is on the cutting edge of technology. Most tour pros today play forged clubs, persimmon woods, and three-piece, balata-covered balls. But as younger players join the tour, more bring with them the investment-cast irons, metal woods, and two-piece balls on which they were weaned. The cast-and-two-piece team has made considerable headway on the women's and senior men's tours, where distance is more in demand than among the younger men. With more options and more sophistication, players at all levels can and do experiment to find the combinations that suit them best.

But some things never change. The USGA and Royal and Ancient continue to be vigilant sentinels, reining in overzealous manufacturers who go too far trying to top the competition by pushing the rules beyond their limits. The immutable truth, as old as the game itself, is that a golfer's skill must not flow from what he holds in his hands but from what he possesses in his head and heart.

Opposite top left:
The iron at right is forged, formed by stamping a heated piece of metal with a die. Forged clubs tend to have their mass concentrated behind the center of the face. Investment-cast clubs, such as the one at left, are formed by pouring molten metal into a mold, which allows the weight to be placed anywhere. Most investment-cast clubs are perimeter-weighted, spreading the weight around the outside of the clubface; this forms a cavity in the back and expands the size of the club's optimum hitting area.

Opposite middle left:
Although metal woods were around as early as 1900, they quickly died out until the early 1970s, when a number of new equipment companies emerged. The heads are hollow, so the walls must be thick enough to withstand contact but not so thick that the club is too heavy to be swung. The heads are filled with foam, which absorbs vibration and helps create the distinctive sound at impact.

Opposite top right:
In 1968, Top-Flite was the name Spalding gave its new two-piece ball. The original Top-Flite was a three-piece ball introduced in 1932. Although some three-piece balls had a solid rubber center, others had a hollow core, which was filled with an interesting assortment of ingredients in trying to guarantee distance and control. In this advertisement, Spalding points out that its rubber core was filled after the ball was constructed; today, liquid centers are filled before windings and cover are put in place.

Opposite bottom:
Many equipment companies turned to computer-aided design, modeling, and manufacturing beginning in the 1980s, thereby saving hundreds of man-hours in research and development. While some industry people lament the loss of a designer's hands-on involvement, improved productivity and bottom-line performance are crucial in the increasingly competitive golf business.

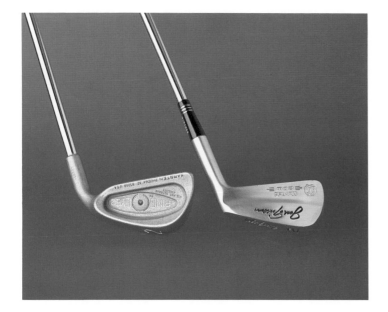

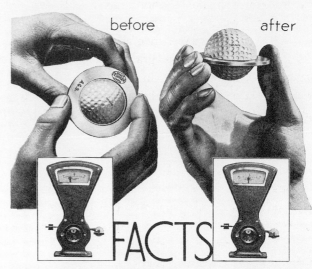

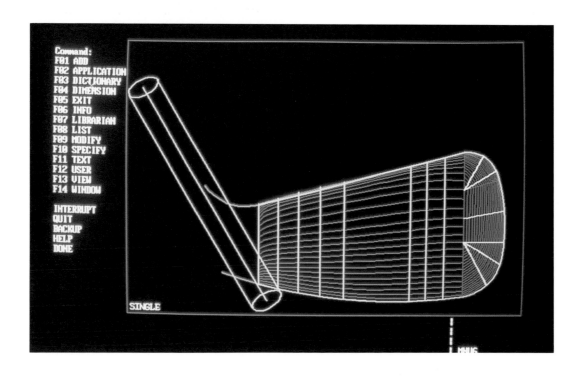

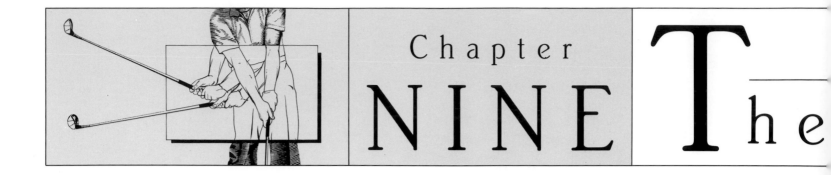

No one knows for certain whether John Reid or his close friend John Upham took the first swing during their historic match on Washington's Birthday in 1888. But whoever it was must have realized straightaway that the seemingly simple act of swatting a small, white ball straight and far was tougher than it looked. Presumably, too, once the two founding members of the Apple Tree Gang hit solid shots, they became obsessed with trying to repeat the wonderful sensation of striking the ball with the sweet spot of the clubface.

A hundred years later, nearly twenty million Americans share the same happy addiction, although they seek improvement through formal lessons as well as through golf instruction books, magazines, and videotapes, which offer tips and swing theories by top professionals and leading teachers.

One of the great joys of watching golf is to witness the myriad swings employed and realize that no *one* method suits everyone. There cannot be one perfect method: players vary in physique, possess individual strengths and play with different made-to-measure equipment. Moreover, not all teachers think alike.

The disciples of the "swingers" school of Ernest Jones include very respected instructors John Jacobs, Bob Toski, and Manuel de la Torre. Jim Flick follows the ideas and teaches the left-sided techniques of Alex Morrison. Jimmy Ballard coaches in the mode of Percy Boomer, the original right-sided theorist. Other instructors stress a two-sided action; still others advocate touch and feel swings. The "mechanics," represented by Paul Bertholy, swear the secret to consistently square clubface-to-ball contact lies in achieving specific positions during the swing. Not to be forgotten is the school of the "mentalists," led by Timothy Gallwey and Charles Hogan, two gurus who view the game as 90 percent between the ears and map out unusual techniques to increase a player's concentration and confidence.

The only bond among these factions is the set of time-tested fundamentals that governs the setup and swing. In capsulizing these basics, teachers generally agree, the student must:

1. Hold the club with a neutral grip, the back of the left hand square to the target, right palm parallel to the left.
2. Set up square to the ball, with feet, knees, hips, and shoulders parallel to an imaginary line extending from ball to target and with the body weight balanced equally between the ball and heel of each foot.
3. Use a smooth, one-piece takeaway by sweeping the club low to the ground for the first foot or two of the swing.
4. Keep the head relatively still and the left arm relatively straight as the wrists cock naturally, swinging the club upward, while rotating the hips forty-five degrees and the shoulders ninety degrees.
5. Arrive at a square position at the top of the swing, the club shaft parallel to the target line.
6. Lead with the lower body on the downswing.
7. Swing through the ball, not at it.
8. Finish facing slightly left of the target.

Nobody has yet discovered when the first golf lesson in America was given, but presumably instruction was imparted in a British accent. The early British pros also brought with

Learning Process

them the St. Andrews swing, popularized by the legendary players from Scotland.

The typical St. Andrean swept the club back swiftly inside the target line and around his body on the backswing. Breaking his left arm and allowing his right elbow to fly up and away from his side, he made a long, loose backswing motion down almost to belt-height at the end of the backswing, with the clubhead dipping past parallel. The reciprocal downswing action was equally flat and wristy and produced a low-flying draw that was a necessity in combating the bitter elements on the windswept seaside links of Scotland. Following the fashion of the day, British golfers generally wore close-fitting overcoats, which restricted their shoulder turn and further encouraged a wristy swing. Cricket was another influence on the swing of those early British players. The motions and muscle movements inherent in that game influenced the way they learned golf.

Those early years in America produced little instruction writing, and the only instruction books available, such as Horace Hutchinson's *Golf: The Badminton Library of Sports* (1890), came from Great Britain.

Two famous nineteenth-century books, *Golf in America: A Practical Manual* by James Lee (1895) and *How to Play Golf* by H. J. Whigham (1897), the first instruction books published in the United States, simply reiterated the fundamentals of the St. Andrews swing. Whigham did recognize and discuss the need for greater teaching ability by suggesting that the golf instructor try to understand the nature of the student, distinguish between "errors of skill" and "errors of emotion," and develop a genuine respect for the student's game.

The first boost to American golf instruction came in 1900 when two supreme British professionals, Harry Vardon and

J. H. Taylor, visited the United States on an exhibition tour. Vardon already had won the British Open three times; Taylor, twice.

This tour gave Americans their first opportunity to watch great golfers, and watch they did. Later, in *The Complete Golfer* (1905), Vardon tells of the "whole-hearted manner in which America was going in for golf. People came to the matches in great crowds and seemed bent on learning all they could from my play. Everybody seemed to be trying to practice my new grip."

Then, as now, the Americans knew a good thing when they saw it. Vardon's grip was truly revolutionary. By placing the tips of both thumbs down the sides of the grip and pinching the club (instead of keeping both thumbs virtually off the handle), and draping his right pinky over the forefinger of his left hand (instead of around the grip, as had previously been taught), Vardon brought a new unity to the hands.

The overlapping, or Vardon, grip calmed the wrists and allowed a player to swing on a more upright plane, setting the club securely in the parallel position at the top. In reducing the wristiness of the action, it quieted the change of direction, allowing a smoother downswing and higher, more controlled shots. This type of shot ideally suited American inland courses, which were not nearly as wind-blown as British links and featured softer greens than those overseas. The Vardon grip initiated the first step in promoting a more upright swing and a higher ball flight. No wonder, then, that the great Ben Hogan, fifty-two years after Vardon's historic visit, was to call the Vardon grip the first, solid fundamental of the swing, even though the analytical Hawk argued that Vardon put pressure on the wrong fingers.

The first American method of swinging came straight from the Old Course at St. Andrews, Scotland. A long, loose, wristy motion, the St. Andrean swing produced the low-flying draw that worked so well on the Scottish links. These illustrations come from Horace Hutchinson's classic book, Golf: The Badminton Library of Sports, published in 1890.

Before golf instruction books became popular, golfers could view the great players through stereopticon slides, such as these that depict Harry Vardon swinging a mashie.

During a 1900 tour of America, Harry Vardon introduced the overlapping grip. The left thumb extended straight down the shaft, gripping the club mainly in the palm. The little finger of the right hand covered the index finger of the left.

Vardon advocated another revolutionary technique: keeping the head perfectly still during the swing. The impact of this idea on the evolution of golf instruction continues to the present time. Jack Nicklaus emphatically states in his book *Golf My Way*: "Keeping the head still is golf's one universal unarguable fundamental."

In the early 1900s, the analysis of Vardon's methods helped spur the development of American golf instruction. Magazines began publishing regular golf instruction articles. The golf fervor spread in 1904 when America's first great player, Walter Travis, stunned the British by winning their amateur championship. With his Schenectady putter, the Old Man put on a masterful display, using the flat stick not only on, but off, the greens, as well as from bunkers when the lie was good and the lip low.

Travis apparently had devised an early scheme utilizing smaller cups on the putting green at Garden City Golf Club, where he practiced until dark. Out on the course, the normal four-and-a-quarter-inch cup looked like a barrel. And one of Travis's main keys to an accelerating putting stroke was to imagine he was driving a tack into the back of the ball with the putterblade. These were classic examples of how practice drills and instructional imagery were starting to develop. Moreover, Travis's inventiveness woke instructors up to an untapped source for getting vital points across to students: the mental side of golf.

In 1916, when the Professional Golfers Association (PGA) of America was founded to introduce golf to the greatest number of individuals, stumbling blocks impeded its goal. For one thing, there were no official practice tees. (They were not introduced on American courses until the twenties.) Consequently, pros walked the course with students, instructing them from shot to shot and hole to hole. Unfortunately, there were drawbacks to the playing lesson, namely, that the student had to perform under the immediate pressure of the golf-course shot and, therefore, could not get into a swing rhythm by repeatedly hitting balls with the same club.

A more pressing problem was the quality of teachers. Although most professionals were themselves fine players, few had the ability to communicate the fundamentals of the setup and swing to students. Worse still, the typical instructor either showed off his skills by hitting shots during the lesson or forced a pupil to learn his idiosyncratic method. Nevertheless, a few good teachers emerged in America; perhaps the best was Alex Smith.

Smith, whose students included Jerry Travers, Walter Hagen, and Glenna Collett Vare, built on a person's inborn strengths and natural tendencies, never forcing a student to adapt to a set method of swinging the club. Smith almost by instinct could spot the weak link in a student's swing, then work on it so effectively and simply that the pupil understood the fault and was thereafter equipped to work on his own. Encouraging golfers to *feel* the movements of the swing so they could repeat a good move or correct a bad one was Smith's trademark.

It was around the same time in 1916 that a young Bobby Jones was modeling his swing after that of his teacher, Stewart Maiden, a man who abhorred "mechanics." Simplicity was the key to his teacher-pupil relationship. Maiden felt that too many maxims in golf instruction only confused pupils. Thus, his simple instruction to swing the club up, down, and through with the hands must have pleased Jones.

Jones was lucky to have Maiden as a model, for the simplicity of his teaching technique and swing discouraged the

Alex Smith, teacher of Jerry Travers, Walter Hagen, and Glenna Collett Vare, among others, had a quick eye for swing faults and an ability to personalize his instruction, never forcing a student to adopt a set method of swinging the club.

Cornishman Jim Barnes won the 1916 and 1919 PGA Championships, then produced his revolutionary book, Picture Analysis of Golf Strokes. Pages such as this one isolated the many intricate movements of the body and enabled the golf swing to be closely studied.

In Golf Fundamentals *(1922), Seymour Dunn provided the first clear
views of what was meant by swing plane, using line overlays to show the
differences among the flat, upright, and correct planes.*

young golfer from theorizing during practice or dawdling over a shot during play. Jones's free, unfettered approach to the swing in turn remains a model to all golfers.

Just before 1920, with golf fever at an ever-increasing pitch, top-class photography came to golf instruction. Jim Barnes, winner of the first two PGA Championships in 1916 and 1919, knew that the human eye was too slow to grasp what was actually happening in the swing. In 1919, he produced the *Picture Analysis of Golf Strokes*, a book that quickly became one of the most widely read instructionals of the day. Featuring full-page photographs of Barnes at key points in the swing, the book revolutionized printed golf instruction. Here was a way of analyzing what actually occurred during the hitting area without depending solely on words to depict the crucial motions. With the large photographs, students could clearly see and recall the correct positions through impact and, theoretically, better understand how to attain them.

By the early twenties, the playing lesson was dying out, chiefly due to the large number of individual and group lessons the better-trained pros were giving on practice tees, which were finally being constructed at courses throughout the country. The first practice tee, named Maniac Hill, opened at Pinehurst, North Carolina, the site of the annual North and South Open and the bailiwick of Donald Ross. The famous golf architect was Pinehurst's head professional and presided over the gathering of other pros as they ex-

changed ideas, experimented with different teaching techniques, and talked about new instruction theories.

In 1922, Seymour Dunn wrote *Golf Fundamentals*, surely the most sophisticated book of its time, for it provided an in-depth study of the swing, including visuals of both flat and upright swing planes.

A year later Ernest Jones, a transplanted English pro, set up the first indoor golf school in New York City. Jones believed that the hands controlled the swing, with the large muscles of the body—upper arms, shoulders, and legs—performing as "admirable followers."

To convey to students the feel of "swinging the clubhead," Jones would attach a handkerchief to a penknife. When he held the hanky at the end and swung the knife back and forth like a pendulum, the hanky stayed taut. When he tried to move the knife through a leverage action, it remained still.

Ernest Jones developed many followers, but it was the other Jones—Bobby—who inspired golfers all over America. In that same year—1923—Bobby won his first major, the U.S. Open.

Jones wrote a meager amount of instructional material during his tournament playing career, and the golf scribes of the day generally seemed more interested in the number of events he won than in how he did it. They glowingly described Jones's motion as "flawless" and "graceful." When Jones was playing his best golf, there was no slow-motion, stop action, or analytical commentary. If there had been, it is

Left:
Ernest Jones, a transplanted Englishman, set up the first indoor golf school in New York City in 1923.

Below:
Ernest Jones was the first to make a strong case for a pure swinging action, a centrifugal-force swing driven by the hands. To make his point, he attached a penknife to a handkerchief and swung the knife back and forth. When he swung it with his hands, the hanky stayed taut, and the knife swung like a pendulum. When he applied any leverage, however, or tried to fight the centrifugal force in any way, the knife remained still.

Opposite:
Shortly after his retirement in 1930, Bobby Jones wrote a number of books and magazine articles and made a series of short instruction films that brought his graceful swing to golfers throughout America.

possible that the average level of golf would have risen considerably.

Jones's retirement ultimately gave him the time to compile all the swing theories and instructions he had learned in works such as *Bobby Jones on Golf* and *Golf Is My Game.* But probably Jones's greatest contribution to the development of instruction came in a series of short teaching films he made in Hollywood in the early thirties. After these were shown at movie theaters around the country, millions of golfers began studying and copying Jones's swing.

The stage was set for a change in equipment that was to have as large an instructional effect on the game as anything ever: the advent of the steel shaft.

Steel did not have as much torque, or twist, as hickory; thus a player truly felt for the first time a "oneness" between the shaft and his left arm as he swung. The club seemed automatically to swing up with the arms instead of around the player's body. This upright plane, as Jack Nicklaus says in *Golf My Way,* "gives the golfer the best chance of swinging the club along the target line at impact."

Another advantage steel had over hickory was this: because the club did not whip as much as with hickory, golfers no longer had to depend quite so much on timing to square the clubface to the ball. Their tempos automatically slowed down, allowing more controlled shots.

The steel shaft truly paved the way for the swing of today, and among the pioneers of the modern, more upright swing, one man stands out: Byron Nelson.

In *Shape Your Swing the Modern Way,* Nelson told of his early experimentation with steel, and how, thankfully, it quieted his hands and allowed him to be more of an arms-legs player. Suddenly, Vardon's dictum, "Golf is all in the hands," together with Ernest Jones's pure swinging motion, applied more to the age of hickory.

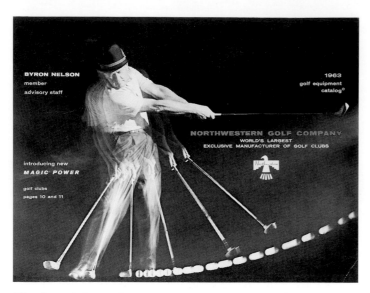

The first of the modern swingers, Byron Nelson led the pros who adapted from hickory to steel shafts.

What became an offshoot of left-sided dominance was the belief in a square left wrist—keeping the back of the left wrist in line with the top of the left forearm on the backswing and follow-through. (More than thirty years later, engineer Homer Kelley in *The Golfing Machine*—a computer-age approach to golfing perfection—reemphasized the square wrist, but renamed it a "flat" wrist. Kelley claimed it kept the clubface trailing, allowing a player to accelerate into impact for maximum power.)

This new key was designed to promote better accuracy, simply because it allowed a player to arrive repeatedly at the same solid, parallel position at the top and to drive the clubface straight through the ball and at the target in the hitting zone. Throughout the forties and fifties, Byron Nelson, Sam Snead, and Ben Hogan proved it worked.

Left-sided theories remained popular until Tommy Armour's best-selling book, *How to Play Your Best Golf All the Time,* entered the marketplace in 1953. Armour's personal

The other major equipment change that took place in the early thirties was the invention of the sand wedge, chiefly brought about by Gene Sarazen. This new club, featuring a bigger flange, revolutionized short-game instruction. Mastering difficult lies around the green could be more easily taught, and these "scoring shots" became less fearsome for the average player. Golfers of below average size and strength, who were incapable of long distance off the tee, could now score as well as, or better than, the big hitters by devoting practice time to finesse shots out of grass or sand.

By the mid-thirties, the golf range business was flourishing. Golfers were busy testing out each new theory, seeing which one suited them. One of these new theories was proposed by Alex Morrison in *A New Way to Better Golf* (1932).

Morrison believed that the key to a true hitting action was in left-side dominance, a swing powered and controlled by the muscles in the left arm, hip, and leg. If the right side were active, he argued, the golfer would lose control and fail to apply the clubface squarely to the back of the ball.

The emphasis of leading from the left grew directly from the steel shaft. American layouts also did not call for as precise a judgment of bounce and roll as did British links. The left-side downswing, which tended to lift the ball higher and quicker than the flatter swing, became *the* shot on America's inland courses, where the wind hardly blew and the greens nearly always held.

Because Bobby Jones, a left-hander playing righty, won the Grand Slam in 1930, it supported Morrison's contention that "golf is a left-handed game for a right-handed man."

Alex Morrison theorized that steel-shafted clubs required a swing powered by the muscles of the left side, especially the left shoulder and arm.

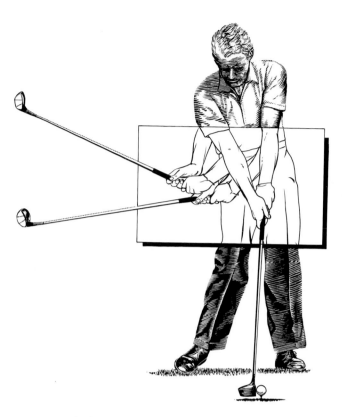

Morrison's method was opposed by Tommy Armour, whose best-selling book, How to Play Your Best Golf All the Time, *claimed left-sided golf was unnatural. The Silver Scot told his disciples to hit the ball hard with the right hand.*

style of writing, for the first time in an instruction book, made readers feel the author was right there, giving instructions. (Ironically, that same year, left-handed players were reading the first book written specifically for them, *Golf for Southpaws* by Henry Gottlieb.)

Armour, a U.S. and British Open champion who possessed unusually large and strong hands, advocated a swing dominated by the right side, specifically, the right hand. The Silver Scot believed that, because the right hand was closer to the clubhead, it should control the swinging action. Moreover, because most individuals are right-handed, Armour stressed it was *unnatural* to lead with the left hand.

Armour's instruction helped many golfers who had silenced the right hand almost completely in trying to adhere to the left-sided theory. But Armour's instruction may have hurt more, for how, his fellow teachers wondered, do you hit it hard with the right hand and still control the shot? Four years later, Ben Hogan was to solve more than that mystery of the swing.

Hogan outdistanced all other theorists, for he had pondered the intricacies of the swing harder than any player and

had mastered them better than any player. The world of golf waited anxiously to read the great man's secrets to a simple, repeating swing and precision shotmaking.

In *Five Lessons: The Modern Fundamentals of Golf,* the second work after *Power Golf,* Hogan told how he discovered that certain long-revered fundamentals were not important at all, while others, often considered secondary, were invaluable, were indeed the true secrets of the golf swing.

Hogan reversed Vardon's emphasis regarding the pressure fingers in the grip by claiming that the pressure should be in the last three fingers of the left hand and in the middle two fingers of the right one, not in the thumb and index fingers of both hands as Vardon had proposed.

Hogan also recommended pointing the toes of the right foot perpendicular to the target line at address, a position, he claimed, that restricted the hip turn (which was at odds with Bobby Jones's ideas on a free hip turn) and increased the backswing to such a degree that Hogan felt his downswing was essentially a reflexive action that *had to happen.*

Hogan also described a key that would turn a hook into a power fade. It involved a roll, or twist, of the hands that

After pondering his swing for years, Ben Hogan revealed his conclusions in Five Lessons: The Modern Fundamentals of Golf. *His greatest contribution to golf instruction may have been the "pane of glass" image, which he used to help show that the arms swing on one plane going back, and on another, slightly less steep, plane coming back down to the ball.*

opened the clubface to the maximum on the backswing. Hogan noted that this roll was called "pronation" and had been taught by the early Scottish professionals who had emigrated to the United States. No matter how hard Hogan "supinated" his wrists on the downswing, the clubface, he argued, could not close fast enough to become absolutely square at the moment of impact. The result: a powerfully hit, controlled, left-to-right shot. (Funnily enough, in 1960 Bobby Jones showed, with the help of a kinesiologist, that by true definition Hogan's pronation and supination theory was "off the wall" because it was impossible for any golfer to employ.)

Hogan's lasting contribution to golf instruction, however, was his image of the swing plane as a "pane of glass." Hogan himself at address visualized this plane tilting from his shoulders down to the ball. And because of this key, on almost every swing as his arms approached hip level on the backswing, they moved parallel with the plane and remained parallel with the plane (just below the glass) to the top of the backswing. On the downswing, Hogan's club dropped into a less steeply inclined plane once he turned his hips back to the left.

Hogan's image was a critical step in the evolution of golf teaching because it "personalized" instruction. Tall people were taught to swing on an upright plane, and shorter people on a less upright plane. Golfers were discouraged from copying other golfers' swings and told instead to swing "their" way. (As inventive as Hogan's pane of glass was, one wonders if he was not influenced by Seymour Dunn, who was the first theorist to review the upright, flat, and correct planes thirty-five years earlier.)

While golfers were busy weighing and practicing the theories of Armour and Hogan, Jack Grout was giving a young Jack Nicklaus lessons on the practice tee of Scioto Country Club in Columbus, Ohio.

Grout taught his pupil the fundamentals of hitting the ball for distance first, knowing that this approach would rid the youngster of any inhibitions. Grout then concentrated on building sound fundamentals, emphasizing a neutral grip, a balanced foundation, and an upright posture at address. In the backswing, Grout advocated a full hip turn, a good extension of the club along the target line in the takeaway, and a parallel position at the top. On the downswing, he told Nicklaus to drive with his legs while maintaining a steady head. Grout ingrained this last fundamental by placing a firm hand on the blond crew cut of his protégé while young Jack took his swing.

Grout viewed the swing as a two-sided affair and de-emphasized the role of the hands. Clearly, Nicklaus heeded

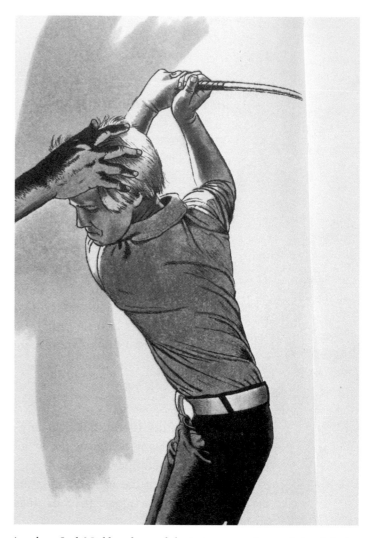

As a boy, Jack Nicklaus learned the importance of a steady head during the swing. His teacher, Jack Grout, ingrained this fundamental by holding a firm hand on Nicklaus's blond crewcut while the youngster hit the ball. Nicklaus later shared the lesson in this illustration from his all-time best-selling book, Golf My Way.

his mentor's advice, for in his classic instruction book, *Golf My Way*, he sarcastically refers to the hands as "limelight huggers." Today Nicklaus still keeps his hands quiet until they reflexively come into action in the hitting area by feeling that they are not moving any faster on the first half of the downswing than they were during the final stage of the backswing.

In the late fifties and early sixties, television showcased the swings of both American and European tournament players. Programs such as Shell's "Wonderful World of Golf" included analyses by Gene Sarazen and tips by players. American golfers were given insights into the swing and into all shot-making departments of the game.

Throughout the sixties and seventies, more professionals became involved in the creation of new methods and simple mental images for communicating the complexities of the golf swing to the average golfer. These methods, in turn, continued to be passed along to the masses of golfers through magazines. Concurrently, an increasing number of instructional golf schools arose. These schools offered consecutive days of intense group instruction, which introduced more families to the game.

In *How to Become a Complete Golfer,* Bob Toski and Jim Flick based their teaching methods on their experiences running the *Golf Digest* instructional schools. In these golf laboratories, working with men and women of all ages, sizes, shapes, and abilities, Toski and Flick proved that the proper way to learn the swing was to start with the short strokes, move on to physical drills for grooving key swing positions, and then enhance shotmaking by learning preswing visualization.

One of the most widely read instruction books to arrive on the modern scene was Carl Lohren's *One Move to Better Golf,* published in 1975. Lohren simplified the swing using this premise: If a player begins the swing by turning his left shoulder inside, the rest of the turn will follow naturally, and the chance of swinging on the correct, inside-square-inside path is greater.

Four years later, in 1979, the first innovative instruction book on the mental side of golf was published: *The Inner Game of Golf* by Timothy Gallwey. Gallwey's "self-one" and "self-two" approach drew attention to the destructive aspects of self-doubt in the learning process. To combat self-doubt, Gallwey taught the pupil to learn in the "awareness mode," to be able to see and feel for himself what was happening. He emphasized that a pupil will not worry about doing something right if his mind is caught up in the process of noting what is happening. When the conscious mind is in touch with the motion of the swing itself, the subconscious mind will allow the body to swing freely and naturally. In Gallwey, golf teachers had an instructor with an acute sensitivity to the learning process of the pupil.

The next of the modern instruction classics, published in 1981, was *How to Perfect Your Golf Swing* by Jimmy Ballard, the teaching director of Doral Country Club in Florida.

As Ballard studied the golf swing, he discovered seven essential movements made by all the great ball strikers: Ben Hogan, Sam Snead, Byron Nelson, Jack Nicklaus, and Seve Ballesteros. These "seven common denominators" became the foundation for his teaching.

Although Ballard and John Jacobs, the famous British instructor, both believe in "swinging" as opposed to "hitting" the ball, their theories are almost diametrically opposite. Whereas Jacobs advocated a definite separation of arms and body, Ballard concentrated on the natural, unified action he found in the great swings. Although he had difficulty at first recognizing and labeling exactly what was responsible for the execution, Ballard eventually identified this action as *connection.*

Jacobs, the author of *Practical Golf,* believed essentially that to swing the club on the proper inside-square-inside path, the arms must swing up and down on a more upright plane than that of the shoulders.

Ballard, by contrast, believed that to swing freely and fully through to the ball, the player's body must work as a team or "connect." To get a student to sense this connection and to feel the seven common denominators working in time, Ballard had him toss a medicine ball or even a shag bag of balls.

Ironically, in 1946, Percy Boomer had written in *On Learning Golf,* "There are a number of *connections* in the swing (such as the wrists and the shoulders) and should any of these connections be broken, should our swing become disjointed, then the feeling of the clubhead cannot be transmitted back to the force—the center."

There is an obvious, clear connection between "right-siders" Boomer and Ballard. "Connection" is the word that describes best the evolution of golf instruction over the past century, for teachers have learned from teachers, players have learned from players, and they all have learned from each other.

Jimmy Ballard's "connection" theory proposed that the golf swing is a unified movement, with the many parts of the body working as a team. To get the feel of this type of swing, Ballard advocated tossing a heavy object, such as a shag bag or a medicine ball.

*Increasingly sophisticated electronic swing analyzers have enabled mod-
ern-day professionals to evaluate their students' swings as never before.*

In most cases, the teachers of the new generation have
improved upon the instruction of the older generation while
adapting to consequent advances in golf equipment. Ernest
Jones ("swing the clubhead with your hands") influenced Bob
Toski ("swing the arms") and John Jacobs ("swing the arms
up as the body turns and swing the arms down as the body
swings through"). Alex Morrison ("left-side dominance is the
number one swing key") influenced Carl Lohren ("turn the
left shoulder inside"). Arnold Haultain, the forerunner of the
mentalists, influenced Timothy Gallwey. The list goes on and
on. There are the occasional mishaps in the evolution of golf
instruction. The biggest flop undoubtedly was *The Square-to-*

Square Golf Swing (1970), written by Dick Aultman, the then
editor of *Golf Digest.*

The major flaw of the square-to-square method, which was
an outgrowth of Alex Morrison's left-side dominance theory,
was the advocacy of a curling under of the left wrist in the
takeaway—a key that led to an overly steep backswing and a
closed clubface position at the top. Unless the player was a
contortionist, he usually returned the clubface to the ball in
an open position and tended to hit high, weak slices. For this
reason, the method was discredited by teachers. John Jacobs
referred to the "American disease," citing a nation of overly
upright swingers.

Above:
For those who have no interest in Jack Nicklaus's swing, it is a simple step to self-tape for home analysis on the video cassette recorder.

Left:
In the past five years there has been a proliferation of instruction videotapes.

Today, the dominant left-side is still around, but Aultman's "square-to-square" has been quietly forgotten.

It would be impossible to review the hundreds—even thousands—of instruction books written to date. That's a shame, for surely hidden somewhere is a nugget of gold that has gone unnoticed, some secret key written down by an obscure author years ago. If that be the case, however, let us not fear, for the track record shows that some teacher or professional of the future will dig it out, turn it into a new theory and produce a book or video promising powerful hits and low scores. True to form, golfers throughout the United States will rush out to purchase this new elixir, because every golfer, from Mr. Average to Jack Nicklaus, longs to master a game that never can be mastered—not now or a hundred years from now.

Chapter TEN Playing Away

In ninety-six years, the first tee at the Homestead has witnessed literally millions of drives.

It is a modest sign, but it is not easily overlooked, and its message comes as something of a surprise to most people at the Homestead Golf Course: "The Number One tee has been in continuous use since 1892. No other tee in the U.S. has been used for a longer period."

Couple that simple fact with another one—two of the five founding clubs of the United States Golf Association were Shinnecock Hills Golf Club and Newport Golf Club—and the message is clear: for about as long as Americans have been playing golf, which is to say for the last hundred years, they have been playing vacation golf.

From Maine to Florida, the East Coast is dotted with places where holiday golf has been played for almost a century. More often than not, it was the spas—Poland Spring, Maine; the Adirondacks' famed Saratoga Springs; Hot Springs, North Carolina; and Magnolia Springs, near Jacksonville, Florida—that seized upon this fashionable new diversion and sparked the growth of the game. The mineral waters were one thing, whether for drinking or bathing, but they were not much fun. Golf was.

In the final decade of the century, golf also gained a foothold along the coasts of Maine (the windswept Tarratine

BY
JIM
FINEGAN

Golf Club at Isleboro commanded the waters of Dark Harbor); of Massachusetts (out on Cape Cod at North Truro on a splendid headland above the Atlantic, the Highland Golf Links opened in 1892); of New York (on one hole on Shelter Island, dubbed Kidd's Treasure, the green was located on a spot where fortune seekers had once dug in hopes of unearthing the notorious pirate's plunder); of New Jersey (at Point Pleasant, at Deal, and at Atlantic City, where, in 1901, Walter J. Travis successfully defended his U.S. Amateur title); of Florida (at Tampa, St. Augustine, Ormond, Palm Beach, and Miami); and of Georgia (where the Rockefellers,

The venerable Pinehurst Hotel and Country Club. From this club-house, the visitor can play 126 holes of golf, including Donald Ross's famed No. 2 course.

Morgans, Goulds, Whitneys, Pulitzers, Goodyears, Vanderbilts, *et al*—in fact, precisely one hundred of the most powerful figures in America—established the Jekyll Island Club).

The game in the East was also played at lakeside (Lake Champlain and Lake Placid, New York) and in the mountains (at Woodstock, Vermont; at Bretton Woods, New Hampshire; and at Stockbridge, in the Berkshires of Massachusetts).

Pinehurst beat the dawn of the new century comfortably when its No. 1 course, sand greens and all, opened for play in 1897. In truth, however, the game itself was an afterthought. James W. Tufts, who had made a fortune manufacturing soda fountains in Boston, bought ten thousand acres of the North Carolina "Pine Barrens" for $7,500 (the seller believed "the rich old Bostonian to have . . . more money than good common sense"). Tufts's plan was to build thousands of homes for those who could no longer endure the rigors of northern winters, selling or renting at rock-bottom prices. Most homes would rent for fifty dollars a year, with some as high as a hundred, depending on location. Tufts never followed through on this philanthropic instinct. Instead, in 1895 he built a great resort hotel, the Berkshire; then, a year later, the Holly Inn; and, in 1898, the Carolina Hotel.

The western part of America, though far distant from the incubators of the game, was not far behind in embracing it. Holiday seekers at Colorado Springs enjoyed golf shortly before the turn of the century. The same was true at the magnificent Hotel del Coronado, where the holes were routed along the shore of San Diego Bay; on the Monterey Peninsula at the Hotel del Monte, which had a course as early as 1893; and, twenty-five miles out in the Pacific Ocean, on Santa Catalina Island.

Top:
Railroads brought the game of golf, and its practitioners, straight down the east coast of Florida to the big hotels. In 1899, the course at Miami's Royal Palm Hotel came equipped with an elevated first tee.

Above:
Near one of America's oldest cities, St. Augustine, were some of America's first golfers. Action here was in the moat of the old Fort Castillo, 1902.

Above left:
Today's architects were not the first to create artificially raised greens. Players needed a ladder to reach this one at the Belleair course in Florida.

Above right:
Exhibition matches brought attention—and guests—to the new hotels. This one at the Biltmore Hotel course in Coral Gables, Florida, pitted Babe Ruth against New York Governor Al Smith.

Railroads frequently played a central role in the development of what might loosely be termed resort golf. The automobile was still several decades away from being a reliable means of long-distance travel, and the horse, for most people, never was such a means. But the train had speed and comfort and availability. One could take it to the Greenbrier and to the Homestead, to the Bon-Air Hotel in Aiken, South Carolina, and, of course, to Florida, which was, purely and simply, a creation of two railroad tycoons.

It was Henry M. Flagler who sent shining steel rails down the Atlantic side of Florida and, as elegant "sidings," erected such landmark resort hotels as the Ponce de Leon at St. Augustine and the Royal Poinciana at Palm Beach. Henry B. Plant laid track down the Gulf Coast to Tampa, Belleair, and St. Petersburg. And perhaps nothing more tellingly illustrates the importance of golf to these rival magnates than the posts held by two immigrant Scottish-born greenkeepers. Alex Findlay served as "golfer-in-chief" for Flagler's Florida East Coast Railroad. In this capacity he designed and built the original courses at St. Augustine Country Club, Ponce de Leon Golf Club, Ormond Country Club, Palm Beach Country Club, and the Miami Golf Links. His opposite number, John Duncan Dunn, held the same post on Plant's Florida West Coast Railroad, leaving his mark on Belleair Golf Club, Coral Gables Golf Club, Oscala Golf Club, and

Tampa Bay Golf Club. It was a fruitful marriage, this union of the train and the game, for, of course, passengers and players were one and the same.

During 1900–1918, the game appeared to be marking time after its lively start. The excellent Ekwanok in Vermont's Green Mountains opened for play in 1900, and Charles Blair Macdonald's landmark National Golf Links at Southampton, New York, bowed in 1911. But both these vacation courses were private. Donald Ross, who had learned his craft on the links of Royal Dornoch in the far north of Scotland, designed and built a number of courses in the eastern part of the country during the first two decades of the century that were open to the traveler: Wentworth by the Sea at Portsmouth, New Hampshire; the Inn at Buck Hill Falls in Pennsylvania's Pocono Mountains; the No. 2 and No. 3 courses at his beloved Pinehurst; and the Bellevue Biltmore at Clearwater, Florida.

The lull that had marked course construction from 1900 through World War I suddenly gave way to a bona fide boom. In 1916, there had been only 742 courses in the United States; by 1923, this number had more than doubled to 1,903. At the end of the decade, there were about 5,700 courses throughout the country. So far as holiday golf was concerned, the Roaring Twenties were precisely that, with at least a dozen truly great resorts vying for the American golfer's patronage.

Chronologically speaking, the West led the way. In 1918, several months before the Armistice, a renegade Philadelphian named Spencer Penrose unveiled his magnificent Broadmoor Hotel in Colorado Springs. He had struck gold in Cripple Creek, Colorado, and parlayed this pile into even greater wealth via copper in Utah, forming Kennecott Copper. Then he erected the Broadmoor. For the grand opening, he hauled a trainload of the rich and celebrated from New

In 1918, the Broadmoor opened in Colorado Springs, Colorado, complete with a Donald Ross golf course. Two courses have since been added.

York and Chicago to his barony. What greeted his guests when they stepped down from their Pullman cars in the foothills of the Rockies was a structure of pale pink stone nine stories in height and Italian Renaissance in style. The accommodations were grand luxe and the cuisine appropriately *haute*. Donald Ross had routed a delightful course through maple, pine, aspen, and spruce. In the years that lay ahead, architect Robert Trent Jones would add eighteen holes and so would the team of Arnold Palmer and Ed Seay. Penrose's stated objective for the Broadmoor was simplicity itself: "I want it to be permanent and perfect."

It is entirely possible that no such aim motivated Samuel F. B. Morse, grandnephew of the inventor. Still, we must applaud the memory of the man who decided that instead of selling the majestic headlands above Carmel Bay for building lots, he would reserve this terrain for a golf course. His legacy is the well-nigh peerless series of holes—6, 7, 8, 9, 10, 17,

and 18—at Pebble Beach. For the American golfer, no destination outranks Pebble Beach. Every wood-topping, iron-shanking, putt-yipping, mulligan-demanding mother's son must, at least once before the biggest divot of all is carefully laid in place upon him, play Pebble. He does not have to stay at the Del Monte Lodge, which was built in 1919 to take care of the spillover from the glamorous Hotel del Monte and is now itself one of the premier inns of the world. However, the golfer must square off against those ferociously intimidating holes high above the Pacific and hurry home to tell about it. And in the telling, he may also be forgiven for taking a perverse pride in reporting that the round required five hours and cost $125.

Down in Phoenix there is a renowned and rather unusual golf resort from this Golden Age. Three MacArthur brothers and the most important American architect of the twentieth century are responsible for the Arizona Biltmore. Charles and Warren MacArthur were determined to build the resort. They commissioned their brother Albert to design it. Albert, who had studied under Frank Lloyd Wright, sought the master's permission to use the ornamental block-style construction that Wright had created for a California house. Not only did Wright grant permission, he also agreed to become a consultant on the project. And, indeed, he was clearly its inspiriting force. Strikingly evocative of the richness and strength and beauty of this country of mountain and desert, the Arizona Biltmore owes no debt to a foreign culture. Like Wright, it is quintessentially American. The golfer can choose between the longer, flatter, more open Adobe course and the much younger (1976) and shorter Links layout, with its hills, narrow fairways, and five water holes.

Meanwhile, back in the last century, two *grande dame* resorts were shaping a rivalry that would redound for decades to the benefit of their respective guests.

Hot Springs, Virginia, has been welcoming people seeking the curative powers of its mineral waters since 1766, ten years before the birth of the nation. Among the guests of the first hotel to be called the Homestead were George Washington, Alexander Hamilton, and Thomas Jefferson.

The original Homestead course, built in 1892, was on the primitive side. During the summer, the 180-yard, downhill tenth could be reached simply by putting from the hilltop tee and letting the ball roll down the clean-shaven rock-hard fairway to the green. Nevertheless, this course was crowded. So much so that in 1923 William Flynn, who only a year earlier had designed Denver's Cherry Hills, was commissioned to lay out the Cascades course (sometimes referred to as the Upper Cascades to distinguish it from the Robert Trent Jones Lower Cascades, built in 1963), which is regarded by many as America's finest mountain course. No two holes are even remotely similar; Swift Run Stream gives pause on eight of the eighteen; and the subtly sloping fairways require precisely placed tee shots to have a reasonable chance of hitting the greens in regulation.

In White Sulphur Springs, West Virginia, golf came into its own at the Greenbrier in 1914 with the completion of the eighteen-hole Old White Course, designed by Charles Blair Macdonald. The nine-hole Lakeside Course had been built in 1910. In the mid-twenties, a second eighteen, the Greenbrier Course, opened for play. Fifty years later, Jack Nicklaus converted this layout into a true championship test for the 1979 Ryder Cup Match.

Sam Snead caddied at the Cascades, developed his game there, then left in 1936 to become the Greenbrier's teaching professional. More than forty years later he returned to the Homestead.

Built in 1919 to accommodate the spillover from the then glamorous Hotel del Monte, the Del Monte Lodge at Pebble Beach is now one of the premier inns in the world.

The entrance to the Arizona Biltmore, as it appeared in 1929.

The Homestead, in Hot Springs, Virginia, has been welcoming guests since 1766.

Not all that far south of these two great mountain spas is the Cloister, a Georgia seaside resort founded in 1928 by a Detroit industrialist who never played golf. Howard Coffin believed the game to be a waste of time. His principal interest lay in the creation of a resort where his friends would feel at home—among them were Calvin Coolidge, Herbert Hoover, and Charles Lindbergh—and golf, he conceded, would probably not get in the way at Sea Island.

It is not easy to say whether, during the Depression, golf at the Cloister was an albatross or a life preserver. The rates would seem ludicrously low even multiplied by ten today—they were $13 a day for two people, all meals included. And for just a dollar a day, a guest was permitted to play all the golf and tennis he or she wanted and to pedal one of the hotel's bicycles from dawn till dusk. There are fifty-four holes (in 1986, when *GOLF Magazine* chose the one hundred best golf

The Greenbrier course was redesigned by Jack Nicklaus in 1979, just in time for the Ryder Cup Matches.

holes in America, the 382-yard fourth on the Seaside Nine made the list).

Hewing to the coast and continuing 374 miles due south is yet another of the great resort hotels built in the twenties. But at this one, there is nothing muted, nothing understated. The Breakers' facade and twin towers were inspired by the Villa Medici in Florence. The lobby, with its intricately decorated vaulted ceiling, was modeled after the great hall in a Genoese palazzo. Fifteenth-century Flemish tapestries adorn the walls, and the fountain in the hotel's forecourt is patterned after one in the Boboli Gardens of Florence.

The Ocean course, where one has the curious feeling of playing on the hotel's front lawn, is an oft-remodeled Donald Ross design. But it is perhaps too short and sweet. The player who normally struggles to break a hundred will clasp it to his bosom. Out Okeechobee Boulevard is the Breakers West, which measures 6,348 yards from the white tee and a little over seven thousand yards from the blue, and where a dunking awaits the unwary on eleven holes.

The Depression and World War II added up to fifteen years in which golf course construction virtually came to a standstill. Further, between 1932 and 1952 there was actually a net loss in the number of courses in play. Only twenty new courses were built, whereas about six hundred closed forever.

So far as vacation courses were concerned, it would not be easy to name three of any distinction that were created during this drought. One that does come to mind, however, is a reflection of America's sweet tooth and the deep pockets of one man, Milton S. Hershey.

The Hershey Country Club's West Course opened in 1930. Little premium is placed on putting. It is consistently sound ball striking that must be summoned, because thirty-yard-wide fairways, seventeen thousand trees, and 117 bunkers leave virtually no margin for error. The Pennsylvania Open has been played there seventeen times. The Lady Keystone Open, an LPGA Tour event, is staged there annually. Over on the East Course, which George Fazio designed in the late sixties, wasted strokes are all too common on the boldly contoured putting surfaces.

The traveling golfer has the choice of staying at either the country club itself or at the Hotel Hershey, which is Spanish Renaissance in style, very grand indeed, and strongly suggestive of Addison Mizner's Palm Beach palazzos.

The recession of 1949–50 followed by the outbreak of the Korean War in 1951 had a dampening effect on course construction, but there was a golfer in the White House ("I like Ike" was the national consensus), and in the last eight years of the decade, an average of a hundred new courses came on-stream annually. And a number of them were de-

The fourth hole of the Cloister's Seaside Nine, a 382-yard par four across White Heron Creek. In 1986, GOLF Magazine *named this hole one of the 100 best in America.*

signed to attract vacationers, who took full advantage of the new interstate highways that made three-hundred-mile driving days easy.

Go back to the dunes of St. Andrews in the sixteenth and seventeenth centuries and you find sand an integral element of the game. But not when it comes in desert-size quantities. For grass has never grown thickly in the desert, at least not until the early 1950s in California's Palm Springs area. First came the Thunderbird course. Then Tamarisk, Indian Wells, El Dorado, and La Quinta.

The La Quinta Hotel—La Quinta means "Country House"—had opened its doors in 1926. Over the years the likes of Clark Gable, Katharine Hepburn, Ginger Rogers, Bette Davis, Errol Flynn, and Greta Garbo have relished its

charming seclusion. It is the hideaway that inspired Frank Capra's *It Happened One Night,* and it now belongs to Landmark Land Company, Inc., one of the movers and shakers, which is to say earth movers and earth shakers, of Palm Springs today. For it is the spectacular new desert courses, most of which are open to the public, that the world is so eager to play.

It would appear that Pete Dye's fantasies have made the biggest impact. At La Quinta Hotel Golf Club, his Dunes Course (water, railroad ties, sand dunes, natural desert vegetation), Mountain Course (water, railroad ties, rockscapes), and Lodge Course (water, railroad ties, clusters of citrus and date trees) are all scandalously beautiful and replete with drama.

One of the grande dames of Florida resort life, the Breakers Hotel.

Action at the ninth green of the Hershey Country Club shortly after it opened in 1930. The course has hosted seventeen Pennsylvania Opens and is the annual site of an LPGA Tour event.

Not since the Haskell ball replaced the gutta percha in the first decade of this century has a single development had as much impact on the game as has the jet aircraft. Suddenly, astonishingly, every golf course on the planet was accessible. The whole wide world of golf was there for the taking. The sixties marked the beginning of what has, with only an occasional recessionary pause, been a case of onward and upward in golf travel. New courses were opening in the United States at the rate of four hundred a year during this first full decade of the jet age.

Once winter sets in, Northeasterners have always been partial to Florida. Their attitude toward Florida resort courses has, however, frequently been somewhat condescending. The Bay Hill Club and Lodge, which opened in late 1960 with, as its centerpiece, a very good Dick Wilson course, quickly won the attention and respect of these fugitives from the frozen greens of Winged Foot and Baltusrol and Oakmont. This Orlando layout has a number of memorable holes, the perilous par-three seventeenth and par-four eighteenth, both over water, being two of the finest holes not only in Florida but in the entire country. One other aspect of Bay Hill is worth noting: It is Arnold Palmer's domain. He revised

Rockscape—an integral element of Pete Dye's Mountain Course at the La Quinta Hotel. This is the par-three sixteenth hole.

Above:
Doral Country Club, where millionaire Alfred Kaskel converted 2,400 acres of Florida swampland into one of the country's most popular golf resorts. This is the treacherous eighteenth hole at the Blue Monster course, host of the Doral Open each winter.

Right:
Part of a four-hole panorama at Williamsburg's Golden Horseshoe that may be the most arresting moment in golf course architecture.

and strengthened the Wilson layout. And there is a nicely masculine feeling about the place that evokes the image of its proprietor. Here, early each spring, the best players in the world assemble for the Bay Hill Classic.

Another celebrated Florida golf resort opened not a year after Bay Hill. It, too, is a stop on the PGA Tour.

Mr. Kaskel's name was Alfred, Mrs. Kaskel's Dora. *Voilà*— Doral!

A man who trusted his instincts—he had not made $200 million in New York real estate by shilly-shallying—he never hesitated when he had the chance to buy the great fountain from the 1964 New York World's Fair and install it at the entrance to Doral. Kaskel, a self-professed "golf nut," came to Florida in the late fifties, turned his back on Miami Beach and bought 2,400 acres of the flattest, swampiest, least prepossessing land in Dade County, out rather near the Miami Airport. He then set to work fashioning "the finest golf resort the world has ever seen." Whether he and his successors ever quite scaled this lofty peak is perhaps a moot point, but Doral is, at the very least, a humdinger of a golf resort and internationally renowned as such.

For a study in contrasts, we turn to Virginia's monument to the eighteenth century, the Williamsburg Inn. By no stretch of the imagination can the Williamsburg Inn be considered a golf resort. Still, just beyond its south terrace, play commences on a course that, for a quarter of a century, has

remained some observers' favorite among the hundreds by Robert Trent Jones that dot the globe.

Set on only 125 acres, the Golden Horseshoe is a succession of holes ranging from very good to superlative, and at the heart of it is perhaps the most audacious moment in golf course architecture. Is there anything that even remotely compares with the scene that stops the golfer dead in his tracks as, for the first time, he crests the fairway on the par-five second hole, uncertain of the location of the green? Then he spots it, on the far side of a generous lake whose very existence comes as an enormous surprise, the green a mere shelf in the steep bank plunging down to the water. But this green is scarcely alone. To its right is the putting surface of the one-shotter twelfth, which likewise traverses the water. To the right of the twelfth is the par-three sixteenth, played from a high bluff to an island green near the opposite shore. And when the flabbergasted player looks to his left, there, on the far hill is the tee of the par-three seventh, which also plays fully across the lake, in the same general direction as the sixteenth but to a well-bunkered green on the opposite hill. It is impossible to take it all in. The eye is confounded. The concept is stupendous. And, what is most important, amidst all the beauty and the drama are four outstanding golf holes, each making reasonable demands on the swing, none in the least gimmicky.

Mention Williamsburg and one thinks instinctively of the Rockefellers. They were the force behind this unique re-creation. Charles E. Fraser, an avowed conservationist, possessed neither the famous name nor the attendant millions, but he did have energy and will and vision. In the late fifties, he took control of the somewhat shaky Sea Pines Company on Hilton Head Island, just off the South Carolina mainland, and set out to create a vacation community for people of means. No fast-food outlets and high-rise concrete condominiums would litter his landscape, and he reserved the right of approval on any home to be built within the Sea Pines

There is arguably more good golf packed into the various compounds of Hilton Head Island, South Carolina, than at any other resort destination in the world. This is the fifteenth hole at the Sea Pines Plantation's Ocean Course.

Set in the hills of Carlsbad, California, La Costa offers thirty-six holes of honest golf and a luxurious spa to go with it. This is the seventh hole of the South Course, home of the PGA Tour's annual Tournament of Champions.

Plantation. Fraser once spent $50,000 to transplant a giant oak that was endangered by a road construction project, and he regularly fed the local alligators raw meat to keep them from fleeing the island as it was being developed.

Less than thirty years ago there was not a golf course on Hilton Head. Today, there are twenty-one courses, many of them private, at least as many open to the public. Among the latter is the celebrated Harbour Town Golf Links. No course in anyone's memory had "greatness" conferred upon it quite so abruptly as this Pete Dye–Jack Nicklaus design, which called for finesse instead of muscle, which featured railroad ties bulwarking the ponds, which was routed through thick stands of pine, oak, elm, and palmetto, and which finally broke free of all that foliage to finish in full view of beautiful Calibogue Sound.

One may reasonably argue that within the rather confined territory of Hilton Head Island there is more first-rate golf than in any comparable-size area in the world. But no more golf courses will be built on Hilton Head, for there is no more room. Of course, there is the nearby mainland and the occasional "islet," such as five-thousand-acre Daufuskie, off

the southwest tip of Hilton Head. Two courses, one by Rees Jones, the other by Nicklaus, have recently opened. In the age of the supersonic Concorde, it is curiously comforting to learn that both these excellent eighteens are accessible only by boat.

Accessibility is scarcely La Costa's problem. Located in Carlsbad, California, it is ninety miles from Los Angeles, thirty miles from San Diego, a very short spin from glamorous La Jolla, and less than an hour from Disneyland. And it modestly proclaims itself to be "one of the world's two great resorts." The identity of the other great resort remains a mystery.

And yes, of course, there is golf on this seven-thousand-acre preserve, with its five hundred rooms, numerous villas, and, for those who want to own a home, condominiums. The Tournament of Champions is played here. Both of La Costa's eighteens are excellent, with turf of a quality to rival the finest private club's. The North, longer and more rolling, has plenty of water and sand. The South's principal challenge stems from its narrow fairways and a stern final four holes that play into the prevailing breezes. There are no tricks, no caprices; it is all classic and honest.

The fiftieth state, 3,300 miles at sea, has more than its share of striking Pacific Ocean vistas. Besides, the days are predictably glorious in Hawaii, the one golf destination above all others that owes its very existence to the development of the jet aircraft. For not only are these islands magnetic to Californians and Oregonians and Coloradans, they are also irresistible to droves of Pennsylvanians and New Yorkers and Michiganders and Illini. Hawaii is paradise here and now.

There are two big problems facing the player on a Hawaiian odyssey: where to begin and how to stop. On Oahu the more challenging layouts can be found at the Sheraton Makaha and the Turtle Bay Hilton (a tough, beautiful George Fazio design), Waialae (a private club that is the perennial venue for the Hawaiian Open), and the Pearl Country Club, which affords spectacular views of Pearl Harbor. On Maui the best golf seems to come in pairs: the Kapalua Golf Club's Bay and Village courses, Royal Kaanapali's North and South eighteens, and the Orange and Blue courses at Wailea Golf Club. Over on the island of Kauai, Robert Trent Jones, Jr., has fashioned a testing and beautiful layout at Kiahuna Plantation. He also has designed three separate and distinctive nines at Princeville, highlighted by the much photographed par-three third on the Ocean nine, where the golfer plays a middle to short iron from the top of the world in the general direction of the often mist-shrouded mountain that Joshua Logan used as Bali Hai in his film version of *South Pacific.* Which leads to the Big Island of Hawaii, where among

Carved from a solid bed of Hawaiian lava, spectacular Mauna Lani puts a premium on accuracy.

the lures are the spectacular Mauna Lani Keauhou-Kona (overlooking Keauhou Bay), Waikoloa Beach (water, sand, lava), Waikoloa Village (mountain panoramas), and, yes, Mauna Kea.

For despite the number of superb golf resorts that have been built on Hawaii during recent years, the *grande dame* of them all continues to be the one that Laurance Rockefeller created almost a quarter century ago.

Located on what was then considered the remote northwestern coast of the Big Island, the hotel at Mauna Kea is, architecturally, uncompromisingly contemporary, but there is nothing minimalist about it. As witness the interior tropical gardens and courtyards, and an extraordinary collection of art and religious objects that reflects the culture of the Orient and the archipelago.

One question, however, might well be asked: Is the golf as good as all the rest of it? The answer is a simple, unequivocal

yes. For this is the old master, Robert Trent Jones, at the peak of his powers. And despite the undeniable majesty of this setting above the Pacific, the task of creating a great course was not easy. Not when you realize that the holes were actually laid out on a five-thousand-year-old lava flow from the great extinct volcano, Mauna Kea, a wasteland so arid that only scattered cacti were growing.

Among the many superlative holes are two of the surpassing par threes of the world. The third hole is Jones's answer to Alister Mackenzie's peerless sixteenth at Cypress Point, with the tee perched on a promontory of black volcanic rock that juts thirty feet into the ocean and the surging Pacific separating the green from the tee. The eleventh is even more rigorous. Off a very high tee, the shot—a drive of 198 yards from the regular tee and generally into the wind—is played to a narrow and subtly crowned green far below against the backdrop of the Pacific.

Mauna Kea, designed by Robert Trent Jones over a quarter-century ago, remains Hawaii's quintessential golf course and resort.

Courses were built at a record-breaking clip in the 1960s. Costs of land, construction, and financing were attractive then. By the mid-seventies, with inflation taking its toll, these costs were soaring. More often than not, new courses were the heart of either a real estate development or a resort. And in the latter instance, renowned skiing centers in both the East and the West caught the golf bug, turning to the royal and ancient game as a means of keeping substantial hotel investments generating income year round and, at the same time, spurring the sale of the obligatory condominiums.

If someone mentions Killington, Woodstock, Mt. Snow, Stowe, Stratton, or Sugarbush, the instant image is of stem Christies and moguls and schussing. In fact, however, each of these Vermont ski resorts is now blessed with first-rate golf courses. And each of these courses is as pretty a place to play as you are likely to find anywhere (the view from the third green at Stowe of Mount Mansfield, Vermont's tallest peak, is

unforgettable). And each course is a solid test. Geoffrey Cornish's fine eighteen at Mt. Snow, with water on eleven holes, has been the site of the New England PGA Championship and the New England Open.

Fly two thousand miles due west out of Dixville Notch and, in the Colorado Rockies, the same word game will produce the same results and for the same reasons. Vail, Aspen, Breckenridge, Winter Park, Crested Butte—these skiing shrines are the homes of a galaxy of splendid courses by Pete Dye, Jack Nicklaus, Robert Trent Jones, Jr., and the team of Ron Kirby and Gary Player. The Vail Golf Club, which opened in 1969, is the granddaddy of them all. And it was Dye who had the honor of designing America's highest course, this one, at Copper Mountain, 9,600 feet above sea level.

Having come this far, we ought to explore a bit more of the West and Northwest. In the heart of central Oregon's high

The Vermont resorts are best known for skiing, but a fall golf excursion to Stowe is a beautiful experience.

Set in a valley in the Colorado Rockies, the Vail Golf Course is itself relatively flat, but its surrounding terrain is impressive.

The spectacular Sunriver Lodge and Resort in the heart of central Oregon's high desert country offers two excellent courses.

desert country, near Bend, is the spectacular Sunriver Lodge and Resort, which offers two excellent courses. The North course has three times been the site of the Oregon Open.

Over on the coast at Gleneden Beach is Salishan Lodge, a series of ground-hugging buildings in natural wood set among fir, hemlock, spruce, and cedar on a bluff commanding Siletz Bay. Each of the 150 rooms features a balcony that looks either to the bay or the golf course and contains a wood-burning fireplace. As for the golf course, it is a pure delight—rolling, with framing pines often giving way to exquisite views of both bay and ocean, the par-three eleventh and par-four thirteenth tight along the bay.

Continue north into Washington to Puget Sound and The Resort at Port Ludlow, twenty-eight miles from Seattle. Carved from a dense forest, its narrow, doglegging fairways are flanked by towering firs. Meandering streams empty into crystalline natural lakes. Many of the greens are huge, some fifty yards in length, but the bunkering is light. Despite the challenge, it is not easy to keep one's mind on the business at hand. For to the west lie the magnificent Olympic Mountains; to the east, snowcapped Mount Baker; below, Puget Sound, studded with hundreds of pleasure craft. And there are times when, dead ahead, as you are about to lace a tee shot, a doe and her fawns will cross the fairway.

California's Monterey Peninsula, site of Pebble Beach and Cypress Point, is also home to sixteen other courses, seven of them open to the public, including the altogether splendid Spyglass Hill. An excellent Pete Dye course opened in 1981 at the Carmel Valley Ranch Golf Club, but it is Robert Trent Jones, Jr., who is chiefly responsible for the two most recent additions to the Peninsula's collection. Strongly suggestive of the British links courses, treeless Spanish Bay is fully exposed to the sea and the wind. At Poppy Hills, fairways wind through the tall pines of the Del Monte Forest. Its creator describes it as "an outdoor sculpture in tune with the eco-system of the forest." On that note, perhaps we would be well advised to proceed in a southeasterly direction, where golf resorts seem to be blooming like flowering cacti in the desert.

The Phoenix-Scottsdale area boasts ten golf resorts, including Camelback (guests enjoy two very good eighteens and lovely adobe *casitas* spotted among the strikingly land-scaped grounds) and Rancho de los Caballeros (long known as a dude ranch, this twenty-thousand-acre resort in Wicken-burg offers testing and very beautiful golf). In Tucson, the Sheraton Tucson El Conquistador is that rarity in the desert, a genuinely rolling layout marked by gullies and ravines. At Tucson National, Bruce Devlin and Bob Von Hagge re-designed the course, improving it markedly. And Tom Fazio's fine new eighteen at the Ventana Canyon Golf and Racquet

The Resort at Port Ludlow, near Seattle, was carved from dense forest, its narrow, doglegged fairways flanked by towering firs.

Club in the foothills of the Catalina Mountains is forcing the long-established resorts to sit up and take notice.

Three hours' drive south of Albuquerque is the unique Inn of the Mountain Gods. It is the jewel of the 460,000-acre Mescalero Apache Indian Reservation. The Indians own it, it provides jobs for many of the tribe members, and it is profitable. The beautiful Ted Robinson course winds through a forest in the very shadow of the snow-capped Sierra Blanca Peak. Most of the Inn's rooms overlook Lake Mescalero.

Let's head east, pausing in the heartland for a couple of stops that are much appreciated by the golfers of Chicago and Milwaukee and Detroit and Kansas City and St. Louis but are perhaps little known to the rest of America.

Wisconsin's Americana Lake Geneva Resort targets the business meetings market, and its two outstanding golf courses make that "afternoon free for recreation" particularly enjoyable. Clearly a child of its time, the Brute, which opened in 1968, is long and tough, with huge greens and more than its share of water. The Briarpatch, three years younger, marked the end of the brief collaboration between Pete Dye and Jack Nicklaus. It is shorter than the Brute, its greens tend to be small, its rough heavy and dotted with heather.

About 170 miles from both St. Louis and Kansas City lies Lake of the Ozarks, which boasts 1,300 miles of shoreline. Marriott's Tan-Tar-A Resort and Golf Club, quite possibly the finest major resort in the Midwest, was built on three spits of land poking into the south central part of the lake. The

Bruce Devlin-Bob Von Hagge course here is hilly, heavily bunkered, tight, and, like most of this team's work, studded with water hazards. Over at the Four Seasons Lodge and Country Club, where a five-story waterfall cascades through the main building and the noted watercolorist Buffy Murai has created a very fetching Japanese garden, Robert Trent Jones has laid out a marvelous course over hill and dale and, of course, water. The thirteenth is a very long par three with a forced water carry followed by a forced sand carry to a plateau green. The tiered bunkering climbing the slope beyond the inlet is distinctly reminiscent of the tiered bunkering at Pine Valley's home green. There is nothing wrong with this kind of reminiscing.

Unlike Lake of the Ozarks, Myrtle Beach *is* a byword among golfers. Not that every golfer has made the pilgrimage to this corner of South Carolina, but every golfer knows that there is a well-nigh inexhaustible supply of courses there, forty-four at last count (only occasionally encumbered by such precious names as Possum Trot, Raccoon Run, Deer Track, Gator Hole, and Robbers Roost). And although there may be a couple of other places in the world with more golf courses per square mile, Myrtle Beach is surely the only place where, simply by checking into a hotel or a motel or a condominium, the golfer can exercise his personal choice of more than forty satisfying eighteens. For if Myrtle Beach is not the golf capital of the world, it is, at the very least, the "golf package" capital of the world. The Grand Strand is a grand collaboration between the innkeepers and the course owners, with the result that virtually no course is off limits.

Perhaps the second-most golf-rich sector of the East Coast is at Cape Cod, where twenty-two courses are open to the traveling golfer. A spurt in course construction came about in the 1970s and 1980s, and it is these more recent designs that have captured the fancy of the vacationer. Cranberry Valley (1974), Dennis Highland (1984), the Captains Golf Course at Brewster (1985), Ocean Edge, also at Brewster and totally redesigned in 1985, are all first-rate. And the Country Club of New Seabury, with its Green and Blue eighteens, has, in the Blue, one of America's outstanding seaside tests. The first nine in particular, essentially treeless and characterized by vast sandy stretches and tracts of marshland, plays tight along Nantucket Sound. Fully exposed to the winds off the water, it is marvelously evocative of the game in its birthplace on the shores of Scotland.

Rawly beautiful Spanish Bay on the Monterey Peninsula, probably the last golf course that will be designed directly along the California coastline.

The basic vacation question is age-old and unanswerable: seashore or mountains? In the Northeast, for every Cape Cod aficionado there must surely be a Pocono Mountains devotee. In these modest hills—the tallest peak tops out at 2,220 feet—there are a dozen courses, including good ones at Tamiment (Wayne Newton, a long way from his Las Vegas home, owns it); the Shawnee Inn (twenty-seven holes at this resort, which for many years was the property of another pop music figure, Fred Waring and today is a bastion of the time-sharing trend); Buck Hill Falls (twenty-seven very hilly, very beautiful, and rather easy holes); Pocono Manor (the only area resort with thirty-six holes and the one where long-time professional Art Wall accounted for thirty-eight of his forty-odd holes-in-one); and the Mount Airy Lodge, where the course took eleven years to build and the result was worth it. This is serious golf at Mount Airy, and at the very outset, the battle is joined: the first hole is 541 yards uphill, with bunkers pinching the fairway in the landing area and a large pond cutting off easy access to the green. Think of the last time you played solidly *uphill* only to arrive at a pond.

Heading south from the Poconos, some eleven hours' drive later, is North Carolina. A new string of courses has sprung

The Sheraton El Conquistador in Tucson is an exceptionally interesting desert course.

New Mexico's Inn of the Mountain Gods is a jewel set in a 460,000-acre Indian reservation.

Above:
Marriott's Tan-Tar-A Resort and Golf Club on Lake of the Ozarks is one of the finest major resorts in the Midwest.

Right:
Island greens are numerous along Myrtle Beach's Grand Strand. This one is at the Heritage Golf Club and Plantation, one of forty-four courses available at this golf mecca.

up along the southern coast at Kitty Hawk (marvelous links at the Sea Scape Golf Club), New Bern (Fairfield Harbour has lateral water on half the holes), Sunset Beach (the new Oyster Bay Golf Links has already established itself in the highest echelon of American courses), and Hampstead (Belvedere Plantation on the Intracoastal Waterway is tight and testing).

Inland, North Carolina has too many outstanding venues to count, ranging from the delightful old courses at the Grove Park Inn in Asheville and the High Hampton Inn in Cashiers to the exhilarating newer eighteens at Hound Ears Lodge in Blowing Rock and Holly Forest in Sapphire, where Ron Garl has fashioned several of the most thrilling golf holes anywhere.

And then there is the king of all mid-South golf resorts, Pinehurst. Never content to rest on its laurels, and despite a couple of disconcerting changes in ownership over more recent years, Pinehurst today is simply better than ever. More and better. Now there are seven eighteens, four of them good; two of them (No. 6 and No. 7) superb; one (No. 2) great.

It was in 1979, not long after Tom Fazio fashioned Pinehurst No. 6, that another Carolina resort, Wild Dunes in South Carolina, nominated him to work his wizardry on the Isle of Palms, just off the coast and only fifteen miles from Charleston. Palms, magnolias, and great moss-draped oaks shade the beautifully undulating fairways as they meander through giant sand dunes and saltwater marshes. The breezes

Sunset at the Country Club at New Seabury, Massachusetts, one of America's finest seaside tests.

and the bunkers—some of the lethal pot variety—provide a continuous test. The last two holes play beside the ocean, with the surf and the sand and the long bents a powerful reminder of the game's origins. Indeed, *GOLF Magazine's* list of the hundred best courses in the world includes the Links at Wild Dunes. And then, almost predictably, the resort asked Fazio to do it again. The result is the Harbor course, the second nine of which begins at the Wild Dunes Yacht Harbor. The front nine is short and tight, much of it skirting what some contend is the world's longest water hazard, the Intracoastal Waterway. The back nine is long and tight, perhaps not as confined as the front, but far from open. This is target golf of the highest order, yet control and finesse are not enough. Raw power is also essential. Is the Harbor course too hard? For all but the top-class player, yes, but it is such splendid stuff that its rigors must be forgiven.

In the last fifteen years, Georgia has come into its own as a golf destination. Along the coast, in addition to the timeless and elegant Cloister at Sea Island, there is first-rate golf in the same neighborhood at the Sea Palms Golf and Tennis Resort. An hour north is the beautiful Sheraton Savannah Resort and Country Club (an excellent old Donald Ross course that Willard Byrd updated in the mid-sixties) and The Landings on Skidaway Island, a community of primary homes with four eighteens that are consistently among the best conditioned in the state. Inland are golf resorts that draw players from all over the East: Callaway Gardens at Pine Mountain, with three very scenic eighteens plus a nine-hole executive course; and Pine Isle on Lake Lanier, where Tommy Aaron heads the golf staff.

Alabama, though scarcely overrun with golf resorts, points with considerable pride to Marriott's Grand Hotel at Point Clear. In the latter part of the nineteenth century, the Grand was a posh gathering place for the well-to-do, who frequently arrived for the season with servants in tow. During World War II, the army used the Grand as a training headquarters.

Gene Sarazen rolling a long one during the 1938 PGA Championship at Shawnee. The imposing inn in the Pocono Mountains of Pennsylvania is now a successful time-share resort.

All soldiers were required to remove their boots before entering the hotel to prevent damage to the handsome old pine floors.

The thirty-six holes are the work of Perry Maxwell (the original eighteen), Joe Lee (nine holes in a pine forest, with a number of stately homes overlooking the fairways), and Ron Garl (the newest and most dramatic nine). At the Grand, the game is enjoyed in the atmosphere of a private club, where—marvel of marvels—no tee times are required!

The wandering golfer is not likely to bump into such a happy circumstance often in Florida. Starting times are a way of life, at least in season. The Sunshine State is, of course, the No. 1 golf destination. South Carolina and Arizona rank second and third, respectively. But more than twice as many people visit Florida for golf as visit the other two states combined. Indeed, Florida sometimes strikes one as a vast proliferation of golf courses loosely strung together by ribbons of concrete. From the three beautiful Pete Dye nines at the Amelia Island complex, just inside the state's northern border at Fernandino Beach, down to the Key West Resort, with its excellent Rees Jones course, Florida is crammed with places that welcome the traveling golfer.

Of course, tourism by American golfers is hardly confined to America. Since resort travel began, golfers have sought foreign fairways, beginning in the resort spas of France in the late nineteenth century. Today, the choice is as wide as the world itself.

Unquestionably, the mecca for true golfers remains the British Isles, specifically Scotland and the Royal and Ancient Golf Club of St. Andrews. Thousands of Americans make that pilgrimage every year. This, after all, is where it all began. Indeed, in a strange way, except for those links-loving residents of the royal burgh of St. Andrews, we are all bag-toting immigrant travelers through this greatest of man's games.

Wild Dunes, South Carolina, offers guests two distinct Tom Fazio courses, the Links and the Harbor.
The view above is of the sixteenth hole at the Harbor course.

Top:
This view of the seventeenth and eighteenth holes at the Links reflects the difference between the two courses at Wild Dunes.

Above:
The Sea Island Golf Club's Avenue of Oaks, a relaxed place to visit, but not with golf club in hand.

WILLIE ANDERSON
(1878–1910)

Willie Anderson was the first player to dominate golf in America. Between 1901 and 1905, he won four U.S. Open Championships, a feat matched only by Bobby Jones, Ben Hogan, and Jack Nicklaus. With the last three of these victories coming consecutively, Anderson set a record as yet unmatched.

Anderson was born in North Berwick, Scotland, the son of the local greenkeeper. At seventeen, Anderson emigrated to the United States, taking a club job at the Misquamicut Golf Club in Rhode Island. (In the fourteen years he lived in America, Anderson would hold nine other club posts, including at the Apawamis Golf Club in Rye, New York, Baltusrol Golf Club in Springfield, New Jersey, and Onwentsia Club in Lake Forest, Illinois.)

Anderson beat close friend and fellow Scot Alex Smith in a playoff for the 1901 Open Championship, and David Brown, another Scot, in a playoff for the 1903 title. The 1904 title came more easily, Anderson pacing the field at the Glen View Club in Golf, Illinois, by five. Finally, Anderson and Smith tussled for the 1905 title before Anderson edged away by two strokes.

Anderson was far from a pretty player. He had a flat swing, swung his hips freely and virtually wrapped his left arm around his right shoulder. But he was an extremely accurate player, especially with the mashie (5-iron) and driver. A greater weapon, though, was his solemn, uncrackable demeanor. And despite the public perception of him as a typically dour Scot, Anderson was well-liked and admired by fellow pros.

Anderson was inducted into the PGA Hall of Fame in 1940 and into the World Golf Hall of Fame in 1975.

TOMMY ARMOUR
(1895–1968)

The ever-colorful Tommy Armour was an internationally known teacher, club-maker, and, eventually, an elder statesmen of the game.

Armour, who was born in Edinburgh, Scotland, played an entire career with one eye and metal plates in his head and left arm—the results of injuries sustained in

the British tank corps in World War I. Although diminutive in stature, Armour possessed huge hands (sportswriter Grantland Rice described them as "two stalks of bananas") that contributed to his excellent control.

"The Silver Scot" entered the public eye by winning the French Amateur in 1920. After a modest amateur career, Armour turned professional in 1924, two years after moving permanently to the United States. He captured the 1927 U.S. Open title at Oakmont Country Club in Pennsylvania in a playoff over Light-Horse Harry Cooper and won a second major, the 1930 PGA Championship, at Fresh Meadow Country Club in Flushing, New York, beating Gene Sarazen 1 up in the final. Armour won the 1931 British Open, the victory he cherished most, at Carnoustie, Scotland.

Ironically, Armour, who suffered from and invented the term "yips"—"that ghastly time when," he wrote, "with the first movement of the putter, the golfer blacks out"—became the most sought-after teacher in America and wrote two of the most influential instruction books ever: *How to Play Your Best Golf All the Time* and *A Round of Golf with Tommy Armour.*

Armour was inducted into the PGA Hall of Fame in 1940 and into the World Golf Hall of Fame in 1976.

SEVE BALLESTEROS
(born 1957)

Seve Ballesteros lit up the golf world in 1976 when he tied for second in the British Open at Royal Birkdale as a nineteen-year-old. That same season, the precocious Spaniard became the youngest golfer to win the European Tour's Vardon Trophy for low scoring average, the European money list, and a European tournament, the Dutch Open. That was just the beginning.

Ballesteros was born in the village of Pedrena, in northern Spain. The son of a farmer, Ballesteros took up golf as a six-year-old, hitting balls around the fields next to his home with one club: a 3-iron. This meager start created in him a versatile imagination. To this day, no shot is beyond him. He hits a long ball, moves it right or left at will, and has a jeweler's touch around the greens. Indeed, there is no "jail" from which Ballesteros cannot escape, which is just as well, for Ballesteros is prone to moments of outrageous wildness. Leading the 1979 British Open with three holes to play, he hit a tee shot at Royal Lytham's sixteenth into an adjacent car park—from which he recovered to fifteen feet and birdied to clinch his first major title and the first Open victory for a continental European in seventy-two years.

The following year, Ballesteros became the youngest Masters champion, winning by four shots. Since 1980, he has added a second Masters (1983) and a British Open (1984). In all, Ballesteros has won more than fifty tournaments worldwide, including five in America, and has made four Ryder Cup appearances. In 1986, he became the first player to surpass $1 million *and* £1 million in career earnings.

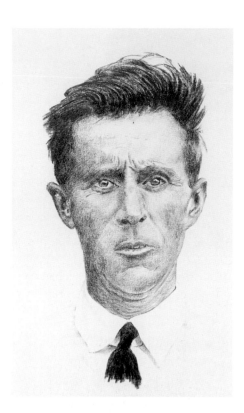

JIM BARNES

(1887–1966)

Six-foot-four Jim Barnes won two PGA Championships, one U.S. Open, one British Open, and three Western Opens between 1916 and 1925, thus capturing every major championship title of the day.

Barnes was made an assistant professional in his hometown of Lelant, England, at age fifteen. Four years later, in 1906, he emigrated to America.

The 1914 Western Open marked Barnes's first professional victory. He finished fourth in the 1915 U.S. Open and third in the 1916 Open. Barnes won the first two PGA Championships, beating Jock Hutchison, 1 up, in the final in 1916 and Fred McLeod, 6 and 5, in 1919. He was runner-up to Walter Hagen in 1921 and 1924.

Barnes earned a second and a third Western Open title in 1917 and 1919 but still lacked a national open crown. That came at Columbia Country Club, Chevy Chase, Maryland, in 1921, when Barnes romped to a nine-shot victory over Hagen and McLeod. Barnes's rounds of 69, 75, 73, and 72 made him one of only four men in the history of the U.S. Open to have led outright after each round.

The only championship that remained was the British Open. Barnes tied for second in 1922, then won in 1925.

Although Barnes's career preceded the organization of a regular, year-long pro tour, an informal circuit existed, and he won a total of seventeen events in the United States. Barnes was one of the original twelve inductees into the PGA Hall of Fame in 1940.

DEANE BEMAN

(born 1938)

In every aspect of the game with which he has been involved, Deane Beman has meant business. He was a top amateur player and a moderate touring profes-

sional. As PGA Tour commissioner, he has been the primary force in making the tour one of the most lucrative organizations in professional sports.

Growing up in Washington, D.C., Beman acquired a reputation as a scrappy competitor and expert golfer. He parlayed this early prowess into a British Amateur title (1959) and two U.S. Amateur titles (1960 and 1963). He also captured four Eastern Amateurs and appeared on the U.S. Americas Cup, World Amateur (Eis-

enhower Trophy), and Walker Cup squads four times each.

A successful insurance broker in Bethesda, Maryland, Beman turned professional in 1967 at the relatively late age of twenty-nine. At five-foot-seven, with a flat swing and a weak shoulder turn, Beman sacrificed yardage off the tee but compensated with one of the finest fairway-wood games of the day. He won four times in six years on the tour, his biggest moment coming when he battled Orville Moody down the stretch only to lose the 1969 U.S. Open by a stroke.

On March 1, 1974, Beman succeeded Joseph C. Dey, Jr., as commissioner of the PGA Tour. Since taking office, Beman has revolutionized the professional game and bolstered the business side of the tour. (Tour assets have grown from $730,000 to well over $50 million.) Beman is responsible for, among other innovations, the Stadium Golf concept; Tournament Players Clubs; the Senior PGA Tour; The Players Championship; PGA Productions, which telecasts the "Inside the PGA Tour" magazine on cable; and a player retirement plan begun in 1983.

PATTY BERG

(born 1918)

Patricia Jane Berg won more than eighty tournaments and helped found the Ladies Professional Golf Association (LPGA) in 1949.

She was born in Minneapolis, Minnesota, and grew up playing on boys' football and baseball teams. She picked up golf at the age of thirteen, and three years later won the 1934 Minneapolis City Championship—the first of twenty-nine amateur victories in seven years. She won the Minnesota State Championship at seventeen and that same year advanced to the final of the 1935 U.S. Women's Amateur Championship before losing to Glenna Collett Vare. Runner-up again in 1937, Berg finally captured the Amateur title in 1938, the year in which she won ten of the thirteen events she entered.

Berg turned professional in 1940, but not until 1941 did she win her first event, the Western Open. A car crash in December in which she severely injured her knee suspended her career for eighteen months.

She came back to win the 1943 Western Open before joining the Marine Reserves that fall. Returning in 1946 to the new Women's Professional Golfers Association (WPGA) tour, Berg won four titles, including her first, and only, U.S. Women's Open. Three years later, she teamed with Babe Zaharias to form the Ladies Professional Golf Association (LPGA) and served as its first president from 1949–52.

Berg went on to win fifty-five titles between 1948 and 1962, including nine of her record fifteen major championships. She won three of the first four Vare Trophies for low scoring average (1953, 1955, and 1956) and was leading money winner three times (1954, 1956, and 1957). She was among the first inductees to the LPGA Hall of Fame in 1951 and to the World Golf Hall of Fame in 1974.

Berg now lives in Fort Myers, Florida.

P.J. BOAT-WRIGHT, JR.
(born 1927)

Purvis James Boatwright, Jr.—known as P.J.—is America's reigning authority on the Rules of Golf. He has been the United States Golf Association's (USGA) executive director in charge of Rules and Competitions since 1981 and has also served as assistant director—his post when he

joined the association in 1959—and as executive director. One of Boatwright's bailiwicks has been to lead the USGA team in the Quadrennial Conferences with its counterpart at the Royal and Ancient Golf Club of St. Andrews in Scotland. The aim of these conferences, which have been held since 1951, is to unify the Rules of Golf throughout the world. Boatwright also is admired for the skill with which he sets up golf courses for championships.

Boatwright, an accomplished golfer himself, at one time held a plus-one handicap. He has qualified four times for the U.S. Amateur Championship, and in 1950 he survived all four rounds of the U.S. Open at Merion Golf Club in Ardmore, Pennsylvania (he finished forty-ninth).

Boatwright was born in Augusta, Georgia, but later moved to South Carolina. He won the Carolina Amateur Championship in 1951 and was the 1957 and 1959 Carolina Open champion. Executive secretary of the Carolina Golf Association from 1955–59, Boatwright has also been inducted into the South Carolina Athletic Hall of Fame and the Carolinas Golf Hall of Fame.

He is a graduate of the Georgia Institute of Technology in Atlanta and Wofford College in Spartanburg, South Carolina.

JULIUS BOROS
(born 1920)

In 1950, at the age of thirty, Julius Boros abandoned his job as an accountant and joined the professional golf tour. Although something of a Julius-come-lately, Boros wasted little time reaching the top. Two years later, he won the U.S. Open at the Northwood Country Club in Dallas, added the World Championship (which was worth $50,000, an outrageous sum for the day), and finished the season as PGA Player of the Year and leading money winner.

At six feet and weighing around two hundred pounds, Boros was an imposing,

but not fearsome, figure. He swung very slowly but whipped strongly through the ball and approached each shot with a gait that verged on the soporific. Although known as "The Moose," Boros was far from clumsy and displayed a delicate touch around the green.

Boros won on and off during the fifties (including another World Championship in 1955). Then, at The Country Club in Brookline, Massachusetts in 1963, he took a second U.S. Open title, at age forty-three. By outdistancing the younger Jacky Cupit (aged twenty-five) and Arnold Palmer (thirty-four) in an eighteen-hole playoff, Boros became the oldest Open winner since Ted Ray won in 1920, also at forty-three. In winning the 1968 PGA Championship at the Pecan Valley Country Club in San Antonio, Texas, Boros became the oldest player to win *any* major.

Boros's final gift to the game came at the 1979 Legends of Golf when he partnered Roberto De Vicenzo to victory over Tommy Bolt and Art Wall in a match that went to six nerve-wracking holes of sudden death. The playoff proved to be the catalyst for the Senior PGA Tour of today.

Boros, a four-time Ryder Cupper, was elected to the PGA Hall of Fame in 1974 and to the World Golf Hall of Fame in 1982. Although he underwent a quintuple bypass operation in 1981, Boros still plays occasionally on the senior tour.

PAT BRADLEY
(born 1951)

Pat Bradley has long ranked as one of the leading players on the LPGA Tour with a reputation for steady if unspectacular play. Not until 1986, when she won three of the four major championships for women, did she dominate the women's tour. She took the Nabisco Dinah Shore, the LPGA Championship, and the du Maurier Classic, while finishing fifth in the U.S. Women's Open, and added two more victories and the Vare Trophy for low scoring average as well as leading the money list and the Player-of-the-Year standings.

Bradley grew up in Westford, Massachusetts, before heading for the warmer climate of Florida International University where she could work on her game year-

round. While her amateur record was mediocre, she improved to the point where it did not take long for her to make an impact with her contemporaries.

Bradley first won in 1976, her third year as a professional. Over the next ten years, she never finished below eleventh on the money list. Prior to 1986, her biggest victory had been the 1981 U.S. Women's Open. Bradley entered 1986 having won sixteen tournaments—but having finished second thirty-five times. Many of these runner-up finishes came after Bradley rose from down the field in the final round, effectively when she had nothing to lose. Before 1986, she often performed poorly when in the lead. That year she learned how to move to the fore and stay there.

Bradley's game has no weak points, but her short game probably is her strength, along with concentration, which fellow players say is the most intense on tour.

JACK BURKE, JR.
(born 1923)

Jack Burke, Jr., won fifteen tournaments in a career that lasted from 1950–63, including The Masters and the PGA Championship in 1956. In 1952 he won four successive tournaments—the Texas, Houston, Baton Rouge, and St. Petersburg Opens—the longest string of victories after Byron Nelson's eleven straight in 1945. Other accomplishments included the Vardon Trophy for low scoring average in 1952 (a

year he also finished second in The Masters) and Player-of-the-Year honors in 1956.

Burke was exposed to the game early by his father, who had tied for second in the 1920 U.S. Open. The son joined the tour in 1950 following service in the Marine Corps and a stint as a club pro. He quickly became known for his putting and as an expert in inclement conditions. His second-place finish in the 1952 Masters came on the strength of a final-round 69—the only subpar score the last two days—amid high winds.

Gale-force winds again plagued the 1956 event, when Burke's 289 equaled Sam Snead's 1954 score as the highest winning total at Augusta. Amateur Ken Venturi led by eight going into the final day, but Burke's closing 71 proved a great round considering the conditions. As Venturi could manage only an 80, Burke won by a stroke. Burke played catch-up in that year's PGA Championship as well, by coming from behind in the semifinal match with Ed Furgol and in the final against Ted Kroll.

In five Ryder Cup Matches, 1951–59, Burke suffered one defeat. But in 1957 he captained the first American team to lose to the British since 1933. He atoned by captaining a victorious squad in 1973.

A wrist injury suffered in the late fifties finally forced Burke to retire from tournament golf, so with fellow Texan Jimmy Demaret, he developed the Champions Golf Club near Houston, which hosted the 1969 U.S. Open and the 1967 Ryder Cup. Burke was elected to the PGA Hall of Fame in 1975.

WILLIAM C. CAMPBELL
(born 1923)

There are few honors in amateur golf that William Cammack ("Bill") Campbell has not won. He has used his long, elegant swing to qualify for thirty-seven U.S. Amateur Championships (only Chick Evans, with forty, played in more), and win in 1964. Campbell played on eight U.S. Walker Cup teams between 1951 and 1975—as captain in 1955—and lost but half a point in all his singles matches. He has played in eighteen Masters and fifteen

U.S. Opens, was runner-up in the 1954 British Amateur, played on the U.S. Americas Cup squad five times between 1952 and 1967, and was the U.S. Senior Amateur champion in 1979 and 1980. Campbell has won four North and South Amateur Championships and has taken the West Virginia Amateur Championship fifteen times, the West Virginia Open three times.

Campbell was born in Huntington, West Virginia, and attended Princeton University, where he posted an unbeaten streak of twenty-two matches. His education was interrupted by World War II, during which time he served as an infantry captain, but he returned to Princeton after the war to finish a degree in history.

Campbell sat on the USGA's executive committee from 1962–65, served as USGA president from 1982–85, and in 1987 was named captain of the Royal and Ancient Golf Club of St. Andrews, Scotland, only the third American (after Francis Ouimet and Joseph C. Dey, Jr.) to be so honored. He received the USGA's highest honor, the Bob Jones Award (for distinguished sportsmanship) in 1956 and the Golf Writers Association of America's William Richardson Award (for outstanding contributions to golf) in 1983.

Campbell runs an insurance agency in West Virginia, a state in whose legislature he served from 1949–57.

DONNA CAPONI
(born 1945)

Donna Caponi reigned as one of the LPGA's most consistent golfers during the 1970s, recording twenty-four official victories, including four majors. Although she did not top the money list, Caponi became the tour's third million-dollar winner in 1981.

Caponi showed her talent early, rising to the top in Los Angeles-area junior programs and winning the Los Angeles Junior Championship in 1956. She turned pro fresh out of high school and joined the LPGA Tour in 1965. She did not win until 1969, when she captured the U.S. Women's Open. She and Peggy Wilson were tied when a thunderstorm delayed Caponi's play of the last hole for fifteen minutes. As soon as it had passed, Caponi nonchalantly birdied. A victory in the Open the following year made Caponi

only the second player after Mickey Wright to win back-to-back.

Caponi's other majors are the 1979 and 1981 LPGA Championships, the latter coming after she broke a three-way tie with Pat Meyers and Jerilyn Britz by sinking a fifteen-foot, uphill, birdie putt on the final hole. (She also won the Peter Jackson Classic in 1976, which was not then considered a major.) Caponi had her best year

in 1980, when five victories helped her net $220,000. Victories not recognized as official by the LPGA include the Portland Ping Team Championship, which Caponi won with Hall of Famer Kathy Whitworth in 1978, 1980, and 1981.

Caponi lives in Tampa, Florida, and still plays the tour. She has cut back slightly on her schedule partly because of knee surgery in 1982.

JOANNE CARNER
(born 1939)

JoAnne Carner is the only golfer to have won the U.S. Girls' Junior, U.S. Women's Amateur, and U.S. Women's Open titles. Robust, gregarious, and immensely popular with LPGA galleries, Carner was known as the "Great Gundy" before her marriage—her maiden name was Gunderson—and later on the tour as "Big Momma."

During a twelve-year amateur career, Carner won five U.S. Women's Amateur titles (1957, 1960, 1962, 1966, and 1968) and played on four consecutive (1958–64) Curtis Cup teams. She turned pro in 1970 after winning the 1969 Burdine's Invitational, making her the last amateur to win an LPGA event.

Carner took Rookie-of-the-Year honors in 1970 by winning the Wendell West Open and by placing eleventh on the money list. Among her forty-two profes-

sional victories—through 1987—Carner can count two U.S. Women's Opens (1971 and 1976). She has won the Vare Trophy for low stroke average five times (1974, 1975, 1981, 1982, 1983), has been Player of the Year and has led the money list three times each. Carner's best year was 1982, when she won five tournaments, $310,399, and was inducted into the LPGA Hall of Fame. Carner suffered back problems in 1984 and 1985, but eclipsed the $2-million, career-earning mark in 1986. She was inducted into the World Golf Hall of Fame in 1985 and received the 1981 Bob Jones Award, the USGA's highest honor, for her contributions to the game.

BILLY CASPER

(born 1931)

During the era of the "Big Three"—Arnold Palmer, Jack Nicklaus, and Gary Player—one other man was as consistently winning both tournaments and money. Between 1956 and 1975, William Earl Casper, Jr., of San Diego, California, won fifty-one events, earned $100,000 or more eight times (and $200,000 once), led in money earnings twice, collected five Vardon Trophies for low scoring average and was PGA Player of the Year twice. He also won two U.S. Open titles (1959 and 1966) and the 1970 Masters.

Casper lacked the charisma of Palmer, the dramatic power of Nicklaus, or the beat-the-odds intensity of Player. Although Casper profited from golf's new exposure and growing affluence, he was too conservative a player to be a media star. Yet this never bothered Casper. He kept winning, drawing strength and support from his family and religion.

Casper won his first season on tour in 1956, and at least once a year through 1971. He was not noted for his heroics through the green, but on them he was a master, if not in style—he employed a very wristy stroke—then in results.

In his two U.S. Open triumphs, Casper needed only 112 (1959) and 117 (1966) putts and averaged fewer than twenty-nine putts per round.

Casper's most famous win was the 1966 Open at the Olympic Club in San Francisco. With nine holes to play, he trailed Palmer by seven strokes. But in chasing Ben Hogan's Open record of 276, Palmer let his lead slip away, and he had to fight just to tie. Palmer led early in the playoff; again he faltered, and Casper won, 67 to 73. It became known as the Open Arnie lost and did little to change the public's perception of the winner.

Casper joined the Senior PGA Tour in 1981, with modest success, highlighted by a 1983 U.S. Senior Open victory.

Casper was elected to the World Golf Hall of Fame in 1978 and to the PGA Hall of Fame in 1982.

FRANK CHIRKINIAN

(born 1927)

The job of a television producer and director goes beyond transferring the action to the television screen. He (or she) should constantly be on the lookout for imaginative ways to present a subject and for technical innovations. Frank Chirkinian, producer and director of CBS-TV's golf broadcasts for the past thirty years, is outstanding in his field.

Chirkinian was born in Philadelphia, the son of an Armenian silk weaver. He studied psychology at the University of Pennsylvania before launching a career in television as an assistant director covering various sports for WCAU, a CBS Phila-

delphia affiliate. He joined the network in 1958 and covered his first Masters that year. Although Chirkinian oversees the network's entire PGA Tour coverage, the annual rite of spring in Augusta, Georgia, remains his tour de force.

During his career with CBS, Chirkinian has been responsible for such innovations as the scoring system whereby a player's score is listed as shots over or under par; the videotaping and editing of tournaments; the introduction of on-course microphones to capture the actual sounds of competition; and the use of cranes to position cameras high above the action.

Chirkinian has received two Emmy awards for his golf coverage, the first coming in 1975 for the CBS broadcast of The Masters, the second for his coverage of the tour in 1981.

HARRY COOPER

(born 1904)

A superb shotmaker and a model of consistency, Harry Cooper won more than thirty times between 1926 and 1942. Ironically, Cooper is better remembered for what he did not win: he had nearly as many seconds as firsts and never won a major.

Cooper was born in England, but his father, a golf pro, moved the family to Texas when Harry was very young. Harry won the Texas PGA Championship in 1922 and 1923, earning the nickname

Light-Horse because of the speed at which he played. Cooper's first big win was the inaugural Los Angeles Open in 1926, and he collected one other first: in 1937, he earned the first Vardon Trophy for low scoring average. That year he won nine tournaments and led the money list with more than $14,000.

It was not as though Cooper never had his chances in the majors. He ended a stroke behind Horton Smith in the 1936 Masters despite leading after three rounds. At Augusta two years later, he and Ralph Guldahl finished two shots behind Henry

Picard. In the 1927 U.S. Open at Oakmont, Cooper three-putted the seventy-first green while Tommy Armour birdied from ten feet to force a playoff; Armour won it, 76 to 79. Cooper's most disappointing defeat came at the 1936 Open at Baltusrol where he shot 284 to break the Open's seventy-two-hole record by two. An hour later, the unknown Tony Manero set a new record, coming in with a final-round 67 for 282 and victory.

Cooper never threatened in the PGA Championships, or made the trip to Britain for the Open. His most prestigious wins were the 1932 and 1937 Canadian Opens (he almost won a third in 1938 but lost in a playoff to Sam Snead).

Cooper was elected to the PGA Hall of Fame in 1959.

FRED CORCORAN
(1905–1977)

Fred Corcoran contributed as much to the tremendous growth of golf in the late 1930s and 1940s as any of the big-name players. The energetic Irishman served as tournament manager of the PGA from 1936 through 1947, during which time the pro tour grew from twenty-two events a year and a total of $100,000 in prize money to forty-five events and $600,000.

Corcoran was a tireless promoter and salesman, who badgered chambers of commerce, resorts—any organization that might be interested in putting on a golf event to attract publicity. He also helped land some of the pro tour's first corporate sponsors.

Corcoran left few stones unturned. When the pros played a fall event in North Carolina one year, they took Saturday off to attend a Duke versus North Carolina collegiate football game. At half time, Corcoran staged a "closest-to-the-pin" competition, with pros hitting from one end of the field to the other, and reminded the football fans that the golf tournament would conclude the next day. He also made sure newspapermen had enough interesting stories to fill their columns.

Corcoran linked up with the PGA when he headed press relations during the 1936 PGA Championship. Shortly thereafter, he was asked to work year-round. Corcoran became Sam Snead's manager dur-

ing his tenure with the PGA and later represented such athletes as Ted Williams, Stan Musial, and Babe Zaharias.

After leaving the PGA, Corcoran helped launch the LPGA in 1949.

BEN CRENSHAW
(born 1952)

No one began a career in quite the way Ben Crenshaw did in 1973. NCAA individual champion at the University of Texas between 1971 and 1973, Crenshaw paced that year's qualifying school by twelve strokes, then won the Texas Open in his first start. The following week, he finished second in the 144-hole World Open in Pinehurst, North Carolina.

Known as "Gentle Ben" because he is soft-spoken and polite, Crenshaw continued to fare better than most on tour, running second on the 1976 money list and fifth in 1979 and 1980. In finishing second in the 1976 and 1983 Masters, the 1978 and 1979 British Opens, and the 1979 PGA Championship, Crenshaw began to acquire a reputation as a pro who could excel in regular tournaments but who was incapable of winning a major. He put that myth to rest in 1984 when, coming off a mediocre 1983 campaign, he won The Masters by two strokes over Tom Watson.

Crenshaw is known for intermittent wildness, due mainly to a swing that goes well past parallel at the top. He compensates for that with a deft touch with his putter. Indeed, sinking a sixty-foot putt on the tenth green at Augusta National set up his Masters triumph.

Nothing related to golf could have salvaged a disastrous 1985, when Crenshaw won only $25,814 and finished 149th on the money list. An overactive thyroid gland was diagnosed; after treatment, Crenshaw returned to finish eighth on the 1986 money list and win two events.

A native of Austin, Texas, Crenshaw is an avid golf historian and collector.

BING CROSBY
(1904–1977)

He was first and foremost an entertainer, but few people have contributed as much to the game as Harry Lillis ("Bing") Crosby. His legacy to the game is capped by the AT&T Pebble Beach National Pro-Am, which before 1985 was known as the Bing Crosby National Pro-Am but which will always be known simply as "The Crosby."

Crosby took up the game as a caddie at age twelve in his hometown of Tacoma, Washington, but expressed little further interest. It was while filming *King of Jazz* in 1930 that he again took up golf. From then on, he could be caught sneaking in practice between takes or in the early morning—anything to maintain a single-digit handicap that once was as low as two.

In 1937, Crosby hosted an informal eighteen-hole pro-am that mixed golf professionals with movie stars at Rancho Santa Fe Country Club outside San Diego. Sam Snead won the inaugural event. The tournament eventually expanded to thirty-six holes, then fifty-four when it moved to California's Monterey Peninsula in 1947. It adopted the present seventy-two-hole format in 1958.

One of Crosby's sons, Nathaniel, won the 1981 U.S. Amateur at the Olympic Club in San Francisco, and Crosby himself, along with Jimmy Demaret, was a powerful force behind the Legends of Golf Tournament at the Onion Creek Club in Austin, Texas, which sparked interest in the Senior PGA Tour. Crosby died of a heart attack in Madrid, Spain, soon after completing a four-ball with Spanish professional Manuel Pinero. In 1978, Crosby was inducted into the World Golf Hall of Fame.

MARGARET CURTIS
(1883–1965)

Among the early top American women golfers were Margaret Curtis and her older sister, Harriot. Margaret was the better golfer, winning three Women's Amateur Championships to her sister's one. Together, they were instrumental in establishing matches between the best women amateurs of America and the British Isles: the Curtis Cup, which began in 1932.

Margaret competed in her first U.S. Women's Amateur in 1897 at age thirteen, losing to defending champion Beatrix Hoyt in the first round. She went on to be low qualifier in 1901, 1902, and 1905, but it was Harriot who won first, taking the title in 1906. The next year, the sisters met in the final, Margaret winning 7 and 6.

Margaret also was a fine tennis player and won the 1908 Women's National Doubles title with Evelyn Sears, making Margaret the only American to hold simultaneous national titles in those sports. A

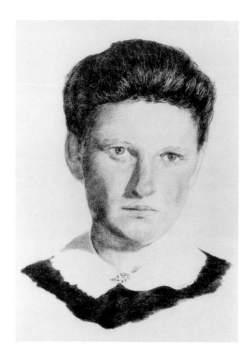

few years passed before she won again at golf, but she added further Women's Amateur titles in 1911 and 1912. She entered the championship twenty-five times, the last in 1949 at age sixty-five.

The sisters donated the prize for the Curtis Cup, the inscription reading, "to stimulate friendly rivalry among the women golfers of many lands." To date, the United States has won nineteen times, the British Isles three times, and two matches have been tied.

In 1958, Margaret Curtis won the USGA Bob Jones Award for distinguished sportsmanship in golf.

JIMMY DEMARET
(1910–1983)

It would be sad if Jimmy Demaret were remembered only for his wisecracking, colorful personality and trend-setting penchant for flamboyant clothes. Demaret was one of the best golfers of the forties, the first to collect three Masters titles, and the winner of forty-four tournaments in all.

Born in Houston, Texas, Demaret was one of nine children and one of three brothers to play professional golf. He joined the tour in 1931, his first victory coming in the 1934 San Francisco Match Play Championship, but quickly left the circuit, repelled by a life that was far from lucrative. He then alternated between playing professionally in Texas and singing professionally in nightclubs.

Demaret returned to the tour in 1938. Two years later, he won his first Masters, taming the back nine at Augusta National in the first round in thirty strokes, a record equaled but still standing. He eventually beat the field by four for a sixth consecutive win that year. Following service in the U.S. Navy during World War II, Demaret returned to the tour to win a second green jacket in 1947 and a third in 1950.

Demaret's accomplishments arose from a considerable outside-to-in, wristy swing that produced a pronounced, yet immaculately controlled, fade. He also was an

expert wind player, whipping the ball low and far—"snake rapers," he called them.

Besides playing golf, Demaret developed the Champions Golf Club in Houston with long-time friend Jack Burke, Jr., the Onion Creek Country Club in Austin, and was a popular host, with Gene Sarazen, on Shell's television series, "Wonderful World of Golf." He was elected to the PGA Hall of Fame in 1960.

ROBERTO DE VICENZO

(born 1923)

Roberto De Vicenzo of Argentina was one of the greatest globe-trotting players ever, collecting national titles the way tourists collect souvenirs. He won more than two

hundred tournaments around the world, including the national opens of twelve countries. Although he never won the U.S. Open, he did make a mark in America by winning various events on the PGA Tour. But De Vicenzo's most memorable moment in the United States came when he signed an incorrect scorecard at the 1968 Masters, awarding himself a 66 instead of the 65 he scored and leaving him in second place instead of in a playoff with Bob Goalby.

De Vicenzo won one major championship, the 1967 British Open, finishing two shots ahead of Jack Nicklaus. De Vicenzo had doggedly pursued the British Open since he finished third in his first attempt in 1948. He added a runner-up finish in 1950 and came in third in 1949, 1956, 1960, 1964, and 1969.

De Vicenzo grew up near a golf course in Buenos Aires and learned the game as a *langunero*, literally a "pond boy," or caddie's assistant. He won the Argentine Open and PGA in 1944 and first played in the United States three years later. De Vicenzo, whose geniality made him very popular, had a long career as a productive player. His wins in the United States spanned seventeen years, from 1951 to 1968, the last coming at the Houston Championship three weeks after his Masters debacle. De Vicenzo was an outstanding striker of the ball but often had trouble with his putting.

He was inducted into the PGA Hall of Fame in 1979.

JOSEPH C. DEY, JR.

(born 1907)

Joe Dey was one of golf's foremost administrators during the latter half of the game's first hundred years in America. He served as executive secretary of the United States Golf Association from 1934 to 1968 and as the first commissioner of the Tournament Players Division of the PGA—later to become the PGA Tour—from 1968 to 1973.

Dey began his professional career as a sportswriter for the *Philadelphia Public Ledger* before moving to the *Philadelphia Evening Bulletin*. While there he covered Bobby Jones's 1930 U.S. Amateur victory, which capped the Grand Slam.

Dey once considered going into the ministry but instead received and accepted an offer to become the USGA's executive secretary. The association had been searching for a young man for the post; Dey had been recommended by Frank Handt, then USGA secretary, who knew of Dey's exploits as a writer.

During Dey's thirty-five years of service, the USGA grew in size and influence. One of his most notable achievements came in 1951 when he spearheaded the move to unify the Rules of Golf with the Royal and Ancient Golf Club of St. Andrews in Scotland.

In 1968, when America's tour pros succeeded in forming their own division

within the PGA, they turned to Dey for leadership. He managed to calm the troubled waters that existed between the players and the PGA administration and sparked a growth in the fortunes of the pro tour that continues to this day. In 1975 Dey became the second American (after Francis Ouimet) to captain the R&A. He was inducted into the World Golf Hall of Fame in 1975.

Leo Diegel
(1899–1951)

A native of Detroit, Michigan, Leo Diegel won consecutive PGA Championships in 1928 and 1929 but was also known for being the best at playing into contention—and losing. Seven times Diegel finished within the top four in the U.S. and British Opens. He needed only to play the final six holes of the 1925 U.S. Open at the Worcester Country Club in Massachusetts in even par to win; he shot nine over. In the 1933 British Open at St. Andrews, Diegel had only to hole a short putt on the final green to tie Denny Shute and Craig Wood. He missed. "They keep trying to give me a championship," Diegel once quipped, "but I won't take it."

In truth, Diegel often was unable to win. He was a bag of nerves on the course, often needlessly worrying about a tough

shot that might materialize several holes later, and he constantly suffered severe bouts of the "yips."

When on his game and in possession of a clear mind, Diegel was invincible. He won a total of thirty-one tournaments, including four Canadian Opens, in 1924, 1925, 1928, and 1929. It was Diegel who in 1928 ended Ben Hogan's string of four consecutive PGA Championships and twenty-two matches without a loss. First Diegel beat Walter Hagen, 2 and 1, in the quarterfinals at Five Farms Country Club in Baltimore, Maryland, then disposed of Gene Sarazen, 9 and 8, and in the final, destroyed Al Espinosa, 6 and 5. Diegel defended his title in 1929, dispatching Johnny Farrell, the 1928 U.S. Open champion, 6 and 4, in the final.

A four-time Ryder Cup player between 1927 and 1933, Diegel was inducted into the PGA Hall of Fame in 1955.

Pete Dye
(born 1925)

Pete Dye is one of the most influential golf course architects of the past twenty years. He is best known for creating the Tournament Players Club at Sawgrass in Ponte Vedra, Florida, home to The Players Championship since 1982 and a template for many new layouts.

Dye first worked on a golf course in the 1940s. His father, Paul, had built a layout near the family home in Urbana,

Ohio, in 1927, and Pete helped maintain it when not attending classes. Although the boy proceeded, very successfully, into the world of selling insurance, he began his move to course design by helping rework his home course, the Country Club of Indianapolis, in the mid-fifties. He soon abandoned the insurance business altogether.

In 1963, Dye and his wife Alice made a pilgrimage to Scotland. Upon his return, Dye began to incorporate in his own projects some of the elements he had seen on Great Britain's classic courses, such as tight fairways or greens (small) and sand traps (large) shored up by railroad ties. These elements can be seen in Dye's first design of note, the Harbour Town Golf Links on Hilton Head Island, South Carolina, on which Jack Nicklaus collaborated.

Dye's Sawgrass design was the PGA Tour's first Stadium golf course, a concept designed to test the best golfers while affording the public excellent viewing areas. Sawgrass also was one of the first to use natural vegetation—which Dye calls "waste areas"—as hazards. A dozen similar courses appeared on the PGA Tour in the ensuing five years, the most notorious being the Stadium course at the PGA West development in California. Just as they had done at Sawgrass, the touring pros complained bitterly about its difficulty.

Dye also was an excellent amateur golfer. He won the Indiana Amateur Championship in 1955 and, eight years later, reached the fifth round of the British Amateur.

Dwight D. Eisenhower
(1890–1969)

It is said that Dwight Eisenhower was the president who taught a nation how to play golf. If that is true, then no finer tribute could be given, for golf was Ike's great love.

Eisenhower, the five-star World War II general who helped plan the Allied invasion of Normandy, was famous—or infamous—for putting out each double bogey as if it were a stroke for the U.S. Open Championship, and he expected his partners and opponents to do likewise. Such devotion was carried into the White

House, where President Eisenhower often could be found chipping on the south lawn or putting in the Oval Office.

Eisenhower first visited Augusta National Golf Club in 1948 as a guest and stayed for eleven days. He soon became a full member and made many trips to the site of the annual Masters Tournament during and after his presidency. A moderately adept player, Eisenhower regularly toured the course with a score in the low 90s. A cottage beside the tenth tee now bears his name.

In later years, Eisenhower split his time between Augusta and Palm Springs, California, where he lived at the Eldorado Country Club. He was a frequent spectator at the Bob Hope Chrysler Classic, a tournament whose charity is the Eisenhower Medical Center in Rancho Mirage and whose championship trophy is named in Eisenhower's honor.

CHICK EVANS
(1890–1979)

Charles ("Chick") Evans, Jr., was one of the leading amateurs of the early 1900s. He was the first player to win the U.S. Amateur and Open Championships in the same year (1916), and he added a second U.S. Amateur title in 1920. Evans garnered many other laurels, including eight Western Amateurs (four in a row between 1920 and 1923), the 1910 Western Open, and the 1911 French Amateur.

Evans also helped break golf's social barriers. Coming out of the caddie ranks around Chicago, Evans proved that a wealthy, country-club background was not a prerequisite for success. With his rhythmic swing and crisp iron play, he was recognized as the finest player in the United States.

Starting with his first national amateur campaign in 1909, Evans regularly found a way to lose the big ones, usually because of poor putting. Between 1909 and 1915, he was knocked out in the semifinals of the U.S. Amateur three times, the final once. Said Jerry Travers, another top amateur, "If Evans could putt like Walter J. Travis [another successful amateur], it would be foolish to stage an amateur tourney in this country."

In 1916, Evans "clicked," winning the U.S. Open with a score of 286, a record

that stood for twenty years, carrying only seven clubs. Three months later, he won his first U.S. Amateur.

Evans never turned pro, instead making his living as a stockbroker. He continued to compete nationally for more than fifty years, qualifying for the 1953 Open and taking part in the 1961 U.S. Amateur. He established the Evans Scholarship Fund, which helps educate Chicago-area caddies. Evans was one of the original inductees into the PGA Hall of Fame in 1940 and was elected to the World Golf Hall of Fame in 1975.

RAYMOND FLOYD
(born 1942)

On June 15, 1986, at Shinnecock Hills Golf Club in Southampton, New York, forty-three-year-old Raymond Floyd became the oldest winner of the U.S. Open Championship at a time when the game was increasingly dominated by long, strong youngsters.

Throughout his quarter century on tour, Floyd, the son of an army officer from Ft. Bragg, North Carolina, has mixed mediocre years with moments of brilliance. When he joined the tour in 1963, Floyd missed the cut in his first ten appearances. Come the eleventh, he won—the St. Petersburg Open victory making him one of the youngest tour winners in history.

Floyd won one event over the next six years, preferring the nightlife of the tour stops to monkish golf practice. Then in 1969, he caught fire, winning three events, including his first major, the PGA Championship.

After these successes, Floyd again went off the boil, winning but one event in six years. When he rebounded this time, he took the 1976 Masters by a record eight strokes while equaling the tournament record of 271, seventeen under par. Notable here was Floyd's use of a 5-wood to float his approaches high and softly onto Augusta National's par fives. (The normal choice of club would have been a long iron, with

similar distance but a trajectory low and ill-suited to the firm, fast greens of Augusta.) He finished the tournament thirteen under par for the par fives and had every amateur in America rushing out to buy the same club. Floyd's third major victory came at the 1982 PGA Championship at Southern Hills Country Club in Tulsa, Oklahoma.

Majors are not the only medals Floyd wears. He has won seventeen regular tour events, has played in six Ryder Cups, and has won tournaments in Brazil, South Africa, Costa Rica, Canada, and Japan. Floyd won the 1983 Vardon Trophy for low scoring average, and only once since 1973 has he won less than $100,000 in official prize money.

GERALD FORD

(born 1913)

Gerald R. Ford, the thirty-eighth president of the United States (1974–77), is an avid golfer with a handicap that slips into the mid-teens. Unlike other presidents who have played—from William Taft to Ronald Reagan—Ford is public about his game, competing in celebrity pro-ams and, like weekend golfers everywhere, talking often about his accomplishments.

A star football player at the University of Michigan in the early thirties, Ford took

up golf after World War II as a young lawyer in Grand Rapids, Michigan. He continued playing while serving as a congressman from his home state and as vice president under Richard Nixon.

His addiction to the game is perhaps exemplified by the fact that four days after becoming president, following Nixon's resignation in August 1974, Ford slipped out to play a round. Ford would often escape the White House, meeting and playing with such greats as Arnold Palmer and Jack Nicklaus. A month after taking office, Ford cut the ribbon at the new World Golf Hall of Fame in Pinehurst, North Carolina. In the round that followed, he outdrove two of his partners—Palmer and Gary Player—off the first tee.

Much has been made of a few incidents when spectators were hit by Ford's errant drives. His good friend and frequent playing partner Bob Hope coined the line, "Ford made golf a contact sport." But no one was ever seriously hurt, and one woman even claimed that being beaned by Ford was "an honor."

Ford still plays as often as he can. He sponsors the Jerry Ford Invitational each summer in Vail, Colorado, where he has a home. Ford winters in Palm Springs, California. Quips Hope, "There are over fifty courses in Palm Springs, and he never knows which he'll play until he hits his first drive."

DAVID FOSTER

(born 1920)

As the president and chief operating officer of the Colgate-Palmolive conglomerate, David Foster helped lift women's professional golf out of sporting obscurity when he injected cash and creativity into the LPGA Tour in the early 1970s.

An Englishman born of American parents, Foster realized that both women's golf and his company's products could benefit from corporate sponsorship. To that end, he created the LPGA's first six-figure tournament, the $110,000 Dinah Shore-Colgate Palmolive Winner's Circle, in 1972, with a first prize of $20,000—double the top check at any other LPGA stop. (With a new title sponsor, the tournament is now known as the Nabisco Dinah Shore and is a LPGA major.) The first winner of the

"Circle," Jane Blalock, became one of many LPGA pros who appeared in television commercials for Colgate-Palmolive products. Both organizations benefited. As Ray Volpe, LPGA commissioner from 1975–82, noted in a recent interview, "David Foster and his emphasis on sports promotion . . . was the initial catalyst to make the LPGA go." True enough. Prize money stood at $558,550 in 1971, the year before Colgate's involvement. In 1987, purses totaled $11 million.

Colgate also sponsored the Triple Crown, a match-play event that was played from 1975–79, the Colgate European Open (1974–79), the Colgate Far East Open (1974–79), and a Colgate Hong Kong Open (1977).

Foster has sat on the board of directors of the World Golf Hall of Fame and the Women's Sports Foundation, and in 1986 received the LPGA's Patty Berg Award for "diplomacy, sportsmanship, goodwill and contributions to the game."

LEO FRASER

(1910–1986)

Leo Fraser held almost every job in golf, from caddie to club owner. He is perhaps best known for his tenure as president of the PGA, seeing the association through a tough period when the tour pros wanted to break from the PGA ranks and form a separate organization.

The son of Jolly Jim Fraser, the Scottish-born professional at Seaview Country Club near Atlantic City, New Jersey, Leo started caddieing at a young age. By seventeen, he was head pro at Saginaw Country Club in Michigan and a respected instructor, clubmaker, and competitor. Fraser became head pro at Seaview when his father died in 1935.

After serving in the army during World War II, Fraser went on to head a consortium that bought the Atlantic City Country Club. As a club owner, Fraser worked with the Philadelphia PGA section and served as its president for seven years in the sixties.

Fraser also became an officer of the national PGA and rose to the presidency in 1969–70. In 1969, when the touring pros

threatened to leave the PGA to take more control over their tour, Fraser forced the parties to work out an accommodation that has evolved into the PGA Tour, a separate division but with PGA officers on its board. He also convinced Joseph C. Dey, Jr., who had been executive director of the USGA, to become the tour's first commissioner.

PGA Professional of the Year in 1957, Fraser was presented the William Richard-son Award from the Golf Writers Association of America in 1971 and the Metropolitan (N.Y.) Golfwriters Gold Tee Award in 1981.

HERB GRAFFIS
(born 1893)

Herb Graffis was a golf journalist, but that term hardly reflects the broad range of contributions he has made to the game. In 1934, he and his brother Joe (a partner on most Graffis projects) founded the National Golf Foundation (NGF), a body that unified a burgeoning industry and spurred further growth. The native of Logansport, Indiana, worked hard behind the scenes to foster progress in the game, always emphasizing the importance of club pros and superintendents to the game.

"Never has a person in the history of American golf contributed so much to the game's overall growth and health," says Robert Rickey, a former NGF president. "His greatest talent was to get people to do what was in the game's best interest—and convince them it was their idea." Graffis was greatly respected by such influential figures as Joseph C. Dey, Jr., long-time executive director of the USGA, and Fred Corcoran, former tournament manager of the PGA.

Graffis, who displayed a wry and often risqué humor, began in golf publishing when he launched the *Chicago Golfer* in 1923. In 1927, he founded *Golfdom*, a trade magazine, followed in 1933 by *Golf-*

ing, a general-interest monthly. Graffis continued to publish the latter two until they were sold to *GOLF Magazine* in 1965.

Graffis worked with Tommy Armour on three instruction books, including the popular and influential *How to Play Your Best Golf All the Time.* He also wrote several books on his own, including a comprehensive history of the PGA. It remains the only history of sport as a business.

Graffis also was a founding member, in 1946, of the Golf Writers Association of America. In his mid-nineties, he is still a consulting editor of *GOLF Magazine.*

RALPH GULDAHL
(1912–1987)

Ralph Guldahl remains one of only five players to win back-to-back U.S. Opens, his victories coming in 1937 and 1938.

A native of Dallas, Texas, Guldahl turned pro in 1930 and claimed his first professional victory in Santa Monica, California, the following year. The tall (six-foot-three) long hitter, who was famous for sledgehammer lunges at the ball, finished second, one stroke back, in his first U.S. Open campaign in 1933 and eighth in 1934. The following year, Guldahl went into a slump, claiming he had lost his putting touch. Frustrated, he quit the tour. He returned to Dallas for the birth of his son, Ralph, Jr., and tried unsuccessfully to sell cars.

A friend soon talked Guldahl into designing a nine-hole course in nearby Kilgore. After practicing hard on the layout, Guldahl returned to the tour in 1936. He won the Western Open and the Radix (forerunner of the Vardon Trophy) for low scoring average (71.65) that year and followed with his first U.S. Open triumph at Oakland Hills Country Club, outside Detroit. Also in 1937, Guldahl won the Western Open again, placed second in seven other events and played on the Ryder Cup team. In 1938, Guldahl won a second Open, by six strokes over Dick Metz at Cherry Hills Country Club, outside Denver, and won a third straight Western title. Guldahl won his only Masters in 1939 and again was named to the Ryder Cup team. He did not play, however, because all Ryder Cup Matches were canceled during the war years (1939–45).

After 1940, by his own admission, the competitive urge left him. A 1963 PGA Hall of Fame and 1981 World Golf Hall of Fame inductee, Guldahl was pro at Braemar Country Club in Tarzana, California, until his death.

WALTER HAGEN
(1892–1969)

Walter Hagen's flamboyance colored both the manner of his play and the style of his clothes. The Haig captured two U.S. Opens (1914 and 1919), four British Opens (1922, 1924, 1928, and 1929), and five PGA Championships (at match play), including four in a row from 1924–27.

Hagen, who was born in Rochester, New York, brought sartorial splendor to the golf course, passing up the traditional tweeds for expensive silk shirts, flannel pants (which he would wear once, then give to bellhops as tips), and white bucks. Win or lose, Hagen left a vivid impression.

Hagen also made an impression on golf's hierarchy in fighting for the fair treatment of professionals. With Hagen spearheading the drive, pros won the right to change in clubhouses instead of caddieshacks.

Hagen showed much less concern for his fellow players on the course. A master of the "psych-out," he would stand on the first tee and declare loud enough for all to hear, "I wonder who's going to take second."

Hagen's swing was anything but classic. He swayed on the backswing and lunged into the ball on the downswing, often sending it wild, especially off the tee. But he had a way of saving himself from seemingly impossible positions, scrambling to reach the green, then more often than not sinking an unmakable putt and shattering a rival's concentration and confidence.

Hagen is a charter member of both the PGA Hall of Fame (1940) and the World Golf Hall of Fame (1974).

FRANK HANNIGAN
(born 1931)

Frank Hannigan has served the game of golf in America for twenty-seven years since joining the United States Golf Association as public information manager in 1961. He moved into his current post as senior executive director in the summer of 1983.

During these years, Hannigan has fulfilled many roles for the association. In 1962, he was appointed tournament relations manager, conferring closely with members of various clubs that hosted the U.S. Open. Four years later, Hannigan became assistant director, involved in the running of the USGA's various championships. Other chores have included the care of the USGA museum and library and assisting in the negotiation of television

contracts for coverage of USGA tournaments with ABC-TV.

Hannigan began working part-time for the USGA in 1976 while pursuing his interest in journalism. He has written articles for various magazines and collaborated with golf pro Tom Watson on *The Rules of Golf, Illustrated and Explained,* which, having sold almost 300,000 copies, is the best-selling non-instruction golf book ever.

Hannigan is modest about any USGA achievements since he returned in 1983 and likens his job of fund-raising and managing a staff of 116 to "that of a small college administrator." But he does accept credit for taking the 1986 U.S. Open to Shinnecock Hills Golf Club in Southampton, New York, one of the oldest clubs in America, for one of the most successful and entertaining Opens in recent memory.

An insightful man with a wry sense of humor—and a handicap that periodically dips into single digits—Hannigan says he has survived his tenure "with only one serious illness"—open heart surgery in 1985. Of that he quips, "This job will do that to you."

COBURN HASKELL
(1868–1922)

Coburn Haskell gave the game the single greatest advancement in the history of golf equipment: the rubber-core ball.

the golf-ball business boomed. Little is known about Haskell himself, other than that he died presumably an even wealthier man than he had begun, thanks to his invention.

SANDRA HAYNIE
(born 1943)

Sandra Haynie should be the envy of many professional athletes, for she has had two successful stints as a player, returning magnificently from illness. Altogether she has accumulated forty-two victories, including four major titles.

Haynie was an amateur success in her native state, winning the 1957 and 1958 Texas Publinx and the 1958 and 1959

Texas Amateur Championships. She also won the 1960 Trans-Mississippi.

Haynie's first career, which ran from the time she joined the LPGA in 1961 through 1976, was worth thirty-nine victories and nearly $500,000. In 1965, Haynie won the LPGA Championship. She won that title again in 1974 and added the U.S. Women's Open, a double accomplished only by Mickey Wright in 1958 and 1961. Haynie recorded at least one victory a year from 1962 to 1975, was the 1970 Player of the Year and finished second on the money list four times.

Haynie pared down the number of events she played to seventeen between

The common ball of the time was the gutta percha, a solid lump of dried tree sap that had been molded into a sphere. Haskell, a wealthy entrepreneur and an average golfer from Cleveland, suspected that a better ball could be made by winding rubber threads around a solid rubber core, using gutta percha for the cover. Haskell built the ball with help from Bertram G. Work, an engineer with the B.F. Goodrich Rubber Company in nearby Akron.

The new invention flew and rolled much farther than guttas but also could curve wildly, hence the nickname "Bounding Billies." It was not until after the cover was molded with a raised bramble pattern and an automatic winding machine was invented that the ball, now offering distance with control, gained favor.

Still, many of the top professionals were reluctant to make the change from the gutta percha to the Haskell ball. Haskell sent a batch to Englishman J.H. Taylor (the eventual winner of five British Opens), who had refused to use one in the 1900 U.S. Open, but who after driving his first wound ball 250 yards—almost fifty yards farther than he could hit a gutta— was converted. Walter Travis then won the 1901 U.S. Amateur using the Haskell. When Sandy Herd took the 1902 British Open with it, the acceptance of the ball on both sides of the Atlantic was all but complete.

When Haskell's patent expired in 1915, many companies entered the fray, and

1977 and 1980 because of arthritis and outside business interests, and went winless. She returned, recovered, to a richer tour in 1981 and won the Henredon Classic. Then she made 1982 her best year ever with two victories, including the Peter Jackson Classic, a major, and $245,000. She placed second on the money list.

Haynie has served as an officer and director of the LPGA. She qualified for the LPGA Hall of Fame in 1977. She lives in Dallas and runs an annual celebrity pro-am with all proceeds going to the Texas chapter of the National Arthritis Foundation.

BEN HOGAN
(born 1912)

Ben Hogan topped the PGA Tour's money list from 1940–42, but it was not until after World War II that the "Hawk" flew highest. Between 1946 and 1953, Hogan won the U.S. Open four times, the PGA Championship twice, The Masters twice, and the British Open once.

Hogan was born in Dublin, Texas, but moved as a boy to Fort Worth, where he caddied and learned to play golf at the Glen Garden Country Club. He turned pro at nineteen, despite the advice of friends who pointed out that his severe hook would handicap him on the pro tour. They were right. Twice Hogan fell off the circuit. Even when he joined for good in 1937, he had to wait several years for his first success.

Eventually Hogan learned the fade, and worked hard to perfect his technique. When he won thirteen times in 1946, including the PGA Championship, Hogan (along with Sam Snead) took over from Byron Nelson as the player to beat. Then, in February 1949, Hogan suffered multiple injuries in a collision with a bus, and his career appeared over.

But Hogan was resolute that he could return, and entered the 1950 Los Angeles Open as a test of endurance. He almost won it, losing to Sam Snead in a playoff. The same year, a still-bandaged Hogan hobbled to his second U.S. Open title, beating Lloyd Mangrum and George Fazio in a playoff at Merion Golf Club.

To say Hogan's approach to the game was clinical would be an understatement. He believed in constant practice, absolute preparation, perfect course management, and a cold, machinelike intensity that erased any outside influences once a tournament began.

The author of one of the top instruction books ever written, *Five Lessons: The Modern Fundamentals of Golf,* Hogan was inducted to the PGA Hall of Fame in 1953 and was an inaugural inductee to the World Golf Hall of Fame in 1974.

BOB HOPE
(born 1903)

Although born in England, Bob Hope did not take a shine to the game until he emigrated to New York City during the era of vaudeville. The popular entertainer played around Westchester County and Long Island before moving to Hollywood in 1937. There he became fast friends with Bing Crosby at Lakeside Golf Club, the course Hope still calls home. Always a respectable player, Hope's handicap has floated from a low of five or six to its present twenty. He has played with presidents (most notably his good friends Dwight Eisenhower and Gerald Ford), kings, sports figures, and celebrities of every distinction. Where Hope travels, golf follows. When entertaining United States forces posted overseas, his driver is often his only prop.

In 1965, at the insistence of Ernie Dunlevie, founder of Bermuda Dunes Country Club, and the late Milt Hicks, president of Indian Wells Country Club, Hope lent his name to the Palm Springs Golf Classic. Since then, the ninety-hole Bob Hope Chrysler (formerly Desert) Classic, held on four Palm Springs area courses, has been the unofficial kick-off for the PGA Tour. Hope still presides over his tournament every year.

A PGA of America Advisory Committee member since 1942, Hope was presented the USGA Bob Jones Award for his contributions to the game in 1979 and was inducted into the World Golf Hall of Fame in 1983.

JOE JEMSEK
(born 1913)

Joe Jemsek is the hero of the public-course golfer. The owner and operator of nine courses around Chicago, Jemsek brings country-club standards to public-fee layouts and is a tireless promoter of the game.

A native of Chicago and one of eight children, Jemsek caddied at Cog Hill (in Lemont, Illinois) and the old Laramie course for 65 cents a round. He turned pro at seventeen, but disliked playing the tour, returning instead to Cog Hill to study club operations. Come winter, Jemsek would work in a restaurant to learn food service and in the sporting-goods department of Sears. Summers, he would work at St. Andrews Golf Club in west Chicago as greenkeeper, caddie master, golf pro, and cook. In 1939, he bought St. Andrews for $100,000 and put his knowledge to the test, offering quality golf and amenities to the daily-fee golfer. He purchased Cog Hill

in 1951 and over the years has acquired seven more clubs and courses.

Jemsek's contributions to golf reach many levels. The USGA has used his courses for staging national qualifying events. Local high-school golf teams have utilized Jemsek courses, and numerous junior championships have been played over them. He helped launch the Illinois PGA in the forties, offering that association sites and purses. He also brought golf to Chicago television in 1949 with a weekly show on instruction and the rules. In 1986, his Pine Meadow Golf Club became the first public course in the United States to employ caddies.

Jemsek is still active in running his empire. He won the National Golf Foundation Herb Graffis Award for contributions to golf in 1977 and in 1986 was awarded a gold medal of appreciation from the Western Golf Association.

BOBBY JONES
(1902–1971)

He played tournament golf for only fourteen years, yet Robert Tyre ("Bobby") Jones, Jr., left a permanent mark on the game. Although an amateur, he concentrated on the major tournaments and won an astounding thirteen of the twenty-seven events he entered, culminating in

1930 with the Grand Slam—the British Open, the British Amateur, the U.S. Amateur, and the U.S. Open Championships. Jones retired from competition after having achieved the goal he had set for himself and having set a standard for all who followed him.

Perhaps most remarkable, Jones essentially was a part-time player. He picked up his clubs only a few months a year, spending the rest of the time first as a student (in engineering, literature, and law), then as a lawyer. Whatever his pursuits, Jones was driven to be the best.

On the golf course, he brought his smooth, controlled, powerful swing into only fifty-two events and won twenty-three of them. Indeed, his presence was such that no matter how other players finished, their first question was, "What's Jones doing?"

Jones also wrote books, both autobiographical and instructional (some with O.B. Keeler, an Atlanta newspaperman and Jones's close friend), and after retiring he made movies, wrote newspaper columns, and spread the gospel of golf over the radio. He co-designed Augusta National (with Scottish architect Alister Mackenzie), which incorporated all the components that Jones felt would make a layout strategically perfect. In 1934, Jones invited some friends to play his creation in a friendly tournament. Under the influence of club president Clifford Roberts,

Jones's intimate get-together became The Masters, golf's annual rite of spring.

Jones played in his tournament (with moderate success) every year until 1947, when his health began to fail. Over the years, even though his arms and legs became paralyzed by a spinal disease, Jones continued to show up at Augusta, albeit in a wheelchair.

Jones is a charter member of the PGA Hall of Fame (1940) and the World Golf Hall of Fame (1974).

ROBERT TRENT JONES
(born 1906)

Robert Trent Jones is the most prolific golf course architect in history. At last count, his tally of courses built or redesigned numbered more than 450, with projects pending in most corners of the United States and in twenty-five foreign countries.

Jones emigrated with his parents from England in 1911. He attended Cornell University in the late twenties, studying a curriculum he himself created of subjects he felt would best suit a career in golf course architecture. Following graduation in 1930, he joined forces with the well-known Canadian designer Stanley Thompson.

Jones established his own firm in the 1930s which, having survived the Depression and World War II, blossomed by the fifties. Jones emphasized the heroic school of architecture, a blend of strategic and penal philosophies. His signature—long tees, massive, undulating greens, and a preponderance of water and sand—became recognized, sought after, and sometimes detested throughout the world. He redesigned Oakland Hills Golf Club outside Detroit for the 1951 U.S. Open. Only the winner—Ben Hogan—and Clayton Heafner returned sub-par scores. When Jones remodeled the Lower course at Baltusrol Golf Club in Springfield, New Jersey, the members complained that the par-three fourth hole, which requires a long carry over water, was too difficult. Jones ended that argument by holing for an ace on his first attempt.

Other Jones projects include Spyglass Hill in Pebble Beach, California; Firestone South in Akron, Ohio; the New Ballybu-

nion course in Ireland; and Hazeltine National Golf Club in Minnesota, a design heavy on doglegs that came in for severe criticism when it was the venue for the 1970 U.S. Open.

In 1976, Jones was the initial recipient of the Donald Ross Award for outstanding contribution to course design from the American Society of Golf Course Architects. Jones now works out of Montclair, New Jersey. His two sons, Rees and Robert Trent, Jr., have also become respected architects.

O.B. KEELER
(1882–1950)

From the time Bobby Jones entered tournament golf, one man followed his every step. Oscar Bane Keeler, or O.B., an Atlanta newspaperman, made his first appearance covering a golf tournament at the 1916 Georgia State Amateur, an event Jones won.

Keeler began professional life as a bookkeeper; that did not last long. In 1909, he secured a job with the *Atlanta Georgia*, then with the *Kansas City Star*, where he became a star reporter and that paper's first to write under a byline. Keeler returned to Atlanta in 1913 to work for the *Journal*, where he spent the remainder of his career.

Jones was big news in Atlanta, so, not surprisingly, Keeler tagged along. Wrote Jones in *Golf Is My Game*, "By Keeler's estimate we traveled 120,000 miles to-

gether, in which travels he watched and reported on my play in 27 national championships here and abroad, in addition to countless less formal appearances. At these tournaments we lived together in the same room most of the time . . . the play and result were as personally his as mine. Indeed, I think he suffered in defeat and reveled in victory even more than did I."

Keeler is often referred to as "Jones's Boswell." They collaborated in 1927 on the now classic book *Down the Fairway*, and following Jones's retirement, Keeler worked with him on scripts for the radio shows and movie shorts that exposed thousands of persons to golf. Keeler wrote a book of his own, ironically titled *Autobiography of an Average Golfer*, in 1925. In 1930, he made the first transatlantic broadcast of a sporting event, describing the British Open over the radio.

JOHN LAUPHEIMER
(born 1930)

As commissioner of the Ladies Professional Golf Association, John Laupheimer is one of the leading administrators in the game today. He took over the post from Ray Volpe in 1982, having previously served as LPGA executive director and as executive director of administration at the United States Golf Association.

If the initial growth of the LPGA was fostered by such stars as Babe Zaharias,

Mickey Wright, Kathy Whitworth, and Nancy Lopez, and such leaders as Fred Corcoran and Volpe, it has matured and stabilized under Laupheimer. When he took office, purses stood at $6.4 million; in 1988 they reached $12.2 million. (Laupheimer maintains that most of his work is dealing with sponsors.) In 1982, there were 185 LPGA members; now there are almost three hundred. Television covered only seven 1982 events; in 1988 alone fifteen are expected to air. In addition, Laupheimer has instituted a player pension plan and has overseen the fruition of the new LPGA headquarters at the Sweetwater Country Club in Sugar Land, Texas, the location also of the LPGA Hall of Fame.

Laupheimer was born in Philadelphia and received a master's degree from Princeton University. He played golf only as a pastime while managing a real estate and banking business, but immersed himself totally in the game when he joined the USGA in 1976. He also sits on the board of the National Golf Foundation.

LAWSON LITTLE
(1910–1968)

Lawson Little reigned over amateur golf in 1934 and 1935, winning the U.S. and British Amateur Championships and putting together an unequaled string of thirty-one consecutive victories at match play.

He turned professional the next year at age twenty-six but failed to reproduce his earlier dominance, winning only seven pro events.

Little was five-foot-nine, stockily built, and one of the longest hitters of the day; he also was famous for his expert short game. If it seemed at times that he had a club for every type of shot around the green, that was probably true, for Little carried as many as twenty-six clubs. This excess contributed to the game's rulemakers declaring a limit of fourteen clubs.

Little reached the semifinals of the U.S. Amateur in 1933 and was named to the 1934 U.S. team for the Walker Cup, held in St. Andrews, Scotland. After helping the team win, Little headed to Prestwick for the British Amateur. In the final against James Wallace of Scotland, Little shot a blazing 66 in the morning round and went on to a 14 and 13 victory.

Little played similarly in the U.S. Amateur, defeating David Goldman, 8 and 7, in the final. The matches were closer the following year, with Little winning the British Amateur, 1 up, over William Twedell and the U.S. Amateur, 4 and 2, over Walter Emery.

Shortly after turning pro, Little won the 1936 Canadian Open. His finest moment as a professional came in the 1940 U.S. Open at Canterbury Golf Club in Cleveland, where Little tied Gene Sarazen after seventy-two holes, then whipped him in a playoff by three strokes.

GENE LITTLER
(born 1930)

Gene Littler owned one of the smoothest swings ever seen, and he used it to rank as one of the top players on the PGA Tour for more than twenty years. Littler's first victory came in 1954, his last in 1977. Only Sam Snead and Jack Nicklaus have stretched victories over a longer span. Littler's twenty-nine wins rank eleventh all-time.

Littler seldom missed a fairway, the main reason he stayed consistently near the top of the money list. The sole blemish on Littler's pro career was the lack of major championship victories: He won only one: the 1961 U.S. Open. He lost the 1970 Masters and 1977 PGA Championship in playoffs.

Littler began with a bang on tour, winning in his native San Diego in 1954 as an amateur (he had won the U.S. Amateur in 1953). He turned pro later that year, then won four times in 1955.

Littler won nineteen tournaments in his first nine years on tour, including five in 1959. While his pace slowed after 1962, Littler remained productive over the next decade, but in 1972 he underwent surgery for cancer of the lymph glands. "Gene the Machine" recovered admirably and won in the next year. In 1975, at age forty-five, Littler won three tournaments and finished

fifth on the money list. He continues his success on the Senior PGA Tour, which he joined in 1980.

BOBBY LOCKE
(1917–1987)

Bobby Locke's career on the American golf tour was short and anything but sweet. The South African played for three seasons in which he recorded fifteen victories. Banned for being too successful, Locke took his game to Europe where he won four British Opens in nine years.

Arthur D'Arcy Locke began playing golf at four. By the age of eighteen, he had won South Africa's Amateur and Open titles. In his first foray overseas after turning professional in 1938, Locke won the Irish and New Zealand Opens followed by the Dutch Open in 1939.

On his return from World War II and service as a bomber pilot, Locke tied for second in the 1946 British Open. Later that year, he played a sixteen-match series against Sam Snead in South Africa, the local winning 12 and 2.

Never a natural long hitter, Locke gained yardage by playing a big hook. His long irons and short game were sharp, but his putting was uncanny; his stance was narrow and closed, and he brought the blade back to the inside, but the style was effective, especially from long distances.

Locke's initial American appearance came in the 1947 Masters, where he tied for fourteenth. He went on to win six of thirteen events in the United States that year and finished second on the money list. He won six more events over the next two years, then was banned from the tour, ostensibly for reneging on commitments to play.

Although the PGA later lifted the ban and apologized, Locke cut back his American schedule and concentrated on Europe. He won the British Open in 1949, 1950, 1952, and 1957, and retired shortly after with more than eighty victories worldwide.

Locke was elected to the World Golf Hall of Fame in 1977.

HENRY LONGHURST
(1909–1979)

Known to American television viewers as "the voice of the sixteenth hole" at The Masters during the late sixties and most of the seventies, Henry Carpenter Longhurst was an expert amateur player, an accomplished golf writer, and a pioneer in the field of radio and television commentary.

Born in Bedfordshire, England, Longhurst took up golf early because of his prep school's proximity to a golf course. He later captained the Cambridge University golf team, won the German Amateur (1936), was runner-up in the French and Swiss

Amateurs and a member of the losing British Walker Cup team (also in 1936).

Following a stint at odd jobs, Longhurst began his journalism career as assistant editor of *Tee Topics,* a small, monthly golf publication in London. Three months later, in 1932, he was approached by the *Sunday Times* in London to start a weekly golf column, which appeared in every edition for the next twenty-one years and sporadically thereafter. Longhurst wrote many books–usually about golf–his most famous being an autobiography, *My Life and Soft Times.* Much traveled, he stated his philosophy as "see everything and do everything once." He almost did, even serving a two-year term as a Conservative Member of Parliament.

Longhurst was the second BBC commentator after Bernard Darwin to cover golf live on radio and television, and he charmed American viewers at The Masters with his brusque shot descriptions and his deep, gravelly voice. At the 1973 British Open, he was presented with the Walter Hagen Award "for furtherance of golfing ties between Britain and the United States." After his death from cancer, an anthology of his writings, *The Best of Henry Longhurst,* became a best-seller in Britain.

NANCY LOPEZ
(born 1957)

Nancy Lopez is the most popular and successful female golfer of recent times. With her outgoing manner, infectious smile, and exceptional shotmaking skills, Lopez has contributed significantly to the growth and image of the LPGA Tour over the past decade.

A Torrance, California, native, Lopez turned professional in 1978 after a fine junior career in which she won two U.S. Girls' Junior Championships (1972 and 1974). She was an immediate success on the women's tour, taking nine tournaments in her first season, five of them consecutively, and winning $189,813 for a single-season record (which has since been broken). Add to these a Vare Trophy for low scoring average, and it becomes obvious why Lopez was awarded both Player-of-the-Year and Rookie-of-the-Year honors, an unheard-of double.

Lopez continued her pace the next year, taking eight more tournaments and a second Vare Trophy. Again, she was named Player of the Year.

Her victory rate has cooled off in subsequent years, but by finishing sixth at the 1983 Nabisco Dinah Shore, she became the fifth woman—and the youngest player, male or female—to pass $1 million in career earnings.

Although Lopez has cut back her schedule in recent years to raise a family, she returned to form in 1985, winning five tournaments and her third Player-of-the-Year award. That season, she also set a seventy-two-hole, LPGA record score of twenty-under-par, at the Henredon Classic, and a Vare Trophy scoring record of 70.73.

In 1987, she was inducted into the LPGA Hall of Fame with thirty-five career victories, among them one major title, the LPGA Championship, which she has won twice. She continues to be the biggest drawing card in the LPGA ranks.

CHARLES BLAIR MACDONALD
(1856–1959)

One of the first Americans smitten with golf was Charles Blair Macdonald. He served this mistress in many ways: first, as one of the finest players, then, as an administrator, author, and golf course archi-

tect. To all these endeavors he brought a keen intelligence, more than a little stubbornness, and an abundant ego.

Macdonald fell in love with the game while a student at St. Andrews University in Scotland in the 1870s. He remained enamored on returning to his native Chicago, but no courses were built there until the early 1890s. Among these was Macdonald's Chicago Golf Club, which opened in 1893. A second eighteen-hole course, also for the Chicago Golf Club and designed by Macdonald, opened in 1895.

Macdonald served as a committeeman of the United States Golf Association, specializing in the Rules of Golf. His lasting reputation is as an architect. His National Golf Links of America, built in 1911 in Southampton, New York, was regarded as the first great course in America. Other Macdonald designs include Mid-Ocean (1924) in Bermuda; Yale University (1926) in New Haven, Connecticut; and

Old White (1914) at the Greenbrier in West Virginia. The courses, like the man, are demanding, intelligent, and influenced by British models. In 1928, Macdonald wrote *Scotland's Gift—Golf,* a summation of his ideas on architecture and a description of life and golf in Scotland and America.

Macdonald designed courses as an avocation, refusing any fees. He made a living as a stockbroker in New York City and died in Southampton near The National.

ALISTER MACKENZIE
(1870–1934)

Many golf course architects have designed and constructed more golf courses than Dr. Alister Mackenzie, but few can boast the quality of his portfolio. Cypress Point in California; Augusta National in Georgia (a joint project with Bobby Jones and the annual venue for The Masters); Royal Melbourne, the finest course in Australia, all came from Mackenzie's drawing board.

Mackenzie was born in Yorkshire, England, of Scottish parents. After gaining degrees in medicine, the natural sciences, and chemistry from Cambridge University, Mackenzie served as a surgeon in Africa during the Boer War. On his return to Britain, he practiced medicine. Then one night he hosted the renowned architect H.S. Colt, who was about to redesign a nearby course. Impressed by Mackenzie's knowledge of the field, Colt invited the doctor to assist in the project. Soon after, Mackenzie abandoned medicine. He eventually moved to the United States.

Mackenzie was the world's first international architect. Although based in America, he also designed or redesigned golf courses in Argentina, Australia, England, Ireland, New Zealand, Scotland, and Uruguay. He was one of the first architects to preach strategic rather than penal design, aiming to provide maximum enjoyment for all golfers. The low handicappers were invited to play heroically, the lesser golfers could, at the cost of a stroke or half-stroke, take an alternate, safer route to the hole. Mackenzie also believed strongly in harmony. He wrote in his 1920 book, *Golf Architecture*, "all the artificial features should have so natural an appearance that a stranger is unable to distinguish them from nature itself."

Among Mackenzie's other designs are the Eden course in St. Andrews, Scotland; Ohio State University's Grey and Scarlet courses (with Perry Maxwell) in Columbus; Crystal Downs Country Club (also with Maxwell) in Crystal Downs, Michigan; and Pasatiempo, an excellent public layout in Santa Cruz, Mackenzie's American "home" in California.

LLOYD MANGRUM
(1914–1973)

Lloyd Mangrum won thirty-four tournaments, good for eighth on the all-time list, but many think his best years may have been stolen by World War II.

A native of Trenton, Texas, Mangrum commanded a faithful following with his Clark Gable appearance, smooth swing, and cool disposition. He finished second in the 1940 Masters after an opening 64—a record that stood for forty-six years. Soon after, he joined the army.

Mangrum won two Purple Hearts during the war after twice being wounded in the Battle of the Bulge. He recovered quickly, however, and prepared for a return to the tour by winning two G.I. events.

Mangrum took the 1946 Open, his single major championship, by one stroke in a thirty-six-hole playoff with Byron Nelson and Vic Ghezzi. He was a master on and around the green, and his name continually appeared among the top-ten money winners between 1946 and 1954. He won eight times in 1948; four times in 1949 (including the Motor City Open, in which he and Cary Middlecoff waged eleven holes of sudden death before calling a halt to the longest playoff in tour history); and four times in 1950 (the same year he and George Fazio lost to Ben Hogan in a playoff for the U.S. Open title).

Despite his success, Mangrum did not top the money list until 1951. He won five times that year and earned the Vardon Trophy for low scoring average. He won five more times in 1952 and a second Vardon Trophy in 1953. A four-time Ryder Cupper (1947, 1949, 1951, and 1953—the last as captain), Mangrum curtailed his playing in the late fifties.

Mangrum was inducted into the PGA Hall of Fame in 1964.

CAROL MANN
(born 1941)

Carol Mann blossomed on the LPGA Tour in the mid-sixties, winning the 1965 U.S. Women's Open and at least two events in the subsequent five years.

Her best seasons came in 1968 and 1969 when, as Mickey Wright wound down her professional career, Mann battled with Kathy Whitworth for bragging rights as the best woman player. In 1968, the pair won ten tournaments each out of a schedule of thirty-two. Mann won the Vare Trophy with a scoring average of 72.04 (a mark that stood until Nancy Lopez won with 71.76 in 1978), but ran a close second to Whitworth on the money list. The following year, Mann won eight tournaments to Whitworth's seven and topped the money list. But the Vare Trophy went to Whitworth.

A natural southpaw who learned to play right-handed and the tallest woman player

ever (six-foot-three, although Mann would joke "five-foot-fifteen"), Mann won a total of thirty-eight events and came in eighth on the all-time money list (through 1987). Her last victory was in 1975, when she won three times.

Mann has always been prominent in the administration of women's sports. A former member of the LPGA Executive Board and LPGA Board of Directors, Mann was inducted into the LPGA Hall of Fame in 1977 and into the Women's Sports Hall of Fame in 1982. She has been a trustee of the Women's Sports Foundation since 1979 and was elected WSF president in 1985.

GEORGE S. MAY
(1891–1962)

This flamboyant millionaire Chicago businessman introduced big money to professional golf. In 1954, he set the first prize for his World Championship at Tam O'Shanter Country Club, a Chicago-area course he owned, at an unheard-of $50,000 and guaranteed the winner another $50,000 for a series of fifty exhibitions. This largess came at a time when the *entire purse* for an average pro tour event was around $25,000.

A carnival-like atmosphere pervaded May's tournaments. He employed clowns, brought in a "masked marvel" golfer, and gave away door prizes. He also held concurrent events for amateurs and women pros.

The 1953 World Championship was the first golf tournament to be broadcast on national television. The timing was perfect, for on the final hole, Lew Worsham holed a 104-yard wedge shot for an eagle to defeat Chandler Harper by a stroke.

Despite the money he paid, May was not a favorite of the players. Many balked when he suggested they wear numbers so specta-

tors could identify them. May subsequently made numbers optional but doubled the entry fee for the holdouts. Finally, he agreed that only the caddies should sport them.

MARK McCORMACK
(born 1931)

Mark McCormack changed the face of golf, not as a player, although he can hold his own on the course, but as chairman of the Cleveland-based International Management Group, which handles sports celebrities and promotes sporting events, including many golfers and golf tournaments.

Born in Chicago to a wealthy magazine publisher, the young McCormack became a top local amateur golfer. He captained the golf team of William and Mary College before heading on to Yale Law School and then into a Cleveland law firm. McCor-

mack remained a proficient enough player to qualify for the U.S. and British Amateurs and the U.S. Open, which became his hunting grounds for up-and-coming players in the early and mid-fifties. He soon formed a golf management company, and in 1960 shook hands with his new client Arnold Palmer. Within two years, the deals that McCormack had cut selling the Palmer name and image had increased the player's income tenfold.

When McCormack signed Gary Player and Jack Nicklaus in the early sixties, the business grew. (Nicklaus went on his own in 1970; Player remains a client.) Today, IMG handles players in golf, tennis, team

sports (such as football and baseball), and such organizations as the USGA (for the U.S. Open) and the Royal and Ancient Golf Club of St. Andrews (for the British Open). IMG also stages a number of foreign golf tournaments.

Called "the most powerful man in sports," McCormack still plays to a single-digit handicap. In 1984, he wrote the bestseller *What They Didn't Teach You at Harvard Business School.*

JOHN McDERMOTT
(1891–1971)

A heroic but ultimately tragic figure, John J. McDermott was the first American-born player to win the U.S. Open Champion-

ship and remains the youngest American to win any men's professional tour event.

The son of a Philadelphia mailman, McDermott dropped out of high school to become a professional golfer. A quiet, intense young man, McDermott practiced rigorously. In the 1910 U.S. Open—his second campaign—at the Philadelphia Cricket Club, McDermott finished tied for the lead with Alex and Macdonald Smith of Scotland. Alex won the ensuing playoff.

At the Chicago Golf Club in 1911, McDermott again went into a three-way playoff, this time with Mike Brady and George Simpson. McDermott prevailed. Then, with his flat, smooth swing, McDermott repeated as U.S. Open champion at the Country Club of Buffalo, New York, in 1912.

As 1913 dawned, life looked good for McDermott. He was endorsing equipment, investing his money, and being compared to the great British players. He placed fifth at the British Open at Hoylake—the highest American finish at the time—but upon his return to America, McDermott's fortunes turned sour. He learned that he had lost heavily in the stock market; he then embarrassed himself with arrogant remarks about American supremacy after winning the Shawnee (Pennsylvania) Open by thirteen strokes over Ted Ray and Harry Vardon. He failed to qualify for the 1914 British Open because he missed the ferry to the train to Prestwick, and on the

return voyage, his ship collided in the fog with a grain carrier and sank, although McDermott survived. In 1915 he suffered a nervous breakdown, thereafter spending much of his life in various sanatoriums.

CARY MIDDLECOFF
(born 1921)

Respected as one of the most intelligent and successful golfers in tour history, Cary Middlecoff won thirty-seven professional tournaments—seventh best on the all-time list—and wrote articles and books on the golf swing.

Born in Halls, Tennessee, Middlecoff originally followed his father and two uncles into dentistry. But while known as the Doctor, he won the Tennessee Amateur four straight times (1940–43) and then became the only amateur ever to win the North and South Open.

Turning pro in 1947, he captured his first tournament in only his third outing and went on to win at least one title a year until 1961. His first big year was 1949, when he won five times, including his first U.S. Open at Medinah Country Club in Illinois. Nineteen fifty-one proved even more lucrative: he won six times on tour, a high. The five 1955 victories included The Masters, where Middlecoff beat Ben

Hogan by seven strokes. A second U.S. Open title followed at Oak Hill, Rochester, New York, in 1956, the same year Middlecoff took his only Vardon Trophy for low scoring average. He narrowly missed repeating as Open champion the following year, losing to Dick Mayer in a playoff.

A three-time Ryder Cup team member (1953, 1955, and 1959), Middlecoff gave up the pro game in the early sixties because of back ailments and constant bouts of the "yips."

A brilliant golf theorist, Middlecoff wrote *Advanced Golf* and *The Golf Swing*. He was inducted into the PGA Hall of Fame in 1974 and into the World Golf Hall of Fame in 1986.

JOHNNY MILLER
(born 1947)

Johnny Miller was a golfer on fire in the mid-1970s. He won eight tournaments in 1974—including the first three of the season—and topped the money list with a record $353,021. He began 1975 with a twenty-four-under-par score at the Phoenix Open—and a fourteen-shot victory—and a score of twenty-five under par in the Tucson Open for a nine-shot victory. No one has started a season so hot.

The San Francisco native, who won the 1964 U.S. Junior Amateur and finished eighth in the 1966 U.S. Open at age nineteen, first made headlines with a final-round 63 that won the 1973 U.S. Open at

Oakmont outside Pittsburgh, Pennsylvania, by a stroke. The slender, blond, twenty-six-year-old phenomenon was the original tour "clone." He won twice more in 1975 to finish second on the money list. Although he won only twice on tour in 1976, Miller added a second major when he won the British Open at Royal Birkdale.

This breakneck pace took its toll on Miller. He attributed his decline to "non-golf" muscles developed while working outdoors on his California ranch. Although he maintained he had disturbed the timing of his explosive swing, the more cynical suggested Miller had lost his drive because he won too much too quickly, including a $1-million-per-year clothing endorsement contract with Sears. Whatever the reason, Miller had slumped to 111th on the money list by 1978.

Since then, Miller has won six times, despite playing fewer tournaments and becoming more of a family man, living with his wife and six children in Salt Lake City, Utah. He remains a popular player with the galleries and every so often displays the uncanny accuracy with approach shots that propelled him to success early in his career.

BYRON NELSON
(born 1912)

Byron Nelson won a record eleven consecutive tournaments, eighteen in all, in 1945, but the tall Texan was no flash in the pan. From 1937, when he won The Masters, to his retirement in 1946, Nelson was one of the best players in the game.

Nelson learned to play as a caddie in Fort Worth, Texas, at Glen Garden Country Club, where Ben Hogan, who was the same age, also caddied. Nelson turned pro in 1932 and struggled to make ends meet for a few years. He stamped himself as a major force in golf by winning the 1937 Masters, then added the 1939 U.S. Open, the 1940 PGA Championship (defeating Sam Snead in the final), and the 1942 Masters, the last coming after a playoff over Hogan. Nelson reached the finals in five out of six PGA Championships starting in 1939, winning in 1940 and 1945 and finishing second in 1939, 1941, and 1944 (the tournament was not held in 1943).

Nelson's peak years were 1944 and 1945, when he won twenty-six tournaments. This success coincided with World War II, when many pros were away serving in the military (a blood disorder prevented Nelson from serving). That should not detract from Nelson's achievements. He alone was responsible for his average 69.67 strokes per round in 1944 and 68.33 in 1945. Today the annual award for low scoring average on the Senior PGA Tour is called the Byron Nelson trophy.

Nelson won five events in 1946 and finished second in the U.S. Open. Finally, the pressure of the tournament grind became too much. At thirty-four, Nelson virtually retired to his Texas ranch, returning to play in a few tournaments a year. Nelson finished his professional career with fifty-four wins, ranking fifth all-time.

Nelson was inducted into the PGA Hall of Fame in 1953 and was a charter member of the World Golf Hall of Fame in 1974.

JACK NICKLAUS
(born 1940)

Jack Nicklaus has played the finest golf of the past twenty-five years. Since his first victory as a professional—the 1962 U.S. Open at Oakmont when he bettered Arnold Palmer in a playoff—Nicklaus has racked up seventy-one victories in the United States and eighteen overseas.

But Nicklaus is known not so much for the quantity of his wins as the quality. "The Golden Bear," a nickname derived from his blond hair and the considerable girth of his youth, owns an unparalleled record in what he has called "the ones that count": the major championships. Nicklaus owns twenty major titles, including six Masters, five PGA Championships, four U.S. Opens, three British Opens, and two U.S. Amateur Championships. His nearest "challenger" in major victories is Bobby Jones, who recorded thirteen.

Nicklaus is a five-time PGA Player of the Year, has played on six World Cup and six Ryder Cup teams (and was non-playing captain for two Ryder Cups), has topped the tour's annual money list eight times, and as of this writing, looked likely to be the first pro to surpass $5 million in career earnings.

He also has become one of the top golf course architects, designing such layouts as Muirfield Village Golf Club, the site of the annual Memorial Tournament near his native Columbus, Ohio; Shoal Creek Golf Club in Birmingham, Alabama, which hosted the 1984 PGA Championship (and will again in 1990); and Glen Abbey Golf Club outside Toronto, where the Canadian Open is held. Nicklaus's other activities include part-ownership of the MacGregor Golf equipment company.

Nicklaus was an inaugural inductee to the World Golf Hall of Fame in 1974.

GREG NORMAN

(born 1955)

If Greg Norman lives up to the potential he displayed in 1986, he soon will become the greatest Australian player ever and one of the finest players to emerge from any part of the world. That year, Norman led every major after three rounds. Although he captured only one, the British Open, which he won by five strokes, he lost The Masters to a Jack Nicklaus playing like the Golden Bear of old and the PGA Championship to a miracle hole-out from sand by Bob Tway.

Norman took up the game in his native Queensland at age sixteen. He was a caddie for his mother, and when she finished Norman would play a few holes. Within two years he was a scratch player, self-taught principally by the writings of Nicklaus and by practicing many hours. He turned professional in 1976 and won the fourth tournament in which he played. Later that year, Norman represented Australia in the World Cup.

Norman had won twenty-nine tournaments around the world—primarily in Australia and Europe—before joining the American tour full-time in 1984. With his ability to drive the ball as long and straight as anyone in the game and his easy rapport with the galleries, Norman quickly became a crowd favorite. "The Great White Shark"—a nickname that grew out of his fondness for deep-sea fishing and his shock

of blond hair—won two events in 1984 and lost the U.S. Open in an eighteen-hole playoff with Fuzzy Zoeller. The Australian slumped the following year, mainly because of a virus, but returned to win three events in 1986 and top the PGA Tour money list.

One of the most exciting players to watch, Norman makes his home in Florida.

FRANCIS OUIMET

(1883–1967)

Francis Ouimet wanted only to watch Harry Vardon and Ted Ray during their 1913 exhibition tour of America, but he ended up beating the pair in a playoff for the 1913 U.S. Open at The Country Club in Brookline, Massachusetts.

Ouimet was born in a modest house adjacent to The Country Club and caddied at the club, playing what golf he could at the nearby Franklin Park public course. He won the Massachusetts Amateur once and only entered the 1913 Open at the behest of the USGA, which wanted to enlarge the amateur field. Shocking the crowd—and himself—the twenty-year-old Ouimet drew even with Vardon and Ray after three rounds, then, after falling behind in the front nine of the final round, staged a remarkable comeback to tie the British veterans by the finish. In an eighteen-hole playoff, Ouimet hammered Vardon by five strokes and Ray by six to be-

come only the second American after John McDermott to win the title. Ouimet's victory was significant. It put the game within reach of the common man.

Ouimet remained an amateur and went on to win the 1914 and 1931 U.S. Amateur titles. He finished fifth in the 1914 Open, then tied for third, one stroke out of a playoff in 1925, but never again threatened.

He served on nine consecutive Walker Cup teams from 1922–49, the last four as non-playing captain.

Ouimet also was respected outside the United States: in 1951 he became the first American to captain the Royal and Ancient Golf Club in St. Andrews, a post since held by only two other Americans.

Ouimet died in Newton, Massachusetts.

ARNOLD PALMER

(born 1929)

Arnold Palmer revolutionized American golf in the late fifties and sixties. With a pants hitch, a lunging swing, and a bold approach to putting, Palmer became a hero for his audacity and final-round charges, and drew adoration from his rabid fans, better known as "Arnie's Army."

The son of the superintendent and pro at the Latrobe Country Club, Palmer won his first major championship, the U.S. Amateur, in 1954. He turned pro in 1955 and won that year's Canadian Open.

Palmer can count seven professional major championships among sixty-one tour victories. He won The Masters four times between 1958 and 1964 and took consecutive British Open titles in 1961 and 1962. His sole U.S. Open victory came at Cherry Hills Country Club in Denver, Colorado, in 1960, when a final-round 65 slingshot him from seven strokes back to win.

Palmer was the first player to eclipse $100,000 in earnings in a single season (1962) and the first to surpass the $1-million mark in career earnings (1968). A four-time leading money winner, Palmer was honored in 1980 when the trophy awarded annually to the leading money winner was named after him. A six-time Ryder Cup member and an inaugural member of the World Golf Hall of Fame (1974), Palmer was inducted into the PGA Hall of Fame in 1980. He now plays on the Senior PGA Tour.

HENRY PICARD
(born 1907)

Henry Picard was one of the leading pros in the tranquil days of the late thirties and early forties after Bobby Jones had retired from tournament golf and before Ben Hogan, Byron Nelson, and Sam Snead came along to dominate.

A tall, lean, quiet pro from Massachusetts with a smooth swing, deadly long irons, and a deft putting stroke, Picard won thirty-four tournaments between 1934 and 1942, including the 1938 Masters and 1939 PGA Championship.

Picard finished well down the field in the first Masters in 1934 but contended in the second, leading by four strokes at the halfway point, only to fall away in rounds three and four. In 1938, he led by a stroke going into the final round, shot a thirty-two on the front nine, and looked as though he would waltz home. But the final nine holes extracted a thirty-eight, and Picard won by only two strokes over Ralph Guldahl and Harry Cooper.

The next year, 1939, was Picard's finest. He captured six titles and was leading money winner with $10,303. In the PGA Championship at the Pomonok Country Club in Flushing, New York, he faced Byron Nelson in the final and drew even at the end of regulation only by birdieing the final hole, nearly driving the green of the three-hundred-yard par four. On the first playoff hole, Picard's drive rolled under a truck, which ran over his ball in moving out of the way. Granted relief, Picard put his approach to ten feet. From the fairway, Nelson hit to six feet, but only Picard holed his putt.

Picard played on the 1935 and 1937 U.S. Ryder Cup teams and was selected for the 1939 matches, which were canceled because of World War II. He cut back his playing schedule during the war because of ill health, resorting to the life of a club pro.

GARY PLAYER
(born 1935)

Gary Player was the first foreign golfer to achieve great success in the United States. While playing a limited American schedule between 1958 and 1979, Player won twenty-one events, including three Masters (1961, 1974, and 1978), two PGA Championships (1962 and 1972), and one U.S. Open (1965). He also won three British Opens (1959, 1968, and 1974), making him one of only four men (the others being Gene Sarazen, Ben Hogan, and Jack Nicklaus) to win the modern Grand Slam.

Player has won more than 120 events worldwide, quite an accomplishment for a

diminutive man from South Africa who first tried his luck in England in the mid-fifties. At that time, while playing with a strong grip, a flat swing, and an intensity that many contemporaries considered arrogant, Player was advised to return home to a club job. But he worked hard at his game, practicing much more than his peers. His deficiencies became obstacles he was determined to overcome. Player became one of the best sand players of all time, a clutch putter, and earned every inch of distance he could muster. And while he occasionally credited a fad diet, the trademark black clothes, even divine intervention for his success, there was little doubt among those who watched Player beat balls for hours on end that only he was responsible.

In the United States, Player became, with Arnold Palmer and Jack Nicklaus, one of the "Big Three" who dominated golf in the 1960s and 1970s. Player became the first foreigner to win The Masters and the PGA Championship and the first foreigner since Ted Ray (in 1920) to win the U.S. Open. His most exciting victory was the 1978 Masters, where he started the final round seven strokes behind Hubert Green, then shot a 64, with six birdies on the back nine, to win by one stroke.

Player is a power on the Senior PGA Tour, playing with much the same intensity and dedication that marked his younger days.

CHARLES PRICE
(born 1925)

Few golf writers have the résumé, either as a scribe or a golfer, of Charles Price. A Philadelphia native who now makes his home in Pinehurst, North Carolina, he has written eight books, was the founding editor of *GOLF Magazine*, for which he continued to write a column long after he stepped down, and played what is today the PGA Tour as an amateur in 1947 and 1948. He has continued to play in a less hectic environment but, with typical self-deprecating aplomb, claims to have "retired" in 1953. "I retired from competition at the age of twenty-eight, the same age as [Bobby] Jones," Price later wrote. "The difference was that Jones retired because he beat everybody. I retired because I couldn't beat anybody."

Price took up golf as a twelve-year-old, playing at Indian Springs, a Donald Ross design outside Washington, D.C., where his father was a member. His education took him to Colgate and Holy Cross Universities, where he studied medicine and played a lot of golf. On his graduation in 1947, he took to the tour. He went to work for the *Pinehurst Outlook,* and later held writing posts with the *Washington Star, Collier's, Esquire, Holiday,* and the *Saturday Evening Post.*

Price became editor of *GOLF Magazine* in 1959 and held the position for three years, during which his "Rub of the Green" columns established him as one of the shrewdest, most forthright, and funniest golf writers ever. He then left the magazine to write *The World of Golf,* a comprehensive illustrated history of the game. That completed, Price began, with Herbert Warren Wind, another of today's finest golf writers, to pen scripts for the successful television series "Wonderful World of Golf," of which he was also an associate producer. Price continued to write for *GOLF Magazine* but ended his affiliation in 1982 when he took a post as contributing editor with the magazine's rival publication, *Golf Digest.*

Price won the Golf Writers Association of America Award for magazine writing in 1978 and 1983; in 1985 he received the Memorial Golf Journalism Award, which is sponsored by Jack Nicklaus. Price also was the first director of golf at the Harbour Town Golf Links on Hilton Head Island, South Carolina, and was instrumental in the launching in 1969 of the Heritage Golf Classic, now one of the most prestigious tournaments on the PGA Tour.

BETSY RAWLS
(born 1928)

Betsy Rawls recorded fifty-five victories that included eight major championships in twenty-two years as a professional. She continues to contribute to the game following her retirement as a player, working with the LPGA, USGA, and various tournament organizers.

Four years after Rawls picked up a club at age seventeen, she won the 1949 Texas Amateur and repeated the following year. Soon after joining the LPGA Tour in 1951, Rawls recorded her first victory, the U.S. Women's Open. She again won the Open in 1953 by defeating Jackie Pung in a playoff, then took the Open once more in 1957 on a technicality: Pung had shot the lower, and one better, score but had signed an incorrect scorecard and was disqualified. Rawls's fourth Open title (a record she shares with Mickey Wright) came in 1960. Her other major victories were the 1959 and 1969 LPGA Championships and the 1952 and 1959 Western Opens.

Rawls's strong short game helped her become the leading money winner in 1952 and 1959, her best season. She won ten times and took home the Vare Trophy for low scoring average. Rawls won at least one tournament a year from 1951–65; her total of fifty-five places her third all-time behind Wright and Kathy Whitworth.

After retiring in 1975, Rawls served as LPGA tournament director for six years, supervising a period of rapid growth. She was the first woman to serve on the Rules Committee for the men's U.S. Open in 1980. The next year she left the LPGA to take over her present post as executive director of the McDonald's Championship, an annual LPGA summer event held outside Philadelphia.

JOHN REID
(1840–1916)

The Father of American Golf emigrated from Scotland in the mid-nineteenth century and made his fortune in iron and steel. Reid never forgot his roots, however, and in 1887 he asked his friend Robert Lockhart, another Scot, to bring back from a business trip to Britain a set of golf clubs and some golf balls.

On February 22, 1888, Reid and some friends went to a cow pasture near Reid's home in Yonkers, New York, to play with the equipment Lockhart had purchased.

Reid played against John B. Upham in the first golf match in America.

A blizzard put a temporary lid on the novel pursuit, but when the weather improved, Reid and his group laid out six holes in a different pasture. In November of that year, Reid and his friends formed the St. Andrew's Golf Club, the first permanent club in America. Reid was elected president.

In 1892, the city of Yonkers extended a road through the new course, forcing the thirteen members to move north to an apple orchard where they laid out another six holes. Because a large apple tree did double-duty as a clubhouse—the players hung their coats on its branches—the group became known as the Apple Tree Gang.

Two years later Reid's group built nine holes on the Odell Farm, three miles north of the orchard. The club moved again in 1897 to its present site, an area large enough to accommodate eighteen holes, in Mt. Hope, New York.

Reid resigned his presidency after nine years but not until the St. Andrew's Golf Club had become a charter member of the United States Golf Association, and although Reid was narrowly beaten out for the post of president by Theodore Havemeyer, he worked with Charles Blair Macdonald to draw up the USGA constitution and by-laws. Reid continued to be a powerful force in the early days of American golf until his death.

GRANTLAND RICE
(1888–1954)

One of the most prolific sportswriters of the first half of the twentieth century, Grantland Rice was as renowned as the heroes whose exploits he chronicled. Although he covered almost all sports, Rice was an avid golfer, and his works contributed greatly to the growth of the game in the United States.

Rice edited *The American Golfer* magazine for fifteen years. A friend of Bobby Jones, Rice was an early member of Augusta National Golf Club in Augusta, Georgia. When the club was planning the inaugural Masters Tournament in 1934, Rice suggested dates in late March when baseball teams would be heading north after spring training—together with the nation's leading sportswriters. His suggestion guaranteed publicity from the outset.

Rice also was partially responsible for bringing Babe Zaharias to the game. After watching her star in track and field in the 1932 Olympic Games, Rice recognized that Zaharias (known as Didrikson at the time) could be a standout golfer and urged her to take up the game. She eventually became a dominant figure in the early years of women's professional golf.

As a writer, Rice could turn a phrase as well as any of his peers. Consider his 1920

description of golf: "Golf is 20 percent mechanics and technique. The other 80 percent is philosophy, humor, tragedy, romance, melodrama, companionship, camaraderie, cussedness and conversation."

CLIFFORD ROBERTS
(1894–1977)

Clifford Roberts left no doubt who was in charge of The Masters Tournament. He ran the event with an iron hand as tournament chairman from its inception in 1934 until his death forty-three years later. Roberts was not particularly liked, but he was respected. And well he should have been, for the autocratic leader molded The Masters into one of golf's four major championships. Roberts created an aura about The Masters as a special invitational event that brought together the world's best golfers in a pure golf setting (no commercialism was allowed) on a great course—the Augusta National Golf Club in Augusta, Georgia. (Augusta National was the brainchild of Roberts and Bobby Jones, the amateur star of the 1920s.) Although a conservative man, he was not afraid to introduce innovations that would improve the tournament, such as installing gallery ropes around the course, or making changes to the course to improve it.

Roberts was born in Morning Sun, Iowa, and reared in small towns in Iowa

and Texas. He eventually became a Wall Street investment banker in the 1920s, and spent his winters in Augusta, where he befriended Jones. Knowing that Jones was interested in funding a club after his retirement in 1930, Roberts suggested the site. He coined the name Masters—even though Jones felt it presumptuous—for the invitational tournament and convinced Jones to play in the inaugural.

By 1977, Roberts had discovered that he was terminally ill. In September of that year, after asking a security guard how to fire a pistol, Roberts was found on the grounds of Augusta, killed by a gunshot wound believed to be self-inflicted. It is said that his ashes are buried somewhere on the golf course, but the location remains a secret.

CHI CHI RODRIGUEZ
(born 1935)

Chi Chi Rodriguez was never the longest hitter, the finest ball striker or, financially speaking, the most successful golfer of his era. But few have played the game with the spirit or heart of this native of Puerto Rico. Since he joined the PGA Tour in 1960, Rodriguez (christened Juan but nicknamed

Chi Chi after his favorite baseball player of his youth) has entertained golf galleries around the world with a quick wit and a deft touch around the greens. Since 1985, he has brought his act to the Senior PGA Tour.

Rodriguez's first club in his native Bayamón, to the southeast of the island, was the branch of a guava tree; his first balls were tin cans. Once equipped with the proper tools, however, Rodriguez improved rapidly and finished as runner-up in the Puerto Rican Open at age seventeen.

Despite his rather delicate build—five feet seven, around 135 pounds—Rodriguez won eight times after joining the tour. He could hit a long, low ball and was a masterful bunker player, but became best known for his wisecracks, his habit of waving his putter the way a fencer wields a sword whenever he holed a putt of any length, and covering the hole with his hat after each birdie. If the antics of the "Clown Prince" of the tour annoyed some, they brought life to a game that had not become totally detached from the robotic style of Ben Hogan.

While Rodriguez continued his success when he joined the senior tour—he was leading money winner in 1987—some would say that his greatest gift to the game has been his work for those less fortunate than himself. Every year the Chi Chi Rodriguez Youth Foundation brings six hundred children from low-income families or broken homes to the Glen Oaks municipal course in Clearwater, Florida. There the children learn everything from the rudiments of golf and course management to the simple need for a foundation in their lives. Despite a hectic golf schedule, Rodriguez maintains close contact with the project. "It means more to me than winning a hundred golf tournaments," he says.

DONALD ROSS
(1873–1948)

Some five to six hundred courses in the world bear the Donald Ross signature, but more important than numbers is the quality of the man's work. Among his American gems are Pinehurst No. 2 in North Carolina, Seminole in Florida,

Oakland Hills in Michigan, Inverness and Scioto in Ohio, and Oak Hill in New York.

Donald Ross was born in Dornoch, Scotland, where he was greatly influenced by the layout of Royal Dornoch, itself one of the world's top courses. As a young man, Ross landed a position under Old Tom Morris at St. Andrews, then became pro and greenkeeper at Royal Dornoch. In 1898, when he was twenty-five, Ross emigrated to the United States, as many other Scottish pros were doing at the time. He is said to have arrived in Boston with two dollars in his pocket. Ross soon landed a job as pro at Oakley Country Club in Watertown, Massachusetts, and two years later found a permanent home as the pro at the Pinehurst resort. Soon he began work on the No. 2 course at Pinehurst, which was to become his masterpiece. He finished a first version in 1903 and continued revising it through 1935. Once Ross's reputation was established at Pinehurst, he became much in demand as an architect.

Many of Ross's courses are subtle layouts that emphasize approach shots and chipping. The greens often are slightly elevated, with crowns and slopes that can run an errant shot right off the green.

Although his work entailed much travel, Ross remained affiliated with Pinehurst until his death.

PAUL RUNYAN

(born 1908)

Few players have been celebrated for their *lack* of distance, but Paul Runyan earned accolades and victories while being regularly outdriven. The native of Hot Springs, Arkansas, was known as Little Poison, because of his height (five-foot, seven-and-a-half inches) and for the deadly ways on and around the greens that made up for any shortfall in length. Runyan won more than fifty tournaments between the mid-thirties and early forties, including two PGA Championships (1934 and 1938). When he left the tour he became a teacher noted for short game and putting instruction.

Runyan exploded on the scene in 1933 and 1934 when he won seven events each year, was the leading money winner both years and was the winner of the Radix Trophy (predecessor of the Vardon Trophy for low scoring average) in 1933. In the 1934 PGA Championship at Park Country Club in Williamsville, New York (near Buffalo), Runyan faced Craig Wood, one of the longest hitters of the day, in the final. The pair went to thirty-eight holes before Runyan blasted from a bunker to eight feet and holed the putt to win.

The rivalry was different but the scenario much the same in 1938 when Sam Snead constantly outdrove Runyan in the PGA final at Shawnee Country Club in

Pennsylvania by about fifty yards. But a sound long-iron game and his usual dexterity around the greens gave Runyan an 8 and 7 victory, the most lopsided in the forty PGA Championships that were held at match play.

Runyan seldom contended in the other majors. He tied for third in the first Masters in 1934 and recorded four top-four finishes in that event's first nine performances. The best he could muster in the U.S. Open was a fifth-place finish in 1941.

Runyan cut back his playing schedule during World War II, turning instead to teaching. Later on, however, he won the PGA Seniors and World Series titles in 1961 and 1962.

Runyan was inducted into the PGA Hall of Fame in 1959.

GENE SARAZEN

(born 1902)

The Squire put together two careers in golf. The first was in the early twenties, the second in the early thirties. This diminutive, stern competitor from Harrison, New York, won the 1922 U.S. Open at Skokie Country Club in Glencoe, Illinois, when he was twenty years and four months old. Later that year he took the PGA Championship and then challenged Walter Hagen to a thirty-six-hole "World Championship of Golf" over Oakmont (Pennsylvania) Country Club and Westchester (New York) Country Club. Sarazen won that, too, 3 and 2. Sarazen repeated as PGA champion in 1923, again defeating

Hagen in the final. For the next nine years, he suffered from a severe hook and did not figure in a major.

Sarazen's invention of the sand wedge in 1931—he added a deep flange and bounce to a straight-faced niblick—kindled his second career. In 1932, wedge in hand, Sarazen romped by five strokes to his only British Open title, at Sandwich. Two weeks later, he fired a final-round 66 to win his second U.S. Open at Fresh Meadows Country Club, New York. Sarazen's third PGA title arrived in 1933, and 1935 brought the shot that helped him become the first player to complete the modern Grand Slam: his 4-wood second shot to the par-five fifteenth at Augusta National in the final round of The Masters rolled into the hole for a double eagle. Sarazen beat Craig Wood, 144 to 149, in the thirty-six-hole playoff the following day.

Sarazen wrapped up his golf career as a commentator with Jimmy Demaret on Shell's "Wonderful World of Golf" television series during the 1960s. Today, he, Byron Nelson, and Sam Snead start each Masters Tournament with a nine-hole tour. Sarazen was an inaugural member of the PGA Hall of Fame in 1940 and of the World Golf Hall of Fame in 1974.

DINAH SHORE

(born 1921)

Just as Bing Crosby did for many years, and Bob Hope still does on the PGA Tour, Dinah Shore stars as the celebrity host of a golf tournament, in her case the Nabisco Dinah Shore, an LPGA major and a popular stop on the women's tour.

Shore first became involved with the tournament in 1972, when it was called the Colgate–Dinah Shore Winner's Circle, and continued as host after Nabisco replaced Colgate as title sponsor in 1982. The tournament, which has always been held in Rancho Mirage, California, has been a major since 1983 and today draws one of the best fields of the year. Shore plays a major role in the running and publicizing of the tournament, playing in the tournament pro-am, hosting dinners, and serving as television commentator with NBC-TV.

Shore rose to fame as a singer on radio and television in the years surrounding

World War II. Born in Winchester, Tennessee (as Frances Rose; the Dinah came from a New York disc jockey who forgot Shore's name but remembered she sang a song titled "Dinah"), Shore began singing in nearby Memphis, where she grew up. In 1938, she won a job with WNEW in New York, singing duets with Frank Sinatra. Three years later, Eddie Cantor discovered her and gave her a regular solo spot on his radio show. He later took Shore to Hollywood, where she met and married film actor George Montgomery.

Shore's popularity increased when she entertained American forces overseas during World War II. After the war, she won national fame on the "Chevy Show," which ran on television from 1951–61. Since then, she has starred on such television shows as "The Dinah Shore Show," "Dinah's Place," and "Dinah!" As a recording artist, Shore has won ten Emmy Awards, nine gold records, and a Peabody Award.

Shore had seldom played golf before becoming associated with the tournament, but in the ensuing years she became the first woman to play the pro-am on the San Diego and Westchester (New York) tour stop. Now her handicap hovers around twenty. "My life's ambition is to shoot 85 or less and then do it consistently," she said recently. "After that I will smile forever. Anyone I'm playing with will not have to cook for a long time. I will buy them breakfast, lunch, and dinner for as long as they can put up with me describing my sensational round."

CHARLIE SIFFORD
(born 1923)

Charlie Sifford was one of the first blacks to play the pro tour and the first to win a tour event. Although a professional since 1948, Sifford made only occasional appearances on tour in the 1950s because the PGA's constitution limited membership to whites. In 1960, that clause was challenged by the State of California and the "all-white" rule erased.

Sifford began in golf as a caddie in his hometown of Charlotte, North Carolina. After a stint in the army, he became the private golf professional for blues singer Billy Eckstine. Playing when he could, Sifford won the Negro National Open six times as well as the 1957 Long Beach Open and the 1963 Puerto Rico Open.

Sifford still faced discrimination when he joined the tour in 1960. He was barred from some hotels and restaurants, kept from entering events and suffered death threats. His first official tour victory was the 1967 Hartford Open, won with a seven-under-par 64 in the final round. His only other victory was the 1969 Los Angeles Open, where he defeated Harold Henning in a playoff. Still, Sifford won more than $340,000 on tour.

In 1975, Sifford won the PGA Seniors title, and in 1980 he joined the Senior PGA Tour. With his trademark big cigar sticking from the side of his mouth, he has enjoyed moderate success, including a victory in the 1980 Suntree Classic. He plays out of the Sleepy Hollow Golf Club in Brecksville, Ohio, where he makes his home.

JAY SIGEL
(born 1945)

Jay Sigel is a throwback, an amateur golfer who is neither a hotshot college kid destined for the pro tour nor a college coach. He is an insurance executive who plays golf as a pastime—and he plays it better than most.

Not that Sigel could not have turned pro. He first shone in the 1961 U.S. Junior Amateur Championship when he finished runner-up and later attended Wake Forest on a golf scholarship. During this time, Sigel accidentally put his left hand through a glass door that had been slammed toward him, severing the nerves in two of his fingers. The injury healed, but not so well that the hand could withstand the rigors of a professional schedule.

Instead, Sigel grew to become one of amateur golf's elder statesmen. He won U.S. Amateur Championships in 1982 and 1983. When he added the 1983 U.S. Mid-Amateur, he became the first man to win two USGA events in the same year since Bobby Jones took home the U.S. Amateur and Open titles in 1930. Sigel added Mid-Amateur titles in 1985 and 1987.

Other achievements by this native of Berwyn, Pennsylvania—where he still res-

ides—include the 1979 British Amateur, six Walker Cup appearances between 1977–87, six U.S. World Amateur team appearances, low amateur honors in the 1980 British Open and 1980 and 1981 Masters, and eleven Pennsylvania Amateur and three Pennsylvania Open titles.

Sigel won the Golf Writers Association of America's Ben Hogan Award in 1984, an honor given to those still active in golf despite a physical disability.

HORTON SMITH
(1908–1963)

In 1929, a twenty-one-year-old named Horton Smith won seven tournaments and finished second four times in nineteen events. Although he never matched such heights again, Smith remained one of the top professionals in the United States throughout the 1930s, winning thirty tournaments, including two of the first three Masters, in 1934 and 1936. Both were dramatic one-shot victories, first over Craig Wood, then over Light-Horse Harry Cooper. Smith took the lead on the penultimate hole each time.

Smith's best finishes in the U.S. Open were third places in 1930 and 1940; his last tournament victory came in 1941. The next year he joined the armed services.

Smith came from Springfield, Missouri, was handsome, sartorially elegant, and popular with the galleries. He had a smooth, slow swing and was one of the better putters of the day. A thoughtful, introspective man, he often experimented with his swing, perhaps to his detriment, because he never quite rediscovered the groove of 1929.

Smith also became interested in the administrative side of the game, chairing the PGA's tournament committee in 1933, and, after his competitive career was over, serving as PGA president from 1952–54.

MACDONALD SMITH
(1890–1949)

Macdonald Smith belongs to that fraternity of outstanding golfers who never have won a major championship.

One of three brothers who emigrated from Carnoustie, Scotland—Willie, the 1899 U.S. Open champion, and Alex, who won U.S. Opens in 1906 and 1910, being the others—Mac was twice runner-up in the U.S. Open. He and John McDermott were beaten in a playoff by Alex at the Philadelphia Cricket Club in 1910, and Bobby Jones edged him by two strokes in the 1930 U.S. Open at Interlachen Country Club in Hopkins, Minnesota.

Smith had lost a major to Jones earlier that year when he and Leo Diegel had gone down by two shots in the British Open at Hoylake. But then, Jones overcame most of the competition in 1930: it was the year of the Grand Slam.

Two years later, Smith logged his fourth runner-up finish in a major, Gene Sarazen wielding his sand wedge to take the British Open at Prince's Golf Club in Sandwich, England. In all, Smith finished within three strokes of the U.S. or British Open Championship on nine occasions.

Not that Smith played without success. He won thirty-five tournaments in the United States, including three Western Opens and four Los Angeles Opens. It galled observers that Smith never achieved major status, particularly because he had a fluid, crisp swing, was an excellent putter and never allowed a disaster of even major proportions to fluster him. "There is no more flagrant case of miscarried justice," H.B. Martin wrote in *Fifty Years of American Golf,* "than in the story of Macdonald Smith, youngest of the Smith clan and the most brilliant. Mac was a stylist with a swing as true and accurate as that of Harry Vardon, the greatest master of them all."

SAM SNEAD
(born 1912)

In 1937, Samuel Jackson Snead came out of the backwoods of Virginia with as smooth a golf swing as had been seen and began a tour career that lasted more than forty years. He is credited with at least 135 wins worldwide, including a record eighty-four on the PGA Tour. He won three Masters (1949, 1952, and 1954), three PGA Championships (1942, 1949, and 1951), and the 1946 British Open. That no U.S. Open is listed remains Snead's greatest disappointment.

Snead learned to play swinging an old 5-iron behind a barn in his native Hot Springs, Virginia. He soon learned to boom the ball straight and long, thereby earning the nickname Slammin' Sammy. Only Snead's putting was weak: he often suffered from the "yips," which led him frequently to switch putters and technique.

In his first year on tour, 1937, Snead won four events and finished second in the U.S. Open. He won seven times in the next year, including the first of eight Greensboro Opens. (The last victory came in 1965 when Snead was two months shy of fifty-three, making him the oldest win-

ner of a regular tour event.) In the forties and fifties, Snead won a handful of tournaments every year in addition to four Vardon Trophies (1938, 1949, 1950, and 1955) for low scoring average while leading the money list three times (1938, 1949, and 1950) and making eight Ryder Cup appearances between 1937 and 1959.

Snead continued to win as a Senior, amassing six PGA Senior and five World Senior titles between 1963 and 1973. In the 1972 PGA Championship, at age sixty, he finished tied for fourth; two years later, he tied for third. In the 1979 Quad Cities, he became the first player to shoot his age in a regular tour event, scoring 67–66 at age sixty-seven.

Snead was elected to the PGA Hall of Fame in 1953 and was a charter member of the World Golf Hall of Fame in 1974.

JAN STEPHENSON
(born 1951)

When Jan Stephenson joined the LPGA Tour in 1974, she brought along more than her golf game; she brought a touch of glamour. The attractive, blonde, blue-eyed Australian quickly became the tour's sex symbol, which helped spur its growth but angered some fellow players.

As an amateur, Stephenson won five consecutive New South Wales Schoolgirl Championships, four straight NSW

Juniors, and three Australian Junior titles. She turned pro in 1973 and won that year's Australian LPGA. The following year, Stephenson came to the United States, finished twenty-eighth on the money list, and earned Rookie-of-the-Year honors. Her first LPGA victory came in 1976 at the Sarah Coventry Naples Classic, and through the end of 1987 she notched fifteen more wins, including three majors— the 1981 Peter Jackson Classic, the 1982 LPGA Championship, and the 1983 U.S. Women's Open. (She was the third non-American to win the Open after Uruguayan Fay Crocker in 1955 and Catherine Lacoste of France in 1967.) In 1985, Stephenson became the LPGA's ninth million-dollar winner.

The controversy over Stephenson's image arose over her alluring poses for the 1981 and 1982 editions of *Fairway*, the LPGA's official magazine. She also ap-

peared in a pinup calendar for one of her sponsors, as well as in posters, which she still does. While a few LPGA players denounced her as demeaning to the game and to women golfers, others applauded her for attracting more spectators. Said tour veteran JoAnne Carner, "If I had a figure like Jan's, I'd show it off, too."

Stephenson's other accomplishments on the course include the 1977 Australian Open (where she beat Pat Bradley in a playoff), the 1981 World Ladies Championship, and the 1985 Nicherei Ladies Cup and French Open. She makes her home in Fort Worth, Texas.

LOUISE SUGGS
(born 1923)

A founder and charter member of the LPGA, Louise Suggs helped Patty Berg, Babe Zaharias, Betty Jameson, and Betsy Rawls affirm the association's presence in its formative years.

Suggs took up the game in her native Atlanta at age ten, under her father's instruction, and went on to forge an amateur career that almost surpassed her success as a professional. Suggs won the North and South Amateur and the Women's Western Amateur three times each before taking the 1947 Women's Amateur, competing on the 1948 Curtis Cup team and winning the 1948 British Ladies Championship.

Suggs turned pro in 1949 and promptly won the U.S. Women's Open by fourteen strokes over Zaharias. Suggs dominated the early years of the LPGA, once noting that watching Berg, Zaharias, and herself battle for tournaments was like "watching three cats fight over a plate of fish."

Suggs won six times in 1952, including a second Women's Open. She won eight tournaments in 1953 and continued her pace of at least one victory a year—adding an LPGA Championship and Vare Trophy for low scoring average in 1957—until 1962, when she won her last tournament, the St. Petersburg Open. She subsequently cut back her competitive appearances.

A three-time president of the LPGA, Suggs was inducted into the Georgia Athletic Hall of Fame in 1966 and into the World Golf Hall of Fame in 1980. Suggs was an inaugural inductee into the LPGA Hall of Fame in 1951 with Patty Berg, Babe Zaharias, and Betty Jameson.

DICK TAYLOR
(born 1925)

Richard Stark Taylor has been a fixture in tournament pressrooms since the late forties. As editor-in-chief of *Golf World,* the only weekly newsmagazine covering the game, he influences how it is viewed by thousands of readers, bringing far-flung events and news to eager fans.

Taylor is a native of Indianapolis, Indiana, where he attended Butler University, following service as a pilot in the air force. Taylor began in journalism in 1948 as a sportswriter for the *Palm Beach Post-Times.* Besides covering University of Miami football, he was assigned the golf beat.

In 1962, Taylor became managing editor of *Golf World,* which was founded in 1947 by Bob Harlow, who had managed Walter Hagen's business affairs as well as the early pro tour. Harlow's idea was to produce a weekly international golf journal that reported everything of consequence in the game to anyone, anywhere, who cared. In 1965, Taylor became the magazine's sixth editor.

Taylor has served as president and secretary of the Golf Writers Association of America and has twice won its annual

writing contest (magazine division). He lives in Pinehurst, North Carolina, and plays to a handicap in the mid-teens at the Pine Needles Resort.

A.W. TILLINGHAST
(1874–1942)

Albert Warren Tillinghast entered the world of golf course design at age thirty-two when a friend asked him to lay out a course at Shawnee-on-Delaware, Pennsylvania. Tillinghast, who was born into a wealthy Philadelphia family and lived the life of an aristocrat, took to golf architecture so readily that he immediately formed a design-and-construction company. He went on to create more than fifty courses, including Winged Foot in Mamaroneck, New York; Baltusrol in Springfield, New Jersey; Somerset Hills in San Francisco; and Baltimore's Five Farms course, all rated among the best in the United States.

Tillinghast preferred to work on site rather than over a drawing board in an office. He always wore a suit, even when tramping through the undergrowth to in-

dicate the placement of tees, greens, and fairways. He involved himself in a project from beginning to end, supervising the construction as well as devising the layout. Although his courses seldom featured spectacular holes, they always provided an excellent test of shotmaking.

Tillinghast had been introduced to golf during visits to Scotland as a young man, and he competed in the U.S. Amateur several times between 1905 and 1915. His architecture business was highly successful through the 1920s but ran into hard times during the Depression.

Tillinghast became editor of *Golf Illustrated* in 1933 but retired to California four years later where he opened an antiques store.

JEROME D. TRAVERS
(1887–1951)

Jerry Travers was the best match player in America before World War I, winning four U.S. Amateur Championships—in 1907, 1908, 1912, and 1913. Only Bobby Jones has ever won more, with five. It was said that Travers honed his mental skills early in his career in a series of cutthroat duels with his close rival Walter Travis.

Travers was born in Oyster Bay, New York, and grew up playing first at the Oyster Bay course and later at the Nassau Country Club. At the latter, Travers came under the tutelage of Nassau pro Alex Smith. After winning a number of local titles, Travers clinched his first U.S. Amateur Championship at the Euclid Club in Cleveland, Ohio. Travers defended successfully the following year at Garden City, New York.

After three winless years, Travers beat the much-fancied Chick Evans in a classic match at the Chicago Golf Club. For the entire first round (the finals were played over thirty-six holes), Travers parried severe wildness with a deft short game and was fortunate to lie only one down going into the eighteenth hole. There, he dropped a thirty-five-foot putt (Travers was a masterful putter) to halve—and shock—Evans. Four holes into the afternoon round, a hooked tee shot from Travers ricocheted off a grassy mound to safety, after which he won the hole and proceeded to trounce a dispirited Evans. Still, that was typical of Travers. When he was behind he never gave up; when he was ahead he never let up. And from his steely countenance, it was impossible to tell which was which.

Travers took the 1915 U.S. Open Championship at Baltusrol and became one of only five amateurs to win the Open and one of ten golfers to win both the Open and the Amateur.

WALTER J. TRAVIS
(1862–1927)

Walter Travis did not play golf until he was thirty-five years old, but there was no more feared amateur competitor at the turn of the century than the Old Man. Travis won the U.S. Amateur in 1900, 1901, and 1903, and struck a blow for American golf by winning the British Amateur in 1904.

Travis was born in Victoria, Australia, but moved to the United States as a boy. He took up golf in 1897, and the following year reached the semifinals of the U.S. Amateur Championship; three years later, he won it.

A slight man, Travis was a relatively short hitter, but was very accurate and a phenomenal putter. He performed best in match play (although he did finish second in the 1902 U.S. Open at stroke play), where his putting demoralized opponents.

In 1904, having won three U.S. Amateurs, Travis decided to test himself overseas. He defeated British Open and Amateur champion Harold Hilton in the quarterfinals of the British Amateur. In the final, Travis was consistently outdriven by Edward Blackwell, one of the longest hitters of the day. But Travis's superior control and putting gained him a 4 and 3 victory.

Although Travis played in tournaments well into his fifties, he was active in golf in other ways, founding *The American Golfer* magazine in 1909 and working as a course designer. Among his layouts are two highly rated New York courses, Garden City Golf Club and Westchester Country Club.

LEE TREVINO
(born 1939)

One of the most entertaining golfers of all time, Lee Trevino has woven a rags-to-riches tale in a twenty-year professional career as player and TV commentator.

Born in Dallas, Texas, Trevino left school before the eighth grade. He spent four years in the Marine Corps, and on his discharge landed a $30-a-week assistant pro job at a Dallas driving range. After turning pro in 1960, he continued to compete in the Dallas area.

Trevino joined the PGA Tour in 1967 and wasted little time in making his presence felt, winning the 1968 U.S. Open at Oak Hill Country Club in Rochester, New York, in a playoff with Jack Nicklaus. With a quirky swing (a writer termed it "agricultural") that produced low fades, Trevino went on to further Tour success, never finishing lower than ninth on the money list between 1968 and 1975.

In 1971, Trevino pulled off an amazing triple, taking the U.S., Canadian, and

British Open crowns in four weeks. He followed that in 1972 with a second British Open victory, a win that dashed Nicklaus's hopes for a one-year Grand Slam. In 1974, Trevino added a PGA Championship, and ten years later—after being struck by lightning in the 1975 Western Open (which injured his back), undergoing surgery for a herniated disc in 1976 and plodding through three-and-a-half fruitless years on tour—he made a dramatic comeback, capturing his second PGA Championship at age forty-four.

Now a golf analyst for NBC-TV, the "Merry Mex" played on six U.S. Ryder Cup teams (1969–71–73–75–79–81) and captained the losing 1985 squad. He has also won five Vardon Trophies for low scoring average (1970–71–72, 1974, and 1980) and was inducted into the World Golf Hall of Fame in 1981.

RICHARD S. TUFTS
(1896–1980)

Richard S. Tufts was born into golf. His grandfather, James W. Tufts, founded the Pinehurst resort in North Carolina in 1897, and Tufts himself learned the game at age eight from Donald Ross, the great golf architect who was then the Pinehurst pro.

JACK TUTHILL
(born 1925)

Jack Clark Tuthill ran the daily operations of PGA Tour events as tournament director from 1964 to 1986. A former professional athlete, a fine golfer, and an expert on the Rules of Golf, he spoke to the players in their language but showed a firm hand when necessary to maintain a smooth-running tournament.

Tuthill, a native of Long Island, New York, caddied and began playing golf as a youngster. His passion was baseball, and he was an outfielder in the Milwaukee Braves farm system from 1947 to 1948. Soon after that, he studied at Cortland (New York) State Teachers College and went on to receive a master's degree in education from Ithaca (New York) College.

Tuthill worked for the New York State Labor Department, the FBI, and Republic Airlines as a labor negotiator. A single-digit handicapper, Tuthill heard through his golf contacts of an opening at the PGA of America and joined the staff in 1960. He became tournament director in 1964.

A newspaper account described him this way: "Tuthill is part agronomist, part meteorologist, part Supreme Court justice and also the man who decides, among other things, how high to let the rough grow and where the pins will be placed each day." Said former USGA Executive

Director Joseph C. Dey, "He, more than any other person, has held the tour together."

Tuthill served on rules committees for The Masters, U.S. Open, PGA Championship, and World Cup. He was honored in 1980 by the Golf Writers Association of America with the William Richardson Award for outstanding service to the game. He lives near Pensacola, Florida.

HARRY VARDON
(1870–1937)

In 1900, twelve years after golf took permanent root in America, Harry Vardon traveled from Britain for an exhibition tour of the New World. He had been hired to promote the Spalding Company's new Vardon Flyer gutta-percha ball, but in losing only one match while pausing briefly to win that year's U.S. Open, Vardon effectively brought golf to the masses when it was in danger of becoming a forgotten fad among the very rich. In any case, the gutta percha would soon be overtaken by the rubber-cored model.

Vardon learned to play as a caddie in Grouville on Jersey, one of Britain's Channel Islands. He moved to the British mainland in 1890, and six years later won his first British Open title, at Muirfield. With ensuing victories in 1898, 1899, 1903, 1911, and 1914, Vardon—who with J.H. Taylor and James Braid formed the "Great

In 1930, Tufts took over the Pinehurst corporation from his father, Leonard, and ran it until the 1960s, during which he supervised its expansion to six courses.

But Tufts was more than a resort manager. He contributed much to the game as an administrator, especially with the USGA. At one time or another, Tufts served on every USGA committee and was its president in 1956–57. As Handicap Committee chairman in 1947, he helped introduce the modern national handicap system, and while chairing the Championship Committee in the early 1950s, Tufts drew up a code that standardized the way courses should be set up for USGA Championships. As head of the Green Section Committee, he instituted the practice of sending USGA agronomists to advise and supervise course management. Most of all, Tufts was an expert on the rules and worked with USGA Executive Secretary Joseph C. Dey in unifying the Rules of Golf with the Royal and Ancient Golf Club of St. Andrews, Scotland, in 1951. In 1960, Tufts wrote a book, *The Principles Behind the Rules of Golf.*

Tufts was a competent enough golfer to compete in the U.S. Amateur on several occasions. A lifelong friend of Donald Ross, Tufts dabbled in golf course architecture and designed Pinehurst's No. 4 course in the early 1950s.

Triumvirate"—set the existing record for Open triumphs.

Vardon popularized the overlapping Vardon grip, in which the little finger of the lower hand overlaps the index finger of the upper hand. This grip remains the choice of top players today. Vardon also introduced method to the golf swing. While players before him had turned on a flat plane, virtually hacking at the ball, Vardon employed a more upright swing that swept through the ball. Combining this motion with superb timing, Vardon was able to put unheard-of spin—and, therefore, movement—on the ball, and was so accurate that it was said he played every second round from the divot holes of his first.

The trophies for low scoring average on the PGA and European Tours were named in Vardon's memory.

GLENNA COLLETT VARE

(born 1903)

Glenna Collett Vare won six U.S. Women's Amateur Championships in the twenties and thirties, a record approached only by JoAnne Carner, who won five in the fifties and sixties.

Vare took up the game at fourteen and was soon under the expert wing of Alex Smith, the transplanted Scot who won the 1906 and 1910 U.S. Opens. "The kid is good," Smith remarked after seeing her raw swing. "If I can't make a champion out of her, I'll be a disgrace to the Smith family."

Vare's exploits disgraced nobody. She defeated Margaret Gavin, an Englishwoman, 5 and 4, in the 1922 final. In 1925, she captured a second Amateur title, beating Alexa Stirling from the Royal Ottawa Club, 9 and 8. In 1928, Vare embarked on a string of nineteen consecutive matches without a loss. That year she trounced Virginia Van Wie, the top Chicago player, 13 and 12, for the second greatest margin of victory in the championship's history (Ann Sander beat Phyllis Preuss by 14 and 13 in 1961). In 1929, Vare outmatched Californian Leona Pressler, 4 and 3, and the following year triumphed again over Van Wie, this time 6

and 5. Vare lost to Helen Hicks, of New York, in the 1931 final, by 2 and 1.

Vare's final Amateur title came in 1935 when she edged an up-and-coming seventeen-year-old from Minneapolis named Patty Berg, 3 and 2.

Vare failed to win a British Ladies Championship, but not for want of trying. She was runner-up to Joyce Wethered in 1929 and to Diane Fishwick in 1930.

Vare, who went by the name of Collett until she married Philadelphia businessman Edwin Vare in 1931, also won six Eastern Amateur titles and six North and South Championships. She played on seven Curtis Cup teams between 1932 and 1948 and was non-playing captain in 1950. In 1953, the LPGA named its prize for low scoring average the Vare Trophy. Vare was inducted into the World Golf Hall of Fame in 1975.

KEN VENTURI

(born 1931)

"My God, I've won the Open!"

So said Ken Venturi when his putt for par dropped on the eighteenth green of the Congressional Country Club outside Washington, D.C., and clinched the 1964 U.S. Open Championship. Venturi, once one of the top players on the tour, had rebounded from more than two years of mediocre play to win by four strokes.

Venturi took up the game as a twelve-year-old in San Francisco and five years

later was runner-up in the first U.S. Junior Championship in 1948. As he improved, largely with help from Byron Nelson, he played on the 1953 Walker Cup team. But as an amateur, Venturi is best known for almost winning the 1956 Masters. Leading the field by four strokes with one round to play, Venturi collapsed with an 80 on the final afternoon, allowing Jack Burke, Jr., to nip him by one.

Four years later, Venturi was pipped at the post at Augusta National again (although by this time he had turned pro). Arnold Palmer birdied the last two holes to win by one.

Venturi's game went south soon after Augusta when he flattened his swing in the search for more length. His play became

erratic: he plummeted from fourteenth on the money list in 1961 to ninety-fourth in 1963.

Venturi had to qualify for the 1964 Open at Congressional, but opening rounds of 72–70–66 left him only two strokes adrift of Tommy Jacobs. The third round was played Saturday morning when temperatures were climbing into the nineties, almost causing Venturi to collapse from dehydration and exhaustion. The afternoon was even hotter, but with Dr. John Everett, a local member, supplying salt tablets and icepacks, Venturi summoned enough strength for an even-par round of 70 and victory.

Venturi now is a GOLF Magazine teaching editor and an analyst on CBS-TV golf telecasts.

TOM WATSON
(born 1949)

By the late 1970s, Jack Nicklaus had set the standard against which other professionals were measured. When Tom Watson, then twenty-seven years old, defeated Nicklaus (thirty-seven) in head-to-head battles for two major championships in

1977—The Masters and the British Open—Watson signaled that he was the next superstar.

Watson lived up to the promise of those victories, especially between 1977 and 1980, a four-year stretch in which he was as dominant as anyone has been in the history of the game. He became the only player to lead the money list and be named PGA Player of the Year for four consecutive years. Watson averaged five victories a year during that span and won the Vardon Trophy for low scoring average three times. The wins have become less frequent since 1980, but through 1987 he had compiled thirty-two career victories, ranking him ninth on the all-time list.

Watson's eight major championships as a professional are surpassed only by Nicklaus (eighteen), Walter Hagen (eleven), Ben Hogan (nine), and Gary Player (nine). He owns five British Open titles (1975, 1977, 1980, 1982, 1983); only

Harry Vardon, with six, had won more. Watson won The Masters in 1977 and 1981 and secured his place in history by stealing the 1982 U.S. Open from Nicklaus with a dramatic chip-in on the seventeenth hole at Pebble Beach. Of the major tournaments, only the PGA Championship has escaped him.

Watson grew up in Missouri, earned a degree in psychology from Stanford University in 1971, and joined the Tour the next year. In his early years, Watson acquired a reputation for "blowing" leads and did not shake it until 1977. Even in his prime, Watson sometimes was a wild driver, but he compensated with a mastery of the putter that the game has seldom known.

JOYCE WETHERED
(born 1901)

Joyce Wethered could be viewed as the female counterpart of Bobby Jones in that just as Jones dominated American golf in the 1920s, then retired, Wethered did likewise in Britain. The one difference was that Wethered came out of retirement to win again. Also like Jones, Wethered possessed a classic swing; in fact, Jones once said Wethered was the best golfer—male or female—he had ever seen.

Wethered learned the game at seventeen from her brother Roger, a leading

British amateur. Entering the 1920 Women's English Championship only "for fun," she defeated Cecil Leitch, Britain's leading female golfer, in the final. Then, starting in 1920, Wethered won thirty-three straight matches in the championship, taking the title every year from 1920–24.

In Britain's other important women's event, the British Ladies Championship, Wethered won three times (beating Leitch in the finals in 1922 and 1925 and losing to her in 1921). Wethered retired in 1925 but returned in 1929 when the amateur was held at St. Andrews. Playing before a huge crowd in the final, Wethered faced America's top woman, Glenna Collett Vare. After a riveting see-saw battle, Wethered won 3 and 1.

Wethered's swing was "the most correct and most lovely swing golf has ever known," wrote the highly respected golf writer Herbert Warren Wind. Her tempo was near-perfect and her accuracy often was compared to that of Harry Vardon. Long off the tee, Wethered also had a deadly touch on and around the greens.

In 1935, Wethered turned pro for an exhibition series in the United States, usually playing with Babe Zaharias, Gene Sarazen, and Horton Smith. In the much-touted contest of the ladies, Wethered regularly topped Zaharias (who had yet to develop into an all-around player) and set a number of course records. Wethered, now known as Lady Heathcoat-Amory, was inducted into the World Golf Hall of Fame in 1975.

KATHY WHITWORTH
(born 1939)

With eighty-eight official LPGA victories, Kathy Whitworth has won more golf tournaments than any other professional: more than Mickey Wright, who won eighty-two times on the tour, and Sam Snead, who captured eighty-four men's events.

A native of Monahans, Texas, who grew up in Jal, New Mexico, Whitworth reigned virtually unchallenged on the women's tour from 1965 through 1973, finishing first on the money list eight times and second one other year, 1969. She won ten tournaments in 1968 and eight each in 1963, 1965, 1966, and 1967. And while she relinquished her throne to Nancy Lopez in the seventies, Whitworth continued to win at least once a year through 1978. After shutouts in 1979 and 1980, it appeared that Whitworth, with eighty wins at the time, might fall short of Wright and Snead. But she rediscovered her game

at age forty-one, winning eight times over the next five years.

Whitworth turned professional in 1959 after capturing the New Mexico Amateur Championship in 1958 and 1959. Her first victory came in 1963, a year she ranked second on the money list to Wright, who soon would curtail her schedule and leave the stage to Whitworth.

Though she began her career when purses were small (she did not earn more than $50,000 in one year until 1972), Whitworth in 1981 became the first LPGA player to pass the $1-million mark in career earnings.

Whitworth captured the LPGA Championship in 1967, 1971, and 1975, and has won the Vare Trophy for low scoring average six times, but she has yet to win the U.S. Women's Open title. Whitworth was inducted into the LPGA Hall of Fame in 1975 and into the World Golf Hall of Fame in 1982. She continues to play on the women's tour.

HERBERT WARREN WIND

(born 1916)

"[No writer] extols the game with more authority and affection than Herb Wind, or more successfully conveys its gracious, fickle, generous spirit to the printed page," wrote novelist John Updike on the cover jacket of *Following Through: Herbert Warren Wind on Golf*, a collection of Wind's essays. It is a sentiment shared by many about America's premier golf historian and chronicler.

Born in Brockton, Massachusetts, Wind took up the game at age ten but never played competitively. He was graduated from Yale University in 1937 before attending Cambridge University in England, where he received a degree in English literature in 1939. During World War II he served as an administrative officer in the U.S. Army Air Corps in China and later was stationed in Tokyo during the occupation of Japan.

Wind settled in New York after the war and had his first book, *The Story of American Golf*, published in 1948. The year before, he was hired as a profile writer for *The New Yorker* magazine but left there in 1954 to help launch a new weekly magazine: *Sports Illustrated*. Wind returned to *The New Yorker* in 1962 to start "The Sporting

Scene," a column encompassing many sports, to which he still contributes about three articles a year, usually on the game's major championships. He is also a contributing editor for *Golf Digest*.

Other golf books by Wind include *Five Lessons: The Modern Fundamentals of Golf* with Ben Hogan; *The Greatest Game of All* with Jack Nicklaus; and *The Encyclopedia of Golf*, edited by Donald Steel and Peter Ryne.

CRAIG WOOD

(1901–1968)

Craig Wood performed best in the twilight years of his career, winning The Masters and U.S. Open in 1941 when he was thirty-nine years old. Until then, Wood had been known mainly for finishing second in majors, often the victim of spectacular play by the winner.

Wood, who was born in Lake Placid, New York, lost three majors in playoffs— the 1933 British Open to Denny Shute, the 1935 Masters to Gene Sarazen, and the 1939 U.S. Open to Byron Nelson. He also lost in overtime (at match play) to Paul Runyan in the final of the 1934 PGA Championship at Park Country Club, Williamsburg, New York, and was runner-

up in the 1934 Masters. Particularly frustrating to Wood were the 1935 Masters, where he was in the clubhouse with what looked like a definite victory until Sarazen tied him with a double eagle on the fifteenth hole, and the 1939 U.S. Open at the Philadelphia Country Club, where he and Nelson tied with 68s in the first playoff before Nelson holed a 1-iron for an eagle two on the fourth hole to gain the edge in the second extra round.

In the 1941 Masters, however, Wood won handily by three over Nelson. He hurt his back two weeks before that year's U.S. Open, but, wearing a corset belt, he won over Shute, again by three strokes.

Wood won seventeen tour events between 1928 and 1944 and was one of the top players throughout that period. He also was a very long hitter; in the 1933 British Open he hit a wind-aided drive 430 yards.

Wood played on three Ryder Cup teams, 1932, 1933, and 1935, and was inducted into the PGA Hall of Fame in 1956.

MICKEY WRIGHT
(born 1935)

In the late fifties and early sixties, when women's professional golf was at last gaining credibility and respect, one of the key figures in the game was Mickey Wright. Her eighty-two career victories, including thirteen major titles and numerous rec-

ords, were instrumental in raising the public perception of the women's professional tour.

Mary Kathryn Wright took up golf at eleven and was a top amateur in her teens, winning the 1952 U.S. Girls' Junior; in 1954 she won the World and All-American Amateurs, made the final of the U.S. Women's Amateur, and was low amateur, finishing fourth in the U.S. Open. After studying psychology for a year at Stanford, Wright dropped out and turned professional in late 1954. Her first victory came in 1956.

In 1958 Wright won the LPGA Championship and U.S. Women's Open, making her the first to win both in the same year; in 1959 she became the first back-to-back winner of the Women's Open. Capturing the 1961 Open, LPGA, and Titleholders (a major tournament from 1937–66 and in 1972) made Wright the only woman to date to win three majors in a single year. Add to those titles the 1964 Open, the 1960 and 1963 LPGA Championships, the 1962 Titleholders, and three Women's Western Opens (1962, 1963, and 1966).

Wright's other accomplishments include twice winning four consecutive events; a record-tying round of 62 in the 1964 Tall City Open; at least one victory a year for fourteen years; and five straight Vare Trophies for low scoring average (1960–64). Most impressive of all, Wright won thirteen of the thirty-two events on the 1963 schedule.

Today, Wright lives in Florida, and although she practices, she rarely plays a round of golf. In 1985, she and Kathy Whitworth made history by playing in the men's Legends of Golf. Twice named Associated Press Woman Athlete of the Year (1963, 1964), Wright is a member of the LPGA Hall of Fame (1964) and a member since 1976 of the World Golf Hall of Fame.

BABE ZAHARIAS
(1914–1956)

Mildred ("Babe") Zaharias, née Didrikson, was the first great female professional, helping to found the Ladies Professional Golf Association in 1949, then dominating it. Before becoming involved in golf, Zaharias held world records in track and

field. After winning two gold medals and one silver at the 1932 Olympic Games in Los Angeles, she played a round of golf—her first in more than a year—with sportswriter Grantland Rice. With the nation's leading sportswriters in tow, Zaharias put on an exhibition of long hitting that convinced everyone present that golf was her calling.

Zaharias, who was born in Port Arthur, Texas, had always hit a long ball. Asked for an explanation, she replied, "I just loosen my girdle and let the ball have it." In 1935, Zaharias toured with Gene Sarazen, pulling in $500 an appearance as she dazzled the crowds with 250-plus-yard drives.

Zaharias knew that her success as a golfer depended on an all-around game. So after marrying professional wrestler George Zaharias in 1938, she sought advice from renowned teacher Tommy Armour. She was reinstated as an amateur in 1944 and two years later embarked on a winning streak of seventeen consecutive amateur tournaments, including the 1946 Women's Amateur and the 1947 British Ladies Championships.

Zaharias turned pro again and helped charter the Ladies Professional Golf Association. Her pro victories included the U.S. Women's Open in 1948 and 1950, and she led the money list every year from 1948 to 1951. In 1952, Zaharias cut back her schedule as she fought cancer, yet still won four tournaments that year and two more in 1953. She underwent surgery the same year and came back to post five victories in 1954, including the Women's Open.

Zaharias died of cancer just before the tour she helped found began to flourish. In 1957, Zaharias was posthumously given the Bob Jones Award for distinguished sportsmanship in golf. She is a charter member of the LPGA Hall of Fame (1951) and World Golf Hall of Fame (1974). She was inducted into the PGA Hall of Fame in 1976.

FUZZY ZOELLER
(born 1951)

Frank Urban Zoeller, or Fuzzy, as derived from his three initials, is a rare animal. In fifteen years as a professional, he has won ten tournaments, including two majors, and has made a remarkable recovery from a complicated back operation. All the while, Zoeller has gone about his business with the relaxed air of a golfer enjoying a quiet eighteen holes at a golf resort.

Born in New Albany, Indiana, which he still calls home, Zoeller became only the third player to win The Masters on his first

attempt. (Horton Smith won the inaugural event in 1934; Gene Sarazen in 1935.) Zoeller birdied the second hole of a sudden-death playoff in 1979 to better Tom Watson and Ed Sneed.

Zoeller captured his second major with one of the great unheralded rounds in U.S. Open history. Tied with Greg Norman after four rounds of the 1984 Open at Winged Foot Golf Club in Mamaroneck,

New York, Zoeller posted a five-under-par 67 in the eighteen-hole playoff and destroyed the Australian by eight shots.

The playoff round went largely unnoticed only because Zoeller had made the previous day's finish so memorable. Standing on the seventy-second fairway watching Norman make an impossible par on the final hole, Zoeller pulled a white towel from his bag and, with typical humor, waved it in mock surrender. That Zoeller thought Norman had *birdied* the hole—making his own defeat more probable—makes Zoeller's gesture the more gallant.

A few months later, Zoeller faced the end of his career. A back injury suffered in a high-school basketball game had eventually forced surgery. But Zoeller returned to the tour in February 1985 and won the Bay Hill Classic in Florida three weeks later.

Zoeller has one of the stranger playing styles in the professional game. He aligns the heel of the club with the ball at address and keeps his hands extremely low. But his swing is relaxed and powerful, and he hits one of the longest balls in golf.

He has made three U.S. Ryder Cup appearances and shares the tour record for most birdies in a row (eight).

CHRONOLOGY

1887   Robert Lockhart purchases six golf clubs and two dozen balls from Old Tom Morris's shop in St. Andrews, Scotland, at the request of John Reid. Lockhart and his sons test the clubs in an open area at the northwest end of Manhattan.

1888   Reid introduces five friends to the game on Washington's Birthday, February 22, playing on a crude three-hole course cut from a cow pasture adjacent to Reid's home in Yonkers, New York. The course is moved in April to a nearby meadow and expanded to six holes. The following November, Reid and seven companions form the St. Andrew's Golf Club at a dinner and meeting at Reid's home. Reid is elected president.

1889   First reference to golf appears in the press, in the *Philadelphia Times*.

1890–   Vacation golf gets off to a brisk start at
1900   such spas as Hot Springs, Virginia, and Poland Spring, Maine; at the seashore (Cape Cod, Atlantic City, Palm Beach, and the Monterey Peninsula); and in the mountains at Woodstock, Vermont, and Colorado Springs, Colorado.

1892   In April, the St. Andrew's Golf Club relocates four blocks north to a thirty-four-acre apple orchard and takes on a new name, the Apple Tree Gang. The membership increases to more than thirty players.

  First reference to golf is made in a magazine, *The Century Illustrated Monthly*.

  Florence Boit, recently returned from France, introduces golf to her Boston relatives.

  Year-old Shinnecock Hills Golf Club in Southampton, New York, opens the first clubhouse in America, designed by Stanford White.

  Julian Curtiss of A.G. Spalding & Bros. sporting goods company visits Britain and returns with $500 worth of clubs and balls.

1893   Shinnecock Hills creates a separate nine-hole course for members' wives and daughters.

1894   In May, the St. Andrew's Golf Club again moves, expanding to nine holes on the site of the Odell Farm in the Grey Oaks section of Yonkers. The membership, numbering more than a hundred, enjoys its first clubhouse.

  Two unofficial and abortive national championships are held at the Newport Golf Club and then at St. Andrew's.

  Representatives from five golf clubs—St. Andrew's, Newport, Shinnecock Hills, The Country Club, and the Chicago Golf Club—meet to form the United States Golf Association (USGA).

  The women golfers of Morristown, New Jersey, open their own seven-hole course.

  The Spalding company sells the first American-made golf club.

1895   The first U.S. Amateur, U.S. Open, and U.S. Women's Amateur are played.

  Designed by Charles Blair Macdonald, the Chicago Golf Club—the first eighteen-hole course in America—opens.

  The first golf book, *Golf in America: A Practical Manual* by James Lee, is published in America.

1895–   The Florida East Coast Railroad and
1915   the Florida West Coast Railroad transform the Sunshine State into a golfer's paradise. Courses open at St. Augustine, Ormond, Miami, Belleair, Ocala, and Tampa.

1896   Robert Cox of Edinburgh, Scotland, donates the Cox Trophy to the Women's Amateur; the USGA assumes conduct of the national women's championship.

1897   The St. Andrew's Golf Club moves permanently to an eighteen-hole course at Mt. Hope, New York, five miles north of Yonkers.

  The first golf magazine, titled *Golf*, is published in America.

  Crawford, McGregor, and Canby (later MacGregor) begins manufacturing wood clubheads, turning them out on lathes used to make shoe lasts.

  The first pure instruction book, *How to Play Golf* by H.J. Whigham, is published.

1898   The U.S. Open expands to seventy-two holes. Beatrix Hoyt wins a third consecutive U.S. Women's Amateur title, becoming the first golfer to win three USGA events.

  Spalding sells the first American-made golf ball, a gutta percha. Coburn Haskell designs and patents a wound-rubber golf ball. It flies longer and straighter than the guttie. The Haskell ball wins acceptance over the next few years, helped by Walter Travis's victory in the 1901 U.S. Amateur and Sandy Herd's victory in the 1902 British Open.

1899   First Western Open is held.

1900   Harry Vardon, under contract to Spalding, comes to America to promote the Vardon Flyer golf ball. While on tour, he wins the U.S. Open and performs in many exhibitions, thereby exposing thousands of persons to the game. The gutta-percha Flyer does not do well in light of the new Haskell ball.

1900–   Donald Ross emerges as the country's
1915   premier golf course architect.

1902   Laurie Auchterlonie shoots 307 using a Haskell ball, the first time eighty is broken in all four rounds of the U.S. Open.

1903   Walter Travis wins a third U.S. Amateur; he is the first man to win three USGA events.

  Golf course architects Henry and William Fownes open Oakmont Country Club in Oakmont, Pennsylvania.

1905   Willie Anderson wins a third successive U.S. Open, his fourth overall.

  Frances Griscom leads a group of eight women golfers, including Harriot and Margaret Curtis, to England to play the British Ladies Championship.

After the tournament, the American and British amateurs play an informal team match.

Englishman William Taylor receives a patent on a dimpled-cover ball design, which proves more aerodynamically sound than the popular bramble cover.

The overlapping, or Vardon, grip becomes gospel as explained by Harry Vardon in *The Complete Golfer.*

1908   The first instruction book to explore the mental side of golf, *The Mystery of Golf* by Arnold Haultain, is published.

1909   Dorothy Iona Campbell of North Berwick, Scotland, the British Ladies champion, wins the United States title and becomes the first double winner.

1910   Smooth-faced irons are almost obsolete. Most irons have some kind of markings, usually punched dots, grooves, or dashes. A.F. Knight obtains a patent for a seamed, tubular steel golf shaft. Steel shafts remain illegal until 1926 (1929 in Britain), but once allowed, are quickly accepted, replacing hickory by the late 1930s.

1911   The first American-born player, John McDermott, wins the U.S. Open at the Chicago Golf Club.

The National Golf Links of America opens in Southampton, New York; the architect is Charles Blair Macdonald.

The East course at the Merion Cricket Club near Philadelphia, designed by Hugh Wilson, opens.

1913   Francis Ouimet, an amateur, wins the U.S. Open by defeating Harry Vardon and Ted Ray in an eighteen-hole playoff. Ouimet's victory starts a surge of interest in the game in America. Jerry Travers wins a fourth U.S. Amateur.

1914   Walter Hagen wins the first of two U.S. Opens.

Eleven holes at Pine Valley Golf Club, Pine Valley, New Jersey, open for play.

1916   Chick Evans becomes the first player to win both the U.S. Open and U.S. Amateur in the same year. Bobby Jones plays in his first national championship, the U.S. Amateur, at age fourteen.

The Professional Golfers Association (PGA) of America is founded. Jim Barnes wins the inaugural PGA Championship.

1918   Pine Valley founder George Crump dies; fourteen of the eighteen holes are now open for play.

The Broadmoor opens in Colorado Springs. It is the first great resort hotel built with a superior golf course (Donald Ross is the architect) as its principal attraction.

1919   Pebble Beach Golf Links, designed by Jack Neville and Douglas Grant, opens in Pebble Beach, California.

Picture Analysis of Golf Strokes by Jim Barnes is published. It is the first instruction book to use high-speed sequence photography.

1920   Ted Ray wins the U.S. Open; he is the last foreign champion for forty-five years.

The USGA creates the Green Section for turfgrass research. The USGA and the Royal and Ancient Golf Club of St. Andrews (R&A) meet to formulate restrictions on the size of golf balls.

The Golden Age of golf course design begins in America, led by A.W. Tillinghast. It will last a decade.

The golf tee is invented by dentist William Lowell.

Throughout the 1920s, the *grand dame* resorts offer great golf—the Arizona Biltmore, the Wigwam, the Homestead, the Greenbrier, the Cloister at Sea Island, the Breakers at Palm Beach, Boca Raton in Florida.

1921   The USGA and R&A agree to a standard ball measuring 1.62 inches in diameter and weighing 1.62 ounces.

1922   An admission fee is charged at the U.S. Open. Walter Hagen becomes the first American-born winner of the British Open, and Americans win the first Walker Cup Match, initiating the American domination of the game. Glenna Collett Vare wins the first of six U.S. Women's Amateurs. The USGA adds the Amateur Public Links Championship.

Gene Sarazen wins the U.S. Open and the PGA Championship. Walter Hagen becomes the first professional to enter the clubmaking field, forming a club company under his name.

First clear explanation of the swing plane, in photographs, is published in *Golf Fundamentals* by Seymour Dunn.

1923   Bobby Jones wins his first U.S. Open.

The Texas Open begins with a purse of $5,000; it is the biggest tournament on the growing winter circuit for professionals.

Ernest Jones sets up the first indoor golf school in New York City.

1924   Bobby Jones wins the first of five U.S. Amateur titles. Sectional qualifying is introduced for the U.S. Open.

1925   First complete fairway irrigation system is installed on a golf course. USGA and R&A ban golf clubs with deep grooves after Jock Hutchison uses them to win the 1921 British Open.

1926   Bobby Jones becomes the first golfer to win both the U.S. and British Opens in the same year. Jess Sweetser becomes the first American-born winner of the British Amateur. The U.S. Open extends to three days, with eighteen holes on each of the first two days and thirty-six on the final. The USGA approves the use of steel shafts.

Walter Hagen defeats Bobby Jones in a highly publicized seventy-two-hole match in Florida.

1927   The American squad defeats the British in the inaugural Ryder Cup Match. Walter Hagen wins a fourth consecutive PGA Championship, his fifth in all.

Golf Architecture in America—Its Strategy and Construction by George C. Thomas, Jr., is published.

1928 Cypress Point Golf Club, an Alister Mackenzie design, opens in Pebble Beach, California.

1930 Bobby Jones completes the Grand Slam by winning the U.S. Open, U.S. Amateur, British Open, and British Amateur.

Bobby Jones retires. The pro game establishes hegemony. The professional tour hires its first full-time organizer.

1930– The Depression and World War II slow
1945 down the development of new golf courses.

1931 Bobby Jones signs with Spalding as a director and advisor. The Bobby Jones Autograph Model, which he helps design, is a big seller for almost two decades. Gene Sarazen perfects his design for the sand wedge.

1932 The USGA approves a new ball measuring 1.68 inches in diameter and weighing 1.62 ounces, which remains the standard, after a one-year experiment with a 1.68-diameter, 1.55-ounce ball.

The USGA and Ladies' Golf Union of Great Britain inaugurate the biennial Curtis Cup Match for women amateurs. The trophy is donated by Harriot and Margaret Curtis.

Augusta National Golf Club, designed by Alister Mackenzie and Bobby Jones, opens in Augusta, Georgia. The course exemplifies the strategic school of golf course design.

Phil Young, owner of Acushnet rubber company, devises a method of making wound-rubber balls with consistently round centers. His new golf ball division, called Titleist, uses x-rays to check every ball produced.

Gene Sarazen uses his sand wedge to win the 1932 British Open and plays the last twenty-eight holes in a hundred strokes to win his second U.S. Open title.

Alex Morrison launches his left-side-dominance swing theory in his instruction book, A New Way to Better Golf.

1933 Johnny Goodman is the last amateur to win the U.S. Open.

Bobby Jones's Hollywood-made instruction films are shown at country clubs throughout America.

1934– Lawson Little wins thirty-two consecu-
1935 tive matches, including the U.S. and British Amateurs, in successive years.

1934 First Masters Tournament is held at Augusta National. Paul Runyan leads the PGA Tour money list with $6,767.

MacGregor Golf signs Tommy Armour to its advisory staff. Armour and his assistant, Toney Penna, will be re-

sponsible for many pioneering club designs for twenty or more years.

1935 Gene Sarazen's double eagle at The Masters becomes the most famous shot in the history of the game.

Glenna Collett Vare wins a sixth U.S. Women's Amateur title. This record still stands.

Donald Ross completes grassing the greens at Pinehurst No. 2 course in North Carolina.

1936 Johnny Fischer wins the U.S. Amateur, the last national championship won with hickory shafts.

1937 Denny Shute wins a second straight PGA Championship; he is the last golfer to accomplish that feat.

First Bing Crosby National Pro-Am is held at Rancho Santa Fe in California.

1938 USGA rules to limit the number of clubs a player may use in one round to fourteen.

Sam Snead, in his second year on the professional tour, wins seven tournaments and leads the money list.

Patty Berg wins the U.S. Women's Amateur and turns pro three months later.

1939 Sam Snead makes eight on the final hole to lose the U.S. Open, a championship that will continue to elude him.

1940 Jimmy Demaret wins the first of three Masters Tournaments.

1940– Ben Hogan leads the professional tour
1942 money list.

1941 The inaugural Tam O'Shanter National Open is held at Tam O'Shanter outside Chicago.

1942 The USGA introduces its Initial Velocity Test, designed to limit the distance a golf ball can be hit to a maximum of 250 feet per second.

Hale America tournament helps raise money for World War II effort. Used golf balls are collected at tour stops to be recycled.

1943 PGA events are canceled. The U.S. Open is not held from 1942–45 nor The Masters from 1943–45.

1945 Byron Nelson wins eleven straight events, a record that still stands. He wins eighteen tournaments during the year.

1946 Byron Nelson retires from regular competition. Ben Hogan wins thirteen tournaments.

The Golf Writers Association of America is formed.

The first Women's Open Championship is played in Spokane, Washington, under the auspices of the Women's Pro-

fessional Golf Association (WPGA). The winner is Patty Berg.

Percy Boomer's "turn in a barrel" theory comes to life in his book, On Learning Golf.

1947 The U.S. Open is first televised on local station KSD-TV in St. Louis, Missouri.

South African Bobby Locke first plays in the United States and wins six tournaments.

Golf World magazine begins publishing.

Babe Didrikson Zaharias, the 1946 Women's Amateur champion, wins the British Ladies Championship at Gullane, Scotland, the first American player to win.

The Dunes Golf and Beach Club opens in Myrtle Beach, South Carolina. It is the first notable resort course built after World War II, and its designer is Robert Trent Jones.

1948 Ben Hogan wins the first of four U.S. Opens, setting a seventy-two-hole record of 276.

1949 Patty Berg, Babe and George Zaharias, Fred Corcoran, and a Wilson Sporting Goods representative meet in Miami, Florida, to organize a new professional women's golf association. Later, eleven women professionals, four of them former amateur champions, convene in Wichita, Kansas, to form the Ladies Professional Golf Association (LPGA).

1950 Ben Hogan wins a second U.S. Open fifteen months after he was nearly killed in an automobile-bus accident.

Sam Snead wins ten tournaments.

1951 The USGA and R&A hold the first joint conference on the Rules of Golf and agree on a single code.

Golf Digest magazine begins publication.

Ben Hogan wins second consecutive U.S. Open; he is the last player to accomplish that feat.

1952 Dwight David Eisenhower is elected president; during his eight years in office, he helps to popularize the game.

1953 Ben Hogan wins The Masters, a fourth U.S. Open, and a British Open but passes up the PGA Championship. Tour purses top the half-million dollar mark.

First nationally televised golf tournament, the World Championship, takes place at Tam O'Shanter. Lew Worsham wins by holing a 104-yard wedge shot for an eagle on the final hole.

The U.S. Women's Open is added to the roster of national championships conducted by the USGA.

Tommy Armour breaks tradition by preaching right-sided golf in *How to Play Your Best Golf All the Time.*

1954 First national telecast of the U.S. Open takes place. Arnold Palmer wins the U.S. Amateur. Babe Zaharias wins her third and last U.S. Women's Open.

1955 Arnold Palmer wins his first professional tournament.

1956 Jack Burke, Jr., makes up an eight-shot deficit to win The Masters.

1957 Ben Hogan reveals his swing secrets in *Five Lessons: The Modern Fundamentals of Golf.*

1958 The World Amateur Golf Council is organized. First World Amateur Team Championship is played at St. Andrews, Scotland.

Arnold Palmer wins the first of four Masters Tournaments. His charisma helps popularize the game in the 1960s. The PGA Championship changes to stroke play. Tour purses top $1 million.

1959 *GOLF* Magazine begins publishing.

1960 Seven strokes behind with eighteen holes to play, Arnold Palmer chews up the front nine at Cherry Hills Country Club in 30, shoots 65, and wins the U.S. Open. It is Palmer's sole Open victory. Amateur Jack Nicklaus finishes second by two strokes. Betsy Rawls wins a fourth U.S. Women's Open.

1960s Investment casting is tried as a way of manufacturing irons, allowing for new designs with the weight distributed around the clubface.

Arnold Palmer jets to Scotland for the British Open, and golfers suddenly realize that now the entire world of golf is only hours away.

A second Golden Age of vacation course construction begins. Bay Hill, Doral, the Catskills' Concord, Williamsburg's Golden Horseshoe, La Costa, and Mauna Kea are all built.

1961 Jack Nicklaus turns professional after winning his second U.S. Amateur. Mickey Wright shoots 69–72 in one day over Baltusrol's Lower course to win her third U.S. Women's Open.

1962 Jack Nicklaus defeats Arnold Palmer in a playoff for the U.S. Open and wins his first tournament as a professional. The USGA adds the U.S. Senior Women's Amateur Championship to its roster.

At Myrtle Beach, the "golf package"—room, meals, and green fees—is born.

1963 Arnold Palmer is the first golfer to win more than $100,000 in one year.

Mickey Wright wins thirteen of thirty-two events on the LPGA Tour.

1964 Ken Venturi wins the U.S. Open at Congressional Country Club outside Washington, D.C., playing the last thirty-six holes in blistering heat. Mickey Wright wins a fourth U.S. Women's Open, the last championship player to do so.

1965 The USGA Executive Committee changes the U.S. Amateur to seventy-two holes of stroke play and extends the Open to four days, eliminating the thirty-six-hole final day. South African Gary Player is the first foreign player to win the U.S. Open since Englishman Ted Ray won in 1920.

Sam Snead wins the last of eighty-four tour events. The tour institutes its qualifying procedure.

1966 Billy Casper wins a second U.S. Open by making up six shots in nine holes against Arnold Palmer.

Jack Nicklaus wins his third Masters in four years.

Bobby Jones in *Golf Is My Game* looks at the ins and outs of his classic swing, citing hip action at the beginning of the backswing as his No. 1 key.

1967 Catherine Lacoste of France is the only amateur to win the U.S. Women's Open.

Ram Golf introduces a golf ball with a cover made of Surlyn, a tough-to-cut, synthetic material created by DuPont.

1968 Tour players form their own division, the Tournament Players Division, with Joseph C. Dey, Jr., as commissioner. Arnold Palmer is the first player to reach $1 million in career earnings. Roberto De Vicenzo comes in second to Bob Goalby in The Masters after a scorecard mistake drops him from a first-place tie.

Spalding introduces the two-piece golf ball. Called Top-Flite, it has a solid core inside a synthetic cover.

1969 JoAnne Gunderson Carner, who won a fifth U.S. Women's Amateur in 1968, is the last player to win an LPGA event as an amateur; she turns professional the following year.

Harbour Town Golf Links opens in Hilton Head, South Carolina. The architects are Pete Dye and Jack Nicklaus.

Homer Kelley, an engineer, publishes the most technical golf instruction book ever written and calls it *The Golfing Machine.*

1970 The square-to-square golf swing makes a big bang in the golf world, then fizzles out.

Condominium and time-sharing are two terms in the golfer's lexicon heard almost as often as birdie and bogey. Golf makes inroads at ski resorts. Thanks to jetcraft and bargain airfares, golf comes into its own in Hawaii, where there are about fifty-six courses, forty-two of them open to the traveler.

1970s Investment casting is used in making woods as well as irons, catapulting numerous new companies into the golf business.

1971 Lee Trevino wins the U.S., Canadian, and British Opens.

Jack Nicklaus wins the PGA Championship, becoming the first player to win the four majors twice.

Astronaut Alan B. Shepard, displaying a swing that truly could be labeled "out of this world," launches a 6-iron shot on February 5 into the thin atmosphere of the moon.

1972 The USGA moves its headquarters from New York City to Far Hills, New Jersey.

Jack Nicklaus wins The Masters and his third U.S. Open. His bid for the modern Grand Slam is dashed by Lee Trevino's British Open victory.

Title IX legislation is enacted by Congress. Colleges, threatened by the withholding of Federal funds, begin to equalize opportunities for female athletes, including golfers. The Colgate–Dinah Shore, the first big-money event for women professionals, debuts.

Practical Golf by John Jacobs is published. The book's central theory is that the arms must swing up while the shoulders swing on a slightly flatter plane.

1973 After eight years at stroke play, the U.S. Amateur returns to match play, with Craig Stadler winning at Inverness. Johnny Miller shoots 63 at Oakmont to win the U.S. Open and set the eighteen-hole record.

Kathy Whitworth is named the LPGA Player of the Year for the seventh time in eight years. Mickey Wright wins the Colgate–Dinah Shore, the last of her eighty-two victories.

1974 The Tournament Players Championship (now called The Players Championship) debuts. The World Golf Hall of Fame opens in Pinehurst, North Carolina. Deane Beman becomes commissioner of the PGA Tour.

Muirfield Village Golf Club opens in Dublin, Ohio. The architect is Jack Nicklaus.

Golf My Way concisely presents Jack Nicklaus's theories and practices.

1975 Johnny Miller wins eight tournaments. Jack Nicklaus wins a record fifth Masters.

Ray Volpe becomes the first commissioner of the LPGA Tour.

1976 The USGA adopts the Overall Distance Standard, another curb on the distance a ball can be hit.

The World Series of Golf expands to four rounds.

Judy Rankin becomes the first woman professional to win more than $100,000 in one year.

1977 The USGA adds the U.S. Women's Amateur Public Links Championship.

Al Geiberger shoots a 59 at the Memphis Classic. Tom Watson outduels Jack Nicklaus at The Masters and British Open.

1978 Tour purses top $10 million. John Mahaffey wins the first sudden-death playoff at a major (PGA Championship). Gary Player shoots a final-round 64 to win a third Masters. Jack Nicklaus wins the British Open, which gives him at least three victories in all four major tournaments. Liberty Mutual Legends of Golf tournament debuts; the senior event is won by the team of Sam Snead and Gardner Dickinson.

LPGA rookie Nancy Lopez wins $189,813 and nine tournaments, five of them consecutively.

1979 Sam Snead beats his age by shooting 66 at the Quad Cities Open at age sixty-seven.

1980 Jack Nicklaus wins a fourth U.S. Open, shooting 272 at Baltusrol, the seventy-two-hole record. He also wins the PGA Championship.

The USGA adds the U.S. Senior Open Championship.

Seve Ballesteros becomes the youngest player to win The Masters. Tom Watson leads the PGA Tour money list for the fourth straight year; he also wins six tournaments and his third British Open. The Senior PGA Tour is established.

1980s Golf booms—and booms—in the Palm Springs desert, where the number of courses grows to more than seventy.

1981 The USGA adds the Mid-Amateur Championship for players twenty-five years of age and over.

Kathy Whitworth is the first woman professional to reach $1 million in career prize money.

1982 Jay Sigel wins the first of two consecutive U.S. Amateur Championships.

Tom Watson wins his first U.S. Open with a chip-in on the seventy-first hole to beat Jack Nicklaus.

The first tournament is held at Pete Dye's Tournament Players Club at Sawgrass (Ponte Vedra, Florida), the first course of a TPC network.

John Laupheimer becomes commissioner of the LPGA Tour.

1983 The USGA introduces its Symmetry Standard, which eliminates balls that correct themselves in flight.

Tom Watson wins a fifth British Open. The all-exempt format is instituted on the PGA Tour.

1984 The video explosion begins in America as teachers and pros launch golf instruction tapes.

1985 Tour purses top $25 million.

Kathy Whitworth captures her

eighty-eighth career title.

Among unusual materials available in golf clubs are beryllium copper, ceramics, titanium, graphite, and boron.

1986 Ray Floyd wins the U.S. Open at age forty-three. Great Britain and Ireland win the Curtis Cup Match, the first time the United States loses an international match on home ground.

At age forty-six, Jack Nicklaus wins a sixth Masters, his eighteenth major professional title.

Pat Bradley is the first woman professional to reach $2 million in career earnings.

Pinehurst unveils its No. 7 course, a Rees Jones design, thus taking an even firmer grip on its ranking as the largest golf resort in the world.

1987 The USGA adds the Women's Mid-Amateur Championship. Judy Bell becomes the first woman elected to the USGA Executive Committee.

Nabisco Championship of Golf is the first PGA Tour event with a $2-million purse. Corporate sponsors help the tour's total purses reach nearly $30 million. The United States loses the Ryder Cup Match for the first time on American soil.

Cruise/golf vacations, with the ship as a floating hotel, bring a new dimension to the concept of vacation golf.

1988 The Arnold Palmer-designed course at the Zhongshan Hot Springs Resort epitomizes China's "open door" policy and reminds us that, on the opposite side of the globe and almost a hundred years later, once again a mineral water spa is giving the game its start.

WINNERS OF MAJOR CHAMPIONSHIPS

United States Open Championship

YEAR	WINNER	SCORE	RUNNER-UP	PLAYED AT
1895	Horace Rawlins	173–36 Holes	Willie Dunn	Newport G.C., Newport, R.I.
1896	James Foulis	152–36 Holes	Horace Rawlins	Shinnecock Hills G.C., Shinnecock Hills, L.I., N.Y.
1897	Joe Lloyd	162–36 Holes	Willie Anderson	Chicago G.C., Wheaton, Ill.
1898	Fred Herd	328–72 Holes	Alex Smith	Myopia Hunt Club, Hamilton, Mass.
1899	Willie Smith	315	George Low, Val Fitzjohn, W. H. Way	Baltimore C.C., Baltimore, Md.
1900	Harry Vardon	313	J. H. Taylor	Chicago G.C., Wheaton, Ill.
1901	*Willie Anderson (85)	331	Alex Smith (86)	Myopia Hunt Club, Hamilton, Mass.
1902	Laurie Auchterlonie	307	Stewart Gardner	Garden City G.C., Garden City, L.I., N.Y.
1903	*Willie Anderson (82)	307	David Brown (84)	Baltusrol G.C., Short Hills, N.Y.
1904	Willie Anderson	303	Gil Nicholis	Glen View Club, Golf, Ill.
1905	Willie Anderson	314	Alex Smith	Myopia Hunt Club, Hamilton, Mass.
1906	Alex Smith	295	Willie Smith	Onwentsia Club, Lake Forest, Ill.
1907	Alex Ross	302	Gil Nicholls	Philadelphia Cricket Club, Chestnut Hill, Pa.
1908	*Fred McLeod (77)	322	Willie Smith (83)	Myopia Hunt Club, Hamilton, Mass.
1909	George Sargent	290	Tom McNamara	Englewood G.C., Englewood, N.J.
1910	*Alex Smith (71)	298	John McDermott (75), Macdonald Smith (77)	Philadelphia Cricket Club, Chestnut Hill, Pa.
1911	*John McDermott (80)	307	Mike Brady (82), George Simpson (85)	Chicago G.C., Wheaton, Ill.
1912	John McDermott	294	Tom McNamara	C.C. of Buffalo, Buffalo, N.Y.
1913	*Francis Ouimet (72)	304	Harry Vardon (77), Edward Ray (78)	The Country Club, Brookline, Mass.
1914	Walter Hagen	290	Charles Evans, Jr.	Midlothian C.C., Blue Island, Ill.
1915	Jerome Travers	297	Tom McNamara	Baltusrol G.C., Short Hills, N.J.
1916	Charles Evans, Jr.	286	Jock Hutchison	Minikahda Club, Minneapolis, Minn.
1917–1918 No Championships Played—World War I				
1919	*Walter Hagen (77)	301	Mike Brady (78)	Brae Burn C.C., West Newton, Mass.
1920	Edward Ray	295	Harry Vardon, Jack Burke, Leo Diegel, Jock Hutchison	Inverness Club, Toledo, Ohio
1921	James M. Barnes	289	Walter Hagen, Fred McLeod	Columbia C.C., Chevy Chase, Md.
1922	Gene Sarazen	288	John L. Black, Robert T. Jones, Jr.	Skokie C.C., Glencoe, Ill.
1923	*Robert T. Jones, Jr. (76)	296	Bobby Cruickshank (78)	Inwood C.C., Inwood, L.I., N.Y.
1924	Cyril Walker	297	Robert T. Jones, Jr.	Oakland Hills C.C., Birmingham, Mich.
1925	*W. MacFarlane (147)	291	R. T. Jones, Jr. (148)	Worcester C.C., Worcester, Mass.
1926	Robert T. Jones, Jr.	293	Joe Turnesa	Scioto C.C., Columbus, Ohio
1927	*Tommy Armour (76)	301	Harry Cooper (79)	Oakmont C.C., Oakmont, Pa.
1928	*Johnny Farrell (143)	294	R. T. Jones, Jr. (144)	Olympia Fields C.C., Matteson, Ill.

*WINNER IN PLAYOFF. FIGURES IN PARENTHESES INDICATE SCORES

YEAR	WINNER	SCORE	RUNNER-UP	PLAYED AT
1929	*Robert T. Jones, Jr. (141)	294	Al Espinosa (164)	Winged Foot G.C., Mamaroneck, N.Y.
1930	Robert T. Jones, Jr.	287	Macdonald Smith	Interlachen C.C., Hopkins, Minn.
1931	*Billy Burke (149–148)	292	George Von Elm (149–149)	Inverness Club, Toledo, Ohio
1932	Gene Sarazen	286	Phil Perkins Bobby Cruickshank	Fresh Meadows C.C., Flushing, N.Y.
1933	Johnny Goodman	287	Ralph Guldahl	North Shore C.C., Glenview, Ill.
1934	Olin Dutra	293	Gene Sarazen	Merion Cricket Club, Ardmore, Pa.
1935	Sam Parks, Jr.	299	Jimmy Thompson	Oakmont C.C., Oakmont, Pa.
1936	Tony Manero	282	Harry Cooper	Baltusrol G.C., Springfield, N.J.
1937	Ralph Guldahl	281	Sam Snead	Oakland Hills C.C., Birmingham, Mich.
1938	Ralph Guldahl	284	Dick Metz	Cherry Hills C.C., Denver, Colo.
1939	*Byron Nelson (68–70)	284	Craig Wood (68–73) Denny Shute (76)	Philadelphia C.C., Philadelphia, Pa.
1940	*Lawson Little (70)	287	Gene Sarazen (73)	Canterbury G.C., Cleveland, Ohio
1941	Craig Wood	284	Denny Shute	Colonial Club, Fort Worth, Tex.
1942–1945 No Championships Played—World War II			
1946	*Lloyd Mangrum (72–72)	284	Vic Ghezzi (72–73) Byron Nelson (72–73)	Canterbury G.C., Cleveland, Ohio
1947	*Lew Worsham (69)	282	Sam Snead (70)	St. Louis C.C., Clayton, Mo.
1948	Ben Hogan	276	Jimmy Demaret	Riviera C.C., Los Angeles, CA
1949	Cary Middlecoff	286	Sam Snead Clayton Heafner	Medinah C.C., Medinah, Ill.
1950	*Ben Hogan (69)	287	Lloyd Mangrum (73) George Fazio (75)	Merion Golf Club, Ardmore, Pa.
1951	Ben Hogan	287	Clayton Heafner	Oakland Hills C.C., Birmingham, Mich.
1952	Julius Boros	281	Ed Oliver	Northwood C.C., Dallas, Tex.
1953	Ben Hogan	283	Sam Snead	Oakmont C.C., Oakmont, Pa.
1954	Ed Furgol	284	Gene Littler	Baltusrol G.C., Springfield, N.J.
1955	*Jack Fleck (69)	287	Ben Hogan (72)	Olympic Club, San Francisco, CA
1956	Cary Middlecoff	281	Ben Hogan Julius Boros	Oak Hill C.C., Rochester, N.Y.
1957	*Dick Mayer (72)	282	Cary Middlecoff (79)	Inverness Club, Toledo, Ohio
1958	Tommy Bolt	283	Gary Player	Southern Hills C.C., Tulsa, Okla.
1959	Billy Casper	282	Bob Rosburg	Winged Foot G.C., Mamaroneck, N.Y.
1960	Arnold Palmer	280	Jack Nicklaus	Cherry Hills C.C., Denver, Colo.
1961	Gene Littler	281	Bob Goalby Doug Sanders	Oakland Hills C.C., Birmingham, Mich.
1962	*Jack Nicklaus (71)	283	Arnold Palmer (74)	Oakmont C.C., Oakmont, Pa.
1963	*Julius Boros (70)	293	Jacky Cupit (73) Arnold Palmer (76)	The Country Club, Brookline, Mass.
1964	Ken Venturi	278	Tommy Jacobs	Congressional C.C., Washington, D.C.
1965	*Gary Player (71)	282	Kel Nagle (74)	Bellerive C.C., St. Louis, Mo.
1966	*Billy Casper (69)	278	Arnold Palmer (73)	Olympic Club, San Francisco, CA
1967	Jack Nicklaus	275	Arnold Palmer	Baltusrol G.C., Springfield, N.J.
1968	Lee Trevino	275	Jack Nicklaus	Oak Hill C.C., Rochester, N.Y.
1969	Orville Moody	281	Deane Beman Al Geiberger Bob Rosburg	Champions G.C., Houston, Texas
1970	Tony Jacklin	281	Dave Hill	Hazeltine G.C., Chaska, Minn.
1971	*Lee Trevino (68)	280	Jack Nicklaus (71)	Merion Golf Club, Ardmore, Pa.
1972	Jack Nicklaus	290	Bruce Crampton	Pebble Beach G.L., Pebble Beach, CA
1973	Johnny Miller	279	John Schlee	Oakmont C.C., Oakmont, Pa.
1974	Hale Irwin	287	Forrest Fezler	Winged Foot G.C., Mamaroneck, N.Y.
1975	*Lou Graham (71)	287	John Mahaffey (73)	Medinah C.C., Medinah, Ill.
1976	Jerry Pate	277	Tom Weiskopf Al Geiberger	Atlanta Athletic Club, Duluth, Georgia
1977	Hubert Green	278	Lou Graham	Southern Hills C.C., Tulsa, Okla.

*WINNER IN PLAYOFF.   FIGURES IN PARENTHESES INDICATE SCORES

YEAR	WINNER	SCORE	RUNNER-UP	PLAYED AT
1978	Andy North	285	Dave Stockton J. C. Snead	Cherry Hills C.C., Denver, Colo.
1979	Hale Irwin	284	Gary Player Jerry Pate	Inverness Club, Toledo, Ohio
1980	Jack Nicklaus	272	Isao Aoki	Baltusrol G.C., Springfield, N.J.
1981	David Graham	273	George Burns Bill Rogers	Merion G.C., Ardmore, PA
1982	Tom Watson	282	Jack Nicklaus	Pebble Beach G.L., Pebble Beach, CA
1983	Larry Nelson	280	Tom Watson	Oakmont C.C., Oakmont, PA
1984	*Fuzzy Zoeller (67)	276	Greg Norman (75)	Winged Foot G.C., Mamaroneck, N.Y.
1985	Andy North	279	Dave Barr T.C. Chen Denis Watson	Oakland Hills C.C., Birmingham, MI
1986	Ray Floyd	279	Larry Wadkins Chip Beck	Shinnecock Hills G.C., Southampton, N.Y.
1987	Scott Simpson	277	Tom Watson	Olympic Club, San Francisco, CA

The British Open

YEAR	WINNER	SCORE	RUNNER-UP	PLAYED AT
1860	Willie Park	174	Tom Morris, Sr.	Prestwick, Scotland
(The First Event Was Open Only to Professional Golfers)				
1861	Tom Morris, Sr.	163	Willie Park	Prestwick, Scotland
(The Second Annual Open Was Open to Amateurs Also)				
1862	Tom Morris, Sr.	163	Willie Park	Prestwick, Scotland
1863	Willie Park	168	Tom Morris, Sr.	Prestwick, Scotland
1864	Tom Morris, Sr.	160	Andrew Strath	Prestwick, Scotland
1865	Andrew Strath	162	Willie Park	Prestwick, Scotland
1866	Willie Park	169	David Park	Prestwick, Scotland
1867	Tom Morris, Sr.	170	Willie Park	Prestwick, Scotland
1868	Tom Morris, Jr.	154	Tom Morris, Sr.	Prestwick, Scotland
1869	Tom Morris, Jr.	157	Tom Morris, Sr.	Prestwick, Scotland
1870	Tom Morris, Jr.	149	David Strath, Bob Kirk	Prestwick, Scotland
1871	No Championship Played			
1872	Tom Morris, Jr.	166	David Strath	Prestwick, Scotland
1873	Tom Kidd	179	No Record	St. Andrews, Scotland
1874	Mungo Park	159	No Record	Musselburgh, Scotland
1875	Willie Park	166	Robert Martin	Prestwick, Scotland
1876	Robert Martin	176	David Strath (Tied, But Refused Playoff)	St. Andrews, Scotland
1877	Jamie Anderson	160	R. Pringle	Musselburgh, Scotland
1878	Jamie Anderson	157	Robert Kirk	Prestwick, Scotland
1879	Jamie Anderson	169	A. Kirkaldy, J. Allan	St. Andrews, Scotland
1880	Robert Ferguson	162	No Record	Musselburgh, Scotland
1881	Robert Ferguson	170	Jamie Anderson	Prestwick, Scotland
1882	Robert Ferguson	171	Willie Fernie	St. Andrews, Scotland
1883	*Willie Fernie	159	Robert Ferguson	Musselburgh, Scotland
1884	Jack Simpson	160	D. Rolland, Willie Fernie	Prestwick, Scotland
1885	Bob Martin	171	Archie Simpson	St. Andrews, Scotland
1886	David Brown	157	Willie Campbell	Musselburgh, Scotland
1887	Willie Park, Jr.	161	Bob Martin	Prestwick, Scotland

*WINNER IN PLAYOFF.   FIGURES IN PARENTHESES INDICATE SCORES

YEAR	WINNER	SCORE	RUNNER-UP	PLAYED AT
1888	Jack Burns	171	B. Sayers, D. Anderson	St. Andrews, Scotland
1889	*Willie Park, Jr.	155 (158)	Andrew Kirkaldy (163)	Musselburgh, Scotland
1890	John Ball	164	Willie Fernie	Prestwick, Scotland
1891	Hugh Kirkaldy	166	Andrew Kirkaldy, Willie Fernie	St. Andrews, Scotland
(Championship Extended from 36 to 72 Holes)				
1892	Harold H. Hilton	305	John Ball, H. Kirkaldy	Muirfield, Scotland
1893	William Auchterlonie	322	John E. Laidlay	Prestwick, Scotland
1894	John H. Taylor	326	Douglas Rolland	Royal St. George's, England
1895	John H. Taylor	322	Alexander Herd	St. Andrews, Scotland
1896	*Harry Vardon	316 (157)	John H. Taylor (161)	Muirfield, Scotland
1897	Harold H. Hilton	314	James Braid	Hoylake, England
1898	Harry Vardon	307	Willie Park, Jr.	Prestwick, Scotland
1899	Harry Vardon	310	Jack White	Royal St. George's, England
1900	John H. Taylor	309	Harry Vardon	St. Andrews, Scotland
1901	James Braid	309	Harry Vardon	Muirfield, Scotland
1902	Alexander Herd	307	Harry Vardon	Hoylake, England
1903	Harry Vardon	300	Tom Vardon	Prestwick, Scotland
1904	Jack White	296	John H. Taylor	Royal St. George's, England
1905	James Braid	318	John H. Taylor, Rolland Jones	St. Andrews, Scotland
1906	James Braid	300	John H. Taylor	Muirfield, Scotland
1907	Arnaud Massy	312	John H. Taylor	Hoylake, England
1908	James Braid	291	Tom Ball	Prestwick, Scotland
1909	John H. Taylor	295	James Braid, Tom Ball	Deal, England
1910	James Braid	299	Alexander Herd	St. Andrews, Scotland
1911	Harry Vardon	303	Arnaud Massy	Royal St. George's, England
1912	Edward (Ted) Ray	295	Harry Vardon	Muirfield, Scotland
1913	John H. Taylor	304	Edward Ray	Hoylake, England
1914	Harry Vardon	306	John H. Taylor	Prestwick, Scotland
1915–1919 No Championships Played				
1920	George Duncan	303	Alexander Herd	Deal, England
1921	*Jock Hutchison	296 (150)	Roger Wethered (159)	St. Andrews, Scotland
1922	Walter Hagen	300	George Duncan, James M. Barnes	Royal St. George's, England
1923	Arthur G. Havers	295	Walter Hagen	Troon, Scotland
1924	Walter Hagen	301	Ernest Whitcombe	Hoylake, England
1925	James M. Barnes	300	Archie Compston, Ted Ray	Prestwick, Scotland
1926	Robert T. Jones, Jr.	291	Al Watrous	Royal Lytham, England
1927	Robert T. Jones, Jr.	285	Aubrey Boomer	St. Andrews, Scotland
1928	Walter Hagen	292	Gene Sarazen	Royal St. George's, England
1929	Walter Hagen	292	Johnny Farrell	Muirfield, Scotland
1930	Robert T. Jones, Jr.	291	Macdonald Smith, Leo Diegel	Hoylake, England
1931	Tommy D. Armour	296	J. Jurado	Carnoustie, Scotland
1932	Gene Sarazen	283	Macdonald Smith	Prince's, England
1933	*Denny Shute (149)	292	Craig Wood (154)	St. Andrews, Scotland
1934	Henry Cotton	283	S. F. Brews	Royal St. George's, England
1935	Alfred Perry	283	Alfred Padgham	Muirfield, Scotland
1936	Alfred Padgham	287	J. Adams	Hoylake, England
1937	Henry Cotton	290	R. A. Whitcombe	Carnoustie, Scotland
1938	R. A. Whitcombe	295	James Adams	Royal St. George's, England
1939	Richard Burton	290	Johnny Bulla	St. Andrews, Scotland
1940–1945 No Championships Played				
1946	Sam Snead	290	Bobby Locke, Johnny Bulla	St. Andrews, Scotland
1947	Fred Daly	293	R. W. Horne, Frank Stranahan	Hoylake, England
1948	Henry Cotton	294	Fred Daly	Muirfield, Scotland
1949	*Bobby Locke	283 (135)	Harry Bradshaw (147)	Royal St. George's, England
1950	Bobby Locke	279	Roberto DeVicenzo	Troon, Scotland
1951	Max Faulkner	285	A. Cerda	Portrush, Ireland
1952	Bobby Locke	287	Peter Thomson	Royal Lytham, England
1953	Ben Hogan	282	Frank Stranahan, D. J. Rees, Peter Thomson, A. Cerda	Carnoustie, Scotland

*WINNER IN PLAYOFF. FIGURES IN PARENTHESES INDICATE SCORES

YEAR	WINNER	SCORE	RUNNER UP	PLAYED AT
1954	Peter Thomson	283	S. S. Scott, Dai Rees, Bobby Locke	Royal Birkdale, England
1955	Peter Thomson	281	John Fallon	St. Andrews, Scotland
1956	Peter Thomson	286	Flory Van Donck	Hoylake, England
1957	Bobby Locke	279	Peter Thomson	St. Andrews, Scotland
1958	*Peter Thomson	278 (139)	Dave Thomas (143)	Royal Lytham, England
1959	Gary Player	284	Fred Bullock, Flory Van Donck	Muirfield, Scotland
1960	Kel Nagle	278	Arnold Palmer	St. Andrews, Scotland
1961	Arnold Palmer	284	Dai Rees	Royal Birkdale, England
1962	Arnold Palmer	276	Kel Nagle	Troon, Scotland
1963	*Bob Charles	277 (140)	Phil Rodgers (148)	Royal Lytham, England
1964	Tony Lema	279	Jack Nicklaus	St. Andrews, Scotland
1965	Peter Thomson	285	Brian Huggett, Christy O'Connor	Southport, England
1966	Jack Nicklaus	282	Doug Sanders, Dave Thomas	Muirfield, Scotland
1967	Roberto DeVicenzo	278	Jack Nicklaus	Hoylake, England
1968	Gary Player	289	Jack Nicklaus, Bob Charles	Carnoustie, Scotland
1969	Tony Jacklin	280	Bob Charles	Royal Lytham, England
1970	*Jack Nicklaus	283 (72)	Doug Sanders (73)	St. Andrews, Scotland
1971	Lee Trevino	278	Lu Liang Huan	Royal Birkdale, England
1972	Lee Trevino	278	Jack Nicklaus	Muirfield, Scotland
1973	Tom Weiskopf	276	Johnny Miller	Troon, Scotland
1974	Gary Player	282	Peter Oosterhuis	Royal Lytham, England
1975	*Tom Watson	279 (71)	Jack Newton (72)	Carnoustie, Scotland
1976	Johnny Miller	279	Jack Nicklaus, S. Ballesteros	Royal Birkdale, England
1977	Tom Watson	268	Jack Nicklaus	Turnberry, Scotland
1978	Jack Nicklaus	281	Ben Crenshaw, Tom Kite, Ray Floyd, Simon Owen	St. Andrews, Scotland
1979	Seve Ballesteros	283	Ben Crenshaw, Jack Nicklaus	Royal Lytham, England
1980	Tom Watson	271	Lee Trevino	Muirfield, Scotland
1981	Bill Rogers	276	Bernhard Langer	Royal St. George's, England
1982	Tom Watson	284	Nick Price, Peter Oosterhuis	Royal Troon, Scotland
1983	Tom Watson	275	Hale Irwin, Andy Bean	Royal Birkdale, England
1984	Seve Ballesteros	276	Tom Watson, Bernhard Langer	St. Andrews, Scotland
1985	Sandy Lyle	282	Payne Stewart	Royal St. George's, England
1986	Greg Norman	280	Gordon Brand	Turnberry, Scotland
1987	Nick Faldo	279	Paul Azinger, Rodger Davis	Muirfield, Scotland

PGA Championship

YEAR	WINNER			PLAYED AT
1916	James M. Barnes	1 up	Jock Hutchison	Siwanoy C.C., Bronxville, N.Y.
1917–1918 No Championships Played — World War I				
1919	James M. Barnes	6 & 5	Fred McLeod	Engineers C.C., Roslyn, L.I., N.Y.
1920	Jock Hutchison	1 up	J. Douglas Edgar	Flossmoor C.C., Flossmoor, Ill.
1921	Walter Hagen	3 & 2	James M. Barnes	Inwood C.C., Far Rockaway, N.Y.
1922	Gene Sarazen	4 & 3	Emmett French	Oakmont C.C., Oakmont, Pa.
1923	Gene Sarazen	1 up (38)	Walter Hagen	Pelham C.C., Pelham, N.Y.
1924	Walter Hagen	2 up	James M. Barnes	French Lick C.C., French Lick, Ind.
1925	Walter Hagen	6 & 5	William Mehlhorn	Olympia Fields, Olympia Fields, Ill.
1926	Walter Hagen	5 & 3	Leo Diegel	Salisbury G.C., Westbury, L.I., N.Y.
1927	Walter Hagen	1 up	Joe Turnesa	Cedar Crest C.C., Dallas, Texas
1928	Leo Diegel	6 & 5	Al Espinosa	Five Farms C.C., Baltimore, Md.
1929	Leo Diegel	6 & 4	Johnny Farrell	Hillcrest C.C., Los Angeles, Calif.

*WINNER IN PLAYOFF. FIGURES IN PARENTHESES INDICATE SCORES

YEAR	WINNER	SCORE	RUNNER-UP	PLAYED AT
1930	Tommy Armour	1 up	Gene Sarazen	Fresh Meadow C.C., Flushing, N.Y.
1931	Tom Creavy	2 & 1	Denny Shute	Wannamoisett C.C., Rumford, R.I.
1932	Olin Dutra	4 & 3	Frank Walsh	Keller G.C., St. Paul, Minn.
1933	Gene Sarazen	5 & 4	Willie Goggin	Blue Mound C.C., Milwaukee, Wisc.
1934	Paul Runyan	1 up (38)	Craig Wood	Park C.C., Williamsville, N.Y.
1935	Johnny Revolta	5 & 4	Tommy Armour	Twin Hills C.C., Oklahoma City, Okla.
1936	Denny Shute	3 & 2	Jimmy Thomson	Pinehurst C.C., Pinehurst, N.C.
1937	Denny Shute	1 up (37)	Harold McSpaden	Pittsburgh F.C., Aspinwall, Pa.
1938	Paul Runyan	8 & 7	Sam Snead	Shawnee C.C., Shawnee-on-Delaware, Pa.
1939	Henry Picard	1 up (37)	Byron Nelson	Pomonok C.C., Flushing, L.I., N.Y.
1940	Byron Nelson	1 up	Sam Snead	Hershey C.C., Hershey, Pa.
1941	Vic Ghezzi	1 up (38)	Byron Nelson	Cherry Hills C.C., Denver, Colo.
1942	Sam Snead	2 & 1	Jim Turnesa	Seaview C.C., Atlantic City, N.J.
1943	—No Championship Played—World War II			
1944	Bob Hamilton	1 up	Byron Nelson	Manito G. & C.C., Spokane, Wash.
1945	Byron Nelson	4 & 3	Sam Byrd	Morraine C.C., Dayton, Ohio
1946	Ben Hogan	6 & 4	Ed Oliver	Portland G.C., Portland, Ore.
1947	Jim Ferrier	2 & 1	Chick Harbert	Plum Hollow C.C., Detroit, Mich.
1948	Ben Hogan	7 & 6	Mike Turnesa	Norwood Hills C.C., St. Louis, Mo.
1949	Sam Snead	3 & 2	Johnny Palmer	Hermitage C.C., Richmond, Va.
1950	Chandler Harper	4 & 3	Henry Williams, Jr.	Scioto C.C., Columbus, Ohio
1951	Sam Snead	7 & 6	Walter Burkemo	Oakmont C.C., Oakmont, Pa.
1952	Jim Turnesa	1 up	Chick Harbert	Big Spring C.C., Louisville, Ky.
1953	Walter Burkemo	2 & 1	Felice Torza	Birmingham C.C., Birmingham, Mich.
1954	Chick Harbert	4 & 3	Walter Burkemo	Keller G.C., St. Paul, Minn.
1955	Doug Ford	4 & 3	Cary Middlecoff	Meadowbrook C.C., Detroit, Mich.
1956	Jack Burke	3 & 2	Ted Kroll	Blue Hill C.C., Boston, Mass.
1957	Lionel Hebert	2 & 1	Dow Finsterwald	Miami Valley C.C., Dayton, Ohio
1958	Dow Finsterwald	276	Billy Casper	Llanerch C.C., Havertown, Pa.
1959	Bob Rosburg	277	Jerry Barber, Doug Sanders	Minneapolis G.C., St. Louis Park, Minn.
1960	Jay Hebert	281	Jim Ferrier	Firestone C.C., Akron, Ohio
1961	*Jerry Barber (67)	277	Don January (68)	Olympia Fields C.C., Olympia Fields, Ill.
1962	Gary Player	278	Bob Goalby	Aronomink G.C., Newtown Square, Pa.
1963	Jack Nicklaus	279	Dave Ragan, Jr.	Dallas Athletic Club, Dallas, Tex.
1964	Bobby Nichols	271	Jack Nicklaus, Arnold Palmer	Columbus C.C., Columbus, Ohio
1965	Dave Marr	280	Billy Casper, Jack Nicklaus	Laurel Valley C.C., Ligonier, Pa.
1966	Al Geiberger	280	Dudley Wysong	Firestone C.C., Akron, Ohio
1967	*Don January (69)	281	Don Massengale (71)	Columbine C.C., Littleton, Colo.
1968	Julius Boros	281	Bob Charles, Arnold Palmer	Pecan Valley C.C., San Antonio, Texas
1969	Ray Floyd	276	Gary Player	NCR C.C., Dayton, Ohio
1970	Dave Stockton	279	Arnold Palmer, Bob Murphy	Southern Hills C.C., Tulsa, Okla.
1971	Jack Nicklaus	281	Billy Casper	PGA National G.C., Palm Beach Gardens, Fla.
1972	Gary Player	281	Tommy Aaron, Jim Jamieson	Oakland Hills C.C., Birmingham, Mich.
1973	Jack Nicklaus	277	Bruce Crampton	Canterbury G.C., Cleveland, Ohio
1974	Lee Trevino	276	Jack Nicklaus	Tanglewood G.C., Winston-Salem, N.C.
1975	Jack Nicklaus	276	Bruce Crampton	Firestone C.C., Akron, Ohio
1976	Dave Stockton	281	Ray Floyd, Don January	Congressional C.C., Bethesda, Md.
1977	*Lanny Wadkins (Won playoff on third extra hole)	282	Gene Littler	Pebble Beach G.L., Pebble Beach, Cal.
1978	*John Mahaffey (Won playoff on second extra hole)	276	Jerry Pate, Tom Watson	Oakmont C.C., Oakmont, Pa.
1979	*David Graham (Won playoff on third extra hole)	272	Ben Crenshaw	Oakland Hills C.C., Birmingham, Mich.
1980	Jack Nicklaus	274	Andy Bean	Oak Hill C.C., Rochester, N.Y.
1981	Larry Nelson	273	Fuzzy Zoeller	Atlanta Athletic Club, Duluth, Ga.
1982	Raymond Floyd	272	Lanny Wadkins	Southern Hills C.C., Tulsa, Okla.
1983	Hal Sutton	274	Jack Nicklaus	Riviera C.C., Pacific Palisades, Cal.
1984	Lee Trevino	273	Gary Player, Lanny Wadkins	Shoal Creek, Birmingham, Ala.
1985	Hubert Green	278	Lee Trevino	Cherry Hills C.C., Denver, Colo.
1986	Bob Tway	276	Greg Norman	Inverness C.C., Toledo, Ohio
1987	*Larry Nelson	287	Lanny Wadkins	PGA National GC, Palm Beach Gardens, Fla.

*WINNER IN PLAYOFF. FIGURES IN PARENTHESES INDICATE SCORES

The Masters Tournament
AUGUSTA NATIONAL GOLF CLUB, AUGUSTA, GEORGIA

YEAR	WINNER	SCORE	RUNNER-UP
1934	Horton Smith	284	Craig Wood
1935	*Gene Sarazen (144)	282	Craig Wood (149)
1936	Horton Smith	285	Harry Cooper
1937	Byron Nelson	283	Ralph Guldahl
1938	Henry Picard	285	Ralph Guldahl, Harry Cooper
1939	Ralph Guldahl	279	Sam Snead
1940	Jimmy Demaret	280	Lloyd Mangrum
1941	Craig Wood	280	Byron Nelson
1942	*Byron Nelson (69)	280	Ben Hogan (70)
1943	No Tournament—World War II		
1944	No Tournament—World War II		
1945	No Tournament—World War II		
1946	Herman Keiser	282	Ben Hogan
1947	Jimmy Demaret	281	Byron Nelson, Frank Stranahan
1948	Claude Harmon	279	Cary Middlecoff
1949	Sam Snead	282	Johnny Bulla, Lloyd Mangrum
1950	Jimmy Demaret	283	Jim Ferrier
1951	Ben Hogan	280	Skee Riegel
1952	Sam Snead	286	Jack Burke, Jr.
1953	Ben Hogan	274	Ed Oliver, Jr.
1954	*Sam Snead (70)	289	Ben Hogan (71)
1955	Cary Middlecoff	279	Ben Hogan
1956	Jack Burke, Jr.	289	Ken Venturi
1957	Doug Ford	282	Sam Snead
1958	Arnold Palmer	284	Doug Ford, Fred Hawkins
1959	Art Wall, Jr.	284	Cary Middlecoff
1960	Arnold Palmer	282	Ken Venturi
1961	Gary Player	280	Charles R. Coe, Arnold Palmer
1962	*Arnold Palmer (68)	280	Gary Player (71), Dow Finsterwald (77)
1963	Jack Nicklaus	286	Tony Lema

YEAR	WINNER	SCORE	RUNNER-UP
1964	Arnold Palmer	276	Dave Marr, Jack Nicklaus
1965	Jack Nicklaus	271	Arnold Palmer, Gary Player
1966	*Jack Nicklaus (70)	288	Tommy Jacobs (72), Gay Brewer, Jr. (78)
1967	Gay Brewer, Jr.	280	Bobby Nichols
1968	Bob Goalby	277	Roberto DeVicenzo
1969	George Archer	281	Billy Casper, George Knudson, Tom Weiskopf
1970	*Billy Casper (69)	279	Gene Littler (74)
1971	Charles Coody	279	Johnny Miller, Jack Nicklaus
1972	Jack Nicklaus	286	Bruce Crampton, Bobby Mitchell, Tom Weiskopf
1973	Tommy Aaron	283	J. C. Snead
1974	Gary Player	278	Tom Weiskopf, Dave Stockton
1975	Jack Nicklaus	276	Johnny Miller, Tom Weiskopf
1976	Ray Floyd	271	Ben Crenshaw
1977	Tom Watson	276	Jack Nicklaus
1978	Gary Player	277	Hubert Green, Rod Funseth, Tom Watson
1979	*Fuzzy Zoeller	280	Ed Sneed, Tom Watson
1980	Seve Ballesteros	275	Gibby Gilbert, Jack Newton
1981	Tom Watson	280	Johnny Miller, Jack Nicklaus
1982	*Craig Stadler	284	Dan Pohl
1983	Seve Ballesteros	280	Ben Crenshaw, Tom Kite
1984	Ben Crenshaw	277	Tom Watson
1985	Bernhard Langer	282	Curtis Strange, Seve Ballesteros, Ray Floyd
1986	Jack Nicklaus	279	Greg Norman, Tom Kite
1987	*Larry Mize	285	Greg Norman, Seve Ballesteros

*WINNER IN PLAYOFF.   FIGURES IN PARENTHESES INDICATE SCORES

The U.S. Amateur Championship

YEAR	WINNER, RUNNER-UP	SCORE	PLAYED AT
1895	Charles B. Macdonald		Newport G.C.,
	d. Charles E. Sands	12 & 11	Newport, R.I.
			All Match Play
1896	H.J. Whigham		Shinnecock Hills G.C.,
	d. J.G. Thorp	8 & 7	Southampton, N.Y.
1897	H.J. Whigham		Chicago G.C.,
	d. W. Rossiter Betts	8 & 6	Wheaton, Ill.
1898	Findlay S. Douglas		Morris County G.C.,
	d. Walter B. Smith	5 & 3	Morristown, N.J.
1899	H.M. Harriman		Onwentsia Club,
	d. Findlay S. Douglas	3 & 2	Lake Forest, Ill.
1900	Walter J. Travis		Garden City G.C.,
	d. Findlay S. Douglas	2 up	Garden City, N.Y.
1901	Walter J. Travis		C.C. of Atlantic City,
	d. Walter E. Egan	5 & 4	Atlantic City, N.J.
1902	Louis N. James		Glen View Club,
	d. Eben M. Byers	4 & 2	Golf, Ill.
1903	Walter J. Travis		Nassau C.C.,
	d. Eben M. Byers	5 & 4	Glen Cove, N.Y.
			All Match Play
1904	H. Chandler Egan		Baltusrol G.C.,
	d. Fred Herreshoff	8 & 6	(original course)
			Springfield, N.J.
1905	H. Chandler Egan		Chicago G.C.,
	d. D.E. Sawyer	6 & 5	Wheaton, Ill.
1906	Eben M. Byers		Englewood G.C.,
	d. George S. Lyon	2 up	Englewood, N.J.
1907	Jerome D. Travers		Euclid Club,
	d. Archibald Graham	6 & 5	Cleveland, Ohio
1908	Jerome D. Travers		Garden City G.C.,
	d. Max H. Behr	8 & 7	Garden City, N.Y.
1909	Robert A. Gardner		Chicago G.C.,
	d. H. Chandler Egan	4 & 3	Wheaton, Ill.
1910	William C. Fownes, Jr.		The Country Club,
	d. Warren K. Wood	4 & 3	Brookline, Mass.
1911	Harold H. Hilton		The Apawamis Club,
	d. Fred Herreshoff	1 up,	Rye, N.Y.
		37 holes	
1912	Jerome D. Travers		Chicago G.C.,
	d. Charles Evans, Jr.	7 & 6	Wheaton, Ill.
1913	Jerome D. Travers		Garden City G.C.,
	d. John G. Anderson	5 & 4	Garden City, N.Y.
1914	Francis Ouimet		Ekwanok C.C.,
	d. Jerome D. Travers	6 & 5	Manchester, Vt.
1915	Robert A. Gardner		C.C. of Detroit,
	d. John G. Anderson	5 & 4	Grosse Point Farms,
			Mich.
1916	Charles Evans, Jr.		Merion Cricket Club,
	d. Robert A. Gardner	4 & 3	(East Course)
			Ardmore, Pa.
1917–1918—No Championships—World War I			
1919	S. Davidson Herron		Oakmont C.C.,
	d. Robert T. Jones, Jr.	5 & 4	Oakmont, Pa.

YEAR	WINNER, RUNNER-UP	SCORE	PLAYED AT
1920	Charles Evans, Jr.		Engineers' C.C.,
	d. Francis Ouimet	7 & 6	Roslyn, N.Y.
1921	Jesse P. Guilford		St. Louis C.C.,
	d. Robert A. Gardner	7 & 6	Clayton, Mo.
1922	Jess W. Sweetser		The Country Club,
	d. Charles Evans, Jr.	3 & 2	Brookline, Mass.
1923	Max R. Marston		Flossmoor C.C.,
	d. Jess W. Sweetser	1 up,	Flossmoor, Ill.
		38 holes	
1924	Robert T. Jones, Jr.		Merion Cricket Club,
	d. George Von Elm	9 & 8	(East Course)
			Ardmore, Pa.
1925	Robert T. Jones, Jr.		Oakmont C.C.,
	d. Watts Gunn	8 & 7	Oakmont, Pa.
1926	George Von Elm		Baltusrol G.C.,
	d. Robert T. Jones, Jr.	2 & 1	(Lower Course)
			Springfield, N.J.
1927	Robert T. Jones, Jr.		Minikahda Club,
	d. Charles Evans, Jr.	8 & 7	Minneapolis, Minn.
1928	Robert T. Jones, Jr.		Brae Burn C.C.,
	d. T. Phillip Perkins	10 & 9	West Newton, Mass.
1929	Harrison R. Johnston		Del Monte G. & C.C.,
	d. Dr. O. F. Willing	4 & 3	(Pebble Beach Golf Links)
			Pebble Beach, Calif.
1930	Robert T. Jones, Jr.		Merion Cricket Club,
	d. Eugene V. Homans	8 & 7	(East Course)
			Ardmore, Pa.
1931	Francis Ouimet		Beverly C.C.,
	d. Jack Westland	6 & 5	Chicago, Ill.
1932	C. Ross Somerville		Baltimore C.C.,
	d. John Goodman	2 & 1	(Five Farms Course)
			Baltimore, Md.
1933	George T. Dunlap, Jr.		Kenwood C.C.,
	d. Max R. Marston	6 & 5	Cincinnati, Ohio
1934	W. Lawson Little, Jr.		The Country Club,
	d. David Goldman	8 & 7	Brookline, Mass.
1935	W. Lawson Little, Jr.		The Country Club,
	d. Walter Emery	4 & 2	Cleveland, Ohio
1936	John W. Fischer		Garden City G.C.,
	d. Jack McLean	1 up,	Garden City, N.Y.
		37 holes	
1937	John Goodman		Alderwood C.C.,
	d. Raymond E. Billows	2 up	Portland, Ore.
1938	William P. Turnesa		Oakmont C.C.,
	d. B. Patrick Abbott	8 & 7	Oakmont, Pa.
1939	Marvin H. Ward		North Shore C.C.,
	d. Raymond E. Billows	7 & 5	Glenview, Ill.
1940	Richard D. Chapman		Winged Foot G.C.,
	d. W. B.	11 & 9	(West Course)
	McCullough, Jr.		Mamaroneck, N.Y.
1941	Marvin H. Ward		Omaha Field Club,
	d. B. Patrick Abbott	4 & 3	Omaha, Neb.
1942–1945—No Championships—World War II			

*RECORD SCORE FOR STROKE PLAY

YEAR	WINNER, RUNNER-UP	SCORE	PLAYED AT
1946	Stanley E. (Ted) Bishop d. Smiley L. Quick	1 up, 37 holes	Baltusrol G.C., (Lower Course) Springfield, N.J.
1947	Robert H. (Skee) Riegel d. John W. Dawson	2 & 1	Del Monte G. & C.C., (Pebble Beach Golf Links) Pebble Beach, Calif.
1948	William P. Turnesa d. Raymond E. Billows	2 & 1	Memphis C.C., Memphis, Tenn.
1949	Charles R. Coe d. Rufus King	11 & 10	Oak Hill C.C., (East Course) Rochester, N.Y.
1950	Sam Urzetta d. Frank Stranahan	1 up, 39 holes	Minneapolis G.C., Minneapolis, Minn.
1951	Billy Maxwell d. Joseph F. Gagliardi	4 & 3	Saucon Valley C.C., (Old Course) Bethlehem, Pa.
1952	Jack Westland d. Al Mengert	3 & 2	Seattle G.C., Seattle, Wash.
1953	Gene Littler d. Dale Morey	1 up	Oklahoma City G. & C.C., Oklahoma City, Okla.
1954	Arnold Palmer d. Robert Sweeny	1 up	C.C. of Detroit, Grosse Point Farms, Mich.
1955	E. Harvie Ward, Jr. d. Wm. Hyndman, III	9 & 8	C.C. of Virginia, (James River Course) Richmond, Va.
1956	E. Harvie Ward, Jr. d. Charles Kocsis	5 & 4	Knollwood Club, Lake Forest, Ill.
1957	Hillman Robbins, Jr. d. Dr. Frank M. Taylor	5 & 4	The Country Club, Brookline, Mass.
1958	Charles R. Coe d. Thomas D. Aaron	5 & 4	Olympic Club, (Lake Course) San Francisco, Calif.
1959	Jack Nicklaus d. Charles R. Coe	1 up	Broadmoor G.C., (East Course), Colorado Springs, Colo.
1960	Deane Beman d. Robert W. Gardner	6 & 4	St. Louis C.C., Clayton, Mo.
1961	Jack Nicklaus d. H. Dudley Wysong, Jr.	8 & 6	Pebble Beach G.L., Pebble Beach, Calif.
1962	Labron E. Harris, Jr. d. Downing Gray	1 up	Pinehurst C.C., (No. 2 Course), Pinehurst, N.C.
1963	Deane Beman d. Richard H. Sikes	2 & 1	Wakonda Club, Des Moines, Iowa
1964	William C. Campbell d. Edgar M. Tutwiler	1 up	Canterbury G.C., Cleveland, Ohio
1965	Robert J. Murphy, Jr. Robert B. Dickson	291 292	Southern Hills C.C., Tulsa, Okla.
1966	Gary Cowan Deane Beman	285–75 285–76	Merion G.C., (East Course) Ardmore, Pa.
1967	Robert B. Dickson Marvin Giles, III	285 286	Broadmoor G.C., (West Course) Colorado Springs, Colo.
1968	Bruce Fleisher Marvin Giles, III	284 285	Scioto C.C., Columbus, Ohio
1969	Steven N. Melnyk Marvin Giles, III	286 291	Oakmont C.C., Oakmont, Pa.
1970	Lanny Wadkins Thomas O. Kite, Jr.	*279 280	Waverley C.C., Portland, Ore.
1971	Gary Cowan Eddie Pearce	280 283	Wilmington C.C., (South Course), Wilmington, Del.
1972	Marvin Giles, III Mark S. Hayes Ben Crenshaw	285 288 288	Charlotte C.C., Charlotte, N.C.
1973	Craig Stadler d. David Strawn	6 & 5	Inverness Club, Toledo, Ohio
1974	Jerry Pate d. John P. Grace	2 & 1	Ridgewood C.C., Ridgewood, N.J.
1975	Fred Ridley d. Keith Fergus	2 up	C.C. of Virginia, (James River Course), Richmond, Va.
1976	Bill Sander d. C. Parker Moore, Jr.	8 & 6	Bel-Air C.C., Los Angeles, Calif.
1977	John Fought d. Doug Fischesser	9 & 8	Aronimink G.C., Newton Square, Pa.
1978	John Cook d. Scott Hoch	5 & 4	Plainfield C.C., Plainfield, N.J.
1979	Mark O'Meara d. John Cook	8 & 7	Canterbury G.C., Cleveland, Ohio
1980	Hal Sutton d. Bob Lewis	9 & 8	C.C. of North Carolina, Pinehurst, N.C.
1981	Nathaniel Crosby d. Brian Lindley	1 up, 37 holes	Olympic Club, (Lake Course) San Francisco, Calif.
1982	Jay Sigel d. David Tolley	8 & 7	The Country Club, Brookline, Mass.
1983	Jay Sigel d. Chris Perry	8 & 7	North Shore C.C., Glenview, Ill.
1984	Scott Verplank d. Sam Randolph	4 & 3	Oak Tree G.C., Edmond, Okla.
1985	Sam Randolph d. Peter Persons	1 up	Montclair G.C., West Orange, N.J.
1986	Buddy Alexander d. Chris Kite	5 & 3	Shoal Creek, Shoal Creek, Ala.
1987	Billy Mayfair d. Eric Rebmann	4 & 3	Jupiter Hills G.C., Jupiter, Fla.

Women's Open Championship

YEAR	WINNER, RUNNER-UP	SCORE	PLAYED AT
Conducted by Women's Professional Golfers Association 1946–48			
1946	Patty Berg		Spokane C.C.,
	d. Betty Jameson	5 & 4	Spokane, Wash.
1947	Betty Jameson	295	Starmount Forest C.C.,
	*Sally Sessions	301–4	Greensboro, N.C.
	*Polly Riley	301–5	
1948	Babe Didrikson Zaharias	300	Atlantic City C.C.,
	Betty Hicks	308	Northfield, N.J.
Conducted by Ladies Professional Golf Association 1949–52			
1949	Louise Suggs	291	Prince Georges G. & C.C.,
	Babe Didrikson Zaharias	305	Landover, Md.
1950	Babe Didrikson Zaharias	291	Rolling Hills C.C.,
	*Betsy Rawls	300	Wichita, Kan.
1951	Betsy Rawls	293	Druid Hills G.C.,
	Louise Suggs	298	Atlanta, Ga.
1952	Louise Suggs	284	Bala G.C.,
	Marlene Bauer	291	Philadelphia, Pa.
	Betty Jameson	291	
Conducted by United States Golf Association as of 1953			
1953	Betsy Rawls	302–71	C.C. of Rochester,
	Jacqueline Pung	302–77	Rochester, N.Y.
1954	Babe Didrikson Zaharias	291	Salem C.C.,
	Betty Hicks	303	Peabody, Mass.
1955	Fay Crocker	299	Wichita C.C.,
	Louise Suggs	303	Wichita, Kans.
	Mary Lena Faulk	303	
1956	Kathy Cornelius	302–75	Northland C.C.,
	*Barbara McIntire	302–82	Duluth, Minn.
1957	Betsy Rawls	299	Winged Foot C.C.,
	Patty Berg	305	(East Course) Mamaroneck, N.Y.
1958	Mickey Wright	290	Forest Lake C.C.,
	Louise Suggs	295	Bloomfield Hills, Mich.
1959	Mickey Wright	287	Churchill Valley C.C.,
	Louise Suggs	289	Pittsburgh, Pa.
1960	Betsy Rawls	292	Worcester C.C.,
	Joyce Ziske	293	Worcester, Mass.
1961	Mickey Wright	293	Baltusrol G.C.,
	Betsy Rawls	299	(Lower Course) Springfield, N.J.
1962	Murle Lindstrom	301	Dunes G. & Beach Club,
	Ruth Jessen	303	Myrtle Beach, S.C.
	JoAnn Prentice	303	
1963	Mary Mills	289	Kenwood C.C.,
	Sandra Haynie	292	Cincinnati, Ohio
	Louise Suggs	292	
1964	Mickey Wright	290–70	San Diego C.C.,
	Ruth Jessen	290–72	Chula Vista, Calif.
1965	Carol Mann	290	Atlantic City C.C.,
	Kathy Cornelius	292	Northfield, N.J.
1966	Sandra Spuzich	297	Hazeltine National G.C., Chaska, Minn.
	Carol Mann	298	
1967	*Catherine Lacoste	294	Virginia Hot Springs G. & T.C., (Cascades Course), Hot Springs, Va.
	Susie Maxwell	296	
	Beth Stone	296	
1968	Susie Maxwell Berning	289	Moselem Springs G.C.,
	Mickey Wright	292	Fleetwood, Pa.
1969	Donna Caponi	294	Scenic Hills C.C.,
	Peggy Wilson	295	Pensacola, Fla.
1970	Donna Caponi	287	Muskogee C.C.,
	Sandra Haynie	288	Muskogee, Okla.
	Sandra Spuzich	288	
1971	JoAnne Gunderson Carner	288	Kahkwa Club,
	Kathy Whitworth	295	Erie, Pa.
1972	Susie Maxwell Berning	299	Winged Foot G.C.,
	Kathy Ahern	300	(East Course)
	Pam Barnett	300	Mamaroneck, N.Y.
	Judy Rankin	300	
1973	Susie Maxwell Berning	290	C.C. of Rochester,
	Shelley Hamlin	295	Rochester, N.Y.
	Gloria Ehret	295	
1974	Sandra Haynie	295	La Grange C.C.,
	Beth Stone	296	La Grange, Ill.
	Carol Mann	296	
1975	Sandra Palmer	295	Atlantic City C.C.,
	*Nancy Lopez	299	Northfield, N.J.
	JoAnne Gunderson Carner	299	
	Sandra Post	299	
1976	JoAnne Gunderson Carner	292–76	Rolling Green G.C.,
	Sandra Palmer	292–78	Springfield, Delaware Co., Pa.
1977	Hollis Stacy	292	Hazeltine National G.C., Chaska, Minn.
	Nancy Lopez	294	
1978	Hollis Stacy	289	C.C. of Indianapolis,
	JoAnne Gunderson Carner	290	Indianapolis, Ind.
	Sally Little	290	
1979	Jerilyn Britz	284	Brooklawn C.C.,
	Debbie Massey	286	Fairfield, Conn.
	Sandra Palmer	286	
1980	Amy Alcott	280	Richland C.C.,
	Hollis Stacy	289	Nashville, Tenn.
1981	Pat Bradley	† 279	La Grange C.C.,
	Beth Daniel	280	La Grange, Ill.

YEAR	WINNER, RUNNER-UP	SCORE	PLAYED AT
1982	Janet Alex	283	Del Paso C.C., Sacramento, Calif.
	Sandra Haynie	289	
	Donna H. White	289	
	JoAnne Gunderson Carner	289	
	Beth Daniel	289	
1983	Jan Stephenson	290	Cedar Ridge C.C., Tulsa, Okla.
	JoAnne Gunderson Carner	291	
	Patty Sheehan	291	
1984	Hollis Stacy	290	Salem C.C., Peabody, Mass.
	Rosie Jones	291	
1985	Kathy Baker	280	Baltusrol G.C., Springfield, N.J.
	Judy Clark	283	
1986	Jane Geddes	287–71	NCR C.C., Dayton, Ohio
	Sally Little	287–73	
1987	Laura Davies	285–71	Plainfield C.C., N.J.
	Ayako Okamoto	285–73	
	JoAnne Gunderson Carner	285–74	

LPGA Championship

YEAR	WINNER, RUNNER-UP	SCORE	PLAYED AT
1955	††Beverly Hanson	220 4&3	Orchard Ridge CC Ft. Wayne, Ind.
	Louise Suggs		
1956	*Marlene Hagge	291	Forest Lake CC Detroit, Mich.
	Patty Berg		
1957	Louise Suggs	285	Churchill Valley CC Pittsburgh, Pa.
	Wiffi Smith		
1958	Mickey Wright	288	Churchill Valley CC Pittsburgh, Pa.
	Fay Crocker		
1959	Betsy Rawls	288	Sheraton Hotel CC French Lick, Ind.
	Patty Berg		
1960	Mickey Wright	292	Sheraton Hotel CC French Lick, Ind.
	Louise Suggs		
1961	Mickey Wright	287	Stardust CC Las Vegas, Nev.
	Louise Suggs		
1962	Judy Kimball	282	Stardust CC Las Vegas, Nev.
	Shirley Spork		
1963	Mickey Wright	294	Stardust CC Las Vegas, Nev.
	Mary Lena Faulk		
	Mary Mills		
	Louise Suggs		
1964	Mary Mills	278	Stardust CC Las Vegas, Nev.
	Mickey Wright		
1965	Sandra Haynie	279	Stardust CC Las Vegas, Nev.
	Clifford A. Creed		
1966	Gloria Ehret	282	Stardust CC Las Vegas, Nev.
	Mickey Wright		
1967	Kathy Whitworth	284	Pleasant Valley CC Sutton, Mass.
	Shirley Englehorn		
1968	†Sandra Post	294	Pleasant Valley CC Sutton, Mass.
	Kathy Whitworth		
1969	Betsy Rawls	293	Concord GC Kiamesha Lake, N.Y.
	Susie Berning		
	Carol Mann		
1970	*Shirley Englehorn	285	Pleasant Valley CC Sutton, Mass.
	Kathy Whitworth		
1971	Kathy Whitworth	288	Pleasant Valley CC Sutton, Mass.
	Kathy Ahern		
1972	Kathy Ahern	293	Pleasant Valley CC Sutton, Mass.
	Jane Blalock		
1973	Mary Mills	288	Pleasant Valley CC Sutton, Mass.
	Betty Burfeindt		
1974	Sandra Haynie	288	Pleasant Valley CC Sutton, Mass.
	JoAnne Carner		
1975	Kathy Whitworth	288	Pine Ridge GC Baltimore, Md.
	Sandra Haynie		
1976	Betty Burfeindt	287	Pine Ridge GC Baltimore, Md.
	Judy Rankin		
1977	Chako Higuchi	279	Bay Tree Golf Plantation N. Myrtle Beach, SC
	Pat Bradley		
	Sandra Post		
	Judy Rankin		
1978	Nancy Lopez	275	Jack Nicklaus GC King's Island, Ohio
	Amy Alcott		
1979	Donna Caponi	279	Jack Nicklaus GC King's Island, Ohio
	Jerilyn Britz		
1980	Sally Little	285	Jack Nicklaus GC King's Island, Ohio
	Jane Blalock		
1981	Donna Caponi	280	Jack Nicklaus GC King's Island, Ohio
	Jerilyn Britz		
	Pat Meyers		
1982	Jan Stephenson	279	Jack Nicklaus GC King's Island, Ohio
	JoAnne Carner		
1983	Patty Sheehan	279	Jack Nicklaus GC King's Island, Ohio
	Sandra Haynie		
1984	Patty Sheehan	272	Jack Nicklaus GC King's Island, Ohio
	Beth Daniel		
	Pat Bradley		
1985	Nancy Lopez	273	Jack Nicklaus GC King's Island, Ohio
	Alice Miller		
1986	Pat Bradley	277	Jack Nicklaus GC King's Island, Ohio
	Patty Sheehan		
1987	Jane Geddes	275	Jack Nicklaus GC, King's Island, Ohio
	Betsy King		

* Won sudden-death playoff
†Won 18-hole playoff
††Won match-play final

GOLF MAGAZINE'S 100 GREATEST COURSES IN THE WORLD

COURSE & ARCHITECT	LOCATION PAR-YARDAGE
1 PINE VALLEY	Pine Valley, N.J.
Crump/Colt, 1913–22	70–6,765
2 MUIRFIELD	Muirfield, Scot.
Morris, 1891; Colt/Simpson, 1926	71–6,894
3 PEBBLE BEACH	Pebble Beach, Cal.
Neville/Grant, 1919	72–6,815
4 CYPRESS POINT	Pebble Beach, Cal.
Mackenzie, 1928	72–6,536
5 AUGUSTA NATIONAL	Augusta, Ga.
Mackenzie/B. Jones, 1932	72–6,905
6 ROYAL MELBOURNE (Composite)	Melbourne, Aus.
Mackenzie/Russell, 1926	71–6,946
7 ST. ANDREWS (Old)	St. Andrews, Scot.
16th Century	72–6,950
8 BALLYBUNION (Old)	Ballybunion, Ire.
Murphy, 1906; T. Simpson, 1936	71–6,542
9 ROYAL Co. DOWN (No. 1)	Newcastle, N. Ire.
Morris, 1889; Dunn, 1905; Vardon, 1919	72–6,968
10 MERION (East)	Ardmore, Pa.
H. Wilson, 1912–25	70–6,482
11 SEMINOLE	N. Palm Beach, Fla.
D. Ross/Watson, 1929	72–6,898
12 ROYAL DORNOCH	Dornoch, Scot.
Morris, 1886; Sutherland/Ross, 1922; Duncan, 1947	70–6,577
13 SHINNECOCK HILLS	Southampton, N.Y.
Flynn/D. Wilson, 1931	70–6,912
14 PINEHURST (No. 2)	Pinehurst, N.C.
D. Ross, 1903–35	72–7,051
15 OAKMONT	Oakmont, Pa.
H. & W. Fownes, 1903	71–6,989
16 WINGED FOOT (West)	Mamaroneck, N.Y.
Tillinghast, 1923	72–6,956
17 OAKLAND HILLS (South)	Birmingham, Mich.
D. Ross, 1917; R.T. Jones, 1950	72–7,067
18 TURNBERRY (Ailsa)	Turnberry, Scot.
M. Ross, 1947	71–7,060
19 OLYMPIC (Lakeside)	San Francisco, Cal.
Reid, 1917; Whiting, 1924	71–6,808
20 MUIRFIELD VILLAGE	Dublin, Ohio
Nicklaus/Muirhead, 1974	72–7,106
21 ROYAL BIRKDALE	Southport, Eng.
Low, 1889; F.G. Hawtree/Taylor, 1931	72–7,001
22 CARNOUSTIE	Carnoustie, Scot.
1842; Braid/Wright, 1926	72–7,101
23 PRAIRIE DUNES	Hutchinson, Kans.
Maxwell, 1937–56	70–6,542
24 SOUTHERN HILLS	Tulsa, Okla.
Maxwell, 1935	71–7,037
25 BALTUSROL (Lower)	Springfield, N.J.
Tillinghast, 1922; R.T. Jones, 1953	72–7,069
26 PORTMARNOCK	Portmarnock, Ire.
G. Ross/Pickeman, 1894; F.W. Hawtree, 1964	72–7,103
27 LOS ANGELES (North)	Los Angeles, Cal.
Thomas, 1921	71–6,811
28 RIVIERA	Pacific Palisades, Cal.
Thomas/Bell, 1926	72–7,101
29 CASA DE CAMPO (Teeth of the Dog)	La Romana, Dominican Rep.
Dye, 1971	72–6,787
30 HARBOUR TOWN	Hilton Head Island, S.C.
Dye/Nicklaus, 1969	71–6,652
31 OAK HILL (East)	Rochester, N.Y.
D. Ross, 1926; G.&T. Fazio, 1978	70–6,964
32 ROYAL ST. GEORGE'S	Sandwich, Eng.
Purves, 1887; Mackenzie, 1925; Pennink, 1975	70–6,829
33 ROYAL PORTRUSH (Dunluce)	Portrush, N. Ire.
Colt, 1929	73–6,810
34 MEDINAH (No. 3)	Medinah, Ill.
Bendelow, 1928; Collis, 1932; Packard, 1986	72–7,365
35 SHOAL CREEK	Shoal Creek, Ala.
Nicklaus, 1977	72–7,029
36 ROYAL TROON	Troon, Scot.
Fernie, 1878; Braid, et al.	72–7,064
37 WOODHALL SPA	Woodhall Spa, Eng.
Hotchkin/Hutchison, 1926	73–6,866
38 THE GOLF CLUB	New Albany, Ohio
Dye, 1967	72–7,037
39 SUNNINGDALE (Old)	Sunningdale, Eng.
W. Park, 1901; Colt, 1920	72–6,566
40 KASUMIGASEKI (East)	Kawagoe, Japan
Fujita/Alison, 1929	72–6,934
41 TPC at SAWGRASS	Ponte Vedra, Fla.
Dye, 1980	72–6,950
42 CASCADES (Upper)	Hot Springs, Va.
Flynn, 1923	71–6,563
43 COLONIAL	Fort Worth, Tex.
Bredemus, 1935; Maxwell, 1940	70–7,142
44 CHICAGO	Wheaton, Ill.
Macdonald, 1895; Raynor, 1925	70–6,553
45 QUAKER RIDGE	Scarsdale, N.Y.
Tillinghast, 1926; R.T. Jones, 1960	70–6,745

	COURSE & ARCHITECT	LOCATION PAR-YARDAGE		COURSE & ARCHITECT	LOCATION PAR-YARDAGE
46	NATIONAL GOLF LINKS OF AMERICA Macdonald, 1911	Southampton, N.Y. 73–6,745	74	ROYAL MONTREAL (Blue) D. Wilson, 1959	Ile Bizard, Que., Can. 70–6,487
47	INVERNESS D. Ross, 1919; G.&T. Fazio, 1977	Toledo, Ohio 71–6,982	75	PGA WEST (Stadium) Dye, 1986	La Quinta, Cal. 72–7,271
48	SAN FRANCISCO Tillinghast, 1915	San Francisco, Cal. 71–6,623	76	GANTON Dunn, Vardon, Braid, Colt, Hutchison, 1891–1930	Ganton, Eng. 72–6,677
49	WILD DUNES (Links) T. Fazio, 1979	Isle of Palms, S.C. 72–6,708	77	THE NATIONAL GOLF CLUB OF CANADA G.&T. Fazio, 1976	Woodridge, Ont., Can. 71–6,975
50	EL SALER Arana, 1967	Valencia, Spain 72–7,108	78	ROYAL ADELAIDE 1904; Mackenzie, 1926	Adelaide, Aus. 73–7,010
51	FIRESTONE (South) R.T. Jones, 1960; Nicklaus, 1986	Akron, Ohio 70–7,173	79	ESSEX D. Ross, 1929	Sandwich, Ont., Can. 71–6,645
52	HIRONO Alison, 1932	Hirono, Japan 72–6,950	80	BALI HANDARA P. Thomson/Wolveridge/Fream, 1974	Bali, Indonesia 72–7,010
53	ROYAL LIVERPOOL G. Morris/Chambers, 1869; Colt, 1920s; Pennink, 1965	Hoylake, Eng. 72–6,979	81	EL RINCON R.T. Jones, 1960	Bogota, Colombia. 72–7,516
54	KINGSTON HEATH Soutar, 1925; Mackenzie, 1928	Melbourne, Aus. 72–6,814	82	CAPILANO S. Thompson, 1937	Vancouver, B.C., Can. 72–6,538
55	NEW SOUTH WALES Mackenzie, 1928	Matraville, Aus. 72–6,688	83	SAUCON VALLEY (Grace) D.&W. Gordon, 1957	Bethlehem, Pa. 72–7,044
56	THE HONORS COURSE Dye, 1984	Ooltewah, Tenn. 72–7,024	84	GARDEN CITY Emmet, 1902; Travis, 1906	Garden City, N.Y. 73–6,840
57	THE COUNTRY CLUB W. Campbell, 1895; Flynn, 1927	Brookline, Mass. 71–6,896	85	BALTIMORE (Five Farms East) Tillinghast, 1926	Baltimore, Md. 70–6,675
58	PHOENIX Ohashi, 1971	Miyazaki, Japan 72–6,991	86	WALTON HEATH (Old) Fowler, 1904	Tadworth, Eng. 73–6,859
59	CRYSTAL DOWNS Mackenzie/Maxwell, 1932	Frankfort, Mich. 70–6,518	87	THE AUSTRALIAN Mackenzie, 1926; Nicklaus, 1978	Sydney, Aus. 72–7,148
60	WENTWORTH (West) Colt/Alison/Morrison, 1924	Virginia Water, Eng. 74–6,997	88	CLUB DE GOLF MEXICO Clifford/Hughes, 1950	Mexico City, Mex. 72–7,250
61	LONG COVE Dye, 1981	Hilton Head Island, S.C. 71–6,900	89	MAIDSTONE W.&J. Park, 1891; Tucker, 1899	East Hampton, N.Y. 72–6,325
62	OAK TREE Dye, 1976	Edmond, Okla. 71–7,015	90	PLAINFIELD D. Ross, 1920	Plainfield, N.J. 72–6,859
63	SCIOTO D. Ross, 1912; D. Wilson, 1963	Columbus, Ohio 71–6,917	91	KITTANSETT Hood, 1923	Marion, Mass. 71–6,545
64	HUNTINGDALE Alison, 1941	Melbourne, Aus. 73–6,955	92	DORAL (Blue) D. Wilson, 1962	Miami, Fla. 72–7,065
65	ROYAL LYTHAM & ST. ANNES Lowe, 1886	St. Annes-on-Sea, Eng. 71–6,673	93	YALE UNIVERSITY Macdonald, 1926	New Haven, Conn. 70–6,628
66	CHERRY HILLS Flynn, 1923	Englewood, Colo. 72–7,148	94	TROON Morrish/Weiskopf, 1986	Scottsdale, Ariz. 72–7,026
67	BUTLER NATIONAL G.&T. Fazio, 1974	Oak Brook, Ill. 72–7,302	95	SUNNINGDALE (New) Colt, 1922	Sunningdale, Eng. 70–6,676
68	DURBAN Waters, 1922; Hotchkin, 1928	Durban, S. Africa 72–6,576	96	SOMERSET HILLS Tillinghast, 1918	Bernardsville, N.J. 71–6,524
69	SOTOGRANDE (Old) R.T. Jones, 1965	Cadiz, Spain 72–6,910	97	SUN CITY Player, 1980	Sun City, Bophuthatswana 72–7,693
70	PEVERO R.T. Jones, 1970	Sardinia, Italy 72–6,485	98	POINT O'WOODS R.T. Jones, 1958	Benton Harbor, Mich. 71–6,949
71	CANTERBURY Strong, 1922	Cleveland, Ohio 71–6,852	99	COMMONWEALTH S. Berriman, 1928	Melbourne, Aus. 72–6,719
72	ROYAL DAR-ES-SALAAM (Red) R.T. Jones, 1971	Rabat, Morocco 73–7,462	100	ROYAL PORTHCAWL Colt/Braid, 1913; F.G. Hawtree/ Taylor, 1925	Porthcawl, Wales 72–6,605
73	VICTORIA Mackenzie, 1927	Melbourne, Aus. 72–6,842			

BIBLIOGRAPHY

Allis, Peter. *The Who's Who of Golf.* Englewood Cliffs, N.J.: Prentice-Hall, 1983.

Amory, Cleveland. *The Last Resorts.* New York: Harper and Brothers, 1952.

Armour, Tommy. *How to Play Your Best Golf All the Time.* New York: Simon and Schuster, 1953.

Aultman, Dick. *The Square-to-Square Golf Swing.* Norwalk, Conn.: Golf Digest, Inc., 1970.

Ballard, Jimmy, with Brennan Quinn. *How to Perfect Your Golf Swing.* Norwalk, Conn.: Golf Digest, Inc., 1979.

Barkow, Al. *Golf's Golden Grind, The History of the Tour.* New York: Harcourt Brace Jovanovich, 1974.

Barnes, Jim. *Picture Analysis of Golf Strokes.* Philadelphia and London: J.B. Lippincott, 1919.

Bertholy, Paul. *The Bertholy Method.* Privately printed. Jackson Springs, N.C., 1977.

Birmingham, Stephen. *Right Places (for Right People).* Boston: Little, Brown, 1973.

Boomer, Percy. *On Learning Golf.* New York: Knopf, 1946.

Brown, Gene, ed. *The Complete Book of Golf.* New York: Arno Press, 1980.

Brown, John Arthur. *Short History of Pine Valley.* Privately printed. Clementon, N.J.: Pine Valley Golf Club, 1963.

Browning, Robert. *A History of Golf: The Royal and Ancient Game.* London: J.M. Dent, 1955. Reprint. New York: Ailsa, Inc., Classics of Golf, 1985.

Campbell, Robert. *The Golden Years of Broadcasting.* New York: Charles Scribner's Sons, 1976.

Charles, Bob, with Roger Ganem. *Left-Handed Golf.* Englewood Cliffs, N.J.: Prentice-Hall, 1965.

Cornish, Geoffrey, and Ronald E. Whitten. *The Golf Course.* New York: The Rutledge Press, 1981.

Cousins, Geoffrey. *Golf in Britain: A Social History from the Beginnings to the Present Day.* London: Routledge and Kegan Paul, 1975.

Crane, Joshua. "Famous Golf Courses of America: Pine Valley, The National, Lido Beach." *Golf Illustrated,* 1927.

Darwin, Bernard. *Golf Between Two Wars.* London: Chatto and Windus, 1970. Reprint. New York: Ailsa, Inc., Classics of Golf, 1985.

Darwin, Bernard, H. Gardiner-Hill, Sir Guy Campbell, Henry Cotton, Henry Longhurst, Leonard Crawley, Enid Wilson, and Lord Brabazon of Tara. *A History of Golf in Britain.* London: Cassell and Co., 1952.

de Koven, Mrs. Reginald. "The New Woman and Golf Playing." *The Cosmopolitan,* August 1896.

Dobereiner, Peter. *The Glorious World of Golf.* New York: McGraw-Hill, 1973.

Dunn, Seymour. *Golf Fundamentals.* Privately printed, 1922.

Fownes, William C. "Oakmont—Where You Must Play Every Shot." *Golf Journal,* May 1973.

Gallwey, W. Timothy. *The Inner Game of Golf.* New York: Random House, 1979.

Glenn, Rhonda. "The Fitful Beginnings of the LPGA." *Golf Journal,* July 1987.

Gottlieb, Harry. *Golf for Southpaws.* New York: A.A. Wyn, 1953.

Graffis, Herb. *The PGA: The Official History of the Professional Golfers' Association of America.* New York: Thomas Y. Crowell, 1975.

Grant, Donald. *Donald Ross of Pinehurst and Royal Dornoch.* Golspie, Scotland: The Sutherland Press, 1973.

Grimsley, Will. *Golf: Its History, People & Events.* Englewood Cliffs, N.J.: Prentice-Hall, 1966.

Hannigan, Frank. "Golf's Forgotten Genius—A.W. Tillinghast." *Golf Journal,* May 1974.

Haultain, Arnold. *The Mystery of Golf.* New York: Houghton Mifflin, 1908.

Heilman, Richard H. *Golf at Merion 1896–1976.* Privately printed. Ardmore, Pa.: Merion Golf Club, 1977.

Henderson, Ian T., and David I. Stirk. *Golf in the Making.* London: Henderson and Stirk, 1979.

Hogan, Ben, with Herbert Warren Wind. *Five Lessons: The Modern Fundamentals of Golf.* New York: A.S. Barnes, 1957.

Hunter, W. Robert. *The Links.* New York: Charles Scribner's Sons, 1926.

Hutchinson, Horace G. *Golf: The Badminton Library of Sports.* London: Longmans, Green, 1890.

Ingalls, Fay. *The Valley Road—The Story of Virginia Hot Springs.* Cleveland and New York: World Publishing Co., 1949.

Jacobs, John, with Ken Bowden. *Practical Golf.* New York: Quadrangle Press, 1972.

Jenkins, Dan. *Sports Illustrated's The Best 18 Golf Holes in America.* New York: Delacorte Press, 1966.

Johnson, William Oscar, and Nancy P. Williamson. *Whatta-Gal: The Babe Didrik-son Story.* Boston: Little, Brown, 1977.

Jones, Ernest, and Innis Brown. *Swinging into Golf.* New York: McGraw-Hill, 1937.

Jones, Ernest, and Dave Eisenberg. *Swing the Clubhead.* New York: Dodd, Mead, 1952.

Jones, Robert Trent. "The Rise and Fall of Penal Architecture." *Golf Journal,* April 1974.

Jones, Robert Tyre, Jr. *Bobby Jones on Golf.* Garden City, N.Y.: Doubleday, 1966.

———. *Golf Is My Game.* Garden City, N.Y.: Doubleday, 1960.

Kaplan, Jim, ed. *Hillerich and Bradsby: History-Catalogs.* Northbrook, Ill.: Vintage Golf, 1983.

———. *MacGregor Golf: History-Catalogs.* Palm Desert, Calif.: Vintage Golf, 1980.

———. *Wilson Golf: History-Catalogs.* Glencoe, Ill.: Vintage Golf, 1981.

Kean, Christopher. *The Tour.* Briarcliff Manor, N.Y.: Stein and Day, 1974.

Kelley, Homer. *The Golfing Machine.* Seattle, Wash.: Star System Press, 1969.

Kennedy, Patrick. *Golf Club Trademarks.* South Burlington, Vt.: Thistle Books, 1984.

Ladies Professional Golf Association. *LPGA Player Guide.* Sugar Land, Tex.: Ladies Professional Golf Association, 1987.

Lawless, Peter, ed. *The Golfer's Companion.* London: J.M. Dent and Sons, 1937.

Lee, James P. *Golf in America.* New York: Dodd, Mead, 1895.

Lohren, Carl, with Larry Dennis. *One Move to Better Golf.* New York: Quadrangle Press, 1975.

Longhurst, Henry. *My Life and Soft Times.* London: Cassell, 1971.

Lopez, Nancy, as told to Peter Schwed. *The Education of a Woman Golfer.* New York: Simon and Schuster, 1979.

Macdonald, Charles Blair. *Scotland's Gift—Golf.* New York: Charles Scribner's Sons, 1928.

Mackenzie, Dr. Alister. *Golf Architecture.* London: Simpkin, Marshall, Hamilton, Kent, 1920.

Mahoney, Jack. *The Golf History of New England.* Privately printed. Framington, Mass.: Wellesley Press, 1973.

Martin, Harold H. *This Happy Isle—The Story of Sea Island and The Cloister.* Privately printed. Sea Island, Ga.: Sea Island Co., 1978.

Martin, H.B. *Fifty Years of American Golf.* New York: Dodd, Mead, 1936.

Martin, H.B., and A.B. Halliday. *St. Andrew's Golf Club, 1888–1938.* New York: Rogers-Kellogg-Stillson, 1938.

McCormack, Mark H., ed. *Dunhill Golf Yearbook 1979.* Garden City, N.Y.: Doubleday and Co., 1979.

———. *Dunhill Golf Yearbook 1980.* Garden

City, N.Y.: Doubleday and Co., 1980.

———. *Dunhill World of Professional Golf 1981*. New York: A.S. Barnes and Co., 1981.

———. *Dunhill World of Professional Golf 1982*. New York: A.S. Barnes and Co., 1982.

———. *Dunhill World of Professional Golf 1983*. London: Springwood Books, 1983.

———. *Ebel World of Professional Golf 1984*. Washington, D.C.: Acropolis Books, 1984.

———. *Ebel World of Professional Golf 1985*. Ascot, Berkshire: Springwood Books, 1985.

———. *Ebel World of Professional Golf 1986*. Ascot, Berkshire: Springwood Books, 1986.

———. *The World of Professional Golf 1968 Edition*. New York: The World Publishing Co., 1968.

———. *The World of Professional Golf: Golf Annual 1969*. Great Britain: International Literary Management, 1969.

———. *The World of Professional Golf: Golf Annual 1970*. London: Hodder and Stoughton, 1970.

———. *The World of Professional Golf: Golf Annual 1971*. London: Hodder and Stoughton, 1971.

———. *The World of Professional Golf: Golf Annual 1972*. New York: Atheneum, 1972.

———. *The World of Professional Golf: Golf Annual 1973*. New York: Atheneum, 1973.

———. *The World of Professional Golf: Golf Annual 1974*. New York: Atheneum, 1974.

———. *The World of Professional Golf: Golf Annual 1975*. New York: Atheneum, 1975.

———. *The World of Professional Golf: Golf Annual 1976*. New York: Atheneum, 1976.

———. *The World of Professional Golf: Golf Annual 1977*. New York: Atheneum, 1977.

———. *The World of Professional Golf: Golf Annual 1978*. Garden City, N.Y.: Doubleday and Co., 1978.

Menzies, Gordon, ed. *The World of Golf*. London: British Broadcasting Corp., 1982.

Middlecoff, Cary, and Tom Michael. *The Golf Swing*. Englewood Cliffs, N.J.: Prentice-Hall, 1975.

Miller, Dick. *America's Greatest Golfing Resorts*. Indianapolis and New York: Bobbs-Merrill, 1977.

Morrison, Alex. *A New Way to Better Golf*. New York: Simon and Schuster, 1932.

Murdoch, Joseph S.F. *The Library of Golf, 1743–1966*. Detroit. Mich.: Gale Research Co., 1968. *Supplement*. Privately printed, 1978.

Nelson, Byron. *Winning Golf*. New York: A.S. Barnes, 1946.

Nelson, Byron, and Larry Dennis. *Shape Your Swing the Modern Way*. New York: Simon and Schuster, 1976.

Nickerson, Elinor. *Golf: A Woman's History*. Jefferson, N.C.: McFarland, 1986.

Nicklaus, Jack, with Ken Bowden. *Golf My Way*. New York: Simon and Schuster, 1974.

Nicklaus, Jack, with Herbert Warren Wind. *The Greatest Game of All*. New York: Simon and Schuster, 1969.

Olman, John M., and Morton W. Olman. *The Encyclopedia of Golf Collectibles*. Florence, Ala.: Books Americana, 1985.

Ouimet, Francis. *A Game of Golf*. Boston: Houghton Mifflin, 1932.

Palmer, Arnold. *Arnold Palmer's Complete Book of Putting*. New York: Atheneum, 1986.

Palmer, Arnold, with William Barry Furlong. *Go for Broke*. London: William Kimber, 1974.

Price, Charles. *A Golf Story*. New York: Atheneum, 1986.

———. *The World of Golf*. New York: Random House, 1962.

Price, Charles, ed. *The American Golfer*. New York: Random House, 1964.

Roberts, Clifford. *The Story of the Augusta National Golf Club*. Garden City, N.Y.: Doubleday, 1976.

Runyan, Paul, with Dick Aultman. *The Short Way to Lower Scoring*. Norwalk, Conn.: Golf Digest, Inc., 1979.

Sarazen, Gene, and Herbert Warren Wind. *Thirty Years of Championship Golf*. New York: Prentice-Hall, 1950.

Scharff, Robert, and the Editors of GOLF Magazine, eds. *GOLF Magazine's Encyclopedia of Golf*. New York: Harper and Row, 1970.

Scott, Tom, and Geoffrey Cornish. *The Golf Immortals*. New York: Hart Publishing Co., 1968.

Seagle, Janet. *The Club Makers*. Far Hills, N.J.: United States Golf Association, 1984.

Shapiro, Mel, Warren Dohn, and Leonard Berger, eds. *Golf—A Turn-of-the-Century Treasury*. Secaucus, N.J.: Castle, 1986.

Smith, Gordon G. *The World of Golf*. London: A.D. Innes, The Isthmian Library, 1898.

Snead, Sam. *Natural Golf*. New York: A.S. Barnes, 1953.

Sommers, Robert. *The U.S. Open: Golf's Ultimate Challenge*. New York: Atheneum, 1987.

Spalding's Athletic Library. *Golf Guide—1924, 1925, 1927, 1931*. New York: American Sports Publishing Co., 1924, 1925, 1927, 1931, and 1932.

Steel, Donald, and Peter Ryde, eds. *The Encyclopedia of Golf*. New York: Viking Press, 1975.

Tatum, Frank D., Jr. "The Decline of Design." *Golf Journal*, May 1976.

Thomas, George C., Jr. *Golf Architecture in America—Its Strategy and Construction*. Los Angeles: The Times Mirror Press, 1927.

Toski, Bob, Jim Flick, with Larry Dennis. *How to Become a Complete Golfer*. Norwalk, Conn.: Golf Digest, Inc., 1984.

Travers, Jerome D., and James R. Crowell. *The Fifth Estate, Thirty Years of Golf*. New York: Knopf, 1924.

United States Golf Association. *USGA Record Book*. 2 vols. 1895–1959, 1960–1980. Far Hills, N.J.: United States Golf Association, n.d.

Vardon, Harry. *The Complete Golfer*. London: Methuen, 1905.

———. *My Golfing Life*. London: Hutchinson and Co., 1933.

Ward-Thomas, Pat, Herbert Warren Wind, Charles Price, and Peter Thomson. *The World Atlas of Golf*. New York: Random House, 1976.

Weeks, Edward. *Myopia*. Privately printed. Hamilton, Mass.: Myopia Hunt Club, 1975.

Wethered, Joyce. "Ladies Golf." *The Game of Golf*. The Lonsdale Library, vol. 9. London: Seeley Service and Co., n.d.

Whigham, H.J. *How to Play Golf*. Chicago and New York: Herbert S. Stone, 1897.

Williams, Gwen. *Unique Golf Resorts of the World*. Corona del Mar, Calif.: Unique Golf Resorts of the World, 1983.

Wind, Herbert Warren. "A Calling for Correct Proportions." *Golf Journal*, July 1977.

———. "Pete Dye: Improving on Mother Nature." *Golf Digest*, May–June 1976.

———. *The Story of American Golf*. New York: Simon and Schuster, 1956.

———. "Understanding Golf Course Architecture." *Golf Digest*, November–December 1966.

Wind, Herbert Warren, ed. *The Complete Golfer*. New York: Simon and Schuster, 1954.

Wishon, Tom W. *The Golf Club Identification and Price Guide*. Newark, Ohio: Ralph Maltby Enterprise, Inc., 1985.

Magazines:

Golf Digest
Golf Illustrated (London and New York)
GOLF Magazine
Golf World

Special Acknowledgments:

Patrick Kennedy, Golf Collectors' Society
Robert Kuntz, Golf Collectors' Society
George Lewis, Golfiana
MacGregor Golf Company, Albany, Georgia
Joseph Murdoch, Golf Collectors' Society
Spalding Sports Worldwide, Chicopee, Massachusetts
Titleist Golf Division, Acushnet Company, New Bedford, Massachusetts
True Temper, Memphis, Tennessee

PHOTO CREDITS

Acme News Pictures: 35 above, 56 below left, 61 above left, 112; Acushnet Titleist: 191 below (both); American Golfer: 34 below, 203; AP/Wide World: 39, 40, 43 below, 59 below, 62 below, 63 below, 67 above right, 68 right, 69, 89 below, 90, 92, 233; Arizona Biltmore: 215 center; The Badminton Library/Horace Hutchinson: 198 above (both); Bensing, Frank: 66 (paintings of Walter Hagen and Gene Sarazen); Ben Hogan Company: 193; Bettmann Archive: 29; Brandon Advertising: 231; Broadmoor Hotel: 214; Carey Florida Archives: 212, 213 right; CBS: 174 right; The Cloister: 217; Culver Pictures: 60 above left, 172 above, 173 below, 190 left; Deane Beman Collection: 121 above; Doak, Tom: 100 below, 104 above, 108 above; Ellis, Jon: 186; Fitz, Morgan: 63 above; Fowler, Frank (original painting): 11 right; Frank Christian Studio: 62 above, 74 below, 75 below left, 76 below; Geeter, Judith: 77 above right; Golfina/George Lewis: 159 below, 160, 164 above (all), 165, 169 above; Golden Bear, Inc.: 118 right; Golf Magazine: 34 above, 56 above, 177, 202 above, 208; Granger Collection: 158 below right; Gustafson ©1967 Sportsman's Eyrie, Wayne, Pa.: 18, 27 below right; Hamilton, Don: 226 below; Harrold, David:

229 above; Hershey Country Club: 218 below; Historical Pictures Service, Chicago: 20; Inn of the Mountain Gods: 229 below; Joseph Murdoch Collection: 162, 184 below; Kamsler, Leonard: 44 right, 47–50, 51, 67 above left, 71, 72 left, 73 left, 76 (top all), 77 above left, 93 above, 94, 97 above right, 100 above left, 101 below, 102, 104 above, 111 below, 116, 119, 120, 159 above, 171, 179 below left, 180, 181, 182 above and below left, 185 above right, 187, 195 above left and center, 209, 216, 220, 223, 226 above, 232; © John P. Kelly/The Image Bank: jacket front; Kinsler, Ray: 66 (painting of Byron Nelson); LPGA: 89 above; Landmark: 118 left; La Quinta Hotel: 219; Lewis, Ken: 189 right, 202 below, 204 below, 205, 207; Macgregor Golf: 190 right; Marriott's Tan-Tar-A Resort and Golf Club: 230; Martin, H. B., *Fifty Years of Golf in America*, Dodd Mead, 1936: 28; Mauna Kea: 225; Mauna Lani: 224; McBride, Jeff: 182 right, 188 above, 191 right; McDonald, Charles Blair *Scotland's Gift: Golf*, Charles Scribner Sons, N.Y. 1928: 27 below left, 100 above right, 106; Mullin, Willard, *The Walter Hagen Story*, Simon & Schuster, 1956: 56 below right; McQueen, Jim, *Golf My Way*: 206; Metropolitan Golf Association:

169 below right; Morgan, Brian: 2–3, 42, 77 below, 104–5, 108 below, 110, 112–15, 117, 121 below, 122–23, 179 above; Morris County Country Club: 79; Mullane, Fred: 222; Newman, Marvin E.: 220–21; New York Tribune ©/Briggs: 163; Northwestern Golf Company: 204 above; Pebble Beach Company: 215 above, 228; Peper Collection: 81 below right, 158 above left and lower left, 166 right; Petrified Films Inc.: 32 above right, 80, 213 left; PGA/World Golf Hall of Fame: 15 above, 18, 23, 26 below right, 27 below right, 30 center right, 36 below right, 44 left, 54 above, 55 above left and right, 58, 64 below, 85 above left, 95, 101 above left, 107 below, 111 above, 170, 172 below, 174 left, 176, 179 below right, 199; Phototeque: 173 above; Pinehurst Hotel and Country Club: 211; Pocock, Philip: photos of The 100 Heroes drawings and the Spitzmiller paintings; Ravielli, Anthony, from Ben Hogan, *Five Lessons: The Modern Fundamentals of Golf*, Simon & Schuster, 1957: 205 below; Ray Davis Collection: 41, 198 left and below; Sea Island Golf Club: 235 above; Shell's Wonderful World of Golf: 175, 178; Spaulding Sports Worldwide: 183 right, 184 above, 195 above right; Sports Illustrated/Walter Iooss Jr.: 70 below; Steshinsky, Ted: 227; St. An-

drew's Golf Club Collection: 10, 11 left, 12, 13, 14 below, 15 below, 16 above left and below, 17, 19 above and below left, 21; Strauss, Richard/Memories of Vail: 226 center; Suffolk County Historical Society: 24, 78; The Boston Traveler: 161 below; The Breakers: 218 above; The Homestead: 210, 215 below; Thomas, George C., *Golf Architecture in America:* 107 above; ©Time Inc.: 166 right; UPI: 67 below, 167; USGA Museum and Library: 11 right, 19 below left, 25, 26 above, below left, 27 top, 30, 31, 32 above left and below, 35 below, 36 above left and below, 37, 38, 43 right, 46 top, 54 above and right, 55 below left and right, 57, 59 right, 60 below left, 61 above left and below, 64 above, 66 (all), 81 above and lower left, 82, 83, 84 above, 85 below and above right, 86–88, 101 above right, 103, 109, 158 above right, 161 above, 164 below, 168 right, 169 below left, 185 left and lower right, 188 below, 189 left, 192, 200, 201; Vance, Fred: 46 below, 72 right, 93 below, 97 above left; Vuich, Fred: 70 left, 73 right, 75 above; Wild Dunes: 234, 235 above; Wills, J. Anthony: 66 (painting of Ben Hogan); Wilson Sporting Goods: 91, 195 below; Walker, Robert: 3 (inset), 74 top, 75 below center and right, 96, 97 below